The Summits of Modern Man

PETER H. HANSEN

The Summits of Modern Man

MOUNTAINEERING AFTER

THE ENLIGHTENMENT

HARVARD UNIVERSITY PRESS   Cambridge, Massachusetts, and London, England

2013

Library of Congress Cataloging-in-Publication Data

Hansen, Peter H.

  The summits of modern man : mountaineering after the enlightenment /
Peter H. Hansen.

      p. cm.

  Includes bibliographical references and index.

  ISBN 978-0-674-04799-0 (alk. paper)

  1. Mountaineering—History. 2. Mountaineering—Philosophy. I. Title.

GV199.89.H36 2013

  796.522—dc23   2012040365

For Allison

Contents

Illustrations

MAPS

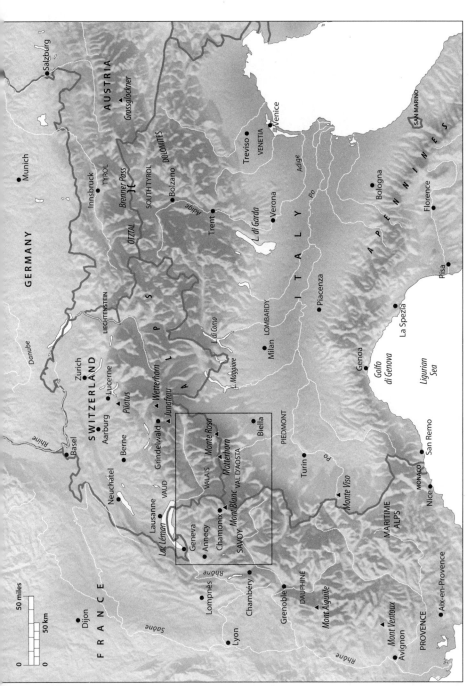

Map 1 The Alps.

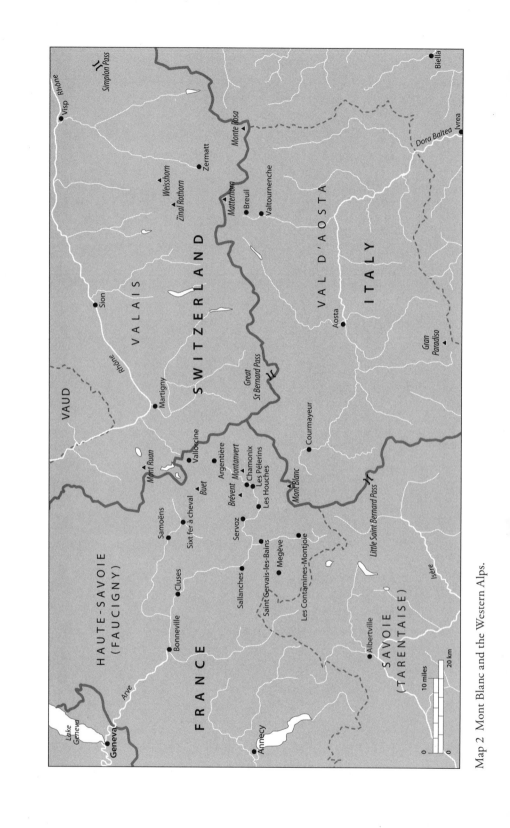

Map 2 Mont Blanc and the Western Alps.

Beginnings

ON BELAY

"On belay!" calls a climber after tying to the rope. "Belay on!" replies a partner, who secures the rope while the lead climber ascends. "On belay" signals that two people have arrived at a threshold. From that moment on, they are no longer autonomous but mutually interdependent. The rope binds them together. Neither occupies a position of superiority. Before proceeding, they acknowledge this partnership with another call and response: "Climbing!" "Climb on!"

Belay signals were standardized by the military in the mid-twentieth century. In the late eighteenth century, climbers tied together during mountain journeys were compared to groups of convicts. In the 1850s, ropes were used on glaciers, but some guides disparaged the rope as "a sign of timidity and over caution."[1] Belay remained a nautical command to fasten a rope around a pin or cleat. As sails unfurled, the rope uncoiled until "belay!" dictated that the rope be held fast and wrapped around the belay pin on the ship. By the end of the nineteenth century, climbers on steep cliffs tied together and looked for "belaying pins," rock spikes or knobs, over which the rope could be passed to provide protection in case of a fall. In the eastern Alps before the First World War, climbers secured the rope with metal pitons, which led to innovations in climbing and belaying techniques.[2] During the Second World War, climbers tested clothing, equipment, and nylon ropes for the U.S. Army and standardized belay commands for the training of mountain troops. The signals were then disseminated by demobilized climbers and publicized in manuals after the war. The brotherhood of the battlefield was knotted with the brotherhood of the rope.[3]

By telling the history of discovery and first ascents of Mont Ventoux, Mont Aiguille, Mont Blanc, the Matterhorn, and Mount Everest, this book seeks to explain a particular strand of modernity in which modern man stands alone on the summit, autonomous from other men and dominant over nature. This modern man envisions the summit as an exclusionary space that may be occupied in succession, but not simultaneously. On this summit, even climbers tied to the same rope must race each other to the top. When and why did such feverish races for unaccompanied achievement, even if fictitious, become such a prominent and defining feature of modernity? During the seventeenth and eighteenth centuries, a diverse group of miners, surveyors, natural historians, and travelers collectively "discovered" the glaciers and mountains of the Alps in vertiginous corners of provincial Europe. Contemporary political debates over the extension of the right to vote in Geneva and the emancipation from feudal dues in Savoy placed men from these communities in competition with one another on an upward trajectory. In the 1780s, multiple people claimed the discovery or conquest of Mont Blanc, which resulted in debates over who was first. Such debates continued long after the French Revolution and the deaths of these climbers by the 1830s. In the mid-nineteenth century, wider groups of people made first ascents of the Matterhorn and other peaks in the Alps. Their achievements served as the model for recalling Francesco Petrarch on Mont Ventoux as the first modern man. Disputes over who was first on Mont Blanc, Mount Everest, and other peaks continued to entangle visions of sovereignty, masculinity, and modernity throughout the twentieth century.

The narratives of modern man imagine that an autonomous individual is first on a hitherto untrodden peak. Yet this modern man on the summit was almost never alone. For many mountaineers and historians, however, the assertion of individual will is the essence of mountaineering and modern man. The will to be first is said to distinguish modern men and women from premodern or nonmodern people who cower in front of mountains. But was premodern man never first anywhere? Could nonmodern man ever be alone in nature? Taken literally, the answer to such questions would be yes, of course. Yet such questions are badly posed and cannot be taken literally, for they are unimaginable without the peculiar emphasis on chronological priority and individual autonomy characteristic of this European modernity. The myth of modern man (or, more precisely, modern Western man) is that he is alone and thereby can be first. Yet the individual climber has never been as sovereign in practice as the mythology of modernity implies. Histories of discovery or mountaineering are usually told as if they follow an ineluctable and inexorable process of enlightenment, disenchantment, secularization, rationalization, and self-assertion when such categories are themselves modern forms of mythmaking.

Verbal signals at the threshold of a belay would be misunderstood if viewed solely as examples of military standardization. In fundamental respects, belay commands belie, if only temporarily, assumptions of individual autonomy. Climbers on belay declare a covenant: we are more entangled and attached than in everyday life and we acknowledge this interdependence for the duration of the belay. It would be inaccurate to say climbers never care who is first when, historically, they clearly did for many years and, some might say, still do. Climbers on the same rope are still asked, "Who was first?" because the question envisages not mutual interdependence but an unencumbered self. Mountain climbing did not emerge as the expression of a preexisting condition known as "modernity," but rather was one of the practices that constructed and redefined multiple modernities during debates over who was first.

PLAYGROUND OF EUROPE

"The rope should be invariably worn on all difficult ice or rock slopes where a fall is possible," advised Leslie Stephen in *The Playground of Europe* (1871). Stephen was a London literary critic and author, as well as a former Cambridge tutor, future editor of the *Dictionary of National Biography*, and the father of Virginia Woolf. The frontispiece of his book depicts a scene during the 1864 first ascent of the Zinal Rothorn, a peak with a knife-edged crest between the Matterhorn and Weisshorn near Zermatt, Switzerland. Stephen scrambles up the crest with his back to the viewer as the rope is held taut from above, and he steps on the shoulders of another climber braced against the rock (Figure 1). Stephen argued that the rope could reduce or eliminate danger and spread the risk from the weakest to the strongest members of the party: "It is essential that there should exist a perfect 'solidarity' between all who join in an expedition. It is the best safeguard against over-rashness to know that if one man loses his life everybody else is likely to lose it."[4]

This solidarity did not always extend beyond the duration of the climb or the length of the rope. Stephen repudiated the view that he should be considered the hero of his Alpine adventures and attributed all his success to guides, whose feats were made more difficult by "taking with him his knapsack and his employer." His favorite Swiss guide, Melchior Anderegg, became a family friend, yet Stephen remained keenly aware that their views of mountains and modernity diverged. Stephen opened the *Playground of Europe* by describing a train ride through London with Anderegg. Looking at a "dreary expanse of chimney-pots" on the edge of "this dingy metropolis," Stephen remarked with a sigh, " 'That is not so fine a view as we have seen together from the top of Mont Blanc.' 'Ah, sir!' was [Anderegg's] pathetic reply, 'it is far finer!' "[5] Was his guide a fool or were his own beliefs folly? Neither, Stephen argued, since a "similar shock" awaited anyone who read Alpine literature from previous centuries.

Stephen contrasted the "old school" of fear and loathing of the mountains with the "new school" of appreciation for mountain beauty. He considered this epochal change the result of the triumph of instrumental rationality, the individual imagination, and the disenchantment of the world: "The history of mountaineering is, to a great extent, the history of the process by which men have gradually conquered the phantoms of their own imagination."[6] As someone who resigned his university position after he had lost his faith and became an agnostic, Stephen not surprisingly viewed this process as an example of secularization. Goblins, fairies, and dragons that populated the mountains in the Dark Ages vanished before the enlightened mountaineers and scientists who classified flora, cataloged strata, and climbed in the Alps.

Figure 1 Ascent of the Rothorn, 1864; frontispiece of Leslie Stephen, *The Playground of Europe* (1871).   HCL, Widener Library, Swi 685.10.3.

Stephen provided an arresting visual image for the "old school" in the
Alpine Journal—the scene of a seventeenth-century man in the Alps recoil-
ing in terror before a dragon baring its teeth, flashing its claws, and rearing
on its hind legs (Figure 2). Stephen reproduced this "most facetious dragon"
from Johann Jakob Scheuchzer's *Itinera Alpina* (1723) along with his own
summary of the Swiss naturalist's descriptions of Alpine dragons: "scaly

Figure 2 Johann Jakob Scheuchzer collected stories of Swiss dragons but considered
them very dubious. In 1723, he published this image of a man encountering a dragon
reported in the 1650s. By the end of the nineteenth century, it had become an iconic
image of superstition in the Alps.   Houghton Library, Harvard University, Swi 607.23*.

dragons and slimy dragons, dragons with wings and feet, dragons with two legs and four legs, with and without wings, and sometimes without wings or legs, but with objectionable heads with semi-human features, and an expression at once humorous and malignant."[7] In the decades after Stephen's retelling, histories of mountaineering compared Scheuchzer in disparaging terms to the contemporary climbers and guides who had conquered such imaginary phantoms. By 1900, the image of the startled man and this feline-reptilian dragon was frequently reproduced in histories of mountaineering as visual shorthand for a narrative of secularization and disenchantment.[8] More than a century later, this image continues to circulate and the emergence of mountain climbing is still sometimes described as "killing dragons."[9]

The ascent of the Zinal Rothorn represented the triumph of the "new school." Stephen viewed this school as founded by Jean-Jacques Rousseau, "the Columbus of the Alps, or the Luther of the new creed of mountain worship." Stephen did not agree with those who said Rousseau was the "first man," but he served as a convenient boundary figure: "The dividing line may be drawn about 1760, and the Alps were fairly inaugurated (in modern phrase) as a public playground by the generation of travelers which succeeded the seven years' war." Scientific observations by Horace-Bénédict de Saussure in the Alps provided a new language for the mountains. Stephen admired "the romantic school of art and literature, and with all that modern revolutionary spirit which we are as yet hardly in a position to criticize." He thought it remarkable that philosophers and poets celebrated savage over civilized life, wild over cultivated scenery, and admired the pastoral life of primitive populations preserved in rural arcadias: "The love of the mountains came in with the rights of man and the victory of the philosophers; and all the praise of Alpine scenery is curiously connected with praise of the unsophisticated peasant."[10]

The Playground of Europe offered the history of mountaineering as a morality tale for modernity. Alpine dragons stood in contrast not only to overly "credulous" figures in the past but also to less-advanced contemporaries. Stephen compared Scheuchzer to children who looked at nature as a toy and to the "British cockney" who went "into ecstasies at a rock shaped like the late Duke of Wellington's nose." For Stephen, the Alps were "places of refuge where we may escape from ourselves and from our neighbors," and the neighbors he wanted to escape were defined as broadly as "respectable human beings" and as narrowly as cockneys, Cook's tourists, and women. In the 1870s, he likened the fate of Alpine dragons to colonized peoples in other parts of the world: "these picturesque beings disappeared before the early dawn of science, much as the natives of Tasmania have disappeared before the English immigrants."[11]

Amid an expanding imperial polity in the mid-nineteenth century, Stephen minimized any political context for his own views and could explain a change in attitudes toward mountains only as the result of a change in individual aesthetic judgment. John Ruskin, in the fourth volume of *Modern Painters* (1856), similarly attributed "mountain gloom" to Catholicism, idleness, and superstition, but for Ruskin, "mountain glory" was not a new development; rather, the "great cathedrals of the earth" had exerted an inspiring influence throughout an intellectual tradition that dated from biblical mountaintops but was developed more fully only after the end of the Middle Ages.[12] Later studies of the dynamics of taste for mountains also took the politics of this periodization for granted. Idealizing and aestheticizing approaches to the love of mountain scenery—the focus of Stephen's and Ruskin's reflections, as well as studies by Marjorie Hope Nicolson a century later—have frequently resulted in histories with the politics left out, not just Rousseau's politics but also Saussure's and Stephen's and Nicolson's and our own.

In the mid-twentieth century, Marjorie Hope Nicolson, the first female full professor at Columbia, offered a similar interpretation in *Mountain Gloom and Mountain Glory* (1959). Nicolson argued that astronomers, geologists and poets in the seventeenth and eighteenth centuries extended an "aesthetics of the infinite" from God to the heavens, then to mountains, and finally to the transcendent individual imagination. Romantic poets completed this process when they envisioned a solitary individual standing on a mountain summit. Her wide-ranging study opened by citing the ascent of Everest as front-page news and locating this autonomous summit position in Wordsworth's poem, "To ____, on Her First Ascent to the Summit of Helvellyn." Wordsworth accompanied a young lady on her first ascent of this peak in the English Lake District and described her amazement at the view and the feeling of possession over all the Alps and the Andes. Nicolson commented: "As she stands on the summit, she is a symbol of something new that has entered into poetry and into human experience only in modern times—the power of hills."[13] If the politics of empire excluded some of Stephen's contemporaries from his history of mountaineering, then the sovereignty of the transcendent individual imagination on multitudinous hills envisioned by romantic poets and embedded by scholars into narratives of "Western civilization" at the height of the Cold War also excluded the wider discourses, practices, and politics that made it possible for the men and women of "modern times" to place themselves in a sovereign position at the summit of history.

AT A THRESHOLD

We are always looking over someone else's shoulder at the threshold of any beginning. I first visited Chamonix in August 1987 during the bicentennial celebrations for Horace-Bénédict de Saussure's ascent of Mont Blanc. The train from Annecy snaked past the foothills of the French Alps and up the narrow gorge of the Arve River before the plain of the Chamonix valley opened between the mountains. The valley is dwarfed on either side by seemingly vertical slopes that rise toward summits topped by rock needles and the snow-covered dome of Mont Blanc. After arriving at the train station with my fiancée (and later wife), we caught a glimpse from behind of the parade of guides walking briskly through the streets. Few people seemed to be paying much attention. Everyone said the real celebration had taken place a year earlier for the bicentennial of the first ascent of Mont Blanc by Jacques Balmat and Dr. Michel-Gabriel Paccard in 1786. Souvenirs from the 1986 bicentennial were available at a discount. Chamonix appeared less interested in Saussure than in returning to business as usual as the *capitale mondial de l'alpinisme* (world capital of mountaineering). For two centuries, business had been good, partly due to ascents in the mountains but mostly on account of visits to the glaciers, initially on foot and later by mule, funicular railway, ski lift, or cable car. By the 1960s, it was possible to reach Courmayeur, Italy, on the other side of Mont Blanc, by floating above the glaciers in cable cars or by driving underneath them in an automobile tunnel. In 1987, statues of Saussure and Balmat pointing to the summit were decorated for this anniversary, but a nearby stone plinth stood vacant. A statue to Dr. Paccard, unveiled the previous year, had been sent out for repair.

At Annecy, a provincial center nestled at the end of a blue lake between verdant hills, an archivist had told us about the Saussure ceremony. I was in search of my own scholarly discoveries through research on British mountaineering in the nineteenth century, and the first ascent of Mont Blanc seemed like well-trodden terrain after the bicentennial.[14] At this early stage, the focus of my research was unclear, but mountaineering and empire looked promising. I perused the register of foreign visitors kept by the Savoyard state, as well as a few miscellaneous sources. Many documents at the departmental archives were in storage at a former lycée while a new facility was being built, so the archivist brought a few documents she thought might interest me because they were in the same series that Emmanuel Le Roy Ladurie had used when he visited the archive to study the glaciers for the history of climate. These recorded the number of cows on farms and other indicators of agricultural productivity, but it was difficult at the time to imagine what any of that had to do with the history of mountain climbing.

At that juncture, the Victorian generation of British mountaineers appeared more interesting for inventing mountaineering as a popular sport in the Alps. The men of the Alpine Club embodied an imperial masculinity in the Alps, but they never had the mountains to themselves and it clearly would be absurd to say the "English invented the Alps."[15] After turning attention to Mount Everest, the Himalayas, and Tibet, such Anglocentric perspectives appeared too narrow for such a collaborative, intercultural, and polyglot endeavor as mountaineering. Parallel disputes over the first ascents of Mount Everest and Mont Blanc suggested that something broader than postcolonial dynamics were at work over a longer period of time. Empire was one dimension of a more complex formation that entwined subjectivity, sovereignty, and the natural world. Modernity rather than empire serves as the analytical anchor for the belay that is this book, which could have been written only in dialogue with postcolonial and subaltern studies and the cultural and imperial "turns" of the last few decades. Indeed, the varieties of scholarly "turns" postulated in recent years are examples of ongoing attempts to conceptualize our contemporary threshold.[16]

Compared with the attitudes of Leslie Stephen or Marjorie Hope Nicolson, or even my own perspective when I began this research, we live now in a postcolonial and post–Cold War world. Stephen recommended "a perfect 'solidarity'" on the rope around 1870, but for at least a hundred years afterward, languages of collective association became politicized and in some jurisdictions were almost unspeakable during the Cold War. Now no longer under the shadow of the Cold War, we live on the threshold of the hot planet. The conquest of nature so often anticipated or celebrated over the previous two hundred years appears to be highly ambivalent. The limited vocabulary to describe solidarities among people or the collectivity of humanity make it difficult for many people to imagine man's relationship with nature in terms other than its conquest by unencumbered individuals asserting their will and autonomy. The consequences of viewing modern man as alone and first on the summit of the natural world will continue to circulate well into the future.

While this book is about mountain climbing, it aims to contribute to wider fields than just the history of mountaineering. The chapters that follow include a review and revision of the historical periodization usually said to constitute the making of the modern world—from renaissance, absolutism, enlightenment, revolution, romanticism, nationalism, colonialism, fascism, decolonization, globalization, and climate change. The longer history of debates over "who was first" suggests that today we face merely the latest in a series of thresholds of modernity. The threshold will always include sacred and secular because these are not discrete periods that take place in sequence but cultural and political formations that mutually produce one another.[17] Despite reminders that humanity has always made room for the sacred in nature, cultural histories of mountaineering and of modernity frequently continue to make secularization the defining feature of the age.[18]

To offer a history of mountaineering after the enlightenment is not to make a claim of chronological or causal priority. Mountaineering did not emerge "after" enlightenment—they arrived together. Mountaineering and modernity mutually constituted one another in the eighteenth century and have continued to do so. Yet these entangled histories are too often separated into linear narratives of the discovery of man and conquest of nature. The uncertainties of our contemporary threshold have called this celebratory sequence into question. Previous histories of mountaineering certainly described mountain climbing as liberating men from fear and establishing their sovereignty, but it is not argued here that the earth radiates disaster. Modernity and enlightenment are not something that we can move "beyond," but neither are the worlds they supposedly left behind. To understand these politics of our own time, we need to recognize our multiple modernities and provincialize the narratives of secularization and disenchantment summarized by *The Playground of Europe.*

IN THE BEGINNING

In the beginning was the "Windy Peak," Mont Ventoux, the highest peak in Provence. Petrarch wrote that in 1336 he climbed Mont Ventoux with his younger brother and two servants. While his brother took the steeper and more direct route, Petrarch tried repeatedly to find an easier way, but each path became longer and more difficult. Regretting his detours, Petrarch told himself that "you must either ascend to the summit of the blessed life under the burden of badly delayed work, or watch yourself sink slowly into the valley of your sins." At the top, Petrarch admired the view from the Alps to the Mediterranean and the valley of the Rhône, and reflected on the years since he had left behind his boyhood studies. After admiring earthly things on the summit, Petrarch thought to elevate his mind as he had done with his body and pulled out a pocket volume of St. Augustine's *Confessions,* intending to read at random. As the spine cracked, the pages fell open and Petrarch read aloud: "And men go to admire the high mountains, the huge waves of the sea, the broad flow of rivers, the expanse of the ocean, and the orbit of the stars, and they pass themselves by."[19]

Petrarch was stunned, closed the book, and asked his brother for silence. As he later wrote: "Then having seen enough of the mountain, I turned my inner eyes toward myself." During his silent descent from the peak, Petrarch recalled that St. Augustine and St. Anthony before him had stopped reading when they heard biblical passages speak directly to them. Petrarch reflected that men "neglect the noblest part of themselves, scattered in many directions and lost in vain spectacles, seeking without what can be found within." When he turned around to look at the summit during the descent, "it looked hardly higher than a cubit compared to the height of human contemplation, if this were not plunged in the mire of earthly filth."[20] Returning by moonlight to the village of Malaucène, Petrarch began to write a letter about his ascent as the servants prepared the evening meal.

For the next five hundred years, Petrarch's ascent remained a minor footnote to his varied career as a lyric poet and humanist scholar better known for his sonnets than his summit. Petrarch's reputation was successively Stoic-Christian sage, Latin writer, initiator of classical revival, Italian lyricist, and the "first modern man."[21] In the eighteenth century, Edward Gibbon expressed amusement at Petrarch's coronation as poet laureate in Rome, but applauded Petrarch's revival of antiquity "as the first harbinger of day."[22] Only in the mid-nineteenth century, as mountaineering became a popular pastime in the Alps, was Petrarch's ascent of Mont Ventoux belatedly recalled and represented by Jacob Burckhardt as exemplifying the discovery of the individual and the arrival of a new epoch, the "first modern man."[23]

Was Petrarch's ascent "first"? When should a history of mountaineering—or modern man—begin? When does any history begin? Burckhardt once mused that anyone studying cultural history "must ask anxiously, 'Where am I to start?'—and the answer is that you have to start somewhere."[24] The conventional response is to beg the question with the tautology that histories "begin at the beginning" or the cliché that any account must begin *in media res.* Beginning statements such as "Petrarch made the first ascent of Mont Ventoux" or "Petrarch was the first ____" (fill in the blank—lyric poet, mountain climber, or modern man) are not merely about chronological precedence or priority. In his study of *Beginnings,* Edward Said averred that a beginning "is the first step in the intentional production of meaning."[25] Many historical statements of beginning also exhibit a preference for what Said termed a utopian simplicity, for a beginning as the first point in a new continuity. Founders, explorers, and discoverers were often represented as exemplary individuals who, through an intentional act, sundered past from present to establish novel continuities. Histories are full of examples prior to an acknowledged "first" that "did not count" either because they did not express a will to be first or they did not establish a new continuity. Said suspected that images of a heroic individual as "first" remain attractive because "the mind prefers contemplating a strong seminal figure to sifting through reams of explanation."[26]

Beyond a preference for simplicity over complexity, the claim that "Petrarch was the first ____" embodies an assumption of an autonomous individual whose will is capable of calling a new epoch of ____ into existence. In this respect, the beginning of an epoch often is represented as resembling the biblical "in the beginning was the Word." Despite family resemblances, images of Petrarch as the "first modern man" are not secularized versions of creation myths. In a critique of secularization theories, Hans Blumenberg argued that the "modern age" was not present in advance of its interpretation because the concept of an epoch was itself a constitutive feature of the modern epoch. The modern age was characterized by "self-assertion," in which "man posits his existence in a historical situation and indicates to himself how he is going to deal with the reality surrounding him." In contrast to viewing historical epochs as distinct periods separated by specific people, dates, or events, Blumenberg envisioned epochs as separated by an imperceptible frontier or threshold, something either not yet arrived at or already crossed. Petrarch's ascent of Mont Ventoux intermeshed humanism with Christian humility and oscillated indecisively between epochs until Petrarch turned away from the mountain toward inward spiritual reflection and concern for salvation.[27]

For Blumenberg, "the ascent of Mont Ventoux exemplifies graphically what is meant by the 'reality' of history as the reoccupation of formal systems of positions." Only by comparing Petrarch on Mont Ventoux to a figure on the other side of an epochal threshold, such as Goethe on the Brocken, a peak in northern Germany, would a change in position be rendered visible: what had been blasphemous lingering became an adventurous undertaking. The self-understanding of the modern age as a new epoch resulted in a preference for a more definitive break. According to Blumenberg, "the demand for an identifiable point where the sheep are separated from the goats and the age of sheep from the age of goats is one that an epoch that wants to have willed itself as an epoch can only see fulfilled by an embodiment of this will by a widely visible and effective boundary figure."[28]

Petrarch has often served this role as boundary figure. Even his conception of history has been localized to an epoch-making event at the Baths of Diocletian in Rome in 1341, when he and a friend divided history into ancient and modern, subsequently adding a middle time of "darkness." Yet it took more than three hundred years for these terms to become widely used and another three hundred years for the claim that Petrarch's Dark Ages were "first" to be advanced in the 1940s.[29] By then, Petrarch's musings among ruins paralleled the intervening view that he was the "first modern man" and another model for beginning—Gibbon's conception of his *Decline and Fall* while listening to barefoot friars chanting in the Temple of Jupiter. The five-hundred-year time lag between Petrarch's ostensible climb of Mont Ventoux and its apotheosis as the ascent of "modern man" appears to be an example of a wider pattern of the representation of modernity. Indeed, terms such as *Neuzeit, modernité,* and modern age became established many years and even many centuries after the beginning of the period they are sometimes said to describe.[30]

Petrarch as modern man on Mont Ventoux was the product of a time knot, a temporal entanglement in which different moments of time are copresent, in conversation, and constitutive of one another. Mountaineers like Leslie Stephen had to begin scrambling among the Alps in the mid-nineteenth century before "modern man" could call himself into existence by re-creating Petrarch in his image on the summit of Mont Ventoux. Claims that Petrarch was "first" disentangle intertwined histories and cut knots of time to locate "modern man" at the apex of a linear sequence of uniform historical development. This summit position became the subject position of modern man as an effect of difference articulated through the semantics of modern time.

The claim that Petrarch was first was seldom, if ever, limited in scope to Petrarch himself, but simultaneously expressed the assumption "first in Europe, then elsewhere." By the mid-eighteenth century, as Reinhart Koselleck has shown, the comparison of coexisting societies that were chronologically simultaneous but culturally diverse or developmentally "noncontemporaneous," globally and within Europe, fostered a new consciousness of time, history, and modernity. Historicist accounts soon classified societies according to temporal and developmental criteria, before and after, too early, or not yet. To be "first" ascribed to the history of Europe or the West a universal character that substituted for more-diverse histories in the world. Assertions of temporal priority created a position of flexible superiority for an idealized Europe that, Dipesh Chakrabarty has argued, remains "the sovereign, theoretical subject of all histories."[31]

Temporal hierarchies framed the development of European conceptions of sovereignty from the sixteenth to the eighteenth century. During this period, the consolidation of "feudal" legal codes and the writing of histories of slavery and individual rights represented the feudal and sacred as part of Europe's medieval past but the non-European present. Kathleen Davis has noted the simultaneous and reciprocal development of conceptions of feudal laws with the growth of colonial slavery in the Americas and of commercial expansion in Asia. These intertwined histories resulted in the division of history into periods of sacred and secular, medieval and modern, and in broader theories of secularization. The self-assertion of modernity as under-stood by Blumenberg and the exclusion of the sacred, eschatological, or the "religious" from the modern world as conceived by Koselleck both repli-cated the advent of modernity as primordial acts of decision. Such an act of decision, according to Davis, reproduces Carl Schmitt's dictum that the sovereign is the one who decides the exception, simultaneously inside and outside of time and the state. The periodization of history itself, especially the break posited between sacred and secular, fills a void to provide the foun-dation for sovereignty: "The idea of a superstitious Middle Ages, in other words, did not preexist the 'superstitious' colonial subject upon which it be-came mapped; rather, they emerged together, each simultaneously making possible and verifying the other."[32]

Alongside "modern man" astride the summit was someone else who made the ascent possible but did not share the same attitudes toward moun-tains. Petrarch accompanied by his brother and servants, or Leslie Stephen by Melchior Anderegg, or even Edmund Hillary by Tenzing Norgay on Mount Everest, are each a case in point. The apparent nonmodernity of such partners in ascent is then taken as a sign of the modernity of the modern man. Yet Petrarch's account of his ascent proffered both self-assertion and self-flagellation, intertwining attitudes that only much later and with much difficulty might be articulated as distinctly secular or sacred. Projections of Petrarch as modern man on Mont Ventoux—and of Scheuchzer's dragons as premodern relics of an "old school"—both exhibit the tensions of translat-ing the sacred time of gods and spirits into the secular time of history. The historian's code of chronology as secular time is not something that developed independent from systems of representation, but presuppose "a particular formation of the modern subject."[33] To provincialize Europe does not require showing that certain developments occurred someplace else first. Chrono-logical priority is itself a peculiar attitude that the "North Atlantic imagina-tion" claims as a universal attribute of modernity.[34]

This Europe may be provincialized from within, from the perspective of its vertiginous provinces. From this point of view, the summit was neither the birthplace of modern man nor reoccupied in a succession of distinct and hierarchical positions. Instead, the summit positions of modern man were multiple and plural, examples of alternative modernities in the world and constellations of modernities in the vernacular.[35] Multiple modernities in first ascents were not residual, archaic, or backward, but integral, constitutive, and reciprocally modern. Modernity is neither a singular and stable entity nor a fixed period of time inaugurated by an act of decision; nor is it the expression of some underlying social or material condition. Rather, modernity is better understood as a cluster of cultural and political formations that are historical—varying by time and place—and performative. Modernity does not already exist "out there," but must be continually enacted and performed. One can only ever be on the threshold of modernity.

Multiple modernities illustrate tensions among self, state, and mountain. These terms should suggest angles of vision and degrees of emphasis rather than a theoretical armature or fixed categories of knowledge. Consider self, state, and mountain as middle-range concepts in the declivities between the summit positions of sovereignty and modernity. Such intermediate concepts mediate between the high-level formations identified with modernity and locations often "deemed as outside of the modern."[36] The summit position has been repeatedly reenvisioned, but self, state, and mountain do not represent a teleological progression. Moreover, they do not indicate a decline and fall from grace posited in a transition from God to state to self.[37] One of the difficulties in conceptualizing modernity is that the diversity and multiplicity within the "modern world" is often concealed by the illusory singularity of certain concepts, such as the self, which are actively redefined and reconstituted. To begin with the mountains is to start not with a place of origin but with a vantage point from which to observe the braiding together of self, state, and mountain in historical knots of time.

THINKING LIKE A SELF

Petrarch became a modern man in the mid-nineteenth century. Ernest Renan, a French Orientalist, wrote in an 1852 study of the Islamic philosopher Ibn Rushd (Averroës) that Petrarch "deserves to be called the first modern man." German historian Georg Voigt argued in 1859 that Petrarch's ascent of Mont Ventoux heralded the arrival of "modern individual man." Jacob Burckhardt, a Swiss cultural historian, viewed the origins of the modern world in the birth of individualism, revival of antiquity, discovery of man and nature, and the decline of superstition and religion in "a civilization which is the mother of our own, and whose influence is still at work among us." Burckhardt's *Civilization of the Renaissance in Italy* (1860) described human consciousness as beneath a veil of faith and illusion that "first melted into air" when man studied the world objectively and recognized himself as a spiritual individual. Renaissance Italians were "the first-born among the sons of modern Europe." Burckhardt cited Petrarch's ascent of Mont Ventoux as an example of the discovery of the individual and the beauty of landscape: "The significance of nature for a receptive spirit is fully and clearly displayed by Petrarch—one of the first truly modern men."[38]

Burckhardt's interpretation of Petrarch as the "first modern man" was itself the product of a time knot. Burckhardt's vision of the "Renaissance man" may be an idealized version of a self-cultivating merchant of contemporary Basel, and his *Renaissance* can be read as a critique of his own time.[39] He was born into the patrician elite of this wealthy city-state, where his family in the eighteenth century had been called "these Medicis," after the Florentine dynasty of bankers and popes. By the revolutions of 1848, Burckhardt lost his religious faith and turned away from the state-centered historicism of Leopold von Ranke and his Berlin teachers to recover the old culture of Europe. Basel had long been a crossroads and its new railway station served as a gateway to Switzerland for the climbers who founded the Alpine Club in London in 1857 and the Swiss Alpine Club in 1863.

Before this period, Petrarch could not have been the "first modern man" on Mont Ventoux, not only because mountain climbing was uncommon but also because the "individual man" was still being constituted as a category of analysis. After the French Revolution, observers developed a philosophical psychology of the self to explain revolutionary upheaval and promote political order. In contrast to eighteenth-century "sensationalism," which was believed to have led to psychological fragmentation and political revolution, Victor Cousin articulated a stable and unitary "self" that balanced sensation, volition, and reason. In an 1820 lecture, Cousin said that "the man of character is a man who makes himself, a man who has a will, which is his own source of life. . . . That is how we can distinguish men of antiquity from modern men."[40] This modern man was distinguished from women and the "people," who were said to possess neither this will nor the capacity of self-reflection.

François Guizot's *History of Civilization in Europe* (1828) elevated this independent individual man who was conscious of "the grandeur of man as man" into the "source of modern civilization."[41] This unitary and stable self was embedded in the philosophy curriculum of state-run lycées in France from the 1830s into the twentieth century. In the German-speaking states of Europe, Burckhardt and others favored Bildung, a comparable model for the self-cultivating bourgeois individual, and these multiple, postrevolutionary concepts of a unitary self were intertwined in representations of "modern man" and "European civilization." To Guizot and his contemporaries, civilization became an object of study and a reality that defined the present. As civilization became an ethnographic category, it was deployed by Renan and others as a sign of European racial superiority.[42]

For a century after Burckhardt's *Renaissance,* Petrarch's ascent of Mont Ventoux served as a foundation myth in histories of the Renaissance, modern man, and Western civilization. By the 1890s, Petrarch was routinely heralded as an epoch-making figure, the "first" humanist, man of letters, or mountaineer. Pierre de Nolhac identified a sketch of Petrarch's "transalpine retreat" at the Fontaine de Vaucluse, reputedly by Petrarch's own hand, as confirming this summit position (Figure 3).[43] James Harvey Robinson reproduced the sketch on the cover of *Petrarch, the First Modern Scholar and Man of Letters* (1898), an anthology that featured Petrarch's ascent of Mont Ventoux. Robinson introduced the Western Civilization course and advocated its expansion throughout American higher education before and after the Great War.[44] In 1927, Ernst Cassirer identified in Petrarch's struggles between self and nature a "newer, deeper concept of 'subjectivity'" and what "might well be called the first presentation of the modern soul and modern man."[45]

Visions of Western civilization provided the framework that sustained the view of Petrarch's ascent as a historical landmark. Generations of students dutifully read Petrarch's account of Mont Ventoux in Cassirer's *The Renaissance Philosophy of Man* (1948), a widely assigned collection of documents throughout the Cold War. For some Renaissance scholars in this period, the "historical definition of humanism was the equivalent of the formulation of an actual paradigm of 'modernity,'" which made an ideological statement with political implications, and even Burckhardt himself was enlisted as a cold warrior.[46] Marjorie Hope Nicolson identified another ascent of Ventoux before Petrarch and regretted that the poet only caught a glimpse of "mountain glory" before falling under the shadow of "mountain gloom."[47] Petrarch's account of the climb was still considered autobiographically

Figure 3 A sketch of the Fontaine de Vaucluse with the inscription, "My most delightful transalpine retreat," perhaps in Petrarch's handwriting, is in the margins of Pliny's *Natural History*, a manuscript he bought in 1350.   BnF, MS Latin 6802, folio 143v.

straightforward, and Morris Bishop echoed twentieth-century Everest climbers in 1963, when he granted Petrarch the laurel of "first recorded Alpinist, the first to climb the mountain because it is there."[48]

By the mid-1960s, scholars doubted the historical accuracy of Petrarch's letters and questioned whether he made the ascent of Mont Ventoux at all. The painstaking preparation of Petrarch's correspondence led Vittorio Rossi and Giuseppe Billanovich to conclude that many of his letters were almost entirely fictitious and his Mont Ventoux letter could not have been written before 1353.[49] By giving prominence to his failed imitation of allegorical precedents on Mont Ventoux, Robert Durling argued that Petrarch called attention to the fictitious character of his account and questioned the possibility of allegorical interpretation. At the very least, most scholars accepted that Petrarch extensively rewrote his letter long after any ascent, and some compared his editorial sleight of hand to a prestidigitator or a cardshark. Hans Baron lamented such skepticism, claiming that Petrarch would not have taken lightly an oath to tell the truth before God or "lied about his life."[50]

Scholarly reassessment of Petrarch's self-fashioning transcended debate over the truth claims of his ascent. As Thomas Greene noted, "If Petrarch never made the climb, his volition to make it is clear; if he did make it, what he left us, whenever written, is a highly stylized version of his experience. In either case, what we have is literature growing out of an existential impulse."[51] Wider latitude for interpretation bypassed empiricist debate over whether Petrarch was the first alpinist or humanist. Petrarch fashioned a self through artifice and style. His once-heralded "desire to see the summit" became an obvious allegory for a sinful wandering eye, a viewpoint repudiated when he turns his gaze inward at himself.[52] The "biographical fallacy" that Petrarch's works corresponded to events in his life was rejected, as well as the theory of a stable and unified self. For Giuseppe Mazzotta, the modernity of "Petrarch's 'invention' of individuality has to be understood primarily as the acknowledgement of the value of the individual fragments composing the whole."[53]

Yet Burckhardtian echoes have sounded very faint after what William Bouwsma called the "collapse of the traditional dramatic organization of Western history." The dramatic "myth of apocalyptic modernization" that connected the Renaissance to the modern world assumed that the modern world was a coherent entity and "modernity has emerged by way of a single linear process."[54] Neither assumption was any longer self-evident by the late 1980s. As the knot tying Petrarch, modern man, and Western civilization frayed with the passage of time, the relationship of Petrarch and the Renaissance was rethought. Renaissance "individualism" took a variety of forms that did not fit interpretations of the "first" self—either autonomous or fragmented—in the Renaissance.[55] Terry Jones, a former member of the British comedy group Monty Python, held a mock public funeral for the "Renaissance man" because "I'm sick to death of that ridiculous assumption that before the Renaissance human beings had no sense of individuality."[56] Despite reassessments in scholarship and popular culture, the naïve view that Petrarch's ascent is an unproblematic empirical record and expression of his "intentions" remains surprisingly persistent.[57] A more persuasive interpretation would recognize that Petrarch's intention appears to have been to repudiate the very notion of individual intention as a form of impiety.

Yet Petrarch is frequently resurrected as the first modern man because the range of interpretations of his ascent is tied to these earlier points of view. Burckhardt might have been intrigued by claims that Petrarch had never made the ascent of Mont Ventoux. He wrote in one of his programmatic statements about cultural history: "Even when a reported act never in fact happened as reported or never happened at all, the way of looking at the world that underlies the representation of it as having happened retains its value for us through the typical character of the representation."[58] Representations of Petrarch as individual modern man on Mont Ventoux were not descriptive of a preexisting self, but actively defined and reconstituted modern individual subjectivity. Petrarch on Mont Ventoux gave salience and prominence to one among many "modern" ways of thinking like a self.

THINKING LIKE A STATE

King Charles VIII of France was on a pilgrimage in the Dauphiné when on November 7, 1490, he saw Mont Inaccessible and ordered his artillery officer, Antoine de Ville, seigneur of Dompjulien and Beaupré, to climb it. The ascent was ordered to manifest the sovereignty of the king over a realm that the twenty-year-old monarch was only beginning to rule without a regent looking over his shoulder. After planning and preparation, on June 26, 1492, Antoine de Ville and seven companions used "subtle engines"— ladders and ropes with grappling hooks that had been used to attack military fortifications—to ascend the peak, which they learned had another local name, Aiguille. He then baptized the peak Aiguille Fort in the name of the Father, Son, and Holy Ghost, as well as in the name of Saint Charlemagne, and for the love of the king. A cleric said Mass three times and they erected three crosses on its high points in honor of the Holy Trinity. Antoine de Ville then wrote to officials at Grenoble to ask for witnesses to testify to his ascent. These depositions reported that the summit featured fabulous birds, fragrant flowers, and fleurs-de-lis; a luxuriant meadow that would take forty men to mow; and chamois that could never descend from their mountaintop prairie—an image of monarchical France as a garden paradise.[59]

For more than three centuries, the ascent of Mont Aiguille was satirized or celebrated as a symbol of monarchical sovereignty. In 1552, François Rabelais quipped that this ascent had led to a mountaintop "so pleasant, so fertile, so salubrious, and so agreeable, that I thought it must be the true garden and terrestrial paradise: the situation about which so many good theologians discuss and debate."[60] The official documents testifying to Antoine de Ville's ascent in the archives of the Chambre des Comptes were published in accounts of the seven wonders of Dauphiné as early as 1656.[61] The Jesuits of Grenoble equated monarch and mountain in *Les sept miracles de Dauphiné* (1701), a book issued to commemorate the visit of two royal princes. The peak was illustrated as an inverted pyramid with Mont Inaccessible as a motto for the mountain and the king. The obsequious caption praised the sagacity, military victories, and glory of the reigning monarch, Louis XIV: "Louis the Great is always ascending; he surpasses himself after being elevated above other monarchs" (Figure 4).[62] By the mid-eighteenth century, the *Encyclopédie* wrote in a debunking mode about visions of the inverted summit and the credulity of anyone who would believe sheep had ever grazed on top. Although it was still well-known in the eighteenth century that Mont Aiguille had been climbed frequently by local shepherds in the 1530s, its next "official" ascent was not recorded until 1834.[63]

The 1892 quatercentenary anniversary of Columbus's discovery of the New World transformed Antoine de Ville's ascent into an epoch-making event. The 1492 ascent of Mont Aiguille was "the real starting point of modern mountaineering," according to W. A. B. Coolidge, a learned but cantankerous American climber who became a historian at Oxford before living in the Alps. He was especially interested in this ascent "because it was completed in 1492, the year when my homeland, North America, was discovered, and because the peak in question rises in Dauphiné, the land that could almost be called my adopted home." Coolidge surveyed the history of mountaineering before 1600 and viewed Petrarch as looking "back to classical antiquity and forward with curious preview of modern times, but he could never liberate himself from the Christian influences tinting the Middle Ages." Coolidge believed that Petrarch was the first to be inspired by the love of mountains, but "we certainly reserve the name of the 'first climber' to Antoine de Ville, the predecessor of all the ardent spirits who love to wrestle with the difficulties in a mountain climb." Since 1492 was "often taken as the beginning of modern history in general, it is certainly

LE MONT INACCESSIBLE.

ON voit cette Montagne à six lieuës de Grenoble dans le Diocéfe de Die ; elle eft d'une hauteur prodigieufe, efcarpée de toutes parts, & feparée des Montagnes voifines, beaucoup plus étroite par le bas ; de forte qu'elle reffemble de loin à une Piramide renverfée.

Ce Mont inacceffible, avec ces deux mots Latins *Supereminet invius*, fait une devife pour le Roy. Dés les commencemens de fon Régne, il s'eft diftingué de tous les autres Souverains, par une longue fuite de victoires & par une fageffe admirable, il s'eft toûjours foutenu pendant le Régne le plus long, & le plus glorieux qu'on ait jamais veu : il fembloit qu'on ne pouvoit rien ajoûter à la grandeur & à la gloire du Roy, qui avoit détruit l'heréfie dans fon Royaume, & qui avoit triomphé de toutes les Puiffances de l'Europe liguées contre la France ; mais LOVIS le Grand, va toûjours croiffant ; il fe furpaffe luy-même, aprés s'eftre élevé au deffus des autres Monarques; il nous paroît toûjours plus grand, plus admirable, plus inimitable.

AVERTISSEMENT.

ON n'a pas prétendu de donner des devifes régulieres fur chacun de ces Miracles ; ny de faire une traduction éxacte des vers Latins, dans les vers François.

Figure 4 Antoine de Ville climbed Mont Inaccessible in 1492 on the orders of King Charles VIII. The caption for this image of Mont Inaccessible in *Les sept miracles de Dauphiné* (Grenoble, 1701) praised Louis XIV and equated both monarch and mountain as unapproachable and towering over all.   Spencer Collection, The New York Public Library, Astor, Lenox, and Tilden Foundations.

appropriate to adopt it for the history of mountaineering, inscribing in letters of gold, at the head of the long list of 'climbers,' the name of Antoine de
Ville."[64]

Coolidge took pride in being "the first foreign mountaineer" to climb
Mont Aiguille, and he located the origins of mountaineering in Antoine de
Ville's letter, "the 'Magna Carta' of mountaineering." Coolidge could find
"no detailed recital of an ascent of an alpine summit" dating from any earlier
period, though he reprinted extracts describing ascents of peaks by Philip of
Macedon on Mount Haemus in 181 BCE, the emperor Hadrian on Mount
Etna in 121 CE, and multiple ascents by later kings or emperors. Around the
turn of the twentieth century, Coolidge and contemporary historians believed published documents were crucial to establish historical objectivity
and to certify "what is a first ascent." Indeed, Coolidge would count as first
only those ascents that could be proven by written documents. Ascents about
which nothing was written were tantamount to no ascent at all.[65]

Apart from one ascent by a "primitive guide," almost all the ascents
Coolidge could document were expressions of monarchical authority—the
sovereign on the summit. Most were undertaken during religious pilgrimages, military campaigns, or for other reasons of state. The requirement for
written documentation of an ascent inevitably limited the voices that could
be heard to those preserved in the institutional archives of church and state.
Antoine de Ville's ascent of Mont Aiguille is a prime example. His witnesses
and retainers only documented the ascent so the royal exchequer would
reimburse his expenses. A note on the reverse of one of the documents in
the Chambre de Comptes itemized the bill—"1533 librae, 8 solidi 5 denarii
unum tercium," of which Antoine de Ville's personal share was more than
575 librae (livres tournois).[66] This amount could be worth tens of thousands, hundreds of thousands, or even millions of dollars today, depending
on assumptions about measuring worth and purchasing power over time,
but is more meaningfully compared to contemporary wages: Antoine de
Ville's personal share of the prize for the ascent was at least sixteen times the
annual wages for a laborer in Paris.[67] The ascent of Mont Inaccessible was
recorded in such copious documentation precisely because the rewards were
substantial and Antoine de Ville had to file an expense report with the ac-
counting office.

The ascent of Mont Aiguille took place on account of "thinking like a
state." James Scott fruitfully offered "seeing like a state" as a metaphor for

the administrative ordering of society and nature by modern states.[68] Scott employed the term to highlight the disastrous effects of high-modernist social engineering during the twentieth century, but he identified similar dynamics at work in earlier state-building projects in Europe and other parts of the world. In seventeenth-century France, for example, lands and people were measured and classified to make them "legible" for the demands of absolutist governance. The ascent of Mont Aiguille took place well before such efforts, during the reign of the Sun King, whose sovereignty was equated with Mont Inaccessible in 1701. The ascent by Antoine de Ville should not be viewed merely as the precursor of absolutist governance, as the first example of something it was not.

Ascents of Mont Aiguille and other peaks by monarchs were demonstrations of sovereignty, ceremonies of possession that varied over geographical territories and terrains. Lauren Benton has convincingly shown that laws of imperial sovereignty in this period took a variety of forms that were profoundly shaped by the topography of the rivers, seas, islands, and landlocked enclaves that they encountered and governed.[69] Ascents in the Alps in the eighteenth and nineteenth centuries were rooted in these contemporary revisions of sovereignty. Ironically, the Chamonix valley is among the best-studied examples of the emancipation from feudal dues in the eighteenth century, but that history is usually divorced from histories of climbing Mont Blanc, as if separated by a *cordon sanitaire.* In contrast, this book argues that aspirations to reach the summit developed as the dynamic consequence of debates over sovereignty and enfranchisement in Geneva, Savoy, France, and other states around the world during the last three hundred years.

After the quatercentenary of the discovery of America in 1892, the ascent of Mont Aiguille symbolized the view that Western civilization really could climb mountains. In 1992, the quincentenary of the Columbian exchange and the ascent of Mont Aiguille were commemorated during the same year, but the ascent had lost this wider resonance.[70] Indeed, the Columbian anniversary celebration was also more contentious than a century before. Petrarch has remained the preferred boundary figure as the first mountaineer and modern man, and not merely because he ostensibly preceded Antoine de Ville by 156 years. During the century from the 1850s through the 1950s and beyond, Petrarch's ascent "solely to see the view" was thought to express his individual will and autonomy. In contrast, Antoine de Ville's ascent was ordered by the king. And that, for later mountaineers, was precisely the problem. The inverted pyramid of Mont Inaccessible visually summarized what later climbers thought was wrong with this picture. The idea that a modern man could be ordered to make an ascent by someone else was anathema. Instead, the solitary individual on the summit was preferred as a symbol for the sovereignty of modern man.

THINKING LIKE A MOUNTAIN

"Mountains come first," declared Fernand Braudel near the beginning of his multivolume work on the Mediterranean world, first published in 1949. Mountains marked the geographical boundaries of the Mediterranean basin and, more important, the methodological gulf between Braudel's total history over the *longue durée* (long term) and the kind of humanist-centered history of events that could hold "Petrarch was first." The Alps were more developed than other mountain ranges around the Mediterranean, but Braudel considered mountains as a rule to be places apart from civilization, refuges of primitive credulity and "aberrant cults." History in the mountains was static and lost in the mist, to be recorded only when mountain dwellers descended to meet lowlanders, who wrote mostly mocking sketches. Even if the mountains themselves were full of variety and bountiful resources, they remained for Braudel a place and a people without history: "Their history is to have none, to remain almost always on the fringe of the great waves of civilization."[71]

A position on the fringe was attractive to Aldo Leopold, who advised "thinking like a mountain" in response to the disappearance of wolves in the North American backcountry. In *Sand County Almanac* (1949), Leopold wrote that the presence or absence of wolves had "a deeper meaning, known only to the mountain itself," but which was felt by all in wolf country and could be discerned in hundreds of small events in the sounds, wind, and shadows of the mountain.[72] Thinking like a mountain preceded Leopold, even if he coined this phrase as a postwar alternate modernity.[73] It was not a restatement of prior religious traditions, but as modern as Braudel's emphasis on material factors in a secular history in which "aberrant cults" had no place. Consider "thinking like a mountain" a metaphor for the network of intersubjective relationships between people and the natural world, spiritual forces, and other people that are not reducible to solipsism of thinking like a self or the system-building abstraction of thinking like a state. Mountains have long been represented as "between heaven and earth," so it should be expected that the effects of "thinking like a mountain" cannot be anticipated in advance, but have to be sought and demonstrated in practice.[74]

Leslie Stephen was uncertain about how to describe his relationship between man and mountain: "Does not science teach us more and more emphatically that nothing which is natural can be alien to us who are part of nature? Where does Mont Blanc end, and where do I begin? That is the question which no metaphysician has hitherto succeeded in answering. But at least the connection is close and intimate." Stephen's scrambles in the Alps embodied his physical interconnection with the mountains: Mont Blanc was part of "the great machinery in which my physical frame is inextricably involved, and not the less interesting because a part which I am unable to subdue to my purposes."[75] Mountains were indomitable forces of nature that confronted man with his smallness and the ephemeral character of his existence. Despite the narrative of secularization in his historical essays, Stephen recommended an attitude of awestruck humility in the mountains. Describing the sunset from the summit of Mont Blanc, Stephen spoke reverently of the "strange threads of association" that had the power to stir like music or plunge him into reveries. His position was like a glimmering threshold "at the quiet limit of the world."[76]

Thinking like a mountain marks the summit as a limit point and renders visible perspectives that otherwise eludes the all-encompassing view claimed by the autonomy of the self or the legibility of the state. A mountain cannot provide the singular perspective of a summit. Indeed, Petrarch's sketch of his transalpine retreat—which was read in the late nineteenth century as symbolizing his summit position as modern man (Figure 3)—looks rather different from this angle. The cross atop the summit chapel suggests a different kind of verticality that is consistent with Petrarch's rejection of individual intentions. More recently, amid the devotional artifacts in the archeological ruins of another mountaintop temple in Provence, Gustaf Sobin observed a "once fervently projected vertical: an invisible axis that ran, infallibly, between the throngs of the devout below and the divinity above." Such a vertical axis joins not only secular and sacred but also past and present and future. Vestiges of archeological artifacts may "speak," Sobin sug gested, if we "reestablish contact with that verticality: to feel ourselves rooted, not merely to the past in general but to our own specific moment within the past's tiered continuum." As the "uppermost layer of a profound compilation" of wind, shadow, and voices, the present is always accompanied by predecessors: "we're not, finally, alone."[77]

"Who was first?" is perhaps the last question to be provincialized. The search for beginnings is perhaps a distinguishing feature of modernity. Thus, the perennial rediscovery of beginnings must lead, necessarily, to a multiplicity of modernities.

CHAPTER TWO

Discovery of the Glacières

MONTAGNES MAUDITES

"Mont Blanc" had to be discovered before the "glaciers" could become a mountain. In 1680, Giovanni Tomaso Borgonio's *Carta Generale de Stati di Sua Altezza Reale,* a map of the Savoyard kingdoms of Victor Amadeus II, was typical in representing *les glacières* as a sweeping mountain massif between Chamonix and the Great St. Bernard Pass (Figure 5). Whether viewed from a distance or up close, the glaciers were little more than an elevated mass of snow and ice. Ecclesiastical visitors a century earlier viewed the valley at the foot of the glaciers as a provincial backwater: "There are a lot of poor people, all rustic and ignorant . . . so poor that in the said places of Chamonix and Vallorsine there is no clock by which to see and know the passage of time. . . . No stranger will come to live there, and ice and frost are common since the creation of the world."[1] In 1580, Archdeacon Bernard Combet visited Chamonix to adjudicate disputes over payment of tithe to the local monastery: "The summits have white glaciers which extend through clefts in the mountains themselves and descend nearly to the

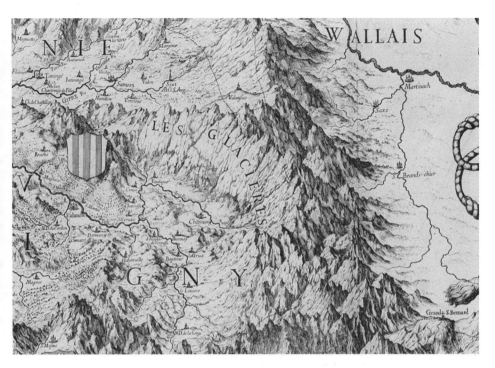

Figure 5 *Les Glacières* form a mountain range between Chamonix and the Great St. Bernard hospice, in G. T. Borgonio, *Carta Generale de Stati di Sua Altezza Reale,* 1680. A dotted line on the glaciers marks the boundary between the province of Faucigny in Savoy and the Valais in Switzerland. HCL, Harvard Map Collection, MA 690.680 pf*.

plain of the valley in at least three places. There the ice accumulates in vast quantities because it remains perpetually frozen, however much it flows in the summer season."[2]

During the seventeenth century, the *glacières* of Savoy acquired another name, *mont maudite,* the cursed mountain. Bernard of Menthon, the founder of Alpine hospices, was named a Counter-Reformation saint in 1681, following new rules for canonization decreed by Pope Urban VIII in 1625.[3] The campaign for sainthood popularized the story that Bernard had banished a demon to mountains that became known as the *montagnes maudites.* The story of the cursed mountain may have circulated in the oral tradition, but appeared more frequently only after this campaign for canonization. In 1685, two Genevans calculated the elevation of the "*montagne maudite* being the *glacières* covered in snow and ice," but they did not publish their measurements until 1730. Eighteenth-century maps of the region often elided "Mont Maudit or St. Bernard" into a single place among the "glaciers" of Chamonix.[4]

The first appearance of "Mont Blanc" is often said to be in a pamphlet by William Windham and Pierre Martel. Inspired by Zurich physician and professor Johann Jakob Scheuchzer's descriptions of the glaciers of Berne, Windham decided to satisfy his curiosity with a visit to the glaciers of Savoy in 1741. He was in Geneva during a grand tour and shared a common room with other Englishmen to economize on expenses and enjoy polite conversation. Richard Pococke, an English traveler returning from Egypt, joined this "tour of curiosity" to visit "the *Glacières* or mountains of ice in the south east in Savoy." Their retinue of servants and string of packhorses resembled a caravan, and Pococke's journals reported that "we all took the name of Arab chiefs and officers." When they reached the village of Sallanches, "we encamped. I dressed myself privately in the Arab dress and surprised the Company, and were all exceeding cheerful."[5] According to Windham, they posted a "sentinel with drawn sword at the opening of his tent" as a joke, which caused "wonder and astonishment" among the locals, who gazed at the travelers. In Chamonix, the peasants took them to see the terminal ends of the glaciers in the valley. Stating that "this did not satisfy our curiosity," Windham asked to go higher, but was told only hunters went there. Nevertheless, he later wrote, "Our curiosity got the better of these discouragements, and relying on our strength and resolution, we determined to attempt climbing the mountain."[6]

The guides took Windham's party to a viewpoint known as Montanvert, which had "a view terrible enough to make most people's heads turn." The *Mer de Glace* had what appeared to be bottomless crevasses and made sounds like claps of thunder: "As in all countries of ignorance people are extremely superstitious, they told us many strange stories of witches, etc., who came to play their pranks upon the glacières, and dance to the sound of instruments. We should have been surprised if we had not been entertained in these parts with some such idle legends." They toasted the health of a British admiral and returned to Geneva. Windham made only a restrained claim of priority: "All the merit we can pretend to is having opened the way to others who may have curiosity of the same kind."[7]

In August 1742, Pierre Martel, an engineer at Geneva, repeated the excursion with his own scientific instruments. Among the peaks, Martel wrote, "'tis this point of Mont Blanc, which is supposed to be the highest in all the Glacières, and perhaps of all the Alps."[8] *Journal Helvétique* published Windham's and Martel's descriptions of the glaciers in French in 1743, and they were translated into English in 1744, with advertisements for Martel's services as a mathematician, surveyor, and mapmaker. This pamphlet secured Windham's election to the Royal Society and Martel's appointment as the harbor master and surveyor in Jamaica. Martel's map of the Chamonix valley labeled one of the nearby peaks as "Mont Blanc" (Figure 6).

MAKING UP MONT BLANC

By 1800, it was widely believed that Windham discovered Chamonix and Mont Blanc. Ebel's guidebook to Switzerland found it unbelievable that "this valley, so singularly interesting, in which one sees the highest mountain in the old world, remained entirely unknown until the year 1741."[9] The view that Windham had discovered Chamonix was so prevalent by the 1820s that a skeptical Markham Sherwill interviewed inhabitants and looked for archives in Chamonix with the assistance of Ambroise Paccard, the son of Dr. Michel-Gabriel Paccard. They found bundles of parchment in a trunk covered with spiderwebs and dust that "appeared as old as the Priory itself."[10] Records included the deed that gave ownership of the valley to a Benedictine priory in 1091, a code of laws that permitted settlement in exchange for payment of dues, charters for public fairs and markets, and reports of many ecclesiastical visits. In 1634, the Savoy Senate permitted horned cattle in the valley for "grazing on those mountains which, by the industry of the peasants, had been cleared of their forests."[11] Despite this longer history, Windham is still, centuries later, sometimes still credited with "discovery."

The discovery of Mont Blanc has served as a foundation myth in narratives of mountaineering and modernity. Windham's curiosity is said to have led to scientific research in the 1760s, exploration of the mountains in the 1770s, and the ascent in the 1780s. In these linear narratives, before Windham is a vacancy that awaits the assertion of individual will and curiosity, as well as the abandonment of self-restriction that ushers in modernity. More recently, scholars have complicated the notion of any singular "culture of curiosity" by investigating diverse languages and sensibilities of curiosity, wonder, and marvels that took a variety of contemporary forms.[12]

Figure 6 Pierre Martel's map and sketch of the Chamonix valley, which labeled one
peak *le Mont Blanc* in *An account of the glacieres or ice Alps in Savoy* (London, 1744), is
reputedly the "first" appearance of Mont Blanc in print.   Beinecke Rare Book and
Manuscript Library, Yale University.

Windham's visit to Mont Blanc is an example of "making up discovery," the process by which "discoveries are made up in the course of making the disciplinary histories of specific scientific practices."[13] Discovery is not an individual, heroic event, but a complex process of negotiation within social networks that results in a retrospective attribution. Discussing examples from the 1660s to the 1840s, Simon Schaffer has shown that none of the ostensibly individual discoveries may be isolated into an unambiguously single-authored event, and "it is impossible to find a criterion for discovery apart from the local practices of contemporary research communities."[14] Indeed, the attribution to Windham or Martel of the discovery of Mont Blanc was the result of particular communities recognizing what counted as success during a series of dynamic economic and political changes in the Alps.

Windham's visit to Chamonix in June 1741 was preceded by the announcement of a mining company in Savoy formed by English and Brabant investors. Mines had been exploited in the area since Roman occupation and the priory of Chamonix and monastery at Sallanches had leased mineral rights or operated mines in the valley since the fifteenth and sixteenth centuries.[15] In May 1741, King Charles-Emmanuel III of Piedmont-Savoy granted rights to all "mines which have been and will be discovered" in Savoy, with certain exceptions, to the "English Company for the Excavation and Exploitation of Mines in Savoy." The *Compagnie Anglaise* received these expansive mineral rights in exchange for providing the Savoyard state at Turin with the metals necessary to manufacture artillery. The company then developed copper, lead, and silver mines throughout the Arve valley, including at Chamonix for thirty years. In the 1780s, coal mines at Servoz became part of the standard itinerary for visitors to the valley.[16]

Windham's "curiosity" declared that he was not an investor in the *Compagnie Anglaise* to readers who were well aware of these mines and the wars that made them profitable. The opposition between curiosity and "interest" was a prominent feature of eighteenth-century British travel writing, and Windham combined the "narrating" and "collecting" tendencies noted in early modern curiosity.[17] Such distinctions were also useful for the *Compagnie Anglaise,* which included investors from the Low Countries and mining engineers from Germany. The intendant of Faucigny was entirely justified to ask the Chamonix village secretary in 1749 to keep a discrete eye on foreigners "calling themselves English" who visited the valley "on the pretext of visiting the glaciers."[18] And yet, the intendant's clear-eyed assessment is too often mistakenly read as an example of cultural backwardness.

These mines were one consequence of fiscal-military reforms undertaken by Victor Amadeus II of Piedmont-Savoy in the wake of almost constant war with Louis XIV's France. During 1690–1696 and 1703–1713, French troops occupied the duchy of Savoy, including the Chamonix valley.[19] Victor Amadeus II, known as the king of Sardinia after Piedmont-Savoy annexed the island in 1720, transformed the Savoyard state from 1690 with a series of administrative reforms that intensified in the 1710s and 1720s. He eliminated tax exemptions, overhauled the educational system, and introduced new legal codes, relief for the poor, and a network of intendants who interposed themselves between peasants and seigneurs and oversaw a new census and detailed land surveys. The authority of the state ran to the lowest levels of activity and the reign of Victor Amadeus II is often considered one of the definitive examples of absolutism at work.[20] The 1741 agreement with the *Compagnie Anglaise* enabled his son, Charles-Emmanuel III, to import foreign workers and up-to-date mining techniques while limiting French influence. The demand for artillery became urgent in September 1742, when Spanish troops occupied the duchy during the War of the Austrian Succession.

Martel's map of "Mont Blanc" followed and copied the Savoyard cadastral survey. During the three hours that Martel spent making a map of the glaciers, he was aided by a guide who had assisted in the Savoyard survey, and Martel used another map exhibited at Chamonix.[21] The cadastral survey of Savoy from 1728 to 1738 recorded the location, value, and ownership of developed land for the *perequazione* (equalization) of land taxes. Indeed, the earliest appearance of "Mont Blanc" on a map is not Martel's sketch, but the military copy of the 1737 cadastral map of Chamonix, now held at the *L'Istituto Geografico Militare* in Florence.[22] The transmission of geographical knowledge involved the translation of preexisting local knowledge into cartographic form. Martel provides a fine example of the process by which cartographic knowledge collected on account of "thinking like a state" was translated into a traveler's narrative as if "thinking like a self." Before the tourist came the state.

Did the state "discover" Mont Blanc? The state—and the church—may have come before the tourist, but to displace Windham with either one would merely substitute an institutional actor for an individual agent while preserving the heroic model of individual discovery. The process of state formation in early modern Europe shaped the "discovery" of the mountain by making the natural world legible through surveys, and it should be emphasized that this was *not* a peculiarly European phenomenon. Chomolungma, the Himalayan peak identified as the highest in the world and renamed Mount Everest by the Survey of India in the 1850s, was first mapped in a Qing survey commissioned by the Kangxi emperor in the 1710s.[23] Although these maps were once considered Western because Jesuits compiled the Kangxi atlas, scholars of eighteenth-century cartography in France, Russia, Qing China, and British India argue that the cartography of this period was early modern rather than Western and applied in similar ways for similar purposes in empires around the globe using a "rhetoric of science and exact measurement."[24]

Blanks on the Savoyard map were no longer outside the scale of legibility created by early modern states. Cadastral maps identified parcels of land along rivers or on arable plains, and mountains were blank spaces of waste in between these ribbons of development. An unanticipated effect of such surveys was to bring the spaces in between into the grid of legibility on which local names of mountains were *recorded,* but not discovered for the first time. When Jacques-Barthélémy Micheli du Crest made a map of Geneva to improve its fortifications in the 1720s, he linked his detailed survey of Genevan landmarks with the triangulation survey of France, but had difficulty in the direction of Savoy: "I drew a provisional map with great precision and consequently saw the empty space that I would have to fill in Savoy."[25]

The population in this empty space possessed knowledge of the area that was neither static nor reducible to a single discovery event. In the 1820s, Markham Sherwill interviewed "older guides whose fathers were present at this first visit of curious travelers," and was told the visitors were entertained by the curate and kindly received by the villagers:

> What seemed most to surprise the peasants was that strangers should come from so far off, though they probably did not know from whence, merely to look at the mountains and the glaciers, in which the natives themselves neither saw nor could understand that any beauty or peculiarity existed, supposing no doubt that the whole world was formed after the manner and fashion of their own.[26]

Early on, the peasants of Chamonix fixed Windham's discovery in the *Pierre aux Anglais*. The young duc de la Rochefoucauld visited the Glaciers in 1762 and reported that the mountains were unknown before Windham summoned the courage to overcome obstacles worse than giants, winged dragons, or windmills: "It had to be an Englishman or a knight errant: it was an Englishman." After resolving to be the first Frenchman "like another Windham," he made the journey and ate lunch at the *Pierre aux Anglais,* a boulder that "takes its name from the English who were the first to use it for this purpose."[27] From the 1770s, guidebooks described "the route of the crystal-hunters" to the rock, which recalled the "first discoveries of Messrs. Windham and Pococke."[28] By the 1830s, their names were chiseled in stone, but the rock was vandalized around 1848 and reinscribed a few years later. By the early twentieth century, historians found even more embellished accounts, and considered "the history of the *Pierre aux Anglais* an excellent joke made by Chamoniards."[29]

Les glacières, Mont Maudit, and Mont Blanc were not mutually exclusive and circulated alongside one another for years. In the early twentieth century, historians once debated whether "Mont Blanc" was owed to the *Rupes Alba* listed as a boundary marker in the prose map in the deed of the priory, but the phrase is usually interpreted as referring to a place in the valley and certainly not to the summit.[30] The canonization of St. Bernard gave prominence to Mont Maudit at the moment when local names were entering a wider geographical lexicon. Not until around 1770, when Jean-André Deluc stood on the summit of the "Glacier of Buet" and measured the elevation of "*Mont Blanc,* which is, so to speak, a single *Glacier,*" was the name Mont Blanc used more consistently to designate the highest peak among the *glacières*.[31] Coming from the Protestant bastion of Geneva, Windham, Martel, Deluc, and Horace-Bénédict de Saussure might have had multiple reasons for preferring Mont Blanc to Mont Maudit, as each framed his encounter with the locals as the triumph over "superstition."

Saussure noted that "the little people" called the snow-covered peaks *montagnes maudites:* "In my childhood I myself heard it said to peasants that the eternal snows were the effect of a curse that the inhabitants of the mountains had brought on themselves for their crimes." Now, he wrote in 1786, this "superstitious opinion, as absurd as it is, could very well serve as the foundation for a disadvantageous idea, which has been accredited even among men far above such prejudices."[32] "Mont Blanc" was neither a Protestant nor Catholic name, and still less a "secular" name, but rather a local name with a wide range of potential meanings. Indeed, the peasants of Chamonix may have preferred Mont Blanc to the disparaging Mont Maudit to resist the implication that the mountains were a curse they had brought upon themselves.

"Making up Mont Blanc" was the result of the encounter of the peasants of Chamonix and visitors from other regions during a period of state formation and the expansion of capitalist mining in the Alps. Eighteenth-century attributions of the "discovery of Mont Blanc" were productive of the very category of "discovery." Yet the role of local initiative was not always invisible. Marc-Théodore Bourrit wrote from Geneva in 1773 that the beauties of the country would have remained unknown

> but for the rude relations of its peasants, who bring us annually their honey and their crystals. The frightful picture which they gave us of their valleys of ice, and of their stupendous mountains; those extraordinary accounts (which procured these snowy precipices the appellation of Les Montagnes Maudites) excited the curiosity of two English gentlemen, who resided some time since in Geneva.[33]

Mont Blanc was discovered by people who lived nearby and brought the fruits of the country to further markets and wider networks of knowledge. We need to clear a space in which to hear the "rude relations" *(récit bizarre)* of these peasants.

THE INDIES IN SWITZERLAND

In 1541, Conrad Gessner found the highest rock on the summit of Mount Pilatus, near Lucerne, carved with the names, dates, and family crests of people who had made previous ascents. Gessner, a Zurich physician and polymath scholar who wrote widely on botany, bibliography, and the natural history of animals, made journeys in the mountains once or twice a year "for my mind and my health" with students and colleagues to observe flowers in bloom. Nowhere besides the mountains was it possible to experience the variety of all four seasons in a single day. Some said Pontius Pilate caused storms from the summit, but Gessner did not believe Pilate had ever visited the mountain or was responsible for violent storms. Such beliefs were a form of superstition and impiety, for "it is impious to attribute the cause of any event or change in the world to an author other than God." For a student and admirer of nature, Gessner believed that "from the contemplation and admiration of so many works of the Sovereign Architect, and such variety of nature in the mountains, as if everything were gathered in one great pile, a pleasure of the mind is conjoined with the harmonious pleasure of all the senses."[34]

Gessner was in the community of sixteenth-century physicians and botanists who developed a "science of describing" to compare accounts from antiquity with the natural world all around them.[35] *De Alpibus Commentarius* (1574), by Josias Simmler, a Zurich theologian and Gessner's first biographer, is a good example of the genre. Simmler compiled references to the Alps from antiquity, cataloged peaks and passes, and added an account of the difficulties of walking on snow and ice and over crevasses using crampons, alpenstocks, ropes, and snowshoes.[36] Other botanists, including Johann Aicholz and Carolus Clusius, also went climbing in the mountains to collect Alpine plants as botanical specimens.[37]

These naturalists were not interested in claiming the summit for themselves. Gessner's early patron was Ulrich Zwingli, and Gessner and Simmler adhered to a Zwinglian theology in which the natural world joined the Bible as a source of God's revelation. The Zwinglian understanding of "the absolute sovereignty and otherness of God" remained consistent with belief in magical prayer, demonic efficacy, and supernatural beings in the world.[38] In the sixteenth and seventeenth centuries, the view from a mountaintop inspired reflection on the vastness of the mountains and the "Sovereign Architect" who made them.

At the beginning of the eighteenth century, Johann Jakob Scheuchzer quoted Gessner and cited his example as an inspiration for his own journeys in the Alps after 1702. The scope of Scheuchzer's work is apparent in the full title of *Ouresiphoites Helveticus, sive Itinera Alpina tria* (1708):

A Swiss Mountain Wanderer: or three Alpine journeys in which the inhabitants, animals, plants, barometric heights of the mountains, temperatures of the sky and sun, medicinal waters, minerals, metals, decorative stones and other fossils; and anything else in the nature, arts and antiquities of the Swiss and Rhaetian Alps, which is rare and noteworthy, is explained and illustrated with pictures.[39]

Published in Latin with illustrations subsidized by Isaac Newton and fellows of the Royal Society, this work reached the same small but learned audience that Gessner's had, 150 years earlier. Scheuchzer's natural histories in German and his illustrated Bible commentary with scenes from Genesis to the Apocalypse reached much wider audiences.[40] Nineteenth-century mockery of Scheuchzer's catalog of dragons or his identification of a fossil as the remnants of a man who witnessed Noah's flood have obscured his influence in reorienting attitudes toward the Alps. Scheuchzer's work entangled natural history and natural theology, the exotic and the local.

Scheuchzer's natural histories went beyond the late seventeenth-century "consensus formula" in the Zwinglian-Calvinist Reformed Churches that the truths expressed in the Book of Scripture and the Book of Nature depended on the Bible for authority and that natural wisdom could not be acquired from nature alone. In contrast, Scheuchzer held that natural theology could independently demonstrate God's existence through the study of nature. Thus, his natural history was a critique of Spinoza, who used mathematics to criticize scripture, and of orthodox clerics in Switzerland, who refused to acknowledge contemporary mechanical philosophy.[41] For Scheuchzer, observations by peasants who could read nature in front of them were as important as those by learned professors. He invited "curious men of the lowest order, fishers, shepherds of flocks, inhabitants of the Alps, farmers, diggers, root-cutters" to contribute observations to his works.[42] His expansive view of natural history in Switzerland, a region that did not correspond to a single state, accommodated the local expertise that was ignored by contemporary state surveys. Scheuchzer's approach was widely emulated in central Europe in studies of local flora, mineralogy, and the natural history of territory.[43]

These natural histories were located in a wider comparative framework that equated the indigenous in Switzerland with the exotic in other parts of the world. As early as the 1690s, Scheuchzer argued that as the English specialized in learning about remote regions of the earth on account of their colonial empire so the Swiss should examine their own native land. *Itinera Alpina* noted that travelers went to India and Africa to admire the exotic and yet neglected to see it in full view every day. *"Europae Provincias"* offered opportunities for such investigation and he chose the provinces of his own country.[44] In a later work on natural history, Scheuchzer noted that all regions of the earth were connected since all were made by God: "All of the lands of the world are joined together as if by a chain. . . . Switzerland must often be sought in the Indies, and the Indies in Switzerland."[45]

The epitome of the exotic was Scheuchzer's account of Swiss dragons. His taxonomy of dragons, compiled from references in previous authorities, local chronicles, and oral reports, demonstrated, through frequent comparison, that the indigenous dragons of Switzerland were as interesting and exotic as those described by Pliny or more recent observers in Africa, the Americas, and Asia. Scheuchzer included an extended discussion of the "Dragon Stone" in a cabinet of curiosities at Lucerne, and his account is best known for its illustrations of monstrous serpents.[46] Although Scheuchzer was later lampooned for excessive credulity, two years before he published these pictures, his own view was quite the opposite: "I myself, although very skeptical about this material, have been assiduous in collecting all the Swiss dragon stories and have had them [the dragons] painted according to the descriptions, but if they [the paintings] should someday become public, I will not give them out as factual but rather as very dubious, and most of them as made-up."[47] In narratives of a disenchanted modernity, however, Scheuchzer must play the role of a credulous deviation from the inexorable path of enlightenment, secularization, and rationalization.

More recent studies of early modern monsters and wonders suggest that such a teleological view depends on exaggerated distinctions between natural and supernatural explanations that were not mutually exclusive, and fails to understand changing intellectual responses to exceptions and anomalies in nature. Dragons and the wonders of nature represented the limits of what observers could know and exhibited a sensibility of wonder and curiosity in natural philosophy. The very strangeness of an account could make it credible. For Newtonians such as Scheuchzer, "to be incredulous was a sign of little learning and narrow experience, not enlightened skepticism."[48] Scheuchzer viewed the dragon stories as subjects of study in their own right, much like a folklorist or anthropologist, and he campaigned against interpreting natural disasters as evil omens.[49]

Most important, Scheuchzer's natural histories restored divine purpose to the mountains. The Alps were not heaps of stones left in the ruins of a flood, as Thomas Burnet had argued, but were useful parts of a harmonious creation that made visible God's deity and power.[50] The illustrations in Scheuchzer's natural histories of Switzerland "reflect awe in the work of the

Master Builder," and have been cited as "one of the first pictorial renderings of the esthetic of the sublime," in which awe, terror, and exultation appropriate to God were transferred to nature.[51] Long before dissemination of rhetorical theories of the sublime, changes in natural theology and natural history articulated this position for an observer of nature.[52]

The primacy Scheuchzer gave to natural theology left him uninterested in reaching the summit. He turned back before reaching the top of Pilatus, "in part due to bodily weariness and in part because the length of the route still to be climbed was not agreeable."[53] For Scheuchzer and for Gessner, the summit position remained for God alone. For both, climbing represented a technique of collecting and a metaphor for field research in natural history. Consider the terms in which Scheuchzer, after his first Alpine journey in 1694, criticized physicians who cultivated their garden but had no interest in collecting specimens: "Instead of climbing the mountains found right in front of their noses, they scarcely look at them, let alone enthusiastically embrace this wonderful opportunity to botanize."[54]

ALPINE IDYLLS AND THE ORDER OF NATURE

For Albrecht von Haller, climbing mountains also meant botanizing in pursuit of natural history and natural theology. Haller traveled in the Alps in search of botanical specimens from 1728 to 1732 before practicing as a physician at Berne, researching anatomy and botany as a professor at Göttingen, and returning to Berne to continue his research while acting as director of a salt mine in the 1750s. In 1728, Haller thought the view beyond a vineyard toward Mont Maudit and the mountains of Savoy was one of the most beautiful in Europe: "the mixture of dreadful and agreeable, cultivated and savage, has a charm which is ignored by those who are indifferent to nature."[55] Haller's poem "Die Alpen" (1732) reworked the idyll and pastoral genres by idealizing a peasant community flourishing in a "happy golden age" in the present. The poem is framed by encomiums to the virtue and innocence of the simple folk of the mountains in contrast to the greed, lust, and ambition of princes at court or burghers in cities. In the Alps, "reason rules with nature as its guide." Much of the poem follows an archetypal peasant couple through courtship and marriage and the seasons of a year tending cows, cutting hay, hunting chamois, and making cheese. Peasants

who can read "nature's mirror" have a practical wisdom worth more than a
thousand books, embodied in an old man who knows every herb and moss,
the location of gold, and the local histories of his homeland, but aspires to
know more.[56]

While Libya offered novel sights and "monsters each day," the Alps lacked
nothing, and even the icy peaks were useful by watering the lands around
them. Yet, for Haller, the diversity of the horizon at sunrise cannot be
encompassed:

> What nature has most magnificently built is seen from a mountain with
> ever-new delight. Through the dispersed vapor of a thin cloud, the theatre of
> the world opens up. A wide abode of more than one tribe shows at once every-
> thing that its area contains; a gentle dizziness forces the all too weak eyes to
> close, eyes that are incapable of penetrating the too broad horizon.[57]

The inability to view all of creation at once led to dizziness, so Haller represented the Alps through a "chain of framed views" of valleys, hills, woods,
glaciers, and flowers. His visual poetics and emphasis on color were similar
to other contemporary poets.[58] As long as the "too broad horizon" was im-
penetrable, the panoramic perspective of the summit remained inconceiv-
able. For Haller, the highest truth was that no object is too small or lowly
that it is not a work of God and wonder in itself: "You will find everything
beautiful and yet different / And you will always dig out the all too rich
treasure, but never fathom it."[59]

By finding the exotic in the local and the sacred in the blossom of a particular flower, Scheuchzer and Haller articulated an aesthetics of difference,
at once geographical, theological, epistemological, and "provincial." The
Alps were as exotic as the Indies, contained all of creation, signs of Providence were in the smallest details, and the provinciality of the mountains
was felt by its residents at home and abroad. Indeed, Martel's images of the
diverse animals of the Chamonix valley are contemporary examples of this
perspective (Figure 6). The aesthetics of difference was the counterpart to
the "aesthetics of the infinite" once celebrated by Marjorie Hope Nicolson.
Early eighteenth-century naturalists, however, were less enthralled by infinite space than by the local, provincial, and different, and this exoticism of
the local was reinforced by comparisons to other parts of the world. Haller's

poem compared the Alps to Libya, Persia, Peru, and Tonkin/China, and later editions added references to Robert Clive's victories in India. The exoticism of the local and provincial was also articulated by mountain residents when they traveled elsewhere: Scheuchzer developed a climatic theory of *Homo Alpinus* and published barometrical readings to show that changes in atmospheric pressure at lower elevations caused "nostalgia" among the Swiss in exile.[60]

Haller was representative of a generation of natural historians whose response to difference was to search for order in nature. If Scheuchzer had reveled in local variety and popular knowledge, the classificatory schemes promoted by Haller, Linnaeus, and others from the 1730s onward depended on detached observers to search for order in nature.[61] Following the model of a Göttingen laboratory, Haller recruited physicians, surgeons, apothecaries, professors, and clergymen to search the mountains for botanical specimens and even paid collaborators like research assistants.[62] The order of nature defined the framework of inquiry across a wide range of philosophical positions and did not necessarily entail a shift away from natural theology toward a rationalization of natural history.

On the contrary, mid-eighteenth-century naturalists in the Alps such as Haller, Charles Bonnet, Jean-André Deluc, and Horace-Bénédict de Saussure all embedded their natural histories in natural theologies.[63] For these naturalists, the order of nature reinforced the existing social order. In another of his poems, Haller argued that reason demonstrated the existence of God in contrast to superstition (in this context, Catholicism) and incredulity (nonbelief in a Divinity). "Humble reason," he wrote, "must confine itself to the genuine expression of timid adoration."[64] Indeed, the popularity of Haller's *Offering of Swiss Poetry* owed as much to his pious odes to his deceased wives and his epistles on evil, vanity, virtue, and reason as to his verses on *The Alps*. From this wider perspective, the search for order in nature reinforced "not so much naturalization as subordination: the subordination of anomalies to watertight laws of nature, of nature to God, and of citizens and Christians to established authority."[65]

The order of nature and aesthetics of difference in the Alps exerted a wide influence, even among contemporaries who were less sympathetic to established authority. Jean-Jacques Rousseau wrote: "I see in nature an admirable physical order always consistent with itself. The moral order should be the same. Yet my life's experience has been the apparent breakdown of this order."[66] Rousseau's varied works reiterated his desire to make moral order as transparent as the physical order of nature. His "Savoyard Vicar" professed the view that the Book of Nature was open to all eyes.[67] His deism and "natural religion" navigated between the reason of philosophers and the revelation of natural theology in defining a religious sensibility or "piety of sincerity."[68] Where Rousseau's *Discourse on Inequality* (1755) and *Social Contract* (1762) posited a natural goodness in man in a "state of nature" in the past, his epistolary novel *Julie, or the New Héloïse* (1761) located a golden age in an Alpine idyll in the present. At the harvest festival at Clarens, for example, "the gentle equality that prevails here reestablishes nature's order, constitutes a form of instruction for some, a consolation for others, and a bond of friendship for all."[69]

More generally, *Julie, or the New Héloïse* provided a summation of the provincial aesthetics of difference and the "Indies in Switzerland." Rousseau said his protagonists were "not French, wits, academicians, philosophers; but provincials, foreigners, solitary youths, almost children who in their romantic imaginations mistake the honest ravings of their brains for philosophy."[70] St. Preux writes to his lover, Julie, that the mixture of wild and cultivated nature in the mountains created harmony and the pure air restored his inner peace: "High in the mountains where the air is pure and subtle, one breathes more freely, one feels lighter in the body, more serene of mind; pleasures there are less intense, passions more moderate. Meditations there take on an indescribably grand and sublime character, in proportion with the objects that strike us." St. Preux later describes the Alps as "more fragrant than the perfumes of the Orient," and the countryside "the most beautiful that ever met human eye; that charming abode like nothing I had found in circling the earth." He asks Julie to "combine in your mind the impressions of all I have just described" to have an idea of a view in the mountains. "Imagine the variety," he continues, "the grandeur, the beauty of a thousand stunning vistas; the pleasure of seeing all around one nothing but entirely new objects, strange birds, bizarre and unknown plants, of observing in a way an altogether different nature, and finding oneself in a new world."[71]

Rousseau's novel reached its emotional peak on a precipice in view of Mont Blanc. After crossing Lake Geneva in a rowboat, St. Preux and Julie climb hills to a "wild and forsaken nook; but filled with those sorts of beauties that are pleasing only to sensible souls and appear horrible to others." A mountain stream fed by melting snows churns nearby with mud, sand, and rocks: "Behind us a range of inaccessible cliffs separated the esplanade where we were standing from that part of the Alps which is named *les glacières,* because enormous crests of ice that are constantly spreading have covered them since the world began." In a note, Rousseau observes that these mountains are so high that their crests are still bathed in light long after sunset. St. Preux finds a protected spot "meant to be the sanctuary of two lovers who alone had escaped nature's cataclysm." He leads Julie to the place where he had once carved her initials and Francesco Petrarch's love sonnets into the rock, and grieved for her love. She pulls him back from the brink, and they return to the boat overcome by emotion. "I see that our hearts have never ceased to understand each other! It is true, she said in a broken voice; but let this be the last time they will have spoken on this register."[72]

Readers responded to Rousseau in the same register and *Julie* would become a best-selling novel of the eighteenth century and "revolutionize the relation between reader and text."[73] Rousseau's presentation of these letters as unmediated and transparent expressions of emotion between lovers, notes Robert Darnton, complemented rather than contradicted the conventions of natural theology that the Book of Nature could be read as the unmediated Word of God. Readers of Rousseau could visit the Alps to see sites from the lives of Julie and St. Preux. As they shed tears and reached emotional heights with these mountain lovers, Rousseau's readers ventured into territory extending far beyond appreciation of the Alps.[74]

Monsieur Wolmar, the landlord who married Julie and had read all the philosophers, embodied the view of the order of nature as social subordination: "Every man has his assigned place in the best order of things, the question is to find that place and not pervert that order." In contrast, Julie articulates another point of view: "Man, she said, is too noble a being to have to serve merely as an instrument of others . . . in order to allocate things appropriately one must not in distributing them look for the job each man is best at, but for the one that is best for each man, so as to render him as good and happy as is possible." The lessons taught by *Julie* should not be underestimated. After walking along the cliffs separating them from the *glacières,* on the most emotional day of his life before Julie's death, St. Preux remarked that "this adventure has convinced me more than all the arguments, of the freedom of man and the merit of virtue."[75]

LETTERS WRITTEN FROM THE MOUNTAINS

Visions of sovereignty inspired a proposal to climb Mont Blanc in 1754. Incarcerated in the elevated Swiss fortress of Aarburg, Jacques-Barthélémy Micheli du Crest estimated the mountain to be the same height as Pichincha, a Peruvian volcano climbed by La Condamine in 1742. Micheli du Crest thought an ascent of Mont Blanc would lead to improved observations and maps: "Although it culminates in a peak always covered with snow at the top, in my opinion that would facilitate the route one could take by revolving around it in order to reach the summit."[76] He was sentenced to life in prison by the canton of Berne to prevent him from continuing in exile the republican agitations that led to his expulsion from Geneva. He used a rain gutter to make trigonometrical observations for what is often considered the "first" panorama of the Alps: *Prospect géométrique des montagnes neigées dittes les Gletscher.*[77]

The panoramic prospect and ascent of Mont Blanc attempted to represent the world transparently. A decade earlier, Micheli du Crest had created a "universal thermometer" featuring a 100-degree scale that was widely adopted in German-speaking Europe.[78] While in prison, Micheli du Crest proposed surveys of Switzerland in letters to Haller and the Swiss Confederation: "To have precise, highly detailed, well-drawn maps of the whole Country is a very useful and convenient thing for the government of a State, since one judges infinitely better from the plan of a place than from the place itself, for the plan represents to the eye not just the lands but also everything that surrounds them for farther than the eye can see."[79] Consider the difference between the cartographer's God's-eye view from above and the panoramic prospect of the horizon from a single viewpoint. The map of the country was useful for seeing like a state, but a panorama put the viewer at the center, as if thinking like a self. It was no coincidence that an outspoken advocate for popular sovereignty envisioned both the panorama of the Alps and the ascent of Mont Blanc. Indeed, Micheli du Crest was in prison because his demands for political transparency were so unsettling.

Debates over sovereignty in Geneva engaged three early mountain climbers—Horace-Bénédict de Saussure, Marc-Théodore Bourrit, and Jean-André Deluc—yet this political context has been sanitized if not neglected altogether in accounts of their ascents. In the early eighteenth century, only a minority of Geneva's twenty thousand people could participate in its political institutions. The General Council of "citizens and bourgeois," a category of citizenship that totaled fifteen hundred male heads of households, elected a Large Council of two hundred members and a Small Council of twenty-five members, and these bodies were increasingly dominated by a small patrician oligarchy. The disenfranchised majority consisted of "natives" born in Geneva, a few "habitants" granted the right of residence, and a small number of "subjects," or peasants in the surrounding villages.[80]

The patriciate came into conflict with the "citizens and bourgeois" over higher taxes to pay for new military defenses. From 1707, the opposition called repeatedly for restoring to the General Council the sovereignty they claimed had been usurped by the smaller bodies. In the 1720s, Micheli du Crest emerged as this group's leader, and he was soon banished for life. A series of *Représentations* in 1734 declared the people of Geneva sovereign and a bourgeois militia briefly took control of the city. Outside the city gates, Micheli du Crest maintained that the people retained sovereignty and magistrates were only "ministers of *the will*" of the sovereign people.[81] The governments of France, Berne, and Zurich brokered a settlement known as the Mediation of 1738, which then held for almost twenty-five years. The opposition split into democrats sympathetic to Micheli du Crest *(Michelistes)* and "moderate" republicans *(Représentants)* led by Jacques-François Deluc. Deluc was a watchmaker who had been a Micheliste in the 1720s but became a Représentant and opponent of civic equality for the natives.[82]

Politically, Geneva was divided into aristocrats, democrats, and merchants, and Saussure, Bourrit, and Deluc were rooted in each of these distinctive milieu. Horace-Bénédict de Saussure was born into the aristocratic patriciate—his mother inherited a great fortune and his father owned an agricultural estate and was a member of the Council of 200. Saussure married an heiress of the Lullin banking fortune and they lived in her family's mansions. In contrast, Marc-Théodore Bourrit was a native, the son of a copyist and arithmetician who was imprisoned for distributing works by Micheli du Crest in 1735. Bourrit married the daughter of a citizen, and their marriage across this social divide later inspired a political novel. Jean-André

Deluc was a textile merchant, the elder son of the leading "moderate" republican, and married the daughter of influential Représentants.[83]

Jean-André Deluc visited the Alps to study natural philosophy and was personally and politically close to Rousseau. In 1754, Deluc and his wife, brother, and father joined Rousseau and his companion on a six-day boat trip on Lake Geneva. Rousseau had recently returned to Geneva to reclaim his citizenship and announce the dedication of his *Discourse on Inequality* (1755) to the Republic of Geneva. The Deluc brothers had visited the *glacières* of Savoy to make barometric observations in hopes of developing a "Theory of our Earth." Jean-André Deluc read everything he could about barometers and then "resolved to put aside these books and consult Nature alone, and follow her step by step as far as she would lead me."[84] Rousseau was impressed enough to offer to publish Deluc's observations in the *Encyclopédie,* but Jacques-François Deluc declined since the aims of that work diverged from his son's hope to "establish a theory of the earth conforming to Genesis, and founded upon the soundest natural philosophy."[85]

Debates over Rousseau's writings overturned the political settlement in Geneva when the Small Council burned *Emile* and the *Social Contract* in 1762. After Geneva banned his *Letter to Beaumont* at the request of a French diplomat, Rousseau renounced "forever my right of bourgeoisie and citizenship in the city and republic of Geneva" in a gesture calculated for maximum political effect. In *Lettres écrites de la campagne* (1763), the attorney-general of Geneva, Jean-Robert Tronchin, defended the government's actions and characterized Rousseau's political works as tending to destroy Christian religion and all governments. Jacques-François Deluc wrote a rebuttal and urged Rousseau to write a reply.[86]

In *Lettres écrites de la montagne* (1764), the longest of his political works, Rousseau addressed the people of Geneva: "I took your Constitution, which I found to be beautiful, as the model of political institutions, and proposing you as an example to Europe, far from seeking to destroy you I set out the means of preserving you." Rousseau provided potted summaries of his other works and remained defiantly heterodox. He praised the Mediation of 1738 and had good things to say about the "negative right," as long as it was counterbalanced by powerful rights of remonstrance by the "citizens and bourgeois." Rousseau defined liberty as individual autonomy under the law: "Liberty consists less in doing one's will than in not being subject to someone else's; it also consists in not subjecting someone else's will to ours."

Letters Written from the Mountain sought to establish disembodied sovereignty in laws and reassert the relationship between sovereignty and government in the *Social Contract:* "My book is in the hands of everyone in Geneva, and would that it were equally in everyone's heart!"[87]

The controversy was on everyone's lips, and "the spirit of the *Social Contract* fills everyone's head," Saussure lamented to Haller at the end of 1765. Saussure and the patrician supporters of the "negative right" became known as *Négatifs* in opposition to the Représentants. But unlike the "ultra-Negatives," Saussure's letters indicate a wider range of sympathies. After telling Haller in 1764 that "the active life of a mountain naturalist singularly pleases me," Saussure offered to send him a copy of Voltaire's *Treatise on Tolerance,* a work he hastened to add was a mélange "of useful truths and pernicious principles."[88] Saussure was named professor at the academy in 1762, a post many left for better-paying political positions, but he remained and also became secretary to the Venerable Company of Pastors in 1766. Even Saussure's journeys in the Alps had a political context. His 1764 "Oration on Glacières," a Latin address to the Geneva Academy, described his visits to Chamonix and closed by comparing glaciers and politics. Ice settles on the highest crags until "changed into steam or water; or rather, growing heavy by the increase of its mass, it is dragged down by its own weight. In science, just as in politics, there is a final point beyond which no further increase is possible, and human affairs seem unable to rise any higher without slipping and falling back."[89]

Further protests led to calls for mediation by outside powers. Rousseau was disappointed at the Représentant response and withdrew, but Voltaire stepped into the breach. Voltaire had lived outside Geneva since 1754, and was friendly with the patricians, but his sympathies now turned to the moderate republicans and then the natives. His *Republican Ideas* (1765) defended republics and freedom of expression and called for outside mediation.[90] Instead, the political stalemate led to sanctions and Jean-André Deluc became chief negotiator for Représentant delegations to Versailles, Berne, and Zurich during 1766–1768.[91] Saussure condemned Deluc as a demagogue and dismissed the Représentant efforts:

> There is all over Europe a fermentation that aims at liberty but which will result in many places in a redoubling of slavery. A half-philosophy aspires to a liberty without limits; a more perfect philosophy, grounded in experience,

will see that the tomb of liberty lies in its extreme, which is Democracy. Our people work on passing a new supporting Memoir and I think it will come to nothing. They make a great folly.[92]

With Voltaire's encouragement, the natives appealed to the "humanity" of the mediators. Early on, Marc-Théodore Bourrit had been a partisan for the Représentants because "he envisioned their cause as that of liberty in general."[93] In 1766, he privately told Georges Auzière, an advocate for native sovereignty, that his views honored his character and humanity, "but, sir, you seem to confuse humanity with politics . . . the two do not always advance together, and for our own safety we are most often in the unfortunate position of having one at the expense of the other."[94] Bourrit allied with the natives in December 1766 and joined their delegation to Berne and Zurich. In 1767, Bourrit intervened with Deluc and led a group of natives who declared their loyalty to the government.[95]

Bourrit lent his name to several epistolary novels debating native sovereignty. *Le Natif, ou lettres de Theodore et d'Annette,* by his friend Jean-Pierre Bérenger, recounts the story of a native who wants to marry the daughter of a citizen. An exchange of letters about the meaning of habitant and native convinces her uncle, but the father consents only after Théodore pays the father's debts: "My son, if all my fellow citizens had a soul like yours, our dissensions would soon be finished; we need less politics and more virtue."[96] *Le Citoyen,* a sequel written by an opponent of the natives, imagined an alternate ending: "To properly judge the distance between a Bourgeois and a Native, would you kindly reflect on this: that each Bourgeois of Geneva is Sovereign, that this quality is indelible within him, that this property accompanies him always." He acquires sovereignty when voting in the General Council and retains it after he leaves: "From whence should come his rights of representation, of carrying weapons, of hunting, except as that which is the effect of an individual Sovereign?"[97] A final rebuttal, *Le Natif à Mr. César J* (1767), claimed that natives were invoking "the rights of nature; she gives us all those rights that legislation has not expressly prohibited to us. We have reclaimed a primordial law that no later state may abrogate." When Annette is told she must marry an old officer like Wolmar, she resolves to retreat to the mountains with Théodore: "Life of my soul! I will live with you among the most sterile rocks and the most awful deserts. There, at least, I will taste peace, liberty, and happiness."[98]

The Edict of March 1768, negotiated by Jean-André Deluc, resembled the views of *Le Citoyen* rather than *Le Natif.* The edict made minor concessions and permitted a small number of natives to buy into the bourgeoisie for a hefty fee. The edict has been interpreted as either conserving patrician dominance or revealing the limitations of a "one party state."[99] Deluc was overjoyed at his own ascent to the upper echelons of the citizens and bourgeoisie, but most people remained disenfranchised. Bourrit was appointed cantor and precentor at the Cathedral of St. Peter in Geneva after auditions in June 1768, but other natives were disappointed. Some natives received demeaning punishments for minor infractions and three were killed and hundreds imprisoned. The "exhortations" of Bourrit were investigated, but charges were dropped after he took an oath of loyalty to the state.[100] Bérenger and others were deported and native rights were again restricted. In 1770, Jean-André Deluc was elected to the Council of 200 and his father and brother wrote pamphlets against the natives. Each member of the Deluc family had become an individual sovereign. Debates about sovereignty in the many letters from the mountains during this period were not distractions from climbing; rather, it was the aspirations for individual sovereignty they articulated that made it possible to envision the summit position.

THE GLACIER OF BUET

With order restored and enfranchisement achieved, Jean-André and his brother Guillaume-Antoine Deluc went to the mountains in search of the order of nature. In 1765, they had chosen a snow-covered peak visible from Geneva to test changes in barometric pressure. They calculated its elevation and were immobilized by "admiration as well as horror" as Mont Blanc presented itself "in all its majesty."[101] Only on their return visit in 1770 did they learn the peak's name, the Glacier of Buet, from villagers at a festival day in the valley of Sixt. The villagers were convinced that anyone with instruments must be looking for mines in the mountains. Deluc noted that his friend La Condamine had encountered the same response in Peru: "By dint of repetition we found people who understood us," including a hunter who knew the peak.[102] This guide attributed everything to the "Author of Nature," and their conversation confirmed for Deluc that man's needs were few and the "sweet calm in his soul when it remains in the hands of

Nature, far from the speculations of Philosophers and from the labyrinth of society."[103]

At the summit of the "Glacier of Buet" in 1770, Deluc experienced a profound silence. He felt as if "suspended in the air, upon one of those majestic clouds," and saw a deep blue sky that produced "a kind of sensation of immensity it is impossible to explain."[104] The brothers determined its elevation with barometers, calculated the height of Mont Blanc trigonometrically, and Deluc used his body as an instrument to observe effects of air pressure. The horizon offered peaks in every direction: "In short they commanded in a manner at one view, all the straights of the Alps, of whose pikes there were but few which raised their points above them . . . and a single cast of the eye, over that immense quantity of ice and snow, which covers the Alps, would amply satisfy a spectator."[105]

Jean-André Deluc's ascent appeared in *Recherches sur les modifications de l'atmosphère* (1772), with popular versions in French, German, and English. He repeated the ascent with his brother and a minister to test a new hygrometer in 1772. Deluc's research wedded his political agenda and investigations in natural philosophy in the service of received opinion.[106] He broke up his textile business in 1773 and left for England where he became reader for Queen Charlotte and lived at Windsor. His departure removed him from Genevan politics only in a narrow sense. Deluc's later works, including *Lettres physiques et morales sur les montagnes et sur l'histoire de la terre et de l'homme* (1778), clearly stated that his ambition in his study of the earth, which he hesitated to call "geology," was to prove the truth of the bible through natural history.[107]

Ascents of the "Glacier of Buet" represented the ascendancy of the coalition that prospered after the Genevan *événements* of the 1760s. Ascents by the Représentant Deluc were followed by the "loyal" Native Bourrit in 1775 and the "moderate" Negative Saussure in 1776. Bourrit experienced the "panorama of the Alps" for the first time when he met his wife at her home outside Geneva in 1761. One of the few natives to prosper after 1768, his cathedral post did not result in admission to the bourgeoisie. Bourrit retained the title of cantor *(chantre)* for fifty years, but its stipend was small and he sometimes paid a replacement to act as cantor while he pursued more-remunerative work as an artist or writer. He made his third journey to Mont Blanc in 1770 and thereafter made almost annual visits to Chamonix. *Description des glacières, glaciers et amas de glace du duché de Savoie* (1773) was widely translated and some editions incorporated Jean-André Deluc's ascent of the Buet. When a Genevan pastor published a competing title, Bourrit attacked him in a heated exchange of pamphlets.[108]

Bourrit toured around Mont Blanc and reached the summit of the Buet. Villagers told Bourrit that the mountain he called the Buet was known locally by a different name, *la Mortine:* "They added, and this ruined my hopes, that this mountain had always belonged to the inhabitants of Vallorcine, that its access was easy and it had been frequented in all times by shepherds and hunters."[109] Within a year, the guides named the large rock where he stopped during his ascent *Table au chantre.* On the summit, the Chamonix guides admired the magnificent spectacle and cried out: "O God! The world is great!" The view of Mont Blanc inspired Bourrit's reflections:

> The image of upheaval and chaos, ideas of eternity and nothingness, of revolutions and order, appear all together at once; the imagination remains silent. What design produced these effects? By contemplating these enormous monuments to the decay of the universe, thoughts are moved back many centuries and fixed on an imposing antiquity so well attested in this place.[110]

Later in 1775, Bourrit was invited to Chambéry by Victor-Amadeus III, king of Sardinia, who was attending the marriage of his son to a French princess. Victor-Amadeus III introduced him to a brother of the bride, the future Louis XVIII, by saying, "I present to you Mr. Bourrit who has made me a greater lord than I was, because he was first to make me aware of the most picturesque of my provinces, a country which was completely unknown to me."[111] Bourrit dedicated his *Description des aspects du Mont-Blanc* (1776) to the king of Sardinia and cultivated many similar patrons. In 1775, the city of Geneva sent four of Bourrit's alpine views to Jacques Necker, an expatriate Genevan who became French finance minister. Bourrit later lived in Paris and received a pension from Louis XVI in exchange for paintings, and he dedicated his 1781 book on the Alps to the French monarch. After the death of Frederick the Great, Bourrit claimed that the king of Prussia had bestowed on him the courtesy title of "historiographer of the Alps."[112] Yet Bourrit's earliest works reserve their most fulsome, almost sycophantic praise for Saussure, his most important patron.

Saussure's ascent of the Buet in 1776 was the literal and figurative high-point of the first volume of *Voyages dans les Alps* (1779). He visited Chamonix in 1760 and made a tour of Mont Blanc in 1767, but his interests took him to other regions rather than the highest elevations. At the height of the negotiations for the Edict of 1768, Saussure left Geneva for a yearlong grand tour of Paris, Amsterdam, and London, as well as the country homes, mines, and caves of England during 1768–1769. He made an extended tour of northern Italy in 1771 and spent a year in Naples and southern Italy for his health during 1772–1773. He climbed Mount Etna to study vulcanology and his family had a private audience with the pope.[113] As the male head of one of Geneva's richest families and living in its grandest mansion, when Saussure traveled around Europe he knocked on doors that were already wide open. He was wealthy enough to cut an imposing figure even in the most fashionable Parisian salons while a neighbor from Geneva felt "small" in the metropolis.[114] He met many aristocrats, naturalists, and men of letters and returned their hospitality in Geneva. Saussure accompanied Lord Palmerston to the glaciers of Chamonix and Grindelwald in 1770, showed his cabinet of natural history to Joseph II of Austria in 1777, and gave Goethe advice for his alpine tour in 1779.[115]

Apart from ascents to elevated viewpoints, Saussure did not try to climb in the Alps until after his return from these grand tours—and after Deluc's ascents of the Buet. In 1779, Saussure cataloged his excursions through the mountains of Europe, but limited his observations to the last few years.[116] Saussure's antipathy for Deluc, whom he considered a demagogue and rival in natural history, motivated his ascents around Mont Blanc including the Buet in 1776. Saussure engaged in a bitter dispute with Deluc over their respective hygrometers in the 1780s, but his concern with rivals was more long-standing. When Saussure met Charles Greville on the St. Gotthard pass in 1775, he hesitated to "talk rocks," because "at first I was afraid he wanted to get the benefit of my observations." He quickly found that Greville was "not a serious student and did not attempt to generalize. . . . I recognized that he was in no sense a formidable rival."[117]

Saussure's ascents in the 1770s also coincided with his active involvement in Genevan politics. Despite earlier misgivings about Rousseau's *Social Contract,* Saussure was deeply influenced by *Emile* and became Geneva's leading educational reformer in the 1770s. Intriguingly, Saussure bought a collection of Rousseau's manuscripts and notebooks from his youthful period in Savoy when they came onto the market, and selections from his dossier of Rousseau papers were published as early as 1776.[118] More significant, during his period as rector of the academy from 1774 to 1776, Saussure proposed a plan to reform the College of Geneva, the school that prepared students to enter the academy. He advocated replacing a curriculum devoted to religion and classical languages with lessons distributed among the sciences, moral instruction, and Latin. "In a Republic such as ours," he wrote after referring to its recent discontents, "an education is called for which will inspire in the young of all classes the love of country, the sense of common interests, and that spirit of equality which the character of our Government implies and demands."[119]

His proposals for educational reform were roundly criticized by the patrician Negatives, but warmly embraced by Représentants headed by Jacques-François Deluc and Natives led by Bourrit, who each presented effusive addresses of thanks. Opponents staged a mock procession of women who protested that they were no longer fit companions for overeducated husbands.[120] Although his education proposals were referred to a committee where they inevitably died, Saussure's daughter became an important advocate for progressive education. Saussure enjoyed more success with the "Society for the Advancement of the Arts and Agriculture," which he founded with a watchmaker in 1776. The society sponsored lectures, prizes, and publications on "useful" arts, and Bourrit and other natives were active participants.[121]

Saussure opened *Voyages in the Alps* with a "preliminary discourse" that placed the natural philosopher in a privileged position on a mountain summit. Observations were the basis of all natural history and the collection of facts alone served as the basis for a "Theory of the Earth." High mountains offered the opportunity to "observe with the utmost precision, and embrace in a moment the order, the situation, the direction, the thickness, and even the nature of the beds of which they are composed." Unfortunately, "the sole object of most travelers who style themselves Naturalists is to collect curiosities; they walk, or rather they crawl, their eyes fixed on the ground, picking up here and there little fragments, without making any attempt at generalization." To obtain more general ideas, "one must leave the beaten track and climb on the elevated summits, where the eyes can embrace at once a multitude of objects." During an ascent, the naturalist may doubt whether the summit can be reached, but the brisk air is a tonic and "the hope of the great spectacle he is about to enjoy, and of the new discoveries which he may gain reanimate his vigor and his courage. He arrives: his eyes, at once dazzled and drawn in every direction, know not at first where to fix themselves." Little by little, his eyes adjust to the light and he selects his objects of study: "But what language can reproduce the sensations and paint the ideas with which these great spectacles fill the soul of the Philosopher? He seems to dominate above our Globe, he discovers the sources of its motion, and to recognize at least the principal agents that effect its revolutions."[122]

Saussure spent *Voyages in the Alps* trying to find the language appropriate for the summit position of the natural philosopher who "seems to dominate above our Globe." This is the theme of his first volume on Geneva and Mont Blanc, which culminates in his ascent of the Buet. Saussure noted that Deluc and Bourrit had considered "neither the Buet itself, nor the view from its summit relative to the Theory of the Earth: this mountain is entirely new in this regard and it will be the principal object of my research."[123] He noted the structure of the rocks, the transitions between strata, the use of crampons by his guides, and the effects of altitude on the body, and compared his exertions and observations with other previous authorities in the Andes and Alps.

THE LIVING EYE

To depict this summit position, Saussure adopted a panoramic point of view. In September 1776, he sketched the view from the Buet as a horizontal circle and commissioned Bourrit to draw a *Vue Circulaire des Montagnes qu'on découvre du sommet du Glacier de Buet* (Circular View of the Mountains from the Summit of the Buet, Figure 7): "The spectator is placed at the center of the image and all the objects are drawn in perspective from this center, as they would present themselves to an eye situated at the same center which successively made a tour of the horizon." Saussure maintained that the variety and unity of the mountains made it impossible to employ ordinary views, so he adopted this new perspective: "The illustrator draws the objects exactly as he sees them by turning his paper as he turns himself. In this manner, anyone wishing to form an idea of the objects he has drawn need only imagine that they are placed at the center of the drawing, enlarged by the imagination. They see from above this center and as they turn the drawing they are able to review all its parts. Thus, they see successively all the objects linked together precisely as they would appear to an observer situated on the summit of the mountain."[124]

Saussure and Bourrit depicted the panorama of the Buet with the transparency of a "living eye." In Rousseau's *Julie, or the New Heloise,* Wolmar

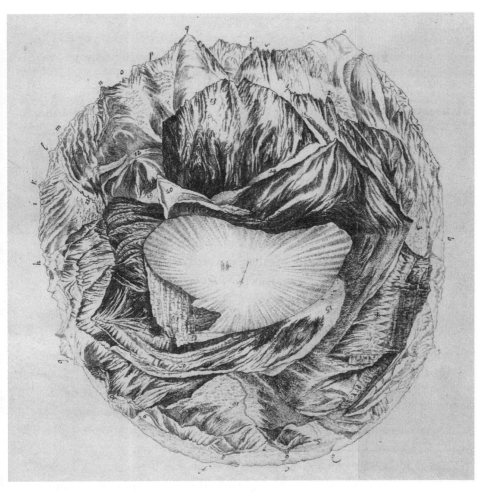

Figure 7 Circular view of the mountains from the summit of the Buet. Horace-Bénédict de Saussure and Marc-Théodore Bourrit collaborated on this panoramic perspective from the summit for Saussure's *Voyages dans les Alpes*, 1779. Beinecke Rare Book and Manuscript Library, Yale University.

said that "if I have any ruling passion it is that of observation," and that he enjoyed observing society but not taking part in it: "If I could change the nature of my being and become a living eye, I would gladly make that exchange."[125] Hovering above the summit, the God's-eye view of Saussure and Bourrit's circular view embodied the sovereign summit position of the natural philosopher who "seems to dominate above our Globe." For Haller, Scheuchzer, and Gessner, the sovereign position had been reserved for God, and the view from the summit was too broad and dizzying to be taken in all at once. This is not to argue that the position formerly reserved for God was simply reoccupied with a secular position, since Deluc, Bourrit, and Saussure all continued to identify themselves and their work in the Alps with natural religion.[126] Nor was this view merely a trick meant to represent a view from nowhere. Rather, it would be more accurate to say that the ascent and the living eye above the Buet were responses to the urgent questions posed by the upheavals of the 1760s and 1770s—who is sovereign and how should sovereignty be represented?

The summit position was difficult to put into words, and Saussure was apprehensive about the power of words in general. In a 1774 essay to clarify his educational proposals, Saussure wrote: "Even in this century, which is said to have arrogated the title of the *century of things,* it is words that govern us. Society is divided into small cabals, each of which scoffs at the sound of a certain *word.* Cry against superficial knowledge and you hear a hundred voices raised in your favor. Why? Because there are indeed superficial men."[127] Saussure was confronted with the problem of representation, and his great-grandson, Ferdinand de Saussure, would posit more complex theories of the structures of language itself. On the summit of the Buet, Saussure and Deluc struggled to articulate the mastery of the naturalist who "seems to dominate above our Globe." For his part, Bourrit could only present the perspective of a sovereign position in the mountains that was still denied to him in "words" in Geneva.

The circular view of the Buet flattered the mountaintop with a sovereign eye, but this panoramic gaze was not the result of an individual discovering inwardness or suddenly inventing himself. The summit position cannot be reduced to the effect of state building, capitalism, governmentality, an aesthetics of difference, or a theology of natural history, even though it emerged during the historical conjuncture that integrated and transformed each of these domains in Turin, Zurich, Berne, Geneva, and Chamonix. Moreover, Genevan visions of the summit were not the work of just one political faction, as each "cabal" struggled, in dialogue with the others, to articulate difference and sovereignty in this corner of provincial Europe. To encompass the view from the summit, they had to see with new eyes. These eyes were not those of another, or any other people, but the "living eye" of the sovereign individual above the summit.

CHAPTER THREE

Ascent and Enfranchisement

AUGUST 8, 1786

A red scarf tied to a baton flapped in the strong west wind after Dr. Michel-Gabriel Paccard and Jacques Balmat des Bots reached the summit of Mont Blanc at 6:30 p.m. on August 8, 1786. From the top, the climbers could see the Chamonix valley, where both men had been born and raised. Paccard had trained to become a doctor in Turin and Paris and was the son of the royal notary in Chamonix. Balmat was a laborer and crystal hunter from a peasant family in the wooded hamlet of Pélerins. Observers in the valley watched through telescopes as the pair trudged up the highest ridges of the mountain. Balmat and Paccard sank deeply in the snow, changed places in the lead, and often paused for rest while standing in their steps. After Paccard raised the red flag, the pair spent the next thirty minutes on the summit. At the top, Paccard took readings with his compass, barometer, and thermometer. They descended by the light of the moon and reached the site of their previous bivouac about midnight. Balmat and Paccard rubbed each other's hands to forestall frostbite and rested for only two hours before resuming their descent in the dark. By daybreak, Paccard was snow-blind, and they reached the outskirts of Chamonix at eight in the morning on August 9. From then on, each went his own way.[1]

Their ascent of Mont Blanc in the summer of 1786 was the culmination of attempts to climb the mountain for ten years and to achieve enfranchisement in Chamonix and Geneva, which extended over a longer period of time. A serious attempt to climb Mont Blanc was made in 1775, but frequent attempts to climb the peak resumed only in the three years before the first ascent. The efforts to climb the mountain in the 1770s and 1780s braided together contemporary definitions of enfranchisement in Savoy, sovereignty in Geneva, and the encounter of competitive masculinities into novel aspirations to reach the summit.

ENFRANCHISEMENT: MAKING UP PEOPLE

Four Chamonix men attempted to climb Mont Blanc on July 14, 1775. The guides Victor Tissay, Michel Paccard, and François Paccard (brothers who were cousins of Dr. Paccard) were joined by *sieur* Jean-Nicolas Coutterand, "son of the respectable Coutterand," the innkeeper who was widow of a former Chamonix notary.[2] According to Coutterand's account, they carried a black flag with the "intention of raising it on Mont Blanc as a monument to their victory." They saw rocks that looked like Egyptian pyramids, ice resembling porcelain, crevasses that reminded them of a fortress moat, and finally, "bristling needles of living ice which did not permit any passage: this place appeared to us as the *non plus ultra*." A detour led to "a cone where we saw the summit of Mont Blanc so close to us that we believed it to be no further than a league distant." Continuing only a few steps, they realized they had misjudged the distance and descended as clouds began to form. Their return to the village restored peace of mind to the people in Chamonix, who could scarcely believe that they were not buried under the snows of Mont Blanc.[3]

Why did these villagers try to climb the mountain? It was not to claim a reward. All too often, however, any attempt to climb Mont Blanc from Chamonix is simplistically attributed to Horace-Bénédict de Saussure's offer of a reward fifteen years before. In 1786, Saussure wrote that he had envisioned the summit of Mont Blanc as absolutely inaccessible: "In my first excursions to Chamonix in 1760 and 1761, I had it published in all the parishes of the valley that I would give a considerable recompense to those who should find a practical route to that point. I had even promised to pay the daily wages of those who would make fruitless attempts. These promises came to nothing."[4] Around 1760, one guide tried without any hope of success and the reward was forgotten until Saussure resurrected the offer in the second volume of *Voyages in the Alps.* By July 1775, Saussure and Marc-Théodore Bourrit had walked around Mont Blanc and Jean-André Deluc had climbed the Buet twice. That month, George Shuckburgh surveyed the elevation of Mont Blanc and one of his sketches marked the high point of Coutterand's attempt. Bourrit climbed the Buet later in 1775, and Saussure did not envision the panorama of the Buet until 1776. Visitors to the valley were less important than local events in inspiring Chamoniards to climb Mont Blanc.

Ascents of Mont Blanc from Chamonix were entangled with *affranchisse-ment,* the emancipation from feudal dues in Savoy, a process distinct from the debates over expansion of individual sovereignty in Geneva. On December 19, 1771, King Charles-Emmanuel III signed a general emancipation for the duchy of Savoy that established a process to abolish all feudal dues, a process that has been called "an exceptional experience in Western Europe" and "an act almost without parallel in the history of the Ancien Regime."[5] The edict provided indemnification for removal of obligations and required seigneurs and communities to negotiate a price for enfranchisement. A regional enfranchisement commission was established at Chambéry to adjudicate conflicts and supervise payments.

On May 21, 1772, a general assembly of Chamonix voted to negotiate its enfranchisement from the fiefs of the Collégiale of Saint Jacques at Sallanches, the monastery that had assumed the right of *mainmorte* (legal restriction on the transfer of real estate that enshrined servitude to the seigneur) after it took control of the priory of Chamonix in 1519. Throughout Savoy, the listing and valuation of all feudal rights began in 1773 and continued actively throughout 1774 and the summer of 1775. After the accession of Victor-Amadeus III to the Savoyard throne, enfranchisement was suspended but not abrogated in autumn of 1775.[6] The process resumed in 1778, and negotiations over enfranchisement for Chamonix continued until a definitive settlement was reached in the summer of 1786. In significant but severely underappreciated respects, the attempts to climb Mont Blanc from 1775 to

1786 should be understood as cultural counterparts to this political process of enfranchisement.

In Savoy and other parts of western Europe, the feudal principle of "no land without its seigneur" had survived into the eighteenth century and peasants continued to owe servile obligations to seigneurs. In the 1750s, residents of Chamonix still owed a variety of feudal payments to the chapter of Sallanches. This "vestigial serfdom" was a remnant of the harsher serfdom that once had been common in western Europe and still prevailed in much of eastern Europe. In a comparative study of the "servile lands" of Europe in this period, Jerome Blum pointed out that it made no difference how people acquired this servile relationship; dependence remained, and "the peasants themselves recognized their unfreedom and servility." Peasants in areas of vestigial serfdom such as Savoy could own land or hold hereditary tenure, but restrictions on its transfer and annual payments of dues forced them to acknowledge their subordination. In contrast to scholars who would hold that such obligations were just another kind of taxation and were neither onerous nor degrading, Blum notes that "if, indeed, the obligations and status of serfdom made so little difference, it becomes difficult to understand why serfs bothered to redeem themselves from it, at sometimes excessively high prices."[7]

Emancipation from feudal dues was proposed at the end of the seventeenth century but was limited in scope before the 1750s. By the 1680s, remonstrances in Savoy complained that royal taxes on top of existing seigneurial dues led to rural poverty and emigration. Royal officials began to argue that removal of seigneurial payments would free capital and increase tax revenue, and reform became urgent during the wars with France. Several communities in the province of Faucigny bought the "rights of the sovereign" or enfranchisement from dues in 1699, the same year that a number of other fiefs in Savoy simply changed hands between noble families.[8]

Officials under Victor Amadeus II initially envisaged the regularization rather than suppression of seigneurial rights, but the cadastral surveys required verification of all privileges, and claims were rejected without documentation that they existed before 1584. In 1731, an official proposed emancipation from the *taille,* the direct feudal tax on individuals, while another warned against steps that could "foster in the imagination of vassals the chimera of petty sovereignty" and make them forget that they are subjects of the king and taxable themselves.[9] Plans for enfranchisement were shelved in 1742 after the invasion of Savoy during the War of the Austrian Succession and not taken up until the end of Spanish occupation. Even in the absence of an overall plan, Chamonix asked for enfranchisement in 1698, 1740, and 1749.

In 1749, the inhabitants of Chamonix elected Joseph-Antoine Paccard, a young royal notary (and father of Dr. Paccard), as a delegate to negotiate on behalf of the village, and he led efforts to achieve enfranchisement into the late 1780s. Paccard was born to a notable family in Chamonix and succeeded his father, also named Joseph Paccard, as a notary and village secretary. Notaries in Savoy were distinguished by their dynamism, multiple roles, and involvement in all aspects of local affairs: they recorded obligations, contracts, the movement of people, and transfers of goods, lands, and animals. During a visit to Paris in the mid-1730s, Paccard attended a lecture on electricity by Abbé Nollet, after which he told the savant that he had seen lightning attracted to an iron rod when building a chalet at Planpraz above Chamonix.[10] In 1749, he visited Turin and Chambéry to ask for enfranchisement and appointment of a priest not connected to the chapter of Sallanches. Ecclesiastical authorities watched these "Chamoniard voyages" with apprehension, but dismissed them as "noise" intended to intimidate them. According to an official at the chapter, "Chamoniards have constantly resisted the sovereigns since the imposition of the *taille* in 1584," refused to participate in the cadastral survey until 1738, and "the same spirit of revolt against the laws of the sovereign is used to justify smuggling in salt, tobacco, and other merchandise by many of these inhabitants, notably those of Argentière."[11]

After an edict in 1752 permitted the purchase of a limited number of fiefs, Joseph Paccard again visited Chambéry and Turin bringing presents of local flax, honey, and wine. An official at the chapter wrote disparagingly:

> The inhabitants of the community of Chamonix, under the most imposing appearance of simplicity, sincerity, moderation, submission, uprightness, and good faith, are, in general, the most clever, tricky, cunning, secretive, defiant, impenetrable, and intractable which are to be found in these States, and perhaps in Europe, and they have not chosen as Administrator someone who has less skill of this nature.[12]

Around this time, one priest was assailed with stones in his parsonage because he would not absolve smugglers for the sins of their profession, and another was thrown into a river. After intervention by a counselor of state in 1757, Chamonix and Vallorcine agreed to pay 30,000 livres of Piedmont over thirty years to the chapter of Sallanches to free without exception all inhabitants and their descendants from any requirement of homage to the liege and to remove feudal payments on their persons or personal property *(taillabilité personnelle)*. As a result, residents were "no longer serfs but they still remained subject to a number of other seigneurial duties," including land and transfer taxes, rights to pasturage, hunting, fishing, mining, and justice.[13]

The 1772 edict of general enfranchisement was greeted enthusiastically and the inevitable protests by nobles and clerics could delay implementation only for a few years. While the process was briefly suspended in 1776, Joseph Paccard argued that enfranchisement would reverse the depopulation of the valley:

> Many inhabitants emigrate to foreign countries, from which several have returned since the enfranchisement from *taillabilité*. But most of them are waiting until general enfranchisement is carried out entirely before their repatriation, having always watched in horror the harshness that the seigneur and curé exerted against themselves and their relations, in respect to both spiritual and temporal matters, during their stay in the country, being obliged to expatriate themselves in order to live in peace and tranquility.

He noted that inhabitants of Vallorcine immigrated to the Valais to tend vineyards in the spring and to the Val d'Isère or Val d'Aosta to make cheese during the summer. Since enfranchisement from the *taille,* "the inhabitants are returning more frequently and the country is a little more populated than before. But if they were not so harassed by their seigneur, they would repatriate themselves even more easily and bring back money to this place. Thus, it is in the interest of the community that enfranchisement be carried out according to the last edict."[14]

The process of enfranchisement classified people in new ways and is an example of "making up people," Ian Hacking's metaphor for the constitution of human subjects.[15] Social categories are too often treated as static and fixed without variation across societies or historical periods. Almost all modernist narratives of mountaineering and "modern man"—whether they exalt Francesco Petrarch in 1336, Antoine de Ville in 1492, Conrad Gessner in 1541, William Windham in 1741, or Saussure in 1760—take such a "static nominalism" as their starting point: a preexisting and stable individual abandons self-restriction and slays the dragons of local superstition in order to inaugurate mountaineering and modernity. In contrast, Hacking notes that naming and labeling people may result in a "dynamic nominalism" in which classification has productive consequences: the categories themselves bring certain kinds of people into existence: "The claim of dynamic nominalism is not that there was a kind of person who came increasingly to be recognized by bureaucrats or by students of human nature but rather that a kind of person came into being at the same time as the kind itself was being invented."[16] Hacking's many works provide examples from nineteenth- and twentieth-century surveys and social categories. Much earlier, the combination of cadastral surveys and campaigns for enfranchisement extended horizons of possibility for personhood. For the people of Chamonix in the 1770s—"no longer serfs" after individual enfranchisement and aspiring to the "rights of the sovereign" through general enfranchisement—debates about enfranchisement opened the space to imagine themselves in a sovereign position.

"Making up people" complemented "making up discovery" of Mont Blanc. Hacking makes a distinction between the interactive effects of labeling people and the apparently indifferent consequences of labeling things. How mountains or microbes are formed or change does not depend on what we call them. One of Hacking's preferred examples is dolomite, a sedimentary rock formed by magnesium carbonate that Déodat de Dolomieu identified in a particular stratum of the Tyrolean Alps in 1791. A year later, Nicholas-Théodore de Saussure, the son of Horace-Bénédict de Saussure, named the rock and the region after Dolomieu despite its previous identification by Giovanni Arduino, a Tuscan mineralogist, who had a better understanding of its geological properties but none of Dolomieu's extensive social network. Over the next two hundred years, the study of dolomite required much debunking of received wisdom in order for the continued formation of this rock by nanobacteria to be observed in places inhospitable to research.[17] At a commonsense level, whether we call a particular mountain *les glacières, mont maudite,* or Mont Blanc represents a mass of rock and snow with a name, but does not intervene in the geological process that led to its formation. The sticking point is to ask whether interactions between people and the natural world can be limited to the effects of a static nominalism. Let us put aside that issue for now. For the moment, the point is that the "discovery of the glaciers" and naming of Mont Blanc may have had indifferent consequences for the mountain yet had significant, interactive effects on the people who lived nearby. These effects complemented enfranchisement and pointed aspirants for sovereignty upward.

This does not necessarily mean that enfranchisement from dues, classification by surveys, or renaming the mountain inevitably put people on an inexorable path to the summit of Mont Blanc. Joseph Paccard wrote to royal officials in a "statistical report" of 1776: "There is nothing remarkable in the valley unless one wanted to say that the glaciers which are here deserve attention, since curiosity attracts many foreigners who look at Mont-Blanc with great respect as being the highest mountain of the earth."[18] Chamonix had few visitors each year before the mid-1770s, but their descriptions inspired others to follow their footsteps. The Englishman John Moore visited Chamonix in 1773 because the glaciers excited his curiosity, "while the air of superiority assumed by some who had made this boasted tour, piqued my pride still more. One could hardly mention anything curious or singular, without being told by some of those travelers, with an air of cool contempt— 'Dear Sir,—that is pretty well; but, take my word for it, it is nothing to the glaciers of Savoy.' "[19] Yet the influence of these visitors has been all too easy to exaggerate and was less important than local changes promoted by the Savoyard state.

MAKING DOCTOR PACCARD

At the end of August 1775, Thomas Blaikie, a Scottish botanist, arrived in Chamonix searching for Alpine flowers and bearing a letter of introduction to the village notary. Blaikie was collecting specimens for a London botanical garden and later spent years as a botanist for French aristocrats. In Chamonix, Blaikie met Joseph Paccard at his home and later recorded in his diary that Paccard "seems to be a man of respect in this place, he has three sons very genteel young men [and] after some discourse there was two of them proposed to go along with me in purpose to conduct me and at the same time to learn plants."[20]

Paccard's three sons were educated at Chamonix, a Barnabite school in Bonneville, and the Royal College of the Provinces in Turin, where they prepared to enter the church, law, and medicine. The eldest, Pierre-Joseph Paccard, born in 1753, defended a theological dissertation at the University of Turin in 1776 and was ordained a priest and appointed at Chamonix in 1777. Mathieu-François Paccard, born in 1755, completed his study of civil and canon law at Turin in 1778 and appears to have pursued a legal career outside the valley. The youngest son, Michel-Gabriel Paccard, was born in 1757, and began his study of medicine at Turin in October 1774. A sister, Marie-Monique Paccard, was born in 1759, the year their mother died. Their father remarried in 1761 and had another daughter and son.[21] The *Collegio Reale della Province* in Turin was founded in the 1720s to offer lodging to deserving students from the provinces and to train the administrative elite for Piedmont-Savoy.[22] The Paccard brothers illustrate the possibilities open to a local notable family and the network of connections through the University of Turin that were more long-lasting and influential than brief encounters with Blaikie in leading one to climb Mont Blanc.

In September 1775, Michel-Gabriel Paccard gave Blaikie a tour of the valley to find plants. They saw the source of the Arveiron, "found many curious plants" along a lake, and heard thunderous sounds that Paccard told him were from an avalanche. Another day, they ascended a needle where Paccard taught him to glissade using an alpenstock. Paccard took Blaikie to the top of the Brévent, where they found a cross on the summit. Blaikie thought "the summit of this mountain is perhaps the most noble perspective in the universe; here you are right over against Mont Blanc and commands a view of all the valley of Chamonix." From the "majestic appearance" of Mont Blanc, whose top "dazzles the eyes," they could see the middle mountain covered in trees and below "cornfields and cottages which is pleasingly dispersed along the bottom of this remarkable valley where there is many mines of different sorts." They continued across the Mer de Glace to collect scarce Alpine plants. They returned to Chamonix, where Blaikie taught Paccard botanical names as he boxed them to be sent to Geneva.[23]

Paccard returned to the second of five years of medical studies at Turin. The first two years included the physical sciences, anatomy, medical institutions, and botany, a wide-ranging subject taught by Carlo Allioni, a celebrated botanist for whom Paccard collected specimens. Paccard passed his "baccalaureate" exams in July 1776, and devoted the next two years to the theory and practice of medicine, including pharmacy, chemistry, laboratory experiments, the inspection of cadavers, and assisting at the San Giovanni hospital in Turin. He passed his "license" exams in June 1778, and defended a thesis for his "laureate" degree in philosophy and medicine in June 1779. Student life at Turin was severely regulated, with lectures in Italian, devotions in Latin, and long hours of social seclusion.[24] Rather than serving a rotation at Turin, Paccard lived in Paris for his hospital residency from 1779 to 1782.

During his medical training and residency, Paccard became connected to wider networks of natural historians. In August 1778, Paccard met the abbé Ermenegildo Pini, a naturalist and Barnabite cleric who taught at the Sant'Alessandro College in Milan and was director of a natural history museum for the Hapsburg Empire.[25] Pini visited Chamonix for mineralogical research and gave Paccard rock specimens for his own cabinet of natural history. In January 1779, Paccard thanked Pini and explained that he added to his collection every day to study nature:

> My aims will not be lower than yours but the difficulties that face a young man whose judgment is not yet formed, whose knowledge is little, and who is without a teacher and must do everything by himself and by means of books halts my progress and often results in the failure of my endeavors. However, I do not stop adding to my collection; it is work that requires less knowledge and the utility of which I measure by future success.

Paccard reported on his voyages in 1778, including an ascent of "the Buet mountain, the highest among those accessible in this area and I saw the beds of slate which compose nearly all this chain of mountains."[26]

In 1779, several visitors to Chamonix expressed an interest in climbing Mont Blanc. Thomas Bowdler, an Englishman later known for his expurgated, family edition of Shakespeare, was delighted by an ascent of the Buet and wished for the wings of an eagle when he looked at Mont Blanc. Bowdler stated that "Saussure, de Luc and all the knowing ones say it will always be inaccessible. I am not of that opinion. The guides say with proper precautions it might be ascended," and he offered a reward for the ascent, but it was foiled by bad weather.[27] An unnamed naturalist from France was surprised his guides could not carry up Mont Blanc the heavy equipment he had brought from Paris. One of the guides, François Paccard, wrote to a naturalist that "we laugh about him every day. Whenever we imagine his *bizarerries,* we laugh."[28] Michel-Gabriel Paccard also wrote to Benjamin Jaïn, the secretary of Morges, near Lausanne, to tell him of his observations during ascents of the Brévent to test for electricity during the day and to view an aurora borealis at night: "I am now cataloging and putting my collection of natural history into systematic order, and gathering my observations to be able to bring a list to Paris where I will go next month."[29]

Paccard spent three years in Paris attending hospitals during the day and occasional lectures in the evening. He spent time with Marc-Théodore Bourrit, who painted his portrait in 1782.[30] Paccard gained enough confidence to publish an article in the *Journal de physique* in Paris in 1781: "Men who study nature to its deepest recesses, who admire its smallest productions and contemplate its entire spectacle, often put aside their books with pleasure, leaving behind all the contents of their cabinets, in order to read only from the Book of Nature. It is only to these naturalists, as simple as they are learned, that I ask to be heard." Layers of rock were sometimes horizontal, oblique, vertical, or folded at angles, for which he gave examples from Servoz, Chamonix, Montmartre in Paris, and formations near Geneva or Turin. Paccard reported on an experiment in something like a laboratory beaker in which he observed sediment mixed with water settling in layers arranged in patterns. These simple deposits in patterns were, by analogy, similar to those left at the bottom of the sea each year and those left by seasonal snows: "The different layers of snow which fall at intervals in the Alps are so distinct that they are not from the same year." Paccard argued that his observations confirmed that minerals were formed by crystallization at the bottom of the seas: "I hope that this discovery will divert and will guide the manifold works of the great many who seek the Philosopher's Stone, and that henceforth their efforts will be more useful to mankind. . . . It is only by closely following Nature that we can finally discover the principles and methods it uses and make progress by analogy." Paccard did not adopt a panoramic point of view as a naturalist. In contrast to those who aspired to develop a general theory of the earth, Paccard wrote that "I have stopped short of a theory above because in these matters we already have more theories than facts."[31]

By the end of 1782, Michel-Gabriel Paccard returned to Chamonix to become its first resident doctor, bringing up-to-date medical care. Paccard's diagnosis of a case of madness as the "alienation of the spirit" in April 1783 and the humane treatments he recommended have been compared to the therapeutic approach of Joseph Daquin of Chambéry.[32] Paccard reportedly wrote papers about ornithology and "diseases of mountain-dwellers and their treatment," but no examples have survived.[33] Bourrit put a blurb about Dr. Paccard's services at Chamonix in his next guidebook and noted that Paccard used the waters of the Arve to purify blood, heal apparently incurable wounds, and treat venereal diseases with some success.[34] In 1783, Paccard sent a list of plants from the Chamonix area to Carlo Allioni, his former professor and director of the Turin botanical garden, for use in a multivolume work on the flora of Piedmont. Paccard invited Dr. Jaïn from Morges to do the same, adding that Allioni was founding a Royal Academy of Science in Turin.[35] Indeed, Allioni nominated Paccard as a corresponding national member of the *Accademia Reale delle Scienze* in Turin, and he was elected in May 1785.[36] Although Paccard stopped short of developing a theory of the earth, his horizon had been extended to the wider republic of letters. When Horace-Bénédict de Saussure first met him in August 1784, he recorded in his diary that Paccard was "a fine fellow, full as it seemed, of intelligence, fond of botany, creating a garden of Alpine plants, wanting to climb Mont-Blanc, or at least to attempt it."[37]

GENEVAN REVOLUTIONS

The Natives of Geneva celebrated civil and commercial equality and the end of feudal dues with the Benevolent Edict of February 10, 1781. This edict admitted natives to the same rights and privileges as citizens and bourgeois for legal punishments, payment of taxes, rights of commerce, and admission to the professions or offices in the militia. Those who had been banished in 1770 were given amnesty. Bourgeois status was open to third-generation natives and a number could be admitted to the bourgeoisie immediately without payment. In later years, groups of natives, a habitant and a subject, could buy admission to the bourgeoisie. In the fiefs controlled by the Republic of Geneva, the "subjects," peasants in the rural hinterlands outside the city walls, were freed from the payment of the *taille* and *corvée* labor, an obligation of unpaid work owed to a seigneur or state.[38]

The Benevolent Edict followed riots that ended the decade-long political stalemate. During the 1770s, the economy of Geneva had prospered, but debates over Geneva's legal code dragged on as different factions dominated each council of the state.[39] Natives remained excluded: they resented the *Représentants'* role in the repression of 1770 and hoped that the ultranegatives, who styled themselves *Constitutionnaires,* would support their civil and commercial equality. Natives received support from the French foreign minister, Vergennes, who expressed sympathy for expanding their economic rights. Many hoped Vergennes, who "aided America to reach the harbor of independence," would preserve liberty in Geneva.[40] Bourrit told the French ambassador in 1780 that his attachment to the natives was subordinate to the peace, tranquility, and independence of Geneva.[41] The crisis deepened when Vergennes promised that France would not neglect the interests of the natives when it pacified Geneva and the Genevan attorney-general condemned the threat of invasion. In the upheaval that followed, a native was assassinated and political circles patrolled the streets. On February 5, 1781, the militias engaged in street fighting that turned in favor of the Représentants when they cut off the city's water supply and seized its artillery. Within days, the General Council approved the Benevolent Edict by an overwhelming margin: *Représentants* and *Natifs* had finally made common cause.[42]

The Negatives coalesced and the smaller councils refused to implement the decree, which they disparaged as the "Edict of the Natives."[43] The syndics considered it illegal and denied that the General Council was "sovereign" in Geneva. France, Prussia, Berne, and Zurich viewed an edict approved under duress to be null and void. Five hundred French troops camped outside Geneva's borders. During the next year, hundreds of pamphlets debated the edict's legality. Even Jean-André Deluc, who had left Geneva for the English royal court at Windsor, offered a memoir that brought forth stern rebuttals from every direction, and François d'Ivernois recorded disdainfully that Deluc "returned to his philosophical retreat, blaming both sides nearly equally."[44] In the broader debate in Geneva, the central issues remained the sovereignty of the General Council and rights of natives as defined in the edict.

Marc-Théodore Bourrit became an agent of the Représentants in Paris. From 1779 Bourrit lived in Paris, where he worked as an artist and musician for a variety of patrons, including a royal pension of 600 livres a year in exchange for paintings. According to one account, Bourrit joined a group that defined the basis for the Benevolent Edict at the home of the Parisian banker Étienne Delessert during their visit to Paris in 1780.[45] Étienne Clavière provided the expenses for Bourrit's diplomatic efforts to counter the influence of the ultranegatives at Paris. Bourrit reported to Clavière that he assured the colonial administrator, Pierre-Victor Malouet, of the difference between a violent revolt in Fribourg and the events in Geneva: "The ones [in Fribourg] are men who claim privileges but who are subjects in all the rigor of the term, while the Représentants, as members of the Sovereign, must maintain the sacred rights." By February 1782, Clavière told Bourrit that the negatives were taking an increasingly arrogant attitude and advised against violence since it could result in repression.[46]

This advice was heeded until the "taking to arms" or "Genevan revolution" of April 1782. The Small Council announced on April 7 that the General Council is not the sovereign of the republic and the edict of February 1781 will never be executed.[47] Groups of Représentants and Natives recalled the militias with the call "to Arms!" Street fighting resulted in casualties. Syndics who tried to intervene were attacked, arrested, or struck by bayonets; respect for their authority had vanished. The tocsin sounded, and Natives marched to the town hall where Negatives and Constitutionnaires were taken hostage. Horace-Bénédict de Saussure, a member of the Council of 200, was held hostage for two days. He was one of the few to be released, while others remained in detention for months. Saussure stayed in the city but sent his wife and children across the border disguised as maids, a workman, and a ragamuffin.[48]

Overshadowed by later events in France, the "taking to arms" in 1782 was no mere riot but a revolutionary government whose first act was to adopt in full the Benevolent Edict of February 1781.[49] The smaller councils were merged and the Constitutionnaires purged. Natives, Habitants, and Subjects were asked to assemble, and more than four hundred people were admitted to the bourgeoisie over the next three months. An eleven-member Committee of Safety was given executive powers, and emancipation from feudal dues brought peasants from the surrounding countryside into the city's political debates. The "mediating powers" of France, Zurich, and Berne rejected the legitimacy of the new government, called for release of the hostages, and threatened military reprisals. Piedmont-Sardinia offered troops and entered into negotiations with France over the pacification of Geneva.[50]

Diplomatic overtures created little external support for Geneva. As the "mediating powers" planned an invasion, potential allies such as Prussia, England, and the United Provinces remained aloof.[51] In Paris, Bourrit's standing in the artistic community enabled him to reach Vergennes with an appeal on behalf of Geneva in May 1782:

> Do not listen to the Negatives. They do not have a monopoly on the truth. The bourgeois of Geneva of which they speak so badly have done some good. The sovereign is master in his own home. The sovereign of the Republic of Geneva is the General Council. The government is in the hands of the large and small councils: if the government becomes abusive and instead of being the guardian of the laws becomes its transgressor, the sovereign has the right to change it.

Bourrit pleaded against the use of force and emphasized the sovereignty of the General Council in the longer history of the republic over the last three centuries. If only Vergennes would declare in the name of the king that he would protect the state and safeguard individuals from all parties, then "the hostages would be released, his person blessed, and altar to him built in the hearts of all Genevans."[52]

These appeals fell on deaf ears. On June 23, 1782, French and Sardinian troops invaded Genevan territory and dug into positions outside the city walls. In the city, five thousand people took up arms and prepared for its defense. The Committee of Safety declared its intentions to "live and die free" rather than do anything that "brings shame on our homeland."[53] Amid rumors that negatives were going to open the city gates, the homes of the negatives were searched and weapons seized. Saussure barricaded himself in his home with provisions, and "according to family tradition, a few servants in the house were ordered to tramp up and down the stairs and show themselves armed at different windows, while the master shouted martial orders in a loud voice." Militia companies advanced on the Saussure mansion with muskets ready, and a standoff ensued. Intermediaries appealed to Saussure to surrender and calmed down the peasants and natives who had gathered outside. The siege lasted until June 28, when formal articles of capitulation permitted the inspection of the residence but made no arrests.[54]

The siege of the Saussure mansion ended only a few days before the siege of Geneva. The French feared that the Genevan revolutionaries would use the hostages as a "human shield" and issued an ultimatum for surrender with a list of Représentants to be banished for life. Amid fears of artillery bombardment, a vote to concede defeat and surrender peacefully passed by a narrow margin. Bourrit had been asked to leave Paris in June, and he arrived in Geneva in time to join the decision for surrender as his friends planned their escape. On July 2, 1782, troops from the mediating powers entered Geneva and declared martial law. In the name of a "sovereign" Small Council and Council of 200, everything done since April 7 was invalidated. The next Edict of Pacification or "Black Code" overturned not only the edict of 1781 but also the reforms of 1768. The constitutional clock had been turned back to 1738. Saussure was surprised to learn that rifles in his apartments were to be confiscated despite his conflicts with the Représentants. Already a member of the Council of 200, Saussure was appointed to committees to develop the Edict of Pacification and revise the legal code, as well as to the Military Council, which controlled the garrison.[55]

The émigrés who fled Geneva created an influential diaspora of refugees. A group went to Ireland with d'Ivernois to found a "New Geneva," an initiative that drew widespread interest but was abandoned for London. Another cluster of refugees, including Bourrit's son, Pierre, who became a pastor in 1788, settled in Brussels or Constance. Still others immigrated to the United States. Clavière and Jacques-Antoine Du Roveray eventually settled in Paris, where they joined the circle around Mirabeau and became leading Girondins during the French Revolution.[56]

Contemporaries viewed the events in Geneva not as a failure but as the culmination of a series of revolutions during the eighteenth century. Unsympathetic to the revolutionaries, Jacques Mallet du Pan argued that corruption, decadence in morals, and an excess of pamphlets and liberty had led to the revolution of 1782: "We were sated with liberty. The recent troubles were a kind of indigestion of it."[57] For Ivernois, Clavière, and Jacques-Pierre Brissot, however, the events of 1782 represented the most recent revolution in a sequence since 1707. The disputes over Micheli du Crest in the 1720s, the representations in the 1730s, the Rousseau affair in the 1760s, and the "last revolution" in 1782 asserted the sovereignty of the people in the General Council.[58] Ivernois' history of Geneva viewed these revolutions as disrupting the confidence of the people in their magistrates, which had been the foundation of the republic. Brissot and Clavière adopted the voice of a "Philadelphian at Geneva" to argue that Genevans had the same right to resist tyranny and oppression and assert their sovereignty that Americans had exercised against the British in North America. "The democratic spirit is based on the principle that all power emanates from the people," they wrote, "Genevans never alienated their political freedom in all times and despite all the turmoil, supremacy remained in the hands of people."[59]

To the extent that the Genevan revolution undermined or transformed an *"ancien régime* of identity," this longer sequence in the eighteenth century as a whole, rather than merely the most recent events, such as the war of American independence, provides the context in which to locate this transformation and to explain the change.[60] It would be a mistake to view the Genevan revolution of 1782 solely as a precursor to 1789, or merely as a "response" to the American Revolution, or even as a "failure," for such framing of events suggests a problematic desire for "revolution" to serve as a boundary figure. Influences on French republicanism by the end of the 1780s have rightly been viewed as multiple, deriving from the "conjunction of Genevan political practice, French political theory, and Anglo-American experience."[61] To understand the broader revision of sovereignty that extended beyond discourses of "republicanism" in this period, we should also add to the list enfranchisement from feudal dues by "enlightened despotism" in provincial Savoy, as well as the ascent of Mont Blanc.

In assessing the revolution in Geneva, Mallet du Pan was struck by the links between Geneva and Savoy: "two sisters set against each other by a change of masters, but closely linked by all kinds of bonds," including kinship, which had once made them part of "the same nation." When Geneva was surrounded in 1782 by foreign armies, "Savoyards wept along the roads, sharing the mourning of the Republic like its own children."[62] The re-vision of sovereignty in the eighteenth century entangled multiple influences and manifold outcomes, not the least of which was the ascent of Mont Blanc. The revolution in Geneva did not "cause" people to climb the mountain in a mechanical or knee-jerk fashion. Rather, when the suppression of the revolution of 1782 appeared to definitively foreclose the possibility that sovereignty could be extended through the political process in Geneva, it had dynamic effects on people in Geneva and Savoy. The Edict of Pacification soon became known as the "black edict," and Représéntants began to refer to the now-defunct Benevolent Edict of 1781 by a new name, the *Edit Blanc,* the "White Edict."[63] Natives in Geneva could not have the white edict, but people from Geneva or Savoy could still climb the "white mountain."

NEW DISCOVERIES, 1783–1785

In the summer of 1783, three Chamonix guides attempted to climb Mont Blanc, and they were joined by Bourrit and Paccard a few months later. On July 11, the day of the festival of St. John of Bergamo, Jean-Marie Couttet, Joseph Carrier, and Jean-Baptiste Lombard, *dit* le Grand Jorasse, left Chamonix using the same route attempted by the Chamoniards in 1775. They received severe sunburn, and the intense heat induced lethargy in one and a loss of appetite in the others. After returning to Chamonix, the guide "Jorasse" told Saussure that it was fruitless to take provisions and he would recommend taking only a parasol and a bottle of smelling salts. Saussure concluded:

> When I pictured to myself this tall and robust mountaineer climbing the snows holding a little parasol in one hand and a bottle of eau sans pareille in the other, this image had something in it so ridiculous and strange that nothing could prove better to me the difficulty of this enterprise and, in consequence, its absolute impossibility to people who have neither the heads nor the limbs of a good guide of Chamonix.

At this time, Saussure also noted, Bourrit "took more interest than me in the conquest of Mont Blanc."[64]

Bourrit and Paccard independently decided to climb the peak, and they tried together in September 1783. Paccard studied Mont Blanc through a telescope and may have watched the guides' ascent.[65] Bourrit planned to climb with Henri-Albert Gosse, a pharmacist who fled Geneva in 1782, but Gosse dropped out before they reached Chamonix. At the moment of Bourrit's departure with guides, Paccard asked if he could join them with his barometer. Bourrit was glad to oblige. After sleeping at a shepherd's hut, they left at dawn and reached the top of the ridge known as Montagne de la Côte. Bourrit stayed on the rocks to sketch the view. The others continued up the glacier's ice until turning back as clouds gathered on the summit.[66]

Paccard and Bourrit each tried again in 1784. Paccard toured the Mer de Glace valley with Pierre Balmat des Barats looking for a route. Paccard took readings with his barometer, tracked chamois, and collected crystals, rocks, and plants. Apart from a very steep couloir, the approach to Mont Blanc from this side was too difficult. En route, they passed a boulder the guides had named the *Pierre à Bérenger* in honor of the Genevan historian and Lausanne publisher, just as earlier rocks had been dedicated to Bourrit, Windham, and Richard Pococke.[67] In September, Paccard scrambled with a guide on the Aiguille du Goûter. After breaking his barometer, Paccard borrowed another and ascended the Bionnassay glacier with yet another guide. He took barometer readings below the top and concluded that the ascent might be possible. The rocks were rotten, however, and before descending, Paccard carved his name into a rock near where he almost perished.[68]

Bourrit and five guides attempted to climb Mont Blanc from a different starting point in St. Gervais. Bourrit hired two local hunters along with a muleteer from Sallanches and two guides from Chamonix. As they tied crampons to their feet, one of the guides, Jean-Marie Couttet, and one of the hunters, François Cuidet, took off in a race and were separated from the others by the clouds. After watching the two men arrive at the summit of the Aiguille du Goûter, Bourrit traversed to a viewpoint and enjoyed the combined beauty and horror of the Chamonix valley. A dog with them jumped about the rocks like a chamois. When the two guides returned, Cuidet reported that they had reached the Dôme du Goûter: "From this height we commanded an immense prospect, with the Alps under us, and so extensive a country, that it was out of our power to estimate it; besides the lake of Geneva and others, all the hills and plains of ice, etc." They descended via the Bionnassay glacier, which confirmed Bourrit's suspicion that it was a better route. Bourrit concluded: "Thus was the Mont Blanc discovered. The way that leads to it is easy; and this success proves that Mr. Bourrit was right in his notions."[69]

This "discovery" of a route was widely celebrated in Europe and North America.[70] Bourrit's *New Descriptions* of the Alps (in multiple editions from 1785) celebrated the discovery and the grandeur of God. At Montanvert, "only one idea remains, but it is strong, it is the Sovereign of nature, who seizes all the faculties of your soul. His idea is sublime; nothing distracts; only he reigns here: that one feels is so strong, so transcendent, that one feels oneself changed. Neither the temples where one gives adoration, nor the view of its altars, produces nearly as profound a feeling of his presence." In conclusion, Bourrit celebrated that "this famous mountain is now accessible! What a conquest for physicists! The wonders and novelties they will furnish by their observations! Oh, you, who admire the beauties of nature, come look at them in the great theatre of the mountains, where the power of the Master of the universe girds you on all sides and where you contemplate with emotion the strangest objects." Bourrit's feeble sketch intended to show "the grandeur and power of God in those of his works, that you cannot discern, and to increase your admiration and your gratitude for his infinite goodness."[71]

Bourrit was by far the most widely read author on Alpine climbing in the 1780s, and his works stimulated broader discussion of the meaning of discovery. Some admired his descriptions as "physical and picturesque at the same time," and others called for further observations with instruments.[72] But "discovery" also spoke to the character of the age. A Lausanne journal commented in 1784: "No, this century is not entirely one of degeneration and selfishness; it is also one of discoveries in more than one arena and especially in the sciences which extend from physics and natural history to geography." Ascents of high mountains had destroyed prejudices and rectified scientific theories. Bourrit now ranked among hardy travelers such as Pierre Bouguer and Charles Marie de La Condamine, Deluc and Saussure.[73]

In 1785, Saussure and Bourrit mounted the largest expedition ever on Mont Blanc. Saussure asked guides to watch for favorable conditions after the heavy snows, and they ventured up the mountain in early September. Bourrit also commissioned Jean-Marie Couttet to build a hut on the mountain where the party could sleep before continuing the ascent. Saussure and his manservant, Têtu, were joined by Bourrit and his son, Pierre, with nine guides and six porters. They carried a tent pole, mattresses, six sheets, five blankets, three pillows, and two loads each of firewood, straw, and provisions, as well as Saussure's instruments.[74] The Bourrits, Saussure, and his servant slept in the hut with a tent roof, while the guides spent the night around the fire. Before Saussure retired to the cabin, he viewed the panorama in the dark and imagined himself as master of the universe:

> The repose and profound silence which reigned in this vast expanse, enlarged still further by the imagination, inspired me with a sort of terror. It appeared to me that I alone had survived in the universe, and that I saw its corpse stretched at my feet. As sad as ideas of this kind are, they have a sort of attraction which is hard to resist. I turned my attention more frequently towards this dark solitude than towards the slopes of Mont Blanc, on which the snows sparkled, and like phosphorics, still gave the idea of movement and life.[75]

The next morning, they stopped below the Aiguille du Goûter where Saussure observed his instruments to coincide with simultaneous readings in Geneva. The guides reconnoitered above and found two feet of fresh snow. The younger Bourrit was eager to continue, but the group decided unanimously to turn around and descended with difficulty. The elder Bourrit's boots had lost their heels, and he and Saussure required assistance from guides above and below holding ropes and placing their feet. Saussure paid each guide six francs per day and the entire cost of the expedition at 15 louis. Afterward, Saussure and Bourrit found consolation in having taken instruments to an elevation equal to the Peak of Teneriffe, and thus climbed to "a height no physical observer had ever attained on a European mountain."[76]

After Geneva's recent revolutions and Saussure's role drafting the Edict of Pacification, stories in Geneva quickly called into question Saussure's skill as a climber. When Saussure asked the Bourrits about these rumors, Marc-Théodore Bourrit told him that "I could not but notice that the way in which you came down was not the happiest," and Pierre Bourrit added: "Sir, do you not envy me my twenty-one years? Who will wonder if a youth of this age, who has nothing to lose, is bolder than a father of a family, a man of forty-six?" Saussure gently chided the father ("your flighty imagination often makes you see things in a false light") and the son ("a moderate amount of boastfulness is no great crime, especially at your age").[77] Both Saussure and Bourrit had depended on the guides and Saussure defended his right to put a stop to stories that caused him annoyance. He gave no sign of this discord when he recounted the journey in 1786, as the culmination of the second volume of *Voyages in the Alps*. The attempt provided the rhetorical high point of the second volume just as the first volume reached its apogee on top of the Buet.

In Chamonix, the guides did not think much of Saussure's mode of ascent and descent, although Paccard was impressed by his observations. Paccard summarized the guide's account in his notebook: "Mr. Saussure was tied like a prisoner for the descent. The rope was tied under his arms and held from behind by Pierre Balmat and François Folliguet. Couttet went in front for him to follow in his steps. Jean-Michel Tournier held Mr. Bourrit by the neck collar and he leaned on the shoulders of Gervais."[78] In the difficult sections, the guides held an alpenstock for Saussure to use as a handrail. Paccard corresponded with Saussure about the height of Mont Blanc and the finer points of using barometers. He told Saussure about his attempt to climb the mountain in 1784 and his barometrical observations at ap-proximately the same location: "Although less accurate than yours, perhaps, they add to the hope that I have formed to raise the elevation of our Mont Blanc." Given their common estimate of the elevation, Paccard concluded that Mont Blanc must be even higher than previously thought: "This brief summary should at least redouble the desire to carry a barometer to the summit of Mont Blanc."[79]

Saussure resolved to return the following year and start from a hut even higher on the mountain. He envied the "aeronauts" who made balloon as-cents in the comfort of their gondolas and speculated on using similar methods to reach Mont Blanc. The prince de Ligne asked Saussure in Oc-tober 1785, "Would it not be possible to approach it by military methods? If your workmen, your hunters, your mountaineers exerted themselves, it seems to me that with spade and axe it would be possible by slow degrees to smooth the rough places, cut down your Aiguilles, destroy your summits, and con-struct little platforms."[80] Saussure instructed Pierre Balmat to build a new hut and improve the path so he could ride a mule as high as possible, and to explore the peak as soon as weather permitted the next year.

JACQUES BALMAT, CRYSTALLIER

On June 7, 1786, two groups of men left Chamonix in a race toward Mont Blanc. One pair slept at the hut built the previous year. The other group of three planned to sleep at a grotto on the Montagne de la Côte. By the time they reached the grotto, the group of three was joined by Jacques Balmat, a peasant laborer and crystal hunter from Pélerins, who was not on good terms with the others and joined this party "almost in spite of them."[81] In Chamonix, the two groups placed a wager on the fastest route, and the Montagne de la Côte group won handily, arriving two and a half hours before the others. On the Dôme du Goûter, they all felt a kind of faintness. Jacques Balmat was rejuvenated after drinking fresh water from the rocks, but kept apart from the others and climbed by himself to look for crystals. As bad weather approached, the others descended without him. The pair of guides descended quickly enough to reach Chamonix, but the group of three slept on a rocky outcrop. Based on their experience, Pierre Balmat advised Saussure to wait another year before trying the ascent.[82]

Balmat stayed long enough that he was forced to spend the night alone on the snows. Dr. Paccard heard about this snow bivouac and recorded in his notebook that Balmat

> followed the tracks of the others, who were sinking to their knees in snow that had been hard in the morning. Having felt with his baton a crevasse which the others had jumped, and not seeing clearly, he did not dare go any further. He placed his bag under his head and his snow shoes under his back, and then passed the night on the snow. His clothes were all frozen the next morning.[83]

According to a fragment written by Balmat, when he reached the crevasse "I was obliged to climb above a crest from fear of being crushed by the ice when passing the night ... I froze my clothing and my handkerchief around my face. There I beat my hands and feet all night and next morning, having seen that the sun could not get rid of the mist on the summit of Mont Blanc, I returned to Chamonix."[84] The scope of his climb has been debated but Balmat was credited at the time by Saussure and others with "discovery" of the route. Saussure noted that "the people of Chamonix also believed that sleep would be fatal at these great heights, but the test, when Jacques Balmat spent the night there, dissipated this fear."[85] When Balmat returned, he was treated by Dr. Paccard. The guides did not welcome Balmat on the mountain, but they certainly acknowledged this: Balmat had slept on the snow and survived.

Jacques Balmat *dit les Bots* was a crystal hunter from the Bots, the wooded upper reaches of Pélerins, a settlement across the river and down the valley from Chamonix. He was born in 1762, the younger son of Jean-François (Zian Fanfouêt in the local patois) Balmat, a peasant proprietor whose family had lived in the area since 1561. Jacques Balmat spent his formative years tending family fields and searching for crystals. His education consisted of his catechism at the Régence des Montquarts, administered by brothers of the Montquarts chapel. Years later, Balmat recalled taking writing lessons that were abruptly interrupted when his father decided they were too expensive. In 1782, Jacques Balmat married Jeanne-Marie Simond and they had a son, Joseph Alexandre, in 1783.[86]

His father owned seven cows, two bulls, several goats and sheep, two pigs, small crop fields, and an area of woods. Such an inventory is consistent with the nineteenth-century view that Balmat was from one of the more comfortable peasant families in the area, and the more recent assessment, based on cadastral returns, that the Balmat family group of thirteen was below average in wealth for Chamonix.[87] The family fortune would have been brighter had his impecunious father not kept going into debt. Jean-François had paid a sum toward communal enfranchisement in the 1760s, took loans to pay dowries for two daughters in the 1770s, and incurred debt to purchase two properties in 1784—one a mountainous parcel for 800 livres in February and the other an even larger property near the river for more than 1,000 livres in September. To complete these purchases, Jean-François borrowed 900 livres from neighbors and nearly exhausted the dowry that Jeanne-Marie, Jacques' wife, brought with her to the family.[88]

As a younger son with no property and few resources besides his own labor, Jacques Balmat's only source of income was to hunt for crystals, minerals, or rock specimens that could be sold to collectors. In 1784, the guide Victor Tissay found three hundred pounds of beautiful purple crystals during three hours on *les Courtes,* cliffs above the Talèfre glacier, and reported "you pull the crystal out of these ruins as potatoes from a garden plot."[89] This was an unusually large find and prompted further exploitation of the area. Above the Tacul glacier, Jacques Balmat and Jean-Marie Couttet also searched for crystals and a route up Mont Blanc, but turned back at an impassable wall. In June 1786, Balmat also climbed alone and spent the night on the rocks.[90]

Balmat had returned from this journey when he learned about a reward offered by Saussure and joined the guides' attempt on Mont Blanc as an interloper. According to an interview around 1820, Balmat was lounging on the bridge in Chamonix when he saw François Paccard making a fuss over something, and "heard that Monsieur de Saussure had offered a reward of two guineas to any person who could find a passage to the summit of Mont Blanc. I dare say, Sir, you think two guineas a small sum for the chance of losing our lives, but in 1786, it was a great deal of money to poor crystal hunters."[91] Indeed, two guineas was a considerable sum and equivalent to the income from four chamois or a very large quantity of crystals, either of which could take several weeks to hunt or collect, equal to eight days' wages as a guide at the exceptional rate Saussure paid for his 1785 attempt on Mont Blanc, or twelve days' pay when employed as a guide in ordinary journeys around Chamonix.[92] By any of these measures, the prize was worth about two weeks' work for a hunter or guide.

Jacques Balmat did not tell the guides about his plan to climb the mountain, but their attitude toward him went beyond mere suspicion of a potential competitor. To the guides of the "Priory," the village of Chamonix
proper, Balmat was a country bumpkin. In his 1785 guidebook, Bourrit
noted that Chamoniards were distinguished from nearly all mountain residents for their sophistication, but peasants from less-frequented districts of
the valley spoke a patois that was nearly unintelligible to foreigners: "In
other districts, such as Montquarts, the men laugh and speak so slowly that
they have become objects of amusement for the inhabitants of the Priory. In
this respect the former are for them as provincials are for the Parisians."[93]

For visitors such as Bourrit and Saussure, however, the guides and hunters of chamois and crystal, like Balmat, exhibited a masculine heroism with
which they strongly identified. In 1786, Saussure waxed eloquent about
their skill in an extended discussion of the people of Chamonix in *Voyages
in the Alps*. Chamonix had no hotels on Saussure's first visit in 1760, but
now three inns bustled with visitors whose money had altered the manners
of the inhabitants. Since seasonal labor took many men abroad, women did
all manner of agricultural labor and the only exclusively male occupations
were crystal hunting and chamois hunting: "The hope of enriching themselves with a strike, of finding a cavern with beautiful crystal, has an attraction so powerful that they expose themselves in this search to the most
frightful dangers, and there is not a year that passes when no one perishes
in the ice or the precipices." Hunters looked for veins of quartz, which they
called crystal, searching grottos and traversing the highest vertical and inaccessible walls by suspending themselves with a rope. In this position, they
would strike the rock with a hammer or drill a hole to fill with gunpowder.
After rocks were dislodged, "young men and even children went searching
on the glaciers in places where rock walls have recently collapsed." Whether
the area was exhausted or because crystals from Madagascar had driven
down the price, now "not a single person at Chamonix makes it his only
occupation." Saussure suggested that someone should write a drama called
the *Crystallier*, about a young crystal hunter who loved a woman and, unable to marry her because of his poverty, searched for crystals in extremely
dangerous places. The savage rocks, avalanches of snow and ice, and the majestic mountains, thought Saussure, could not fail to inspire sublime music
and a theatrical staging.[94]

Chamois hunting was equally exhausting and dangerous and had an irresistible attraction to young men—and to Saussure. In *Voyages in the Alps*,

Saussure recalled the story of a married man from the village of Sixt: "My grandfather died in the hunt, my father died, and I am confident that I will die. That sack of mine that you have seen, Sir, and that I carry hunting, I call my funeral shroud, because I am sure I shall have none other. And even if you offered to give me my fortune, on condition that I renounce the chamois hunt, I would not renounce it." This man demonstrated dexterity and strength, but more temerity, and Saussure later learned that he had slipped on a cliff and met his fate: "What is the attraction of this way of life? It is not cupidity, at least it is not a rational cupidity, for the finest chamois is not worth more than twelve francs to anyone who kills it, even including the value of its meat." Now that the number of chamois had fallen, the time it took to hunt far outweighed these meager returns: "But there are the dangers themselves, the alternation of hope and fear, the continual agitation that these emotions nourish in the soul, which excite the hunter as they animate the gambler, the soldier, the sailor and even, to a certain point, the Alpine naturalist, whose life resembles in some respects that of the chamois hunter."[95]

These heroic masculinities of hunter and naturalist were not just complementary but also in competition. It is striking how frequently the early climbers on Mont Blanc entered into an explicit race or competition. In 1783, after joining Bourrit in his attempt on Mont Blanc, Paccard wrote acidly in his notebook, "Bourrit never set foot on the ice." In 1784, while their companions were still putting on their crampons, two guides took off to race each other for the first ascent of the Aiguille du Goûter. The aftermath of Saussure's expedition of 1785 was dominated by sniping over the amount of assistance he received. In June 1786, the guides placed a bet and raced to be first to the Dome du Goûter via different routes. Competition has remained so consistent a strand in mountaineering narratives throughout the twentieth century that Sherry Ortner has posed the question whether competition is "the base, the core, the—dare one say it—essence of Western masculinity."[96] Of course, as Ortner and many other scholars have shown, masculinities take particular forms at different periods and change over time. Indeed, such changes suggest it is problematic to take Saussure's characterization of the "alternation of hope and fear" as a timeless feature that defines mountaineering in general.[97] Without locating an essence of mountaineering or masculinity in Saussure's comparison of the hunter and naturalist, it remains fruitful to view the ascent of Mont Blanc as an encounter between competitive masculinities.

ENFRANCHISED MEN, 1786

Paccard and Balmat each intruded at the last moment on ascents organized by others that left them dissatisfied. The subsequent collaboration of naturalist and guide was certainly due to Balmat's recent experience in the snow bivouac. Balmat was far from the only guide who aspired to climb the mountain, and the reward and higher rate of pay offered inducements for many that should not be discounted. Michel Carrier, the son of a guide and nephew of Jacques Balmat, recalled in 1854 that "Balmat was not the only guide who ardently desired to make the first ascent of Mont Blanc. Many others tried at different times and by different routes to arrive at the same goal."[98] Paccard had climbed with many other guides, yet he invited Balmat to join him in the ascent shortly after the snow bivouac. Why?

For the next thirty years, visitors to Chamonix heard the following explanation for their collaboration. Balmat was treated by Dr. Paccard after his snow bivouac and "told the doctor on his recovery that he was unable to repay him for his kind attention in the usual way but that in his late expedition he had discovered a practicable path by which to reach the summit of Mont Blanc, and that if he felt any ambition to be the first man that ever stood upon that spot, he would conduct him to it."[99] This is consistent with accounts that Balmat refused to be paid by Paccard after the ascent. Paccard told the astronomer Jérôme Lalande in 1795 that he had been planning the ascent for three years and "already had three projected routes when Balmat made me prefer this one."[100] Balmat was also very fit, later describing his younger self as strong and robust. Paccard almost certainly read Saussure's description of the heroic guides and hunters of Chamonix in *Voyages in the Alps* after it was published in May or June 1786. Paccard's correspondence with Saussure leaves no doubt that he shared the aspiration to make observations as well as the heroic masculinity of an Alpine naturalist.

As Paccard and Balmat arranged to make the ascent, the village of Chamonix received its enfranchisement. Negotiations to remove feudal obligations that reached an impasse in the 1770s were brokered by official mediators in the 1780s. In July 1785, Joseph Paccard, the doctor's father who had led these negotiations, was authorized to reach a comprehensive settlement for the valley. On May 21, 1786, the syndics, councilors, and administrators of Chamonix and Vallorcine gathered at the Paccard home to discuss a document in these negotiations. The assembled notables reviewed the acts by which the count of Geneva gave the Chamonix valley to the Benedictines of Saint-Michel de la Cluse, who were succeeded by the chapter of Sallanches. A decree of 1330 required Chamonix to pay feudal dues, and another from 1562 ordered the chapter to give alms to the poor. As terms of the tentative settlement had been announced for three months, "in consequence the public is informed of its contents and all the rights that the Chapter offers to divest from itself in favor of these communities."[101]

For Joseph Paccard, the process of enfranchisement created a "public" and redefined their rights as men. In a "Memoir for the community of Chamonix," the royal notary subversively reinterpreted the regulations in which the chapter had defined *"their men"* as those *taillable* to the chapter: "This was necessary to be a *man.*" The residents of Chamonix and Vallorcine had not been taillable since July 18, 1757, and with this transaction "the canons continue to take the *rights* of *their men* only." They no longer had any claim on men in these communities, as "the right vanishes with this quality of their *men.*"[102] Paccard did not specify a status encompassing the rights of man nor did he assert rights to a sovereign position. Either would have been politically unspeakable in the Sardinian-Savoyard state, so the royal notary employed discourse that remained at the edge of this cliff.

In Chamonix, the end of feudal obligations in 1786 was viewed as crossing a threshold as irrevocable as birth or death. Joseph Paccard wrote in the same memoir: "These men would rather go back into the belly of their mother than become taillable again to the Chapter."[103] On June 14, 1786, the Delegation General for Enfranchisement at Chambéry fixed the price of emancipation from the fiefs of the chapter of Sallanches at 52,000 livres for Chamonix and 6,000 livres for Vallorcine. After appeals from each side, the total of 58,000 livres for both jurisdictions was approved and signed by the chapter of Sallanches on July 15, 1786. On August 9, the chapter of Sallanches decided to maintain only one member of the order at the priory for curial functions. After the first payment, a record keeper in Chamonix made the following entry in the register of deaths: "On 30 October 1786, the administration of the Priory of Chamonix died at the hour of midnight, and was buried the following day."[104]

Ascent and enfranchisement arrived almost together in the summer of 1786. In early August, when the weather had cleared and around the time of the full moon, Balmat and Paccard left their respective homes with alpenstocks, provisions, and other equipment for a journey in the mountains.

They met on August 7 and continued to the usual bivouac site on the Montagne de la Côte. On the morning of August 8, they proceeded up the mountain and paused periodically for Paccard to take readings with his barometer and thermometer. Four times they nearly fell into crevasses, which were crossed only by placing both alpenstocks in parallel and sliding across to the other side. Rather than following the route of previous attempts, they took a different path and crossed the Grand Plateau. Each climber later claimed that he had chosen this route. From below, observers could see two figures scaling the highest slopes of the mountain in the early evening. As they approached the highest point, the two men broke into a run and raced each other to the summit.

CHAPTER FOUR

Who Was First?

CONQUERORS OF MONT BLANC

The ascent of Mont Blanc was watched with excitement in Chamonix, but there was no celebration after the climbers returned home. Jacques Balmat returned to learn that his eighteen-day-old daughter, Judith, had died at 4:00 p.m. on the day of the ascent, and she was buried a day later on August 10. Dr. Michel-Gabriel Paccard went to bed immediately and convalesced with severe sunburn and temporary blindness. He was well enough later in the day to receive Baron Adolf Traugott von Gersdorf, a naturalist from Görlitz in Upper Lusatia, who had watched the ascent through a telescope with Karl Andreas von Meyer. At the request of Joseph Paccard, the two savants signed a certificate that they had seen Dr. Paccard and Balmat on the summit.[1] Gersdorf showed a sketch of their route to the reigning Duke of Mecklenburg-Schwerin, who arrived in Chamonix that evening. A few days later, the Sardinian envoy in Geneva reported the news to Turin: "Two individuals of the place have climbed to the highest summit, and that is the point of Mont-Blanc. This is regarded in the area as an epochal event, which will attract even more foreigners and the curious to the Glaciers."[2]

Gersdorf as well as the guides and innkeepers of Chamonix gave the news to Horace-Bénédict de Saussure and Marc-Théodore Bourrit, who could barely contain their excitement. Gersdorf reported that Paccard planned to make another ascent of Mont Blanc and to publish a description of the journey. "I wish for the sake of the public," Gersdorf wrote in his notebook, "that in addition to his very robust frame, the Herr Doctor had a really good knowledge of physics and natural history."[3] Gersdorf acknowledged Paccard's interest in botany, but was unimpressed by his knowledge of mineralogy, his insignificant collection of minerals, and his barometer, which was without a calibrated scale and had broken during the descent. Based on these reports, the Genevan naturalist Charles Bonnet looked forward to Paccard's publication, but feared the inferior instruments had not yielded any useful results. In contrast, Bonnet hoped his nephew, Saussure, would profit from the discovery of a safe route to the summit.[4]

An ascent with physical instruments remained the immediate objective for Saussure and Paccard. On August 15, Balmat went to Geneva with François Paccard, a guide and cousin of the doctor, to claim the prize that Saussure had announced earlier in the summer. Saussure paid the reward and asked them to build another cabin, higher on the mountain. On Saussure's first day in Chamonix, he learned that Dr. Paccard had already left to climb Mont Blanc again with the guide Jean-Baptiste Lombard, *dit* Jorasse, taking with him a working barometer and thermometer. In his journal for August 19, Saussure expressed consternation at the news, for he had expected Paccard to remain in Chamonix to make observations while Saussure made them on the summit. Instead, Saussure now feared "the pain of having come here only to see with my telescope this devil, the Doctor, ascend for a second time." Paccard returned after deep snow thwarted his ascent, and Saussure hastened to make his own. Before leaving, Saussure became frustrated while trying to teach Paccard and his brother how to use his instruments for the corresponding observations in Chamonix: "He made me impatient because instead of listening to me, he asked questions and raised evasive objections; but his brother, the lawyer, followed me very well, and this was important because he stays in the valley while the Doctor goes perhaps I know not where."[5] After Saussure's attempt with sixteen guides and almost as many instruments also ended without success, Joseph Paccard invited Saussure to dinner, where he finally heard about the first ascent directly from the doctor.

News of the ascent of Mont Blanc traveled quickly through the networks of an enlightened Europe. Gersdorf and Meyer wrote about the ascent by

Paccard and Balmat to *Leipziger Zeitung,* the *Mercure de France* published a brief notice, and Marc-Auguste Pictet, director of the Geneva observatory, spread the word to *Nouvelles de la République des lettres.* "The honor of this perilous enterprise," reported the *Affiches de Dauphiné,* "was due to the young Doctor Paccard from Chamonix following a guide named Balmat." They were seen through telescopes at "the top of the mountain, the highest of the old world and after Chimborazo of Peru, the most beautiful belvedere in the universe."[6] The *Affiches* also reprinted a commemorative verse from *L'Année littéraire* that compared Paccard to Jean-Pierre Blanchard, a balloonist who had made several ascents in hot air balloons between 1784 and 1786: "If true courage is the measure of glory, then the name of Paccard, and that of Blanchard, will be engraved together in the temple of memory."[7]

Paccard promoted himself as a conqueror of the mountain. George Cumberland, a British writer who visited Chamonix after the ascent, sent Joseph Banks a copy of Paccard's original barometrical observations during the first ascent. Above the readings from his barometer, Paccard scribbled that Mont Blanc was "Conquered by Dr. Paccard."[8] Banks sent these observations out for peer review and they were used in a "rude computation" to calculate that "the height of Mont Blanc comes out nearly 3 miles, as it has commonly been supposed to be."[9] In Lausanne, Paccard arranged with Jean-Pierre Bérenger to publish a leaflet to attract subscribers for a forthcoming book, *Premier Voyage à la cime de le plus haute montagne de l'ancien continent, le Mont-Blanc.* Paccard promised to provide a short history of attempts to climb the mountain, descriptions of its rocks, insects, rare plants, physical and medical observations, and the information necessary to visit the glaciers of Savoy. Booksellers from Amsterdam to Zurich were designated to receive subscriptions to underwrite its publication and as a prize to reward "the Conquerors of Mont Blanc."[10]

After initial reports, the first detailed account of the ascent was published by Marc-Théodore Bourrit in a letter dated September 20, 1786. According to Bourrit, during the ascent at about three in the afternoon, Dr. Paccard became breathless, his knees stiffened, and he was incapacitated by the cold. The climbers could see a summit above them, but were unsure if it was the last: "Balmat, resolute to make certain, dashes on alone: as he advances on the route the difficulty lessens; the snow is firm, and he sees that only a few steps remain to arrive at the summit of the mountain: he gains it. What joy, what triumph which compensates for his fatigue! All nature is at his feet; all that is most strange before his eyes!" Balmat shouted to his companion and descended to assist Paccard before they returned together to the summit at 6:30 p.m. The view was immense, but the cold and approach of darkness prevented the travelers, according to Bourrit, from taking as much advantage of the situation as would a naturalist like Saussure or an artist like himself: "Our voyagers had nothing more to show for their zeal than the satisfaction of being the first human beings who could reach so high."[11]

Bourrit admired the courage of the climbers, awaited Saussure's observations, and noted that Balmat has "a right to expect an honest reward." Visitors to the valley had often said they would contribute to a prize for whoever was first on Mont Blanc. Paccard needed none, as his father was the richest man in the valley. Saussure would be rewarded by his discoveries and a richly deserved celebrity: "Balmat could only be rewarded by money which would ease his circumstances and it need not be much for a man of his station [état]." Bourrit complained that Paccard had announced himself at Lausanne "as the conqueror of Mont Blanc and promised a description for which one can subscribe, while the poor Balmat, to whom he owes this discovery, is almost unknown." In a second edition of the letter, published a few weeks later, Bourrit added a postscript stating that Paccard should not take offense since Paccard's own publication would be enriched by his knowledge of mineralogy and botany and "the glory of being the first to have reached a summit attacked so often in vain." Bourrit's pamphlet was reprinted in *Mercure de France* and translated into German, English, Spanish, and Dutch.[12]

Privately, Bourrit told Saussure that he was inspired to publish his letter in the interest of justice and truth. Bérenger told his longtime friend Bourrit that Paccard's prospectus was poorly written and when he suggested changes, "the doctor responded in a trenchant tone 'it must be so.'" Around this time, the doctor's cousin, François Paccard, spread rumors about Bourrit that were considered malicious enough by regional officials to have him imprisoned in Bonneville for three days for slander. Those comments remain unknown, but Michel-Gabriel Paccard certainly told Gersdorf that Bourrit had stopped well below the highest point he claimed to have reached. Bourrit thanked Saussure for interceding on his behalf with Paccard and for suppressing rumors among the guides in Chamonix when Saussure told them: "I know everything and I want to know nothing more; you are all nothing but chatterboxes." Saussure replied to Bourrit that he was only glad to help: "The description of his voyage, whatever it may be, will be read from one end of Europe to the other, and I would have been sorry to see anything that caused you pain." Bourrit believed his postscript had rendered justice to Paccard and "it will be easy for him to see that my goal is for Balmat as well as him to enjoy the glory due to *the conquerors of Mt. Blanc*." And yet, disputes between the two climbers had occurred as early as the day after their return. Bourrit also reported that Paccard insulted Balmat by offering to pay him a single *écu,* worth six livres, on the day of his daughter's funeral. To this, Balmat replied: "I did not guide you, neither for six livres nor for 20, nor for 50—keep your six livres."[13]

HONEST REWARDS

Rewards for Balmat were soon forthcoming in Germany and Savoy. After the ascent, Balmat accepted an écu as a gift from Gersdorf in Chamonix, as well as the reward of 48 livres from Saussure in Geneva. Gersdorf reprinted Bourrit's letter in Görlitz and distributed it with an appeal to contribute to a subscription for Balmat from the German-speaking states. Gersdorf noted that all lovers of natural history knew the works of Saussure and Bourrit and the "exact knowledge" they obtained at great cost and risk during ascents of Mont Blanc. Who would not want to reward such efforts that promised so many important discoveries and the perfection of natural history? "Certainly they deserve a reward, at least the poorest among them, the guide Balmat." As two *Oberlausitzer* (residents of Upper Lusatia) had the unexpected pleasure to be eyewitnesses to such an extraordinary event, Gersdorf asked all lovers of natural history among his countrymen to contribute to a gift for "poor Balmat."[14] Friedrich Franz I, the reigning Duke of Mecklenburg-Schwerin who visited Chamonix after the ascent, contributed 10 louis d'or, more than half the total that Gersdorf raised of 102 *Thaler* of Saxony, equivalent to almost 17 louis d'or, a little more than 400 livres of France.[15]

In Savoy, Jean-François Garnier d'Alonzier, the intendant of Faucigny in Bonneville, asked the finance minister in Turin for a reward for Balmat in December 1786. As the ascent by Dr. Paccard and Jacques Balmat

> caused a stir in Europe, and was the result of the courage and fearlessness of the latter, a peasant of Chamonix, aged 23, who, having made up his mind

that he could do it, hazarded everything to succeed. I hope, sir, that you do not disapprove of the liberty I take to recommend him to your generosity, to procure the happiness of feeling the beneficence of our august master, whose heart is always inclined to reward remarkable deeds.

Garnier d'Alonzier apologized for taking so long to recognize Balmat's merits—spending a night on the ice of Mont Blanc, seeing it was possible to reach the summit, and leading Dr. Paccard who engaged him for the ascent: "The news of this voyage cannot but be useful and beneficial for the province; the foreigners who already come in droves in the summer to visit the glaciers of Chamonix will be even more eager to race there in hope of a climb to the summit, where the view offers so many beautiful objects to contemplate."[16]

Balmat's youth, poverty, and humble status made him an especially deserving object of royal charity. In an annex to this letter, Garnier d'Alonzier further identified Balmat as twenty-three years old, married to Jeane Marie Simond, with a two-year-old son named Joseph Alexandre: "He has only one cow and two goats and has been obliged to leave his father and mother for income with little regard for his wife. His father assigned him a small plot of ground to cultivate, of very modest production, which does not suffice to support his family, such that he is forced to go for day labor in the parish and to serve as guide for foreigners who come to see the glaciers."[17] In Turin, the finance minister promised to show the letter to King Victor Amadeus III and was hopeful a gratification would be given to Balmat.[18]

The Sardinian-Savoyard government hoped the state itself would reap rewards through more visitors to the glaciers of Savoy. For several months, the Sardinian ambassador to Geneva, Jean-Baptiste d'Espine, remained impressed that so many foreigners passed through Geneva "with the singular goal of travel," especially the English who "visit the Glaciers or make a journey to Switzerland, which had become very fashionable." He forwarded copies of Saussure's map of the glaciers and Bourrit's letter about the ascent: "In the summer, curiosity attracts a prodigious quantity of foreigners, and this voyage is beginning to become easy even for the most delicate ladies, and of the highest rank. The Intendant of Burgundy went there last week with his wife and several other ladies. They were more than 30 masters and the servants were in proportion."[19]

The arrival of visitors with such extravagant entourages would only enrich the province and fill the coffers of the state. By the end of 1786, Garnier d'Alonzier followed up his request for a reward with statistics on the number of notable foreign visitors to Chamonix during the last forty years: "I thought worthy of your attention the progression that has been made year by year since 1746." The progression was easy to discern. Only two or three notable visitors to Chamonix were named in any year through the 1760s, while the number of notable visitors increased rapidly, from about 30 in 1772 and 70 in 1773, to more than 200 in 1775, 300 in 1776, 500 in 1780, 1,300 in 1782, fewer than 500 in 1783 due to the recent revolution in Geneva, 1,960 in 1784, and more than 2,000 in 1785. Writing at the end of 1786, when about 1,680 foreigners had visited Chamonix, the intendant promised to supply "a very exact notice of all who will go to see the glacières" in the future.[20] Provincial officials also looked favorably on requests to improve the road to Chamonix, now used less for the mines than for visitors to the glaciers.

Thus, the Sardinian-Savoyard monarchy in Turin was persuaded to reward Balmat. In February 1787, the king's verdict was reported through the finance ministry in the usual bureaucratic formula:

> The intendant of Faucigny, having described the courage and intrepidity of the peasant Jacques Balmat of Chamonix, who led doctor Paccard to the summit of Mont Blanc, which had been unsuccessfully attempted many times, said this brilliant action could inspire a great quantity of travelers to visit the glaciers and produce some benefits to the province, that Balmat is married and has one son, that the small plot which he has to cultivate cannot suffice for his subsistence and he works as a day laborer, and that he seems worthy by his honesty to feel some effects of your Majesty's beneficence.

A marginal note added: "His Majesty is disposed to accord Balmat the sum of 240 livres by way of recompense."[21] Local authorities were informed, the sums were transferred to Chamonix, and Balmat was asked to sign a receipt.[22]

The financial rewards that Balmat received after the ascent totaled between 500 and 700 livres. The largest sums were collected in the German subscription organized by Gersdorf. Unlike such foreign largesse, which took several years to be delivered and came with no strings attached, the gift from the king of Sardinia represented an act of incorporation into the Savoyard state. But what does it mean to be incorporated into a state without citizenship? At a practical level, it meant that Balmat was now at the beck and call of the monarchy. In August 1788, the intendant in Faucigny received a request from Turin for examples of the most beautiful "curious crystals" to be found by Jacques Balmat or other men who would know where to find them, for which the prince of Piedmont would pay an honest price.[23] At a more profound level, to receive the king's charity on account of his poverty and limited prospects established Balmat's subaltern status as a subject of the king and object of the generosity of "our august master."

Almost a century later, historians speculated that the king granted Balmat the right to use *"dit le Mont Blanc"* after his name as "a veritable title of nobility," but diligent research in the state archives in Turin has failed to find any royal patents for this designation.[24] The absence of any official sanction should not be surprising. Other prominent guides in Chamonix were already known as *"dit le Grande Jorasse"* and *"dit le Géant,"* and the honorific that Balmat adopted was clearly a local name, his own honest reward with a name that he made for himself. The surname distinguished him from his formerly provincial status as Jacques Balmat *des Bots,* as well as from fellow guides who shared the same name—a less distinguished Chamonix guide at this time became known as Jacques Balmat *des dames* (for the ladies). To become Jacques Balmat *dit le Mont Blanc* had nothing to do with joining an aristocratic order of the state, but everything to do with asserting that he was not merely a subject of the king but a man among guides.

FIGHTING WORDS

The Paccard family defended the doctor against Bourrit's version of events. In October 1786, shortly after François Paccard was released from prison for slandering Bourrit, Paccard had Balmat sign a certificate drawn up by one of the notaries in the family. The certificate attested that Paccard had planned the route, shared the load, and kept Balmat from turning back when he wanted to return home to his wife and sick child. According to the statement signed by Balmat,

> The doctor continued to climb with agility; we reached a small rock behind which I sheltered from the wind, while Mr. Paccard examined it and loaded himself with some stones. We were near the summit of the mountain; I went to the left to avoid a steep slope of snow, which the said Mr. Paccard crossed with courage to reach right to the summit of Mont-Blanc. The line that I took delayed me a little, and I was obliged to run in order to be almost as soon as him at the aforesaid summit.[25]

Balmat later signed another statement, notarized in Chamonix in March 1787, that Paccard had given him a new écu as a gift from Baron Gersdorf as well as his wages on August 10.

After the royal reward for Balmat was announced in February 1787, Paccard's version of events was published in an anonymous article in the *Journal de Lausanne,* a periodical for the dissemination of knowledge about science, agriculture, and medicine to a regional audience.[26] Under the heading of *"Variétés,"* the article claimed that Bourrit had suppressed Paccard's history of previous attempts on Mont Blanc and "the doctor alone had indicated the route which in the end led to the summit." In 1784, Paccard had attempted Mont Blanc via the Aiguille du Goûter, a route that Bourrit followed a week later. The article continued: "Why do men, who have so many other titles to glory, envy the doctor for what he has earned by his own efforts?" Since Bourrit could not claim the glory of the ascent of Mont Blanc for himself, he "wishes to give it solely, or almost solely, to the companion in these efforts." Paccard had chosen Balmat only because others were unavailable, and "he was engaged not as a guide but as a porter [*ouvrier*]." Instead, Paccard had guided and encouraged Balmat: "He was useful, no doubt, but not for reaching the summit, which was reached at the run. Balmat was not the first to reach the summit, Dr. Paccard has certificates which prove this; Balmat was not unrewarded, the doctor himself gave him money."[27]

Bourrit sent a spirited reply to the *Journal de Lausanne.* The description of an exhausted Paccard "seems very natural, especially when one thinks of the advantages which guides have over us in these sorts of ascents." Bourrit claimed that Gersdorf had seen the indifference Paccard had shown toward his companion and opened a subscription for "poor Balmat." Balmat had been on the route of the ascent earlier in the summer and was engaged by Paccard because no one else had seen the mountain from such close range. Bourrit mocked "the certificates of the *Chancellerie du Mont Blanc*," which said that Paccard "was the first to reach the summit of Mont Blanc *at the run,*" a feat Bourrit claimed to have accomplished on other peaks with the help of guides when only a few paces remained. He continued, "Let us tell the truth: Mr. Paccard is angry that he has shared his glory with the honest Jacques Balmat, whom he tries to rob of his rights; this jealousy seems to me to be ungenerous."[28] In reply, Paccard sent the certificates signed by Balmat, which the *Journal de Lausanne* printed with a note that it would no longer be occupied with this issue.[29]

This correspondence remained largely unknown in Chamonix outside the Paccard family until the summer of 1787. Paccard wrote to Gersdorf to ask what indifference he had shown to Balmat (to which Gersdorf replied that he could remember none) and said he had not yet published his own account due to "a thousand obstacles," mainly his conflict with Bourrit, whose letters had turned nasty and mean-spirited.[30] Saussure commissioned Balmat to let him know when the winter snows had receded enough to make an ascent possible. On July 5, 1787, Jacques Balmat made the second ascent of Mont Blanc with fellow guides Jean-Michel Cachat *le Géant* and Alexis Tournier. They planted a black flag on the summit that was distinctly visible in the valley.[31] After hearing news of this ascent, Saussure arrived in Chamonix on July 9 and stayed at Coutterand's inn, where many guides had gathered in preparation for his attempt.

Balmat and other guides were taking shelter from the rain at the inn when some of Paccard's relatives asserted that he had been the first on Mont Blanc, citing the certificates published at Lausanne. Balmat maintained that he had signed a blank sheet of paper on which Paccard must have added a statement written to his advantage. The group marched to Paccard's home and met the doctor en route. Balmat said, "Is it not true that you made me sign that?" and Paccard struck him between the eyes with his umbrella and knocked him to the ground.[32] The two men were separated by the other guides. The next day, Dr. Paccard left Chamonix with a guide to explore the mountains on the other side of Mont Blanc near Courmayeur for almost three weeks. On his return to the valley, he learned that his father, Joseph Paccard, had slipped off a narrow plank footbridge in bad weather while crossing the swollen torrent of Houches and died from complications. The doctor returned to Chamonix in the early hours of July 27, the night after the funeral.[33]

SAUSSURE'S HOMERIC VOYAGE

Saussure consoled himself during weeks of rain in Chamonix by avidly reading Homer's *Iliad,* which he had never read from beginning to end. When he found a beautiful passage in the Latin translation, he would look it up in the original Greek to copy it and learn it by heart. Since Paccard had left for Courmayeur just after his arrival, Saussure did not see him again until after the death of Paccard's father and gave his condolences. He then learned that the doctor had visited many sites from Saussure's earlier voyages. Saussure noted in his journal: "It appears he deliberately went everywhere where he could go higher and further than I had been." Saussure walked in the valley to break in his new boots, met an illustrator for Captain Cook's voyages who was touring the Alps, and visited Montanvert with his family. Even in bad weather, Saussure tested his barometer and hygrometer and perfected new instruments such as a *diaphonomètre* to measure the transparency of air. During this period of reading and testing, Saussure wrote in his journal: "I finish my *Iliad,* I make various preparations."[34]

The weather finally cleared in early August, and Saussure proceeded up the mountain with a large caravan of eighteen guides and his valet, Têtu. The first night, they camped at the edge of the snows at the Montagne de la Côte so Saussure could make observations with his instruments. While his feet were firmly on the slopes of Mont Blanc, his head was still in the clouds of ancient Greece. The next day when the guides had to be persuaded to leave a resting place on isolated rocks in the glaciers, it was "for my guides a place of delight, an island of Calypso," as he transformed the island in the snows into a place from the voyage of Odysseus. Saussure used the occasion to contrast his own determination with the guides' fear of cold temperatures, and won them over by promising to erect a tent to protect them from the frost. When his servant dropped the pedestal for his barometer at the top of a crevasse, it slid rapidly on the slope and "planted itself to a great depth in the opposite side, where it remained fixed, quivering like the lance of Achilles on the bank of the Scamander." As this pedestal was also used for his compass, telescope, and other instruments, he was relieved when a guide retrieved it after being lowered into the crevasse. From the sleeping place on the Grand Plateau, he could see Jupiter above the peaks and paid tribute to his predecessors: "When I pictured to myself Doctor Paccard and Jacques Balmat arriving, the first, at the end of the day in these deserts, without shelter, without assistance, without having even the certainty that men could live in the places where they were attempting to go, and continuing nevertheless on their route intrepidly, I admired their resolution and courage."[35]

After much effort, Saussure reached the summit at 11:00 a.m. on August 3, 1787. He looked to Chamonix, where his family hoisted flags to show they had seen his arrival, and his greatest satisfaction on the summit was to allay their concern for his safety. Since he had been able to see almost everything visible from the top for the last two hours, "this arrival was no *coup de théâtre;* it did not even give me all the pleasure one might have imagined." The memory of the long struggle was more poignant than the physical pain, but left him irritated: "At the moment when I attained the highest point of snow that crowns this summit, I trampled it with feelings of anger rather pleasure. Besides, my goal was not merely to reach the highest point, it was necessary above all to make the observations and experiments which alone would give some value to my voyage." He first scanned the horizon with the eyes of a natural philosopher finally able to see the peaks whose organization he had desired to know for so long: "I could not believe my eyes. I thought I was in a dream when I saw, below my feet, those majestic summits, the formidable Aiguilles—the Midi, Argentière, and Géant—whose bases had been so difficult and dangerous of access for me. I understood their proportions, their connections, their structure, and a single view removed doubts that years of work had failed to clarify."[36]

Saussure spent four and a half hours making a series of experiments. The guides erected a tent in which he boiled water, tested alkali sticks, and observed his thermometer, hygrometer, electrometer, and two barometers to compare with simultaneous observations in Chamonix and Geneva. He observed the shape of the summit as well as its rocks, snow, animals (butterflies), and vegetation (lichen). He judged the color of the sky with a "cyanometer," and used himself as an instrument to record his taste, smell, and response to the sound of a gunshot. Saussure's pulse raced faster than his guide, Pierre Balmat, but slower than his servant, Têtu. At length, clouds gathered below and Saussure was forced to leave earlier than he intended, even though he had completed only a fraction of his planned experiments. As he wrote in his journal: "Despite the admiration that this superb spectacle caused me, I felt the painful sense of not being able to take full advantage and even to know my rate of respiration. I was like a gourmet invited to a superb feast whose extreme loss of appetite prevents him from enjoying it."[37]

The descent was easier than expected and after spending another night on the snows they were greeted enthusiastically on their return to Chamonix. Bourrit met them at the edge of the ice and tried unsuccessfully to convince some of the guides to return with him to the summit, for they were too tired and wanted to attend Mass. In Chamonix, Saussure was greeted with "great emotion and very tender embraces" by his wife, her sisters, his children, and other relatives. The eighteen guides were jubilant at *each* receiving 5 louis (120 livres) as payment for assisting him. The intendant of Faucigny watched the ascent through a telescope from Chamonix, and reported to Turin the amount that Saussure paid his guides, as well as news of the construction of two "barracks" on the route: "It is certain that he spared no expense to have every possible comfort in this enterprise, and it is to be hoped that his discoveries encourage foreigners to visit this valley. There is no doubt of the number who have come in the last few years nor the amount of money they bring to this province."[38]

Saussure reported his ascent in the *Journal de Genève* and the *Relation abrégée d'un voyage à la cime du Mont-Blanc*, which was widely reprinted in journals throughout Europe.[39] Saussure paid warm tribute to his predecessors, Paccard and Balmat, but his elaborate expedition with its multitude of experiments and observations easily overshadowed the first ascent and those that followed for many years. A week after his ascent, an Englishman named Mark Beaufoy, the son of a Quaker vinegar distiller in London, followed Saussure's tracks to repeat the ascent with many of the same guides. Beaufoy established the latitude of the summit with a sextant, for which he was elected to the Royal Society in 1790, but did not publish his account of the ascent for several decades.[40] Bourrit was able to report on both ascents, but none of his own. He regretted that English visitors had promised to reward the discovery of a route to the summit, but no one from England had yet come forward to reward Balmat: "Balmat not only was the first arrive on Mont Blanc, but he has been three times, and these ascents have exhausted him enough to take away the urge to go a fourth."[41] Saussure attracted more attention than the other climbers even in Turin, where Carlo Allioni translated the abridged relation into Italian.

Saussure's ascent was the culmination of the twenty-seven-year odyssey he described in *Voyages in the Alps* and the embodiment of the masculine heroism he celebrated in those volumes. Consider the terms in which Madame Necker, the wife of the French finance minister whose nephew was married to Saussure's daughter, wrote to the savant shortly after the ascent: "It is not the cadaver of the universe, as you said with so much energy, that you have seen lying under your feet; it is, on the contrary, the noble and colossal figure of a frightening and sublime nature." She and Jacques Necker had followed his ascent past every precipice and danger:

You made us all experience the sentiments of hope and fear that make the life of the chamois hunter so delicious and so terrible; we cried with joy at the magnificent view when you, a new Enceladus, scaled Mont Blanc. Certainly, the chaos of Milton, the underworld of Virgil, and the palace of Gnomes in the Arabian Nights, are only childish inventions beside the wonders you have made known to us, for nature and the truth have a character to which the imagination cannot aspire.

Saussure had mastered the anatomy of the world, the "living body" that served as his object of study: "Columbus did not expose himself to more dangers than you, but he opened Pandora's box in America, and you tell us from Mont Blanc of the most beneficial plants." In the midst of chaos, Saussure had discovered "the imprint of the divine hand that created the universe." She regretted that her lack of strength did not permit her to follow his footsteps, "but my imagination compensates for my weakness."[42]

RENDERING JUSTICE: MONT SAUSSURE AND MONT PACCARD

Saussure's ascent was honored with celebratory and satirical poems in Geneva, Lausanne, and Paris. Jean-Étienne-Francois Marignié, a Parisian playwright visiting Geneva at the time of Saussure's return from Chamonix, published *Hommage à Mr De Saussure sur son ascension et ses expériences physiques au sommet du Mont Blanc,* a flattering tribute that began: "Finally, on the summit where nature ends, Saussure leads as science ascends. The proud giant of the old Continent lowers its snowy brow under instruments of the Arts, vainly defending its slopes from mortals." In reference to how Saussure scattered the rocks to make a route to the summit, Marignié continued: "Neither craggy rocks nor ramparts of ice can intimidate the daring Saussure: 'O Nature,' he has said, 'whatever the danger on this piercing summit, I will interrogate you!'" Twenty eager and courageous guides share the perilous work like Titans scaling the heavens. In a long section, Saussure's devoted wife and family watched through a telescope among the spectators in Chamonix. Breaking the silence, a cry of victory reaches the heavens to the beat of drums and the sound of brass: "Yes, triumph! Triumph! He has conquered: Saussure around him and beneath him, sees all of nature." Saussure makes several observations with the instruments scattered around him: "this cylinder, measuring the cold, testifies in a word to the death of nature." Marignié closed by placing Saussure's ascent alongside recent maritime voyages and the discovery of Uranus, and asked that Mont Blanc be renamed in his honor:

> I ask for a prize that the name of the conqueror be attached to the famous peak which tested his mettle. May my voice reach our race in the future with the finest name, the name of Mont Saussure. Citizens, foreigners, savants, neighbors of the mountain, repeat after me, and confirm this name! Thus in our time the whole universe comes alive, and everywhere I see places consecrated with respect. The wake of Cook rolls over the seas, and the name of Herschel is written in a golden register in the heavens.[43]

In response to this verse, the *Journal de Lausanne* published a quatrain proposing to rename the mountain Mont Paccard "as a joke rather than an epigram," which was reprinted in a variety of Parisian journals under the heading of a "Letter from an inhabitant of Chamonix." *L'Année littéraire* and *Nouvelles de la République des lettres et des arts* pronounced Saussure's abridged relation "written with the noble simplicity of a great man, for whom the most perilous enterprises are the most familiar things. Thus it was that Caesar wrote his commentaries." They noted Marignié's success onstage in Paris and reprinted the final stanzas of his poem calling for Mont Blanc to be renamed Mont Saussure:

> As if the glory of Mr. de Saussure were not great enough by itself without having need for this strange *éclat,* we report another quatrain, produced by the final tirade of these verses. It is a justice due to Doctor Paccard of Chamonix, who had the honor to ascend Mont Blanc before all others, justice that Mr. de Saussure is the first to render to him: "Mortals! Do not seek after an empty renown. Injustice and error overcome nature; Vespucci to America has given his name, and the Mount of Paccard is named Mount Saussure."[44]

"Cuique Suum" (to each his own), responded Étienne-Salomon Reybaz, a pastor who left Geneva for Paris in 1782. Reybaz opened his *Epître à Messieurs Balmat et Pacard sur leur ascension au Mont Blanc* with a reply to Marignié: "A Poet sung in harmonious verse of a daring scientist, his glorious exploits, and the conquest of the amazing wonders of Mont-Blanc. I listened: beautiful verse was pleasing to my ear and my heart shared the

perils of these heroes. But Paccard, I said to myself, and Balmat, where are they?" Reybaz cited Bourrit's account of the first ascent, and advised poets not to dispense honors to anyone other than Balmat and Paccard: "Your audacity made the first conquest; and the first laurel must garland your head." He compared Balmat and Paccard to others who did not receive credit for their discoveries. Christopher Columbus preceded Amerigo Vespucci, and the work of Francesco de' Marchi came before the military fortifications of Sébastien Le Prestre de Vauband. Reybaz cited the contemporary dispute between Aimé Argand of Geneva and Antoine-Arnoult Quinquet in Paris over credit for the discovery of the oil lamp: "Friends, do not fear envy and controversy; when you name a rival, it gives you the prize." He noted that Saussure's abridged account of his ascent had "rendered brilliant justice to his two predecessors."[45]

Reybaz also sang the praises of Bourrit as a painter and writer of picturesque descriptions, and followed his account of the first ascent. After reaching the top, Balmat descended to his friend who had succumbed to toil and terror: " 'Companion,' he said, 'I have conquered without you. A secret sorrow saddens my victory. We should share all, the dangers and the glory. Courage! Come, follow me, the danger is everywhere, but Balmat will sustain you, and honor is at the end!' " Paccard was revived and the valiant pair reached the top. In the most widely quoted passage from any of the poems, Reybaz compared Saussure and his guides to Jason and the Argonauts taming the hydra of Colchis. Their victory did not surprise him, but Hercules alone had choked the Nemean lion: "Hercules is more than a man, and alone is worth an army." Reybaz concluded: "The guide was emboldened; Balmat rises to the clouds. The observer followed him and the Alps are known. Everything is subject to man, and his curious eye confronts the underworld and pierces the heavens."[46]

The anonymous author of *Scène dialoguée entre Balmat et l'auteur de l'Hommage* offered Alexandrine verses to mock comparisons with discoverers and to defend the priority of Saussure as a scientist on Mont Blanc. Balmat introduces himself to the author by quoting Reybaz's poem and asks why nothing was said about him for more than a year until after Saussure's ascent: "then it is a chorus, an uproar of verse and prose in my praise. I'm Brutus, Columbus, Marchi: I'm an angel. But I am not a dupe, and I say to everyone: You raise me then you must lower someone else." The author replies, "Balmat, your common sense delights me and enchants me."

To be a real hero, "believe that your victory enhances less merit and glory. They say: 'After all, he did his job. As galloping exercises the steed, the mountaineer exercises by climbing on peaks—he is made for danger and for abysses.'" In an extended note, the author of the dialogue surmises Bourrit's polemical purpose and criticizes Paccard for failing to publish his own account. Bourrit's "real purpose was to put in his place Mr. Paccard, who according to Bourrit made too much of himself and too little of his companion. I know that this is called rendering justice. One is a rectifier of wrongs, a fine title. But praise for praise and for no other purpose, pleases me even more. The author of the *Hommage* was given this pleasure in all its purity." There was nothing to redress, as Saussure had already praised his predecessors: "The first ascent was well known, and those who made it had plenty of time to describe and celebrate it in every way. It was otherwise, and we have taken care to mark clearly the distinctive and particular character of the second enterprise." That is, the first ascent had done nothing for science: "In this regard, Mont Blanc was still virgin. But Paccard and Balmat, where are they, you ask? They are not there, where science is; it is a different genre." *"Age quod agis"* (do what you are doing), the author advised, and the Balmat character as portrayed in *Scenes of Dialogue* was happy to oblige: "I return to the village, where I hope to forget all this nice verbiage."[47]

But these poems should not be forgotten, for they aired fundamental issues about the politics of the summit position in 1787. Seemingly the most ephemeral of the Genevan poems came from a prisoner named de Coponnex, who wrote occasional satirical verses from his captivity. In his own *Hommage à Mr De Saussure,* he mocked the pomposity of Marignié and the profound wits who wrote about the ascent. Saussure's glorious ascent merited the homage of a learned people since his fame eclipsed everyone who had ever previously been admired in Geneva. The poem envisioned the mountain itself envying the savant's name: "That he give me his name and takes the mien, I want to unite myself to him by a double lien." Nature replied: "You will be named Mont Blanc de Saussure; and Saussure will be Saussure du Mont Blanc," as surrounding mountains echoed their approval like vassals paying their respects. Saussure was more careful than Icarus and Empedocles, wiser than Socrates and Sophocles, nimbler than Sisyphus, and happier than Enceladus. Unlike these audacious Titans who failed to climb into the sky, Saussure did not succumb but returned victorious to be elevated to immortality. If Saussure had the courage, Coponnex cunningly concluded, he would be a "generous Seigneur" and reduce the unhappiness of those groaning in slavery: "To soften their awful fate if he himself in these places of SOVEREIGNS the power shared, without doubt, we would say still more, SAUSSURE IS A GREAT PERSON."[48]

PORTRAITS OF ENLIGHTENMENT

Miniature portraits of Balmat and Paccard were painted on round medallions above allegorical mantles by Louis-Albert Ghislain Bacler d'Albe in 1788 (Figures 8 and 9).[49] Bacler d'Albe, a French artist who later became a general and cartographer in the Napoleonic army, lived at Sallanches and painted scenes of the Alps from 1786 to 1793. Balmat sat for the artist in July 1788 to create a portrait to match one that he had already made of Paccard. The watercolor portraits were engraved in Basel and offered for sale at 24 livres for the pair. The head and shoulders of each man were shown in profile, Balmat facing to the right and Paccard to the left. *Jacque Balma dit le Mont Blanc* hangs above a rustic tableau with alpenstock and crystal hunter's ax, and explanatory text that Balmat had ascended Mont Blanc with Paccard in 1786 and since then served as guide to de Saussure in 1787. The portrait of Dr. Paccard, adorned with an elaborate ribbon, rests on a mantle with its own miniature reproduction of Bacler d'Albe's view of Mont Blanc from Sallanches and a quotation in Latin from Claudian: "He ascended those mountains, inaccessible in winter, with no thought for the season or the weather."[50]

One assessment of the medallions posited that "the symmetrical opposition of the two figures offered the contrast between a reflective savant and the energetic man."[51] Rather than opposition, however, this symmetrical pairing illustrated the complementarity of the masculinities of the savant and energetic man that remained in tension with neoclassical representations of a singular masculine heroism. On Paccard's medallion, the quotation from Claudian came from a passage that honored the exploits of General Flavius Stilicho during the Gothic Wars around 402: "Thou and thou alone, Stilicho, has dispersed the darkness that enshrouded our empire and restored its glory." In Claudian's panegyric, Rome was vexed with discord, enervated with luxury, and misread portents when the Visigoths crossed the Alps and marched on to the city. After a stirring speech, Stilicho crossed

Figure 8 Louis Bacler d'Albe, *Jacque Balmat dit le Mont-Blanc*, 1788.　Collection Paul Payot, Conseil Général de la Haute-Savoie.

Figure 9 Louis Bacler d'Albe, *Michel-Gabriel Paccard, docteur en médecine à Chamouni en Savoie,* 1788.   Collection Paul Payot, Conseil Général de la Haute-Savoie.

lakes and ascended those mountains where men had been frozen to death, engulfed in snow, or plunged into crevasses. A shepherd and rustic family admire him as he recuperates: "From out of those Alpine huts, Rome, came thy salvation."[52] The frequent references in poetry and prose and on the medallions to precedents from classical antiquity stemmed in part from neoclassical assumptions that heroic individuals acted alone.[53]

The savant *was* an energetic man in the ascent of Mont Blanc and thus assumed some of the characteristics of his climbing partners, Alpine hunters, and peasants. Representations of this partnership departed from neoclassical models and began to be called "modern." The prospectus for Bacler d'Albe's views of the Alps remarked that Haut Faucigny, a region enveloped in clouds and located in the middle of Europe, was unknown for years, even to its neighbors: "This region, known to the ancient Romans, forgotten by their successors, had escaped modern observers, and seems to be reborn, as it were, upon the globe. Doctor Paccard, in going to the summit of Mont Blanc, Mr. de Saussure, in analyzing many of these elevated mountains, and finally Mr. Bourrit, by his works, have all opened our eyes toward this country."[54] Unlike Claudian's verses in which Alpine peasants remained a passive audience, these "modern observers" achieved their success in partnership with the peasants of the Alps. Bacler d'Albe's portrait showed Balmat not as a Rousseauvian primitive as much as Saussure's active *Crystallier* come to life.

Saussure's position was commemorated in models of Mont Blanc and depicted in several commemorative prints. In 1787, Charles-François Exchaquet, the director of mines in Faucigny, sold painted relief models of the valley of Chamonix and Mont Blanc for 30 louis, which offered to any observer the position above the summit.[55] In 1788, Saussure camped for several weeks on a pass between Chamonix and Courmayeur to make a series of experiments and brought an artist to create illustrations of the ascent of Mont Blanc for a new edition of his "abridged relation." A young Genevan artist, Henri L'Évêque, created several sketches of Saussure's ascent and descent that were refined by Marquardt Wocher and engraved by Chrétien de Méchel in Basel. In the first version of the ascent, a white-haired and potbellied Saussure climbs in hobnailed boots with very long spikes. In the companion piece for the descent, Saussure slides down a gentle slope on his rear end as guides secure him on a short rope from above and below (Figure 10). After Saussure saw these prints, he insisted that the copperplates be destroyed

Figure 10 Marquardt Wocher, *Voyage de Mr de Saussure à la cime du Mont Blanc au mois d'août 1787—La descente—2ème planche, 1er état,* 1790.   Collection Paul Payot, Conseil Général de la Haute-Savoie.

and "changed to represent me in a standing glissade on the snow in the attitude of a guide that we see in the vignette in the first volume of *Voyages*."[56] In the revised version of the prints, published in 1790, Saussure is fit and trim with darker hair and a younger countenance. Balmat watches from a respectful distance. Saussure's boots have lost their spikes and rippling leg muscles propel his purposeful stride in the ascent. In Take 2 of the descent, instead of being tied like a prisoner, Saussure stands like a guide in full command above the crevasse.

These portraits "rendered justice" to the climbers and articulated different definitions of enlightenment. Consider the manner in which Saussure's interactions with Alpine peasants informed Immanuel Kant's vision of enlightenment and aesthetic judgment. In 1784, Kant had written that "enlightenment is mankind's exit from its self-incurred immaturity," and offered

Sapere aude!—Dare to know!—as a motto of enlightenment and shorthand for the courage and resolution to use one's own understanding rather than rely on the guidance of others.[57] Saussure's Alpine voyages embodied such daring—a common refrain in the Genevan poems and other commentary—and Kant made a hero of Saussure. Kant cited Saussure's example and adopted his summit position to envision a transcendental aesthetics in *The Critique of Judgment* (1790). Kant argued that when viewed from safety, overhanging cliffs, volcanoes, oceans, and lofty waterfalls all demonstrate the power of nature, elevate the soul, and allow men to "discover within ourselves a capacity of resistance of quite another kind." Despite the inability to measure aesthetic sensations, the faculty of reason "has that very infinity under itself as a unit against which everything in nature is small, and thus find in our own mind a superiority over nature itself even in its immeasurability." Thus, "sublimity is not contained in anything in nature, but only in our mind, insofar as we can become conscious of being superior to nature within us and thus also to nature outside us (insofar as it influences us)."[58]

Kant argued that Saussure's inspired description of an "insipid sadness" on the Col du Bonhomme required an awareness of an interesting sadness and demonstrated that even sorrow "can be counted among the vigorous affects if it is grounded in moral ideals." Saussure's voyages fostered these ideals and a sensibility that Kant believed was repellant to unrefined Savoyard peasants:

> Thus the good and otherwise sensible Savoyard peasant (as Herr de Saussure relates) had no hesitation in calling all devotees of the icy mountains fools. And who knows whether that would have been entirely unjust if that observer had undertaken the dangers to which he there exposed himself, as most travelers usually do, merely as a hobby, or in order one day to be able to describe them with pathos? But his intention was the edification of mankind, and this excellent man experienced the elevating sentiment that he gave to the readers of this travels as part of the bargain.[59]

This edification and these sentiments elevated Saussure's ascent into a portrait of the enlightened natural philosopher.

Saussure encouraged Kant and others to view his ascent as the "first" of its kind. In the final volume of *Voyages in the Alps*, which appeared in 1796, Saussure clarified the moment he trampled the highest point of Mont Blanc with feelings of anger rather than pleasure with the following footnote to Lucretius: "_____ Pedibus submissa vicissim Opteritur."[60] Lucretius had surveyed the nature of things in *De rerum natura,* and claimed that humanity had been crushed under the weight of religion or superstition until Epicurus became the "first mortal man" to raise his eyes to defy the gods. Undeterred by myths and thunderbolts, he was "first" to disclose the secrets of nature by voyaging across the cosmos and returning with knowledge of the powers of nature and the boundaries that marked their limit. Saussure changed the quotation slightly, but his classically educated readers would have had no trouble filling in the blank—*religio*—religion or superstition. Even if Saussure and many other eighteenth-century admirers of Lucretius remained committed to a natural theology, the full quotation from Lucretius clearly placed Saussure in the position of the eye above the summit: "By this victory superstition is trampled underfoot and makes us equal to the heavens."[61] Kant employed the same Lucretian phrase to dismiss mystics in 1796, and in lectures on *Physical Geography,* published in 1802, Kant declared that "Saussure was the first mortal to climb to the summit of Mont Blanc."[62]

WHO WAS FIRST?

The guides of Chamonix were aware of the position occupied by their clients and actively competed to be "first." In August 1787, Bourrit crossed a pass from Chamonix to Courmayeur and hailed the event as its "first" ascent and more difficult than Mont Blanc.[63] The oral tradition in Chamonix held that the crossing had been made frequently in previous centuries, and Charles-François Exchaquet, the director of mines, had made the same journey two months before Bourrit. Indeed, when Chamonix guides learned of Exchaquet's plans to cross the pass at the end of June 1787, Jean-Michel Cachat *le Géant* and Alexis Tournier raced to cross the pass before him in a single day. At Courmayeur, they hurried to find local officials to sign certificates testifying to their accomplishment. A week later, both guides joined Jacques Balmat in the second ascent of Mont Blanc and, later in the summer, they were among the guides for Saussure and Beaufoy. Cachat *le Géant* led Bourrit over the pass at the end of August and returned a year later in 1788, when Saussure camped on the pass for weeks to make observations. At that time, Saussure proposed renaming the pass the *Col du Géant,* ostensibly after the nearby Aiguille du Géant. In the wake of aborted proposals to name Mont Blanc after Saussure or Paccard, it must have been satisfying for the guides to know that the Col du Géant now bore the name of one of the "first" people to cross it. Cachat *le Géant*'s terse description of the journey in his *livre de raison* (record book) scrupulously noted the length of time spent in ascent and descent and added of the crossing with Tournier: "We were the first to pass through in more than a century."[64]

Jacques Balmat *dit le Mont Blanc* also claimed to be first. The snow bivouac was widely recognized by contemporaries as giving him an undisputed claim to priority, even if the circumstances of the first ascent were contested. The fistfight with Paccard leaves little doubt that he took the claim to be first more seriously than he took signing pieces of paper. The claim that Balmat reached the top before Paccard should not be attributed merely to the jealousy of Bourrit. In Bourrit's letter, the prizes from Germany and Savoy, and the verses in Geneva, the guide was frequently represented as "poor Balmat"—the subaltern figure and noncontemporaneous contemporary in the pairing of climber and guide. And yet, the effects of poverty were not merely the consequence of representations by others, but framed his ability to exercise agency and occupy a position of his own. Balmat's prize winnings did not make him wealthy or even financially independent from his father. In 1791, Jacques Balmat finally received most of the funds raised in Germany and he plowed the money into several plots of land that he bought from his father as an advance on his inheritance. On this property, Balmat then built the first home of his own at the summit of the village of Pélerins.[65]

Neither Balmat, Bourrit, nor Paccard could occupy the same position as Saussure. In Bourrit's case, it was not for lack of trying. Bourrit remained disenfranchised in Geneva and fell deeply into debt. In December 1787, Bourrit was brought before the Genevan Council for singing the canticles for communion "with such rapidity that the listener could not follow and one thought one heard a profane song rather than a religious hymn."[66] In the summer of 1788, Bourrit tried again to climb Mont Blanc with an Englishman and Dutchman who were visiting Chamonix.[67] Only the Englishman William Woodley, the son of a plantation owner and governor in the Leeward Islands, reached the summit with his guides. A few years later, Gersdorf became irritated with Bourrit for failing to deliver a set of prints for which he had paid in advance and for not remitting to Balmat the full reward collected on his behalf. After Balmat wrote to Gersdorf to tell him that the reward he received from the subscription, as transmitted via Bourrit, amounted to 10 louis rather than almost 17 louis, Gersdorf berated Bourrit. In his defense in 1792, an intermediary asked for additional time for Bourrit to repay his debts and pleaded extenuating circumstances: Bourrit had spent more than 25,000 livres over the years on his Alpine journeys, was without a fortune, and had recently lost his French royal pension: "In a word, Sir, he was among those men who had enriched a great number of others but ruined themselves." It is unknown whether Bourrit ever paid the balance he owed to Balmat. Jakob Samuel Wyttenbach, a Bernese savant and conservative patrician, told Gersdorf amid further revolutionary upheavals in 1793: "All who know him realize Bourrit to be an inflated toad, an airy fool, a boastful braggart, a worse man."[68]

Paccard's humility and intelligence impressed visitors, even if his amateur observations could not match those of Saussure. The German poet Friedrich Matthissen described meeting a humble doctor at Chamonix in 1788:

> We also visited Doctor Paccard, who gave us a very plain and modest account of his ascension of Mont Blanc, for which bold undertaking he does not appear to assume to himself any particular merit, but asserts that anyone with like physical powers might have performed the task equally well. He is at present employed in a work upon the Glaciers, which will contain the results of many years examination into their origin: from an intelligent man, who lives at their foot, and can observe them at every season, we may reasonably be led to expect something satisfactory relative to so important and curious a subject.[69]

Yet Paccard never published this work. Why? As a doctor, Paccard had training as a naturalist and was connected to a regional network of savants, but he faced a variety of obstacles to publication beyond his disputes with Bourrit and Saussure. His professional contacts were primarily in the Francophone areas of Savoy, France, and Switzerland, but he was not as well plugged in to the Italian- and German-speaking areas of the Alps or to the wider networks of Europe. Paccard used inferior equipment during the first ascent, and Gersdorf, Bonnet, Saussure, and Joseph Banks were each underwhelmed by his results. Paccard himself must have been disappointed; why else would he make plans to climb the peak a second time with new instruments within days of returning from the first? Paccard claimed to reach the top first, but even for him, the first ascent remained incomplete without making detailed observations.

Philippe Joutard has argued that Paccard did not receive the credit he deserved because he did not fit the "model for alpine travel" established by Albrecht von Haller, Jean-Jacques Rousseau, and Saussure. As a local client, Paccard was neither the foreign client nor the local guide and thus in a position outside the assumed partnership between peasant and philosopher: "The tragedy of Paccard was to be an intermediary, a *'metis culturel,'* too notable to be assimilated to the guides, an indigene of a social and cultural level not high enough to be considered a traveler. The guide-client binary was in the process of formation and this division of roles implies the Chamonix doctor has no place."[70] This is an astute analysis, but Paccard's ambivalent position "in between" had less to do with inside-outside or local-foreign than with disparities in power relations stemming from contemporary forms of subjectivity and sovereignty available to Paccard at the end of the 1780s. In this respect, Paccard resembles colonial subjects whose elevated positions in a provincial context were considered but pale imitations by the standards of the metropole: almost the same, but not quite. Despite his education in Turin and Paris, Paccard's role in the first ascent received little notice in Piedmont: the prize from the king of Sardinia honored Balmat as the representative subaltern subject of the monarch's enlightened rule, and Saussure rather than Paccard was lionized in Turin after their respective ascents.[71]

After Saussure's ascent, Paccard took to traveling in the mountains alone, aspiring to a kind of autonomy that was distinct from the perspective provided by either Kant's aesthetic interiority or Saussure's panoramic totality. When Paccard reported a curious observation on the Glacier des Bossons to the *Journal de Lausanne* in 1788, he emphasized, "I was alone." Walking on the glacier in the dazzling winter sun, Paccard looked at a piece of paper and all the letters turned a very lively red: "I had taken a few drops of liquid laudanum Sydenham, and I was at the height of dizziness that opium often provides. It seems to me therefore that I ought to attribute this phenomenon to the effect of opium on the retina."[72] Although it is unclear how often Paccard medicated himself with opium, his chemically enhanced trips appear to have had medicinal rather than transcendental purposes.

The most important obstacle for Paccard was epistemological and, in a broader sense, political. In his article for the *Journal de physique,* Paccard preferred "facts" to theories and this standpoint underscored political differences that further distinguished him from Saussure. The enfranchisement that Paccard and the village of Chamonix had purchased in Savoy was not the same as the sovereignty that Saussure possessed and to which Bourrit aspired in Geneva. In Savoy, enfranchisement removed servile obligations, but each person remained a subject of the king. Enfranchisement in Savoy did not create an "individual sovereign" equivalent to the status of citizen and bourgeois in Geneva. The interactive effects of "making up people" vary with different kinds of classification, and "enfranchisement" and "sovereignty" produced different representations of individual subjectivity, or put another way, brought different sorts of people into existence. The attempts to climb Mont Blanc in the eighteenth century were braided with these revisions of sovereignty, but the early ascents of Mont Blanc resist incorporation into a singular narrative of the emergence of a particular category of individuality or "modern man" because the very constructions of individual selves among Paccard, Balmat, Saussure, and Bourrit remained distinctly different.

The ascent of Mont Blanc had diverse meanings and significance in relation to different networks, cosmologies, and practices at the end of the eighteenth century. The ascent did not embody one representation of enlightenment, modernity, masculinity, or individuality, but entangled competing and mutually constitutive contemporary visions of each. Differences between these representations of the ascent have remained in tension, even as they continued to evolve and change in later years. The certificate that Paccard obtained from Balmat said he had to run to be "almost as soon as him at the aforesaid summit." To reach the summit almost together marks a limit in their partnership, and articulates a tension that cannot be resolved as a question of discovery or by asking who was first. Rather, it appears that both were first since each occupied a position distinct from the other. We cannot assimilate the positions of Paccard and Balmat into one view from the summit. We need to stay with both, and the differences that remain between them. Let us recognize that even when two people reach the highest point together, they do not necessarily occupy the same summit position.

CHAPTER FIVE

Temple of Nature

EDGE OF A CLIFF

À LA NATURE was carved in stone above the door of the Temple of Nature. The "temple" was built in the summer of 1795 at Montanvert, the scenic viewpoint above the Mer de Glace, by Marc-Théodore Bourrit at the suggestion of Charles-Louis Huguet de Sémonville, a French revolutionary diplomat (Figure 11). Sémonville toured the glaciers in July 1793, with Bourrit as a guide. The entourage was too large to take shelter at a primitive cabin, so Sémonville suggested that Bourrit construct a hospice dedicated to nature as a refuge for visitors. The temple was intended to honor man as well as nature: "Carved on its four equal faces, let one receive the imprint of these words: *à la nature* by a friend of liberty; let three others recall to posterity what it owes to Bourrit, [Horace-Bénédict] de Saussure, and [Jean-André] Deluc: their names are inseparable from this frozen ocean and these elevated mountains whose dangers they had to forget for the benefit of humanity." Visitors would read these names with reverence and a pious respect: "Misfortune to anyone whose soul is unmoved by these sentiments

Figure 11 The temple dedicated to nature was built at Montanvert at the request of
French diplomats in 1795. Marc-Théodore Bourrit published this sketch in *Description
des cols* (1803). The building provided shelter to travelers and extolled the virtues of
the French Revolution and the savants who ventured beyond the edge of the cliff.
HCL, Widener Library, Swi 685.21.7.

and leaves this place without having taken another step towards the love of
letters and of virtue! This is, Citizen, the sketch of a plan which only awaits
your approval and care to be executed."[1] Flattered by the invitation to build
his own monument, Bourrit took up the challenge of creating this alpine
pantheon.

At the end of the path from Chamonix, the Temple of Nature stood on
the edge of a cliff, at the limit of normal terrain. Beyond, nothing but the
sea of ice. The Temple of Nature also stands at the limit of normal theoretical terrain, the "edge of a cliff" where Michel de Certeau located Michel
Foucault "when he attempts to invent a discourse that can speak of non-
discursive practices."[2] Although the contrast between "non- or pre-verbal
domains in which there are only practices without any accompanying discourse" has been rightly criticized, the "edge of a cliff" remains a fruitful
metaphor for the intersection of discourse and practice at this particular
moment. In debates over this metaphor, Roger Chartier argued that not all
practices can be reduced to discourse, and William H. Sewell noted the

"semiotic heterogeneity" of human practices that are always "meaningfully constructed and therefore available for interpretation," manifesting diverse forms of historical logic.[3] Talal Asad once asked when the notion of culture was "transformed into the notion of a *text*—that is, into something resembling an inscribed discourse," and James Chandler suggested that it became prominent during "the Romantic period."[4] Indeed, the edge of a cliff defined the limits of discourse during years when the Temple of Nature was constructed and rebuilt. As Percy Shelley wrote at the time in a fragmentary essay on life: "We are on that verge where words abandon us, and what wonder if we grow dizzy to look down the dark abyss of how little we know."[5]

Limits of discourse have restricted the scope of histories of mountaineering, which trivialize the French Revolution and Napoleonic periods by viewing them as merely restricting visits by otherwise assertive individuals during an unpleasantness between the states of Europe. Yet the entanglement of sovereignty and the summit during the French Revolution transformed Mont Blanc. The mountain became a contested symbol for revolutionaries and counterrevolutionaries, monarchs and emperors, peasant guides and romantic poets. The extension of the French revolutionary state into the Alps and the appropriation of Mont Blanc as a "temple of nature" transformed the mountain into a "temple" in a wider sense. In particular, political contests of this period gave prominence to religious and political practices that cannot be reduced to discourses of individual romantic "transcendence."

The edge of a cliff during the revolutionary and Napoleonic periods suggests overlapping lines of inquiry, less an alternate route of ascent than a traverse across terrain that is separately well traveled but seldom linked together. A traverse of this cliff embraces a diversity of perspectives. Visitors to the mountains translated their encounter with the popular piety of people who lived among the mountains. Even poetry once read as the "mind" encountering "nature" incorporated the peasants of the Alps, sometimes in the foreground and sometimes in the fissures of literary discourses. These provincial or "local" histories of Chamonix, Savoy, and the Alps more generally were constitutive of the "literary" representations at the edge of the cliff that they shared with one another. Well beyond the revolutionary and romantic periods, the men and women of Chamonix continue to haunt Mont Blanc.

CRIES FOR LIBERTY IN "MONT BLANC"

Events of the French Revolution in 1789—the Estates General, the fall of the Bastille, the abolition of feudal privileges, the Declaration of the Rights of Man and Citizen—were felt throughout Europe and deeply divided communities in Savoy. The assertion that men were free and equal in rights disrupted political settlements and expanded horizons of possibility. French aristocrats and émigrés hoped to use Savoy as a base from which to overturn the revolution, and after the Civil Constitution of the Clergy in France required priests to take an oath of loyalty to the state, many clerics joined them in exile. Refusal to pay the church tithe *(dîme)* multiplied in northern Savoy after it was abolished in France. Some Savoyards crossed the frontier into the Dauphiné on July 14, 1790, to join the Festival of Federation to celebrate the anniversary of the fall of the Bastille. By then, Piedmontese magistrates viewed much of the "Third Estate" in Savoy as sympathetic to French ideas, and they blamed the "malice of lawyers, procurers and notaries."[6] Reform of feudalism from above by "enlightened despotism" had not resulted in a new equilibrium in Savoy, but rather, as Jean Nicolas has argued, unleashed forces of division that made reconciliation difficult after the revolution in France. Two-thirds of all communities in Savoy had negotiated enfranchisement from vestigial feudal rights by 1792, and antagonisms over the sale of communal land to pay for enfranchisement remained contentious.[7]

Le Premier Cri de la Savoie vers Liberté (a 1791 pamphlet) lamented that Savoy "has been poorly described by our travelers and geographers. The friend of humanity is very little satisfied with their observations." It blamed Savoyard poverty on Piedmontese despotism: agriculture was poor, industry was shackled by government, and too many of the region's limited resources were devoted to the church, military, or legal professions. The highest administrative posts were filled by appointees from Piedmont: "there remain for Savoyards only some of the least lucrative and subaltern positions." The mountains separating Savoy from Piedmont created physical, political, and moral barriers: "These enormous masses placed here and there on the globe seem to be natural barriers that liberty always opposes to despotism." More generally, the *Premier Cri* asked Victor Amadeus III to establish a Savoyard Estates General: "If this sublime project does not enter in the virtuous heart of your monarch, or rather if it is rejected by the councils that surround him, do not despair," for in time the people will weary of despotic government and "find the old valor of the Allobroges and reverse everything that opposes their happiness."[8] The state increased surveillance by informers and secret agents who reported that in Chamonix a notary obtained this pamphlet and gave it to the curé (the senior parish priest), Joseph Revillod, who was unsympathetic, and Dr. Michel-Gabriel Paccard, who became a leading Jacobin in the village.[9]

The French National Convention abolished the monarchy and declared France a republic on September 22, 1792. French troops immediately invaded Savoy and encountered little resistance. Piedmontese troops, French émigrés, and refugee priests fled in panic and disarray across the mountains. By mid-October 1792, the communities of Savoy held votes on "reunion" with France, and it was approved enthusiastically in Chamonix.[10] By contrast, at Megève, a nearby village with a sizable clerical population, the cantor recorded that when the gathering of three hundred was asked for a show of hands in favor of reunion, he could count barely twenty arms raised. The fine lace and colored buttons on their sleeves led him to remark: "Without seeing the faces, it was easy to conclude that these were not our peasants. However, with a strike of the gavel they shouted with glee that the general will was for reunion to the France, and the vote was called accordingly."[11]

Savoy was thus annexed to France and renamed the *Département du Mont Blanc,* as the mountain itself symbolized the new regime of liberty. Abbé Grégoire told the National Convention in 1792 that Savoyards demonstrated that "the man of the mountains is truly a man of liberty. . . . Our union, our liberty and the sovereignty of peoples will be as durable as your mountains, as immutable as the heavens."[12] The new representative body in Chambéry renamed itself the "National Assembly of the Allobroges" in honor of the Alpine peoples who were never conquered by the Romans. This assembly abolished remaining seigneurial privileges, eliminated the *dîme,* seized the property of émigrés, and reorganized municipalities with new offices, including mayor, assessor, and justice of the peace, each unknown in the former regime.

The Department of Mont Blanc was run by many of the same local notables whose families had been prominent in Savoy earlier in the eighteenth century. Dr. Paccard became a member of the communal council in 1792, a justice of the peace in 1793, and mayor in 1794, and exercised executive authority under a variety of titles for several years. By the end of 1795, Paccard was "ex-mayor" and commissioner with executive power, and in 1796, he became "officer of health and commissioner with executive power for municipal administration in the canton of Chamonix."[13] Although he reached the top of Mont Blanc in 1786, only under the regime of the French revolutionary state was Dr. Paccard able to occupy the summit position.

In larger cities of the region, "Mont Blanc" symbolized the new union in civic festivals in March 1793. In Annecy, a statue of liberty stood on a pyramidal altar surrounded by flames while, on another peak, symbols of feudalism and Catholicism collapsed as a choir sang hymns to reason and danced on the debris. At Chambéry, Mont Blanc was festooned with flames, and torrents of water flushed away crowns, banners, and symbols of Italy from its slopes. At the summit, a woman dressed as the Goddess of Liberty stood triumphant over anarchy, and "Mont Blanc" took its place among the departments of France. It is difficult to know what those who saw these spectacles thought of them. An unsympathetic observer of the festival at Chambéry wrote: "the people were frozen, mortified. There was not a single cry of joy."[14]

THE WHITE MOUNTAIN

During 1793, the Department of "Mont Blanc" was divided by the introduction of a new French currency, policies toward Catholicism, and military conscription for the revolution. The Civil Constitution of the Clergy nationalized church property and required the clergy to take an oath of allegiance and preach sermons of loyalty to the state. The Roman Catholic bishop for the Diocese of Geneva, who had resided in Annecy since the Reformation, was replaced by an elected "Bishop of Mont Blanc." These actions crystallized unease into active resistance and open hostility. In Faucigny, more than 85 percent of vicars and curés refused to take the oath or preach the sermon. In Chamonix, the vicar and brother of the doctor, Pierre-Joseph Paccard, refused, and the curé, Joseph Revillod, told the municipality in March that he could not take the oath "without hurting his conscience."[15]

Military conscription was met with revolt in the name of defending the church and king. In the upper valley of the Arve, the tocsin was sounded to protest conscription in April 1793. Protestors included many seasonal servants returned from Paris and former soldiers in the royal armies of France and Sardinia, who refused to send soldiers and demanded more priests.[16] At

Chamonix, young men from Argentière invaded the recruiting rooms, trampled tricolor cockades, tore up the mayor's sash in the name of the Sardinian king and Roman Catholic religion, and forced the resignation of the Jacobin-dominated Chamonix council. The youth manhandled and beat several of the notables, "among others Doctor Paccard, who was nearly beaten to death."[17] Volunteers marched to Sallanches, trampling liberty caps and wearing cockades of white paper. A mannequin representing the Goddess of Liberty, painted by the Jacobin Bacler d'Albe for a festival, was burned with a liberty tree in counterrevolutionary effigy.[18]

This "revolt of the shepherds" was followed by French reoccupation and repression led by the National Guard. Sémonville's visit to Mont Blanc in July 1793, when he proposed the Temple of Nature, took place during one of the extended periods when French troops were stationed in Chamonix and provided de facto military escort. The Montagnard arrest of Girondin members of the National Convention followed the pattern of seizure of power that had been used in the Alps. The town council of Annecy, which Hérault de Séchelles had purged in the spring, announced its approval of the Montagnard coup he joined in Paris that summer: "O unforgettable day! We will engrave it in ineffaceable characters on the majestic summit of Mont Blanc. This summit was inaccessible to slaves, but she never will be so for free men!"[19]

Simultaneously, Mont Blanc symbolized freedom to the refugees and clergy who crossed into Piedmont after the French invasion of Savoy. Pierre-Joseph Paccard, the Chamonix vicar and the doctor's brother, fled to the Vaud in May 1793 and then to Lausanne. Fugitives were said to be so numerous that "the way from Chamonix to the Valais by the Tête-Noire was obstructed and blocked with caravans."[20] A sketch from the early 1790s depicts a column of émigrés stretching into the distance through the Chamonix valley. The line of people is so crowded that faces in the procession blend into the white snows of the mountain. As the mountain provided sanctuary to royalists and clergy, Mont *Blanc* carried connotations similar to the royalist white flag or white cockade.

Piedmontese-Sardinian troops used the same passes to invade in mid-August 1793. Soldiers disguised as muleteers entered the Arve valley from the Valais via Chamonix and from the Val d'Aoste via Saint Gervais. In many villages, peasants greeted returning troops and priests with pails of milk, cries of *vive le roi* (long live the king), and arms uplifted in prayer. In

Chamonix, by contrast, the royal troops were greeted with long faces, and residents seized a bridge to prevent their advance. On August 14, the marquis Maurice de Sales ordered soldiers to set fire to houses in Chamonix to the beat of military drums, as people who had been holding the bridge fled into the hills. Documents of the republic were seized and the Paccard residence was burned along with the liberty tree.[21]

This retribution was not indiscriminate. Before the invasion, the Piedmontese army collected intelligence from priests and émigrés to identify the respective royalists and democrats in each village. Informants reported that Chamonix was divided between a number of committed royalists led by Jacques Balmat and other guides, and the more numerous and influential democrats including the innkeepers, magistrates, and the extensive Paccard family.[22] Paccard's notoriety was such that Joseph de Maistre wrote in 1795: "there are at Chamonix four cancerous houses [*maisons gangrenées*], among others that of the famous Paccard, the first climber of Mont Blanc."[23] Royal troops were joined by volunteers from surrounding villages led by an architect from Saint Gervais and the curé of Chamonix, who returned from exile. Their advance to Sallanches led to pro-Piedmontese demonstrations in Annecy and other cities, which often featured cutting down liberty trees.[24]

The French "Army of the Alps" moved from suppressing a rebellion in Lyon to defeating the royalist forces at Sallanches in September 1793. Two members of the French National Convention were surprised to see "peasants armed with the crucifix, the cross, and signs of their invulnerability; in this pious disposition a national fusillade sent their souls to eternal glory."[25] Despite attempts by revolutionaries and some historians to view religion as a pretext for revolt due to other causes, this insurgency should be seen, like others described by Ranajit Guha, as in large part the consequence of religious consciousness.[26] In a similar register, anti-*philosophe* and Catholic polemicists offered providential interpretations of the French Revolution as divine punishment long before Joseph de Maistre synthesized their views in his influential *Considerations on France* (1796). The anxieties of counter-revolutionaries were, as Darrin McMahon has shown, "first and foremost" motivated by attacks on religion; they were not relics of "tradition," but as modern as the Jacobin revolutionaries whose rhetoric was a mirror image of their own.[27]

After Piedmontese troops were pushed beyond the boundary of Mont Blanc, French troops remained stationed in the Chamonix valley for years.

Liberty trees were replanted, sacred objects confiscated, church bells melted, and steeples destroyed. Although revolutionary festivals were celebrated in many cities, the campaign against Christianity met with significant resistance and clandestine worship of Catholicism continued in all the mountain areas.[28] So many insurgents emigrated that few were executed, and retribution in Savoy was far less violent than in other areas of France. Only Marie Couttet *dit Moutelet,* a guide who had cut down the liberty tree at Servoz, was condemned to death, and he escaped execution by fleeing over the Col du Géant.[29] Overall, the tempered French response to revolt may have resulted from the proximity of Piedmont as an escape route, the "prudent milieu" of the region's political culture, or what a nineteenth-century cleric and historian called Savoy's "aversion to spill blood."[30]

MONTAGNARDS AND ESCALADES

In Paris, the French government incorporated Mont Blanc into the new regime of festivals and practices that constituted the revolution. The revolutionaries marked their break in time and space with new calendars and weights and measures based on nature. The revolutionary calendar introduced in 1793 included weeks of ten days each to break with Christian observance of Sunday. The metric system replaced a patchwork of local measures with the meter based on a fraction of the distance from the pole to the equator. The revolutionary government celebrated the principles in whose name the revolution had been carried out with ecumenical festivals in honor of reason, nature, unity, and the Supreme Being. Although the repertoire of symbols used at each festival were almost interchangeable, the "mountain" became especially prominent during the Year II (1793–1794).[31]

The mise-en-scène that Sémonville envisioned for the Temple of Nature was exhibited later the same year at the Festival of Reason in Paris. On 20 Brumaire Year II (November 10, 1793), the National Convention held the Festival of Reason in Notre Dame, rebaptized the Temple of Reason. In the middle of the sanctuary stood a large white mountain with a temple at the summit displaying the inscription: *À LA PHILOSOPHIE* (Figure 12). Young women dressed in white with tricolor waistbands traversed the mountain, saying: "crossing the altar of Reason, each of us bows before its flame and rises again in the same direction on the summit of the mountain." Liberty

Figure 12 The temple dedicated to philosophy was placed at the summit of a white mountain for the Festival of Reason in November 1793. This image of the mountain in the Temple of Reason, formerly Notre Dame Cathedral, appeared in *Révolutions de Paris*. HCL, Widener Library, Fr 1325.914.

emerged from the temple holding a pike as an alpenstock. The conquest of the monarchy was represented through the conquest of the white mountain, or to give its proper name, *le Mont Blanc.* The hymn concluded: "Come, conquerors of kings, Europe you survey; Come, on false gods extend your success; You, Holy Liberty, come live in this temple: Be the Goddess of the French!"[32]

The mountain remained a dynamic symbol during the revolution. The Jacobin faction was nicknamed the "mountain" since its deputies sat on the highest benches in contrast to moderate deputies on the "plain," but the word did not merely signify a seating chart. Mountain imagery in partisan rhetoric evoked the "holy Mountain," biblical images of Sinai, and the explosive power of a volcano. "The ingenious axiomatics of altitude" underlying mountain images gave this terminology wider significance.[33] Mountains appealed to the revolutionary imagination by representing liberty, freedom, and direct democracy of the Swiss Alps, works by Jean-Jacques Rousseau, and the legends of William Tell. Yet even as certain political parties in Savoy and the Pyrenees suggested a link between mountains and patriots, the mountains themselves served as havens of refuge for counterrevolutionaries.

In Savoy, revolutionaries sponsored *Montagnard* festivals and destroyed churches around Mont Blanc. After French authorities ordered the destruction of chapels, crosses, oratories, or other public signs of religion, Joseph-Marie Devillaz pulled down the church bell towers at Servoz, Houches, and Chamonix. He organized a civic festival at Servoz with his nineteen-year-old sister playing the role of the Goddess of Reason. As the procession proceeded, Devillaz's brother smashed a Christ figure, shouting, "If you are stronger than me, prove it!" before the event concluded with a bonfire of crosses, statues of the Virgin Mary, and church furnishings.[34] In Chamonix, the church bells were melted to make cannons. Within months, "nothing remained except the four walls" in the church, and the guide Cachat *le Géant* lamented the absence of sounds from the belfry: "It is very sad, especially for the departures for Mont Blanc."[35]

In France, images of the "mountain" fell from favor just before the Montagnards fell from power. The mountains at revolutionary festivals had paths to the top and could be climbed easily by children, but the inaccessibility of Mont Blanc meant some mountains could be viewed by revolutionaries as anti-democratic. Mona Ozouf astutely notes that "verticality was scandalous" to revolutionaries of the Year II. The revolutionary statue, column, or tree provided moral elevation without visual constraint, but the heavy mass of the mountains on which they were planted caused unease. In the departments of the Ain and Mont Blanc, the demolition of church bell towers was ordered by Antoine-Louis Albitte in January 1794 because "their height is a sign of pretension which offends the republican eye." The campaign to abolish crucifixes and "calvaries" confirms that this unease was not merely architectural or an artifact of political rhetoric. After the fall of the Parisian Montagnards in Thermidor (July 1794), mountains were dissociated from liberty trees and other revolutionary symbols. Liberty trees provided a verticality of dominance without humiliation and adapted folk traditions of the maypole as well as the Christian cross, combining multiple forms of verticality.[36]

The revolutionary mountain also came to Geneva. "In view of the new ideas set afloat by the French Revolution, and the political ferment resulting from them," Horace-Bénédict de Saussure told the Large Council of Geneva on February 1, 1790, "it is impossible not to realize that we have need of a

Constitution carefully framed and acceptable to the commonality."[37] This was a volte-face for Saussure, who had opposed a mild edict of reconciliation a year earlier. After Saussure's more favorable intervention, Marc-Théodore Bourrit was among a large group of natives "promoted" to the bourgeoisie and citizenship in Geneva on February 15, 1790. Exiles rallied the natives, who remained excluded as well as subjects in the countryside to form the *égalisateurs,* a party devoted to the egalitarian principles of the French Revolution.[38]

The Egalitarians led Geneva's revolution in December 1792. The new regime in Geneva proclaimed liberty and equality, created a new constitution, and annulled the judgments against Rousseau. Saussure was named to the provisional committee of thirty citizens that exercised executive authority and constituted a National Assembly. The elected assembly included older figures such as Saussure and Bourrit, who both viewed the revolution with dismay, but was led by a younger generation including Pierre Bourrit, who served terms as president. Saussure was respected for his mixture of flexibility and firmness and even designed a lightning rod for the liberty tree in Geneva.[39] In June 1793, members of the assembly were required to take an oath to liberty, an oath Saussure swore even as the revolution ruined his finances. Much of his fortune had been invested in French government securities that were now effectively worthless.[40]

On December 12, 1793, Geneva reestablished the *fête de l'escalade,* a festival abolished in 1782 that had celebrated the defeat of Savoyard forces attempting to surmount the city walls in 1602. At festivals in Geneva, the National Assembly sang a hymn to peace to the tune of the *Marseillaise,* but French battalions singing the lyrics of the original *Marseillaise* were far more threatening to Geneva's independence than the Piedmontese forces that had been defeated in Savoy. As Genevans prepared to defend themselves again, the *fête de l'escalade* symbolized the independence of Geneva and the ascent of democracy. At the same time, revolutionary clubs organized themselves under the umbrella of the *Club fraternel de la Montagne.* The club's insignia depicted a woman atop a mountain resembling the Salève, a peak just outside Geneva across the border with France, who waved slogans that conspicuously dropped the claim for Genevan independence.[41]

Saussure and Bourrit did not join the ascent of this mountain. During a debate in the National Assembly on renaming churches, Jean Desonnaz, one of the Genevan Montagnards, was amused to hear "a philosopher, de

Saussure, praising the Saints" and "Bourrit, the man of the Alps, also judiciously argued that what Calvin had not reformed must not be changed. And you tell me that this man has not the wit of four! It is without doubt on Mont-Blanc where he learned so much."[42] The assembly approved a new constitution that provided political equality to members of the Reformed Church in February 1794. A month later, Saussure suffered a stroke and retired from politics. He published the final volumes of *Voyages in the Alps* in 1796, writing that in his scientific publications, "I find relief from the troubles and anxieties which desolate at this moment almost the whole world."[43] After suffering yet another stroke, Saussure remained in genteel poverty in Geneva to ensure that his mansion was not confiscated, until he died in 1799.

In the summer of 1794, the revolutions in Paris and Geneva escalated in violence and collapsed on themselves. Genevan Montagnards established revolutionary tribunals to make an example of aristocrats, and seven prisoners were hastily convicted and summarily executed. After the fall of Robespierre in Thermidor, the Genevan Montagnards fled the city before they too were sentenced to death in absentia by the next round of tribunals. By the end of 1794, the latest revolutionary government in Geneva marked the year's events by burning the registers of habitation and bourgeoisie of Geneva on the day of the Festival of the Escalade.[44]

TEMPLE OF FAME

In Chamonix, the oscillation between revolutionary and counterrevolutionary images of the mountains continued after the bloodshed ended in Paris and Geneva. As war loomed at a distance, revolutionaries competed with religious practices rather than military forces. On 22 Nivôse Year III (January 11, 1795), the commune received a patriotic gift. Citizen Michel-Gabriel Paccard, the mayor, donated 190 livres toward the construction of a ship to be named "Mont Blanc" for use in the war against England.[45] He also presided in April over the Chamonix Communal Council that approved construction of the Temple of Nature.

Construction of the hospice was paid for by the French ambassador at Geneva, Félix Desportes, who hoped the "small temple" would appear as if "deposited by a miracle."[46] The site was communal land and the Chamonix

council approved the hospice for traveling savants stocked with "all the instruments of physical science necessary for observation of the rare beauties
of nature." The council noted Bourrit's distinguished reputation as a traveler and had no doubt that the building would benefit travelers, savants,
and the commune, which would become its owner: "Resolved and resolve
that Citizen Bourrit, celebrated historiographer of our mountains, be com-
plimented on the felicity of his object and his sentiments of goodwill towards the Commune, and that our approval be given to his request by
authorizing him to construct the hospice and observatory on the mountain
of Montanvert."[47]

Bourrit supervised construction of the Temple of Nature by a hotelier and
two guides. The building contained two windows, a chimney, and the pedi-
ment above the door dedicated to nature. Inside, Bourrit mounted medallions high on each wall with names of savants who had distinguished themselves in the mountains. When the naturalist J. J. Lalande visited Chamonix
in the summer of 1795, he regretted the destruction of churches, but was
pleased to see inscribed on the walls of the hospice the names of Saussure,
Deluc, Bourrit, Déodat de Dolomieu, and Marc-Auguste Pictet. Other savants made scientific pilgrimages to Mont Blanc and added their own names
to the walls. Visitors could leave comments in an album or sign their names
on the walls, which became "one of the ceremonies of the expedition."[48]

Sometime after 1797, the Temple of Nature was pillaged and vandalized,
its windows broken, interior wrecked, and furnishings taken away. After
France granted limited freedom of worship in private, émigrés returned
within a few years. This post-Thermidor religious revival widened the arena
for worship in France more generally. Popular devotion led to protests to re-
open churches, ring bells, and celebrate festival days. In Savoy, missionaries
reopened churches from 1797, but freedom for religious practices were not
secured more fully until after Napoleon's concordat with the Roman Catholic Church in 1801. In Chamonix, the guide Cachat *le Géant* recorded faithfully in his *livre de raison* (record book) in 1797 that it had been "three years,
10 months and 12 days without Mass in the church," and later noted periods
of continued suppression of religious festivals after the concordat.[49]

In 1803, Bourrit did not propose reestablishment of the Temple of Nature.
Much had changed in the decade since the temple was proposed to teach
the love of virtue. Bourrit wrote during an armistice that visitors returned

to Chamonix and described an ascent of Mont Blanc by climbers from Lausanne and Courland (Latvia). The grandeur of the Temple of Nature elevated
the self "closest to his creator" and above political conflict: "Elevated, so to
speak, above nature, one feels perfectly new sensations, the soul is purified
and all one's thoughts ennobled. Men whose political opinions had rendered
them enemies, cannot resist forgetting their grievances, and the mutual
opening of their hearts to one another attests to the influence of this climate."
In this spirit, Bourrit buried the hatchet over the first ascent, and declared
that Dr. Paccard rather than Balmat was primarily responsible for the first
ascent.[50]

French officials proposed restoring the "Temple of Hospitality," but took
no action for years. Louis-Gustave le Doulcet de Pontécoulant, a regional
prefect and later senator, saw the temple in 1802 and offered to pay for its
restoration, which was duly completed in 1808.[51] Whitewashing the walls
had obscured the names of the savants and covered the signatures of visitors.
In 1810, P.-X. Leschevin made rubbings of the whitewashed medallions to
discover and restore the names of those "diverse savants of Europe, to whom
the history of the earth and mineralogy are most obligated." By then, signing the walls was discouraged and replaced by the visitor's book or register.
A decade later, the temple was in disrepair and Desportes again paid for its
restoration. The most prominent inscriptions in 1818 were to Desportes, de
Pontécoulant, and Isaac Newton, with other medallions grouped by nationality. By 1821, visitors to the Temple of Nature could immortalize themselves
by signing "our names in a sort of temple of fame."[52]

MONTS RELIGIEUX: TRANSLATED BY FEELINGS

Mont Blanc itself became a temple during the revolutionary and Napoleonic periods. Indeed, the sacking of the "Temple of Nature" at Montanvert
was the corollary of the sacralization of Mont Blanc during and after the
revolution. Mont Blanc became the "monarch of mountains" and inspired
religious and romantic poetry. Charles-Jullien Chênedollé popularized this
"monarchical" language in an ode to Mont Blanc and an epic poem after
visiting Chamonix in 1797. Chênedollé had emigrated in 1791, served tours
of duty with royal armies, and lived in Hamburg and Switzerland before
returning to France in 1799. The ode, which begins "here is Mont Blanc,

the monarch of mountains," portrays the peak with royal scepter, "throne of rocks," and "diadem of snow," language that Bryon later borrowed word for word in *Manfred*.[53]

Similarly, the Danish-German poet, Friederike Brun, wrote "Chamounix beym Sonnenaufgange" after visiting the valley in 1791: "Out of the deep shade of the silent fir-grove / trembling I survey thee, mountain head of eternity, / dazzling summit." The poem then proceeds with a series of rhetorical questions (who sank the pillars of the earth?) before answering: "Jehovah! Jehovah! Crashes in the bursting ice; / avalanche thunders roll it down the chasm."[54] Samuel Taylor Coleridge adapted and lengthened her work in his celebrated poem, "Hymn before Sunrise in the Vale of Chamouny" (1802). Coleridge's hymn to "thou first and chief, sole sovereign of the Vale" paraphrases the rhetorical questions before providing the same answer: "God! Let the torrents, like a shout of nations, / Answer! And let the ice-plains echo, God!" The earth fills the hills with praise: "Earth, with her thousand voices, praises God."[55]

Since Coleridge never visited Chamonix and never acknowledged his debt to Brun, he was accused of plagiarism after his death in 1834. Byron's borrowing prompted similar charges in the nineteenth century. Coleridge claimed he had been inspired to write his poem on Scafell in the Lake District before transferring his sentiments to the grander setting of Mont Blanc. More constructive than viewing this as a case of plagiarism is attention to wider political contexts and dialogue among poets. This suggests that critical suppression of common experiences was necessary to sustain the "myth of the unique, solitary individual of the romantic period."[56] Coleridge's "Hymn before Sunrise" deserves consideration on its own merits, but as Elinor Shaffer points out, "its roots remain in translation, and it is not necessarily a better poem than its source."[57]

Coleridge's debt to Brun is more interesting as a problem of translation than as a question of plagiarism. But who, and what, is being translated? Translation did not mean simply rendering Brun's German into Coleridge's English. Visitors to Chamonix encountered the peasants of the Alps at the same time they encountered the landscape of Mont Blanc. Even poets who knew Mont Blanc only secondhand—from reading the accounts of others who had visited the mountain—were implicated in the cross-cultural poetics of this encounter. The translations of popular piety into literary discourse could figure prominently or appear in the fissures of discourse.

Consider Chênedollé's 1802 hymn to earth and mountains, *Le génie de l'homme,* which features the voice of an Alpine peasant as an oracle of wisdom. Such a voice should be considered as a translation of encounters with peasants in the Alps as much as a reworking of prior literary models such as Rousseau or Albrecht von Haller. In the poem, the narrator travels to Mont Blanc, the *"monts sourcilleux,"* where Saussure demonstrated his daring and audacity. Alone on these heights, he meets an old man who asks why he seeks peace for his soul in the mountains. The poet replies that he meditates on the Alps "to observe their structure and search for the hand that raised their ramparts." The old man had worked at court in Versailles and had known Buffon, Voltaire, and other savants, but their "vain systems" did not provide wisdom. The *"monts religieux,"* whose summits bring us nearer the sky ought to inspire the poet: "These mountains want a hymn and not a system." After summarizing geological theories of Buffon and Saussure, the old man pauses to chastise the young man for pretending to conquer his ignorance: "How did God elevate the summits? Here is the great mystery."[58]

Other writers in Madame de Staël's circle in Switzerland were caught between revolutionary and religious associations of the mountain. François-René Chateaubriand, then well known as the author of *Génie du Christianisme* (1802), visited Chamonix in 1805, but preferred the view of Mont Blanc from Lake Geneva to the view from its adjacent valleys: "For monuments of nature as for works of art, to enjoy their beauty one must be at the proper point of perspective." He also did not enjoy his excursion to Montanvert: "The grandeur of these mountains, about which so much fuss is made, is based only on the fatigue which they give you."[59] Chateaubriand's reputation as "detractor of the mountains" has caused confusion among critics. The target of his antipathy was not just mountains in general, but rather the aesthetics and politics represented by the revolutionary "mountain."[60]

Chateaubriand's *Voyage to Mont-Blanc* offers eulogy as well as critique, and he celebrates the association of high places with religious belief: "In only one circumstance do mountains inspire one to forget the troubles of the earth: when one retires from the world for the consecration of religion." In language that inverted revolutionary discourse, Chateaubriand contrasted Rousseau and his followers with "the *montagnards* (mountain dwellers) who call the plain the good countryside." The attachment of local people to the mountains had to do with marvels of God, memories of childhood, sentiments of the heart, loyalty to home, and religious devotion: "The instinct of man has always been to worship the eternal on elevated places." Chateaubriand preferred the Passion of Christ and mountains of Judea to the "interior passions" of tourists on mountains in Switzerland: "Mountains are the source of rivers, the last asylum of liberty in an age of slavery, a useful barrier against invasion and the scourge of war."[61]

William Wordsworth translated his encounter with the Alps and its peoples differently during and after the French Revolution. "Among the more awful scenes of the Alps," Wordsworth wrote to his sister in 1790, "I had not a thought of man, or a single created being; my whole soul was turned to him who produced the terrible majesty before me."[62] When he put this into verse three years later, Wordsworth demonstrated ambivalence about the religiosity of people in the Alps. *Descriptive Sketches* (1793), Geoffrey Hartman noted, "depicts a vacillation between mighty opposites" exemplified in Mont Blanc.[63] But the most striking contrast provided by Mont Blanc is not internal to each couplet but with the preceding section on the pilgrims to Einsiedeln, the Swiss Benedictine monastery. Wordsworth's notes on Einsiedeln mingles admiration with contempt, contrasting the muttering prayers, chafe of feet, and weeping cries of the "multitudes, from every corner of the Catholick [*sic*] world" with the "sentimental traveler and philosopher [who] may find interesting sources for meditation" in sheds built for the pilgrims' ascent. Wordsworth's verses continued, "My heart, alive to transports long unknown, / Half wishes your delusion were its own. / Last let us turn to where Chamouny shields, / Bosom'd in gloomy woods her golden fields." He blends his hope for freedom, liberty, and the "emancipation" of Savoy with outrage at the "blasphemous" occupation of the Chartreuse monastery by French troops after his visit.[64]

Wordsworth registered disappointment in the revolution in *The Prelude* in verses on the Chartreuse monastery, Mont Blanc, and the Simplon Pass. The solitude of the monastery was broken by "arms flashing, and military glare" of revolutionaries come to expel the monks from "this one temple last" devoted to eternity. The summit of Mont Blanc presented "a soulless image on the eye," but the rivers of ice in the valley of Chamonix "made rich amends, / and reconciled us to realities." On the Simplon Pass, he and his companion were separated from their guides and continued walking until they were lost. They met a peasant who told them to continue downward: "We questioned him again, and yet again; / But every word that from the peasant's lips / Came in reply, translated by our feelings, / Ended in this,—that we had crossed the Alps."[65]

Commentary on these passages makes a jump cut from Wordsworth's tour in 1790 to later moments of the *Prelude*'s composition in 1799, 1804, and 1816—from the Festival of Federation in 1790 to Napoleon's seizure of power in 1799.[66] Critical attention to Napoleon's seizure of power on 18 Brumaire Year VIII (November 9, 1799) has skipped 20 Brumaire Year II (November 10, 1793) and the "mountain" of the Festival of Reason and the Temple of Nature. Wordsworth inserted these events not only with the sacking of the Chartreuse monastery but also the "soulless image" of Mont Blanc, which should be read as a critique of the politics of revolutionary montagnards. Critics of Wordsworth, Chateaubriand, and other "romantic" poets have been confused by the assumption of a narrowly discursive formula: mountains = sublime. Alan Liu rightly reads a "muted story of predation here, of some spoliation or usurpation in the area of Chamonix."[67] However, the spoliation of "a soulless image on the eye / Which had usurped upon a living thought / That never more could be" was Jacobin as much as Napoleonic, the usurpation by the revolutionary mountain.

Wordsworth's translation of every word "from the peasant's lips" into crossing the Alps as a tribute to imagination, arising "like an unfathered vapour" from his mind, represents an intercultural encounter on the edge of a cliff in which the peasants remain visible in the vapor. Wordsworth and other visitors to the Alps were almost constantly accompanied by guides while in the mountains, and similarities between literary descriptions may owe less to reading one another than the shared experience of hearing the same stories from guides in the same terrain. By the 1790s, guides of Chamonix had a reputation for leading clients over routes that used surprise to heighten sentiment.[68] Indigenous imagery hovers above representations of Mont Blanc. M. H. Abrams read Wordsworth's image of "the eagle soareth in his element" as consolation for the French Revolution and an "emblem of the poise of human aspiration between impossibility and despair."[69] In the Alps, however, the eagle was a common emblem of the monarchy, Christianity, and the sovereignty of nature in mountain communities, with connotations similar to royalist interpretations of Mont Blanc. The eagle also was not alone, according to Wordsworth: "There doth the reaper bind the yellow sheaf, / The maiden spread the haycock in the sun."[70] How would these lines be read if the reaper and the maiden could speak?

ASCENSION DAYS

Changes in local administration enabled the guides of Chamonix to assert new verticalities on Mont Blanc during the Napoleonic regime. The church bell tower, destroyed in 1794, was resurrected in June 1807.[71] By then, the communal council changed hands and peasant proprietors like Jacques Balmat were in the ascendant. Former "democrats" left office, and Paccard stepped down as justice of the peace in the year VIII (1800). In 1810, Paccard petitioned the communal council for 1,900 francs back pay as justice of the peace, but the council, including Balmat, disclaimed any responsibility and denied the claim.[72]

Balmat was honored by the French Empire for agricultural improvements despite his limited resources. In the year IX (1801), Balmat bought two male merino lambs from Charles Pictet in Geneva and they prospered in the communal pastures above Chamonix. Other villagers petitioned against the use of communal land by Balmat's purebred Spanish merinos, and Balmat was required to visit other communities with similar sheep to document that they were free from contagious diseases. The next year, Balmat bought three female merinos from Pictet and crossbred them with the local sheep.[73] Despite local opposition, the high-quality wool from Balmat's small flock was in demand for the manufacture of stockings. For his success, the prefect of the Department of Léman presented Balmat with a gold medal on behalf of the minister of the interior. In 1809, the Agricultural Society of the Department of the Seine also awarded Balmat a silver medal for his zeal in the improvement of wool-producing animals as an example to other less fortunate farmers that perseverance could overcome modest means.[74] Balmat showed his medals to Empress Josephine when he escorted her on the Mer de Glace in 1810, a few months after her divorce from Napoleon. The Genevan naturalist Henri-Albert Gosse considered writing a biography of Balmat in this period, but nothing came of it.[75]

Balmat made two ascents of Mont Blanc, suggesting resistance to the revolutionary mountain and ambivalence toward the French Empire. Such ambivalence may have stemmed from the service of Balmat's sons in the French Grand Army. In 1809, the eldest, Joseph Alexandre, disappeared during a battle in Spain and was presumed dead. In 1813, his son Ferdinand died at a French military hospital from wounds at the battle of Leipzig, but the Balmat family was not informed of his death until 1820, an event Balmat recorded bitterly in one of his fragmentary papers: "He was dead 6 years 4 months 15 days when we heard the news."[76] Beyond resentment about these sacrifices, Balmat's ascents in the Napoleonic period had religious overtones. Yet the uncertain status of religious worship after the concordat and before the restoration of the monarchy has obscured the "religious" dimensions of these ascents. Indeed, his 1808 and 1811 ascents are often omitted from lists of ascents since they were made by the guides without clients from outside the valley.

The 1811 ascent had a clear purpose—the construction of a trigonometrical signal on the summit of Mont Blanc at the orders of the Napoleonic state. In Balmat's list of Mont Blanc ascents, he recorded on July 25, 1811, "five men in order to plant the signal by order of the French government of Napoleon."[77] In 1811 the minister of war ordered a triangulation survey from the Atlantic to the Adriatic using the summit of Mont Blanc as an anchor point. The signal erected for this purpose was described as an "obelisk," a "pyramid," and a "column of wood," but most often simply as a "cross." By the 1820s, Chamonix guides frequently told visitors that "Napoleon ordered a cross to be erected on the top of Mont Blanc," and it was even described as an "iron cross."[78] A detailed description of the structure in 1831 reported a "simple pyramid" made of local trees with "four strong posts, squared and closely joined together by eight solid iron hoops, on one of which was engraven the name of Napoleon; on the second, that of the chief engineer of the district; and on the third and fourth hoop, the names of Joseph Couttet and J. Balmat (dit le Mont Blanc), the two guides of Chamonix who were charged to fix the pyramid on the summit."[79] Whatever the intentions of Napoleon and his cartographers, Jacques Balmat, Joseph-Marie Couttet, and the guides of Chamonix who carried out these orders appropriated the signal for multiple purposes. The guides erected the cross with every care, but reported that it was carried away or overturned by a storm a few days later.

What did the summit cross say? After the destruction of religious icons and sacred objects during the revolution, crosses rose again with layers of meaning and significance.[80] Elsewhere in Europe, summit crosses came with captions. On first ascents of the highest peaks of the Grossglockner in the eastern Alps, Franz Xaver von Salm, the prince-bishop of Gurk, erected crosses in 1799 and 1800 with Latin inscriptions to exalt the cross and spread the faith.[81] Although the "cross" on the summit of Mont Blanc did not have such inscriptions, it would be wrong to say there was no accompanying discourse. As Mona Ozouf observed of crosses resurrected to replace liberty trees, "such a cross spoke without benefit of writing."[82] In 1808, Vallorcine erected a cross on its pastures for the first time since 1794. Crosses proliferated at the edge of other cliffs around Chamonix. Perhaps the most prominent was *croix de la Flégère,* directly across the valley from Montanvert, which it rivaled as a destination for pilgrims who placed stones at its base. Samuel Birmann captured the scene *À la Flégère,* with the cross and a shepherd watching over his flock before a view of the mountains, themselves as temples of nature (Figure 13).[83]

The 1808 ascent of Mont Blanc by Marie Paradis also served multiple purposes and combined festive and religious practices. By all accounts, a party led by Balmat dragged and carried Marie Paradis to the summit on

Figure 13 Samuel Birmann, *À la Flégère,* ca.1826. Birmann's post-Restoration images of churches, oratories, and crosses in the Chamonix valley represent the return of religious worship after the French Revolution, and the mountains themselves have become temples of nature.   Paul Mellon Collection, Yale Center for British Art.

July 14, 1808, and the first woman on top became known as *Marie du Mont Blanc*. The mayor of Chamonix, J.-J. Bossoney, wrote to the subprefect at Bonneville on September 12 that "a young woman aged 28 years named Marie Paradis has reached the summit without fear of the precipices, passing the crevasses with boldness. About a quarter hour before arrival the thin air made her feel weak. Assisted by her companions, she reached the summit of Mont Blanc where they stopped for 20 minutes."[84] The mayor reported that Balmat was joined by his two sons, and two innkeepers along with an ex-hussar officer. In 1810, Jacques Balmat told the empress Josephine that "only one woman had ever made the ascent," but her courtesan later recalled "it is inexcusable for me to have forgotten the name of this village heroine."[85]

Paradis remained largely unknown outside the valley until visitors interviewed Marie and her guides in the 1820s. The 1828 memoirs of Josephine's courtesan recalled that Balmat described the ascent by "a servant girl of an inn who felt ashamed that our sex was not more courageous." Despite becoming ill midway, "she swore she would rather die than descend without having placed her foot upon the spot where M. de Saussure had placed his." She vomited and was seized with nervous attacks, but insisted: "Drag me, carry me, only let me touch the stone erected to commemorate that never to be forgotten journey and I shall die content."[86] Henriette d'Angeville met Paradis after she repeated the ascent in 1838, and reported that Marie told her guides in the local patois, "Throw me in a crevasse and go where you wish," and claimed that Marie climbed Mont Blanc to make money from tourists.[87] While this explanation of her motives painted a stark contrast with Angeville's own, and seemed plausible when many tourists visited Chamonix thirty years later, it must be supplemented by other practices and discourses—sacred and profane—that were more legible in 1808.

Marie Paradis played multiple roles in the ascent. According to an oft-repeated version from the 1830s, Jacques Balmat refused to take Euphrosine Ducrocq, who was "nursing a seven month old infant" and instead chose Marie because she was "still unmarried."[88] In fact, at the time of the ascent in July 1808, Marie-Françoise Paradis *"dite l'aînée"* (the elder) was twenty-nine years old and the unmarried mother of a four-month-old son; she also had a younger sister with the same name, which has led to much confusion about her age at the time of the ascent.[89] Nonetheless, Marie's sobriquets, *Marie du Mont Blanc* and *la Paradisa,* named a role for her to play. In several respects, the interviews she gave in the 1820s and 1830s were parallel to interviews given by women who had played the Goddess of Liberty at revolutionary festivals. Over the next century, many Virgin Mary statues were erected on summits—Marie de la Meije, Vierge des Drus, and Notre Dame du Grépon—but Marian worship in the area had a much longer history.[90] Pilgrims had attended the festival of the Assumption of the Virgin Mary on August 15 at Notre Dame de la Gorges since the fifteenth century, and visits to Notre Dame du Lac, a pilgrimage site since 1091, resumed with even greater fervor after the revolutionary hiatus.[91]

And yet, the summit scene was described as more festive than pious. Versions of their banter invoked the woman out of place and mocked the ceremonial weddings and public dowries then staged at Napoleonic festivals.[92] On the summit, guides recalled that Marie Paradis recovered and could see the horizon: "We told her laughing that we were giving her for a dowry all the countryside which she could see. Then Balmat added: Now, since she has a dowry, it is necessary for her to marry. Messieurs, which is the lad that will take a wife here? Why! We are not making false gallantry: still no one presents themselves, except Michel Terraz, who asks for half an hour." As they could remain only ten minutes, "the proposition was not acceptable," and they descended as quickly as the setting sun.[93]

The sexual innuendo of the "woman on top" has long had disturbing spillover effects in "serious" life.[94] Marie Paradis's ascent was not "prepolitical" but at the edge of a cliff, representing an act of defiance through practice rather than discourse. This defiance may have been in response to "local" ascents of Mont Blanc. *Sieur* Joseph-Marie Simond *dit Montillet,* a proprietor of Chamonix, returned from a solo ascent of Mont Blanc during July 8–10, 1808, and made much of sustaining himself with a piece of oat bread and a small bottle of brandy. On July 12, the guide Jean-François Simond reached the summit with four companions, and told the mayor: "Mont Blanc is not forgotten, its virginity seems reborn as the head of a hydra as measured by the efforts we made to surmount it"; he claimed his success encouraged a woman, two children, and four grand personages to follow his footsteps.[95] A plausible interpretation is that Balmat took a woman to the top to humiliate the boastful proprietor.[96] Balmat may have dragged a woman to the top to show he could have done the same during the first ascent. Paccard's reputation was at a low ebb a few years later, in 1815, when he sued Victor Desailloux, his brother-in-law, and Victor Terraz for calling him a "cheat, villain, thief, pig, pillager, beggar, a scoundrel" in a public square.[97]

Whether demonstrating female courage, enacting Marian veneration, lampooning Napoleonic festivals, or acting as an intervention in local politics, the ascent by *Marie du Mont Blanc* had seditious potential on July 14, 1808. The *fête du 14 Juillet* commemorating the fall of the Bastille was celebrated in the 1790s, but disappeared with the founding of the Napoleonic Empire. From 1806 to 1813, it was replaced as a national holiday by the festival of St. Napoléon, observed on August 15, Napoleon's birthday as well as Assumption Day. For a committed royalist like Balmat, the 1808 ascent also may have reclaimed the cycle of the Virgin from mid-July to mid-August.[98]

The multiple contexts, logics, discourses, and practices in Marie Paradis's ascent resist attempts to reduce it to a singular act of transcendence. To some critics, however, the detail required to make such figures visible provides an allegory for individualism in which "the local threatens to go transcendental" and "sublimes all the underlying voices of the world."[99] On the contrary, to the extent that Marie Paradis's ascent exhibited "local transcendence," it mocked the transcendent individualism exhibited at the Temple of Nature, by ascents of Mont Blanc, and through contemporary poetry. Shahid Amin is surely right to ask "must non-literates always exemplify a code when they speak?"[100] Marie Paradis was ill when she returned to Chamonix, but made a full recovery. All the women of the village asked her for details of the voyage: "She told them that she had seen so many things that it would take too long to recount; but if they were very curious to know them, they could only make the voyage themselves. Not one of them did."[101]

CHAMONIX IN 1816: GHOST STORIES

By 1816, officials in Savoy insisted that the French Revolution was over. The Congress of Vienna returned Savoy to Piedmont-Sardinia and another treaty settled its boundaries with Geneva, which became a canton in the Swiss Confederation. The return of the Savoyard old regime was more complete and less ambivalent than the restoration of the monarchy in France. With the restoration in Savoy, residents and visitors looked for moral images in the mountains. In his promenades around Mont Blanc, for example, Charles Moulinié, a protestant pastor from Geneva, viewed the landscape itself as the "temple of nature."[102]

Amid the revival of older regimes, Percy Bysshe Shelley and Mary Woll-
stonecraft Shelley also sought moral lessons in a tour of the Alps in July
1816. "I never knew—I never imagined what mountains were before," Percy
Shelley wrote from Chamonix. The summits excited "a sentiment of ecstatic
wonder, not unallied to madness. And remember this was all one scene, it all
pressed home to our regard and our imagination." Shelley's panoramic point
of view embraced the mountains, pines, and ravine of the Arve—"all was as
much our own, as if we had been the creators of such impressions in the
minds of others as now occupied our own. Nature was the poet, whose harmony held our spirits more breathless than that of the divinest."[103]

The Shelleys visited the tourist sites of Chamonix over several days. They
climbed to the "cabin" at Montanvert and the "sea of ice, a scene in truth of
dizzying wonder." The avalanches never stopped, and "one would think
that Mont Blanc, like the god of the Stoics, was a vast animal, and that the
frozen blood for ever circulated through his snowy veins."[104] They walked a
distance on the ice and enjoyed an open-air picnic near the cabin. After
returning to Chamonix, each wrote works inspired by the deep and powerful feelings excited by these scenes, a poem about Mont Blanc and a story
that became *Frankenstein*.[105]

In Percy Shelley's "Mont Blanc, Lines Written in the Vale of Chamouni," the sounds of the Arve and the silence of the snows flow through the
poet's mind with the universe, and Mont Blanc dwells apart from living
things. The poet muses on his own "separate fantasy" that these primeval
mountains teach a lesson to the refined mind: "The wilderness has a mysterious tongue / Which teaches awful doubt, or faith so mild, / So solemn, so
serene, that man may be / But for such faith with nature reconciled. / Thou
has a voice, great mountain to repeal / Large codes of fraud and woe." The
poem closes with a question that has been the subject of much debate: "And
what were thou, and earth, and stars, and sea, / If to the human mind's imag-
inings / Silence and solitude were vacancy?"[106]

Throughout the nineteenth century, Shelley's "Mont Blanc" was read as
an atheist's credo and radical revision of the *monts religieux*. In visitor's
books at Chamonix, Shelley's declarations of atheism affirmed a radical
skepticism. At the Hôtel de Londres in Chamonix, Shelley listed his place
of origin as England, destination Hell, and added, in Greek, "I am a demo-
crat, philanthropist, atheist." In the visitor's book at Montanvert, Shelley's
party signed themselves "atheists one and all."[107] For a decade, Shelley's
inscriptions were seen by visitors from across Europe and entered what

was arguably a wider discursive field than his "Mont Blanc" poem, which appeared in an obscure account of their continental tour before being reprinted in his posthumous poems and later anthologies.

In the mid-twentieth century, Shelley's poem was read as the manifesto of philosophical idealism or the transcendent individual imagination. During the Cold War, it became conventional to read this "Mont Blanc" as exemplifying a transition from the political to the aesthetic and negotiating tensions between idealism and the material world. From that perspective, Shelley's poem "makes an implicit argument for the transcendent existence of man."[108] Such idealizing interpretations were part of the same cultural formation that viewed Francesco Petrarch as the first modern man. More recently, critics have investigated wider historical and scientific contexts and the materiality of the mountain itself, but an emphasis on materiality often preserves a mind/nature dichotomy that excludes space for the other. Shelley's radical skepticism has been recovered, so much so that "Mont Blanc is his Mount Fuji or Sainte-Victoire" and the "counter-Sinai" of his ode is viewed as an amplification of his declarations of atheism.[109]

Debate about the voices in Shelley's head has drowned out the cacophony of voices to which he responded in the "many voicèd vale" of Chamonix.[110] Shelley's closing question—what if "silence and solitude were vacancy?"— exhibited the same rhetorical gesture that Ranajit Guha noted in James Mill: "The author's textual strategy required that the ancient indigenous culture of the colonized should be demolished on intellectual and moral grounds, so that he could then go on to posit his own system into that vacancy."[111] By substituting vacancy for voices, Shelley composed poetry in a language that he described as "created by that imperial faculty, whose throne is curtained within the invisible nature of man."[112] This "imperial faculty" mediated Shelley's encounter with the inhabitants of Chamonix. In his letters, Shelley considered the degradation of "half deformed or idiotic" inhabitants of the Alps a "subject more mournful and less sublime; but such as neither the poet nor the philosopher should disdain to regard." He also reviled the population of Chamonix as "the vilest species of quack that together with the whole army of aubergistes [innkeepers] and guides and indeed the entire mass of the population subsist on the weakness and credulity of travellers as leeches subsist on the blood of the sick."[113] If Shelley disdained the local community in his letters, he also displaced these figures in his poetry into the shadows, margins, and the "spaces between words."[114]

Ghosts were "endemic" to Shelley's poetry and phantoms haunt his 1816 poem: "In the still cave of the witch Poesy, / Seeking among the shadows that pass by, / Ghosts of all things that are, some shade of thee, / Some phantom, some faint image." A reading of this passage ought to find not secondhand Platonism, but rather a firsthand account of a personal encounter with the people of the Alps, translated through the composition of poetry.[115] Shelley's mythmaking in this passage echoed geological theories and local descriptions of the source of the Arveiron as "this fairy dwelling, or this cave of Fancy" and the "Temple of the God of Frost."[116] The temptation remains to view his mythmaking as the teleological progress of philosophical cogitation and to argue that Shelley replaced one "code" of natural grandeur with one more politically progressive.[117] Yet his reactions to the restoration and legacies of the French Revolution were more complicated and ambivalent.

The edge of the cliff produced multiple modernities for Mont Blanc that critiqued Enlightenment rationality as well as religious discourses on the mountain. Shelley's panoramic view of the valley envisioned power dwelling in remote tranquility on the mountain: "Mont Blanc yet gleams on high;— the power is there." Shelley denied the summit position to any god, whether the Christian God or Zoroastrian deity of darkness. Instead, Shelley located "Power in likeness of the Arve," but refused to name or to personify it: "the still and solemn power of many sights, / and many sounds, and much of life and death."

In Geneva, the Shelleys talked of ghosts with Lord Byron and essayed a friendly competition to write ghost stories that summer. Byron visited Chamonix shortly afterward and composed *Manfred,* a play about a man tormented by guilt. Manfred is saved from jumping off a cliff by a chamois hunter and speaks to spirits of the earth, the witch of the Alps, and nemesis on the summit of the Jungfrau before dying in a mountain castle.[118] But the most famous phantom of Chamonix in 1816 appears in Mary Shelley's *Frankenstein; or, The Modern Prometheus* (1818), which she began to compose during her visit. Dr. Victor Frankenstein creates a "hideous phantasm of man" that escapes into the world, educates himself, and vows revenge on his creator. The scientist travels to Chamonix where the mountains "towered above all, as belonging to another earth, the habitations of another race of beings." He walks to Montanvert, crosses the Mer de Glace alone, and perceives a man advancing across the glacier "at superhuman speed." They take refuge at the "hut" at Montanvert, where the "daemon" tells his mournful life story to Victor Frankenstein. The creature recalls that he had first sought happiness through "the love of virtue," but his "dreams of virtue, of fame, and of enjoyment" had been degraded by vice.[119]

The force of this critique of science, rationalism, and the French Revolution was all the stronger for being delivered beneath the medallions honoring natural philosophers in the "hut," which nineteenth-century visitors to Chamonix would have recognized as the Temple of Nature. The introductory material to *Frankenstein* referenced theories of vitality discussed by Erasmus Darwin's *The Temple of Nature* (1803) as evidence that the novel was "not of impossible occurrence."[120] Despite fruitful interpretations of *Frankenstein* as embodying wider critiques, Mary Shelley's novel did not espouse a "philosophy" or "agenda" of Enlightenment, Romanticism, science, or progressive good causes. In such interpretations, Mary Shelley's "modern Prometheus" is shackled to later formations of individual "modern man" perpetually in the ascendant. By contrast, the novel's sympathetic portrayal of Christianity and critical depiction of the rationalism of Frankenstein—and of her father and husband—suggest a more ambivalent work, a search for a standpoint between positions that have been rejected.[121] Indeed, Mary Shelley's "refusal to place humanity at the center of the universe" in *Frankenstein* or in *The Last Man* (1826) has been viewed as a rejection of biblical authority and the Romantic imagination and "a profound and prophetic challenge to Western humanism."[122]

Percy Shelley's "Mont Blanc" and Mary Shelley's *Frankenstein* were both composed at the edge of a cliff and remain open to multiple interpretations. Perhaps it is only fair to ask: Must literates always exemplify a code when they speak? The ghosts of Chamonix continue to haunt more recent commentary as well as works written in 1816. Consider Alan Liu's remark that the whiteness of Mont Blanc "is the space in which history can ghost into the present; it is not no meaning but a panic of too much possible meaning."[123] Or note the oscillation between seriousness and satire that Susan Wolfson identified in Byron's and Mary Shelley's ghost stories: "Literary imagination is always coursing between self and other, mediating possession by spirits—'inspiration' by another name."[124] Yet mediation has received less attention than imagination. Percy Shelley reserved to himself and others with an "adverting mind" the ability to interpret and feel the mysterious tongue of the wilderness and voice of the mountain, but he did not articulate an "egotistical sublime" that John Keats identified with Wordsworth's poetry only a few years later. On the contrary, Shelley identified the "secret strength of things which governs thought" as inhabiting the dome of the mountain at the end of his poem, but it remains unclear whether he envisioned the human mind or this "secret strength of things" as occupying the vacancy otherwise known as the summit of "Mont Blanc."

TEMPLE OF NATURE

In the early nineteenth century, Mont Blanc became a temple and the Alps cathedrals of the earth. Marc-Théodore Bourrit had compared Montanvert to a temple, but this language underwent a transformation by the time he died in 1819. Where Bourrit had envisioned worship of the "Sovereign of nature" in 1785, the sovereignty represented in revolutionary temples and mythologized in some romantic verse envisioned the sovereign individual above and apart from nature.

When Mary Shelley revised *Frankenstein* in 1831, the scenes in Chamonix taught more comforting lessons than earlier editions. The sound of the Arve "spoke of a power mighty as Omnipotence" and the rush of the river serves as a lullaby for the tired Victor Frankenstein: "The very winds whispered in soothing accents, and maternal nature bade me weep no more." The mountains consoled Frankenstein, but the reassurance disappeared when the peaks were shrouded from view: "Still I would penetrate their misty veil, and seek them in their cloudy retreats."[125] In the 1830s, Mary Shelley marked a contrast between maternal nature and female characters who appreciated its beauty on the one hand, and Victor Frankenstein's masculine aspiration for mastery and conquest of nature on the other, a contrast accentuated later in the nineteenth century.[126]

In the 1860s, John Ruskin criticized mountaineers for despising the "deep and sacred sensations" of the Alps that "our poets used to love so reverently." Ruskin's comment that "the French revolutionists made stables of the cathedrals of France; you have made race-courses of the cathedrals of the earth,"[127] contains an insight that could be framed more strongly as a statement of causality. It was precisely the redefinition of sovereignty and the contests between revolutionaries and royalists over the mountains that transformed these Alpine peaks into temples. A traverse of the revolutionary and Napoleonic periods suggests that the transformation of Mont Blanc into a "sacred" space by popular religious piety was coeval with attempts to make it "secular" by revolutionaries, scientists, and poets. The sacralization of the highest peaks in the Alps was one of the effects of modernity, not something overcome or replaced by it.[128]

The Temple of Nature at Montanvert became a tourist canteen serving wine, liquors, and strawberries and cream in the 1820s. After considering expansion of *la Maisonette,* the municipality of Chamonix built a new hotel between the hut and the Mer de Glace in 1840. This hotel was replaced by a Grand Hotel in 1879, after which the former temple became a shepherd's hut and stable for mules or goats. In the 1920s, the temple was restored by a tourist association that cleaned the interior and whitewashed the walls.[129] In the standard French history of Mont Blanc from the 1870s to the 1940s, Charles Durier wrote that the visitor to Montanvert looks up and "discovers the weathered black marble plaque with the inscription: *À la Nature.* He smiles—and why? The worship is out of fashion but the divinity is not dead."[130]

The edge of this cliff remains. Divergent responses to Mont Blanc may be recognized because they still confront us as ways of being in the world. In the early twentieth century, the guides of Chamonix began to dress in traditional costumes for an annual blessing of ice axes at the *fête des guides* on August 15, the Festival of the Assumption, which celebrates the purity of the Virgin Mary. The nearby village of Saint-Gervais celebrated a similar festival, the *fête de l'Alpe,* in 2004, to launch a long-term campaign for *la montagne à l'état pur* (the pure mountain). The campaign promoted sustainable development in the village and "leave no trace" in the mountains. According to a press release from the tourist office of Saint-Gervais, the campaign had another purpose: "The nineteenth of June, the festival day at Saint-Gervais, will be equally the occasion to render homage to the first woman climber to reach the summit of Mont Blanc, Marie Paradis, the celebrated Saint Gervaolaine."[131] The modern self is haunted by mountains.

CHAPTER SIX

Social Climbers

DUMAS'S CONQUESTS

Alexandre Dumas recounted the first ascent of Mont Blanc as the triumph of the sovereign individual. Dumas himself was a young man in a hurry. The son of a Creole general in the Napoleonic army, he ascended from a position as a clerk to become a playwright and best-selling author of novels such as *The Count of Monte Cristo* and *The Three Musketeers*. In the summer of 1832, Dumas was forced to flee Paris for the Alps after the outbreak of a cholera epidemic and a friendly warning that he faced arrest for his support of an insurrection against the July monarchy of 1830. His publisher refused to give him an advance for a book about his journey to Switzerland since "everyone" had visited already and there was nothing left to say.[1] Dumas would need a more compelling narrative to find a buyer for his travel writings.

Dumas found what he needed in panoramic sketches about the people and places of the Alps, and whimsical adventures told in dramatic dialogue. After eating a steak of bear meat, he learned that the bear had killed and eaten the hunter who had shot it before its own death. He descended into a salt mine and ascended to elevated viewpoints above Chamonix. There, he wrote to Jacques Balmat and invited him to dinner. Dumas met the seventy-year-old guide and shook hands: "It was Jacques Balmat, the intrepid guide who amid a thousand dangers had been the first to attain the highest summit of Mont Blanc and paved the way for Saussure. Courage preceded science." Dumas introduced himself with formal courtesies that made Balmat uncomfortable: "I thanked him for giving me the honor of accepting my invitation. The brave man thought that I was making fun of him; he did not understand that he was for me a figure as extraordinary as Columbus, who found an unknown world, and Vasco da Gama, who rediscovered a world that was lost."[2]

After dinner, they enjoyed a bottle of wine as Dumas recorded Balmat's "pure and simple" recital of his exploits. Balmat recalled the first ascent of the mountain:

> I perceived that I had finally arrived at the summit of Mont Blanc. Then I looked all around me, trembling that my eyes deceived me and would find some needles, some new peak, that I did not have the strength to climb. The joints of my legs seemed to be held together only by my pantaloons. But no, no. I was at the end of my journey. I had arrived where no one had ever been before, not even the eagle or the chamois. I arrived alone, without any help other than my own strength and my own will. Everything around me seemed to be mine. I was the king of Mont Blanc. I was the statue of that immense pedestal!

Balmat turned toward Chamonix, waved his hat on his baton, and saw a reply from below: "My subjects of the valley had seen me; the whole village was on the plaza." Balmat then descended to revive Dr. Michel-Gabriel Paccard, and they returned together to the summit about six o'clock. From the top, they could see only ice, snow, rocks, and emaciated peaks. On the descent, Balmat assisted the doctor: "Paccard was merely a child without energy and without will that I guided through the good routes and carried in the bad."[3]

Dumas published his interview with Balmat in essays about the Alps in *Revue des deux mondes* and *Impressions of Swiss Travel* (1834), which sold well enough to entice his publishers to commission other travel books. By

the early twentieth century, the Dumas account was widely read as a transcript of what Balmat had actually said, as if Dumas's role was merely to
take dictation. Such a naïve empiricist reading is difficult to sustain, as the
interview appears to be a pastiche of earlier narratives and Dumas's own
dramatizations. Dumas certainly interviewed Balmat, but it is more difficult to say where Balmat's recital ended and Dumas's embellishments began. Twenty years later, for example, Dumas confessed in his memoirs that
he had used dramatic license to create the bear steak scene, with its macabre
hints of cannibalism by proxy, when he transformed the tale of a bear that
ate its hunter into his own evening meal.[4]

By the early 1830s, Dumas already had a reputation for taking liberties
with the works of others and was accused of plagiarism in dramatic and
historical works. In later years, Dumas outsourced much of his writing and
engaged in disputes with his collaborators, coauthors, and ghostwriters.
Dumas's contribution to some later works amounted to little more than allowing his name to appear on the title page. In the early 1830s, Dumas still
wrote his own material and argued that the rearrangement of existing work
was the essence of creativity: "For it is mankind, and not any man, who
invents; each arrives in his turn and at his hour to take the things known to
his forefathers, arrange them in new combinations, and then dies, after
having added a few pieces to the sum of human knowledge." After selective
quotations from Shakespeare and Molière, Dumas summed up in his own
inimitable style: "The man of genius does not steal, he conquers. He incor-
porates into his empire the province he annexes: he imposes on it his laws,
peoples it with his subjects, extends over it his golden scepter, and no one
dares tell him, as he surveys his good kingdom: 'This parcel of land is not
part of your patrimony.'"[5]

When Dumas portrayed Balmat as the king of Mont Blanc, alone on the
mountain pedestal waving his alpenstock/scepter to his subjects below, it
was Dumas rather than Balmat who "conquered." Dumas appropriated
Balmat's story of the ascent to place himself in the summit position. Claude
Schopp astutely remarked that *Impressions of Swiss Travel* rejuvenated the
genre of travel writing as "an epic of the self . . . an affirmation of subjectivity."[6] For Dumas, the ascent represented the triumph of individual will and
Balmat and Paccard were rendered as mirror images: one reached the top
"without any help other than my own strength and my own will" and the
other stumbled "like a child with no energy or will." These dual portraits

represented neither "enlightenment" discourses of individual daring nor revolutionary representations of popular sovereignty, and still less counter-revolutionary doctrines of monarchist loyalty or religious devotion. Rather, Dumas's depiction of Balmat's ascent as the triumph of individual will and self-assertion bore the stamp of the same postrevolutionary discourses of the autonomous self that were then recasting Francesco Petrarch as the "first modern man."

The image of Balmat as king of Mont Blanc was possibly the product of the imagination of Dumas rather than the memory of Balmat, and this poses interpretive dilemmas. In the mid-nineteenth century, Venance Payot, a Chamonix naturalist who was the son of Dumas's guide, frequently reprinted the Dumas-Balmat interview in guidebooks and recalled that his father frequently told him "the story of the famous novelist was not only accurate, but more accurate than he would have done. He added, however, that 'Balmat was sparing with words and Dumas had padded.'"[7] Another visitor recalled listening to Balmat speak: "When at a loss for a word to express his thought, he uses a gesture that makes you understand."[8] Dumas's "padding" should be understood as a translation, not a transcript, and not simply the invention of a fertile imagination. Some readers may be tempted to pick and choose: this came from Dumas, but that's really Balmat! In contrast, other critics have argued that voices like Balmat's are so heavily filtered that he cannot speak at all. Yet interviews hardly speak with one voice, and the problem of translation should not be framed as one "conquering" the other. As Sherry Ortner noted in a similar context—Sherpa autobiographies based on interviews with ghostwriters—"let us assume a surplus of truth rather than an absence of truth."[9] The presence of so many collaborators in Dumas's wider opus of dramas, chronicles, and histories has posed a related question in acute form: who is the author? Michel de Certeau was surely correct to observe that others insinuate themselves into Dumas's work and "define and occupy Dumas' place as much as he colonizes theirs."[10] Dumas's work was haunted by the other and his "conquest" remained deeply ambivalent.

Dumas's virtual conquest of Mont Blanc resembled the actual ascents by social climbers who reached the top of the mountain. From the 1820s to the 1850s and beyond, new masculinities and subjectivities continued to transform mountaineering. In these years, the ascent of Mont Blanc became regulated by the state, commercialized by guides, and a commodity of leisure time. Dumas attempted to annex this mountainous corner of provincial Europe, but his experience should be provincialized. The climbers of the early nineteenth century could reach the summit only in partnership with Alpine guides, and narratives of conquest never achieved the mastery they intended. When Dumas asked to meet one of the guides who survived a fatal climbing accident in 1820, his own guide was reticent to raise the subject: "On clear nights, above the crevasse where they are buried, you will see three flames hovering. These are their souls returning because a coffin of ice and a shroud of snow is not a Christian burial." Dumas pressed further to ask if the survivor would talk to him: " 'Certainly, though it is not a happy subject, but it is curious, and we are here to satisfy the curiosity of travelers.' I did not appear to pay attention to the kind of bitterness with which he uttered these words."[11] The bitterness of this "backstage" talk needs to be made visible, for it is a sign of resistance by the guides to the heroic individualism of the "curious" travelers.

THE HAMEL AFFAIR

"We are all lost!" cried Joseph-Marie Couttet, when he heard a horrible cracking sound above his head, felt his feet slip, and saw a giant avalanche of fresh snow engulf a group of climbers above the Grand Plateau on Mont Blanc. He tried in vain to support himself with his alpenstock, but the weight of the avalanche forced him to roll down the hill like a ball in the snow. Couttet was leading the ascent of Dr. Joseph Hamel, a savant and counselor of state to the Russian emperor, along with Joseph Dornford and Gilbert Henderson, students at Oxford, on August 20, 1820. Couttet was carrying one of four barometers on his back, and the straps broke as he reached the bottom and launched him into a small crevasse along with Julien Dévouassoud, who landed nearby. As he tumbled down the slopes, Dévouassoud thought to himself: " 'I am lost, goodbye my wife and children,' and I asked forgiveness from God. I thought of absolutely nothing else." Dévouassoud used an alpenstock to extricate Couttet, who was buried up to his neck and turning blue in the face. The two men climbed out of the crevasse to learn that the three gentlemen had survived, but three guides at the head of the line—Pierre Carrier, Pierre Balmat, and Auguste Tairraz—had been plunged into a massive crevasse now covered with snow.

Mathieu Balmat, the only person to arrest his fall during the avalanche, watched the guides disappear into the void and pointed out the place. They spent two hours in a fruitless search by sounding with poles, shouting names, and digging by hand in the snow.[12]

The journey ended in disaster because Dr. Hamel was investigating the science of high altitudes with a distinctly haughty attitude. Trained as a physician in St. Petersburg, Hamel had been sent to England by the Russian interior minister in 1813 to research science and industry. He had already published works on coal mining, education, and the manufacture of potassium, and engaged in the kind of industrial espionage typical of its time by sending back to Russia 35,000 pamphlets on English patents. A polymath savant, he later helped establish railways in Russia and wrote about armaments factories, cochineal dyes, daguerreotypes, magnetoelectrical machines, skeletons of extinct birds, and the history of arctic exploration. On Mont Blanc, Hamel wanted to confirm Mont Blanc's elevation as the highest in Europe and test his theory that reduced levels of oxygen in the thin air at higher altitudes contributed to muscle weakness. Hamel planned experiments to measure oxygen levels in the blood and in breathed air, and even hoped to carry compressed oxygen with him to test its restorative effects, but could not find a useful apparatus.[13]

On the morning of the accident, Hamel wrote two letters to announce his arrival on the summit, leaving a blank only to insert the hour, which he planned to tie to a carrier pigeon being carried by a guide. Hamel also envisioned his own summit position: "I saw myself already on the summit. I was breaking off specimens of the highest rock in Europe to place in the cabinet of our Imperial Academy of Sciences at St. Petersburg." One of the Englishmen announced that he could not be induced to turn back for any amount of money, and they were soon debating whether the first toast on the summit should be to the king of England, the emperor of Russia, or the memory of Horace-Bénédict de Saussure.[14]

Hamel, Dornford, and Henderson were last in the line when the avalanche struck and they came to a stop on the brink of the crevasse. Hamel portrayed himself heroically directing the rescue efforts until the guides called a halt: "The guides intervened and forced us, so to speak, to come out of the crevasse. They declared our search useless; they even refused the money that we offered if they would wait." An inquest took statements from the gentlemen and the guides. Dornford commented on the despair and silence of the grieving guides in the immediate aftermath of the avalanche, but he also thanked a guide for saving his life, contributed money to the families of the victims, and admired the honesty, courtesy, and solicitude of the guides more generally.[15] Hamel showed no such generosity.

The guides told quite another story. When Dévouassoud emerged from the crevasse, "he immediately blamed Mr. Hamel saying that he had been the cause of all that had happened by his imprudence, since he obstinately made the ascent despite the bad weather," according to a note written by Dévouassoud's father-in-law, Michel-Gabriel Paccard.[16] After two nights on the mountain in heavy winds, rain, hail, and a ferocious electrical storm, the conditions on the second day, a Sunday morning, remained unsettled and the mountain was covered in fresh snow. The guides deliberated and decided everyone should return to Chamonix. Hamel objected: "We were under his orders; our time and our lives were his, since he paid us. We did not insist, but only cast lots to see which of us would return to Chamonix in search of food." Hamel said he would not lose the fruits of his journey, reproached the guides for their exaggerated fears, and insisted on continuing without waiting for the food or the weather. "If one of us had had this idea," recalled Couttet, "we would have taken him for a fool and tied his legs together and not taken one step further. But the doctor was a foreigner, ignorant of the dangerous caprices of the mountain. So we contented ourselves to respond that to try to go another two leagues, despite the warnings the sky was giving the earth, was to defy Providence and tempt God. Dr. Hamel stamped his feet, turned towards Henderson and muttered the word *cowards*."[17]

After that, there was no more hesitation and everyone prepared silently for departure: "After five minutes, I asked the doctor if he was ready to follow. He gave a nod with his head, because he was still angry with us." More than forty years later, Couttet and Dévouassoud still recalled that after Hamel's tantrum, "we climbed in anger."[18] Another gentleman who had been a member of the climbing party, Alexandre François Gilles-Selligue, an optician, engineer, and inventor from Geneva, stayed behind and descended with two guides. Selligue tested a new barometer and had planned to use a camera lucida to make a panoramic view on the summit. But Selligue felt unwell, feared the bad weather, and decided that a married man should not risk his life. In Geneva, Selligue told the same story as the guides about the decision to continue the ascent.[19]

The guides also recalled the search of the crevasse despite injuries and the seriousness of the situation. Years later, Couttet recalled: "I have seen many battlefields and I have assisted in real human slaughter on a warship, but I have never suffered what I suffered in the presence of this horrible hand-to-hand combat" during the search of the crevasse. Henderson stood by, wringing his hands, while Hamel was impassive and offered cold encouragement. In time, their frostbitten fingers could no longer grip the batons. "'It is useless, my friends,' Hamel said, 'we will not see our poor companions in this world. The abyss would kill us; we can do nothing more for them.'"[20] The deceased guides had been unmarried, though one provided financial support for his parents. A subscription for the families was opened and visitors to Chamonix and the nearby baths at Saint-Gervais contributed generously. The king of Piedmont-Sardinia, Victor Emmanuel I, also authorized a pension for the families of the victims.[21]

COMPANY OF GUIDES

After the Hamel accident, the communal council established the *Compagnie des guides de Chamonix* on July 24, 1821. The intendant of Faucigny provided the governor of Savoy with an explanation for the new rules that identified accidents on the glaciers and the deaths in 1820 as the motive for establishing the company: "A great number of the members of the Company almost became victims of this misfortune, which they generally attribute to the obstinacy of foreigners wanting to go beyond the advice of the guides, and threatening them to withhold their wages if they would not lead them to the summit of Mont Blanc." The Company of Guides ensured confidence in the qualifications of the guides and gave them the legal authority to make decisions by majority vote during an ascent.[22] New rules established a fixed price for journeys, a regular rotation among qualified guides, and fees and fines to provide mutual aid for victims in the case of accidents.

The Savoyard state affirmed and strengthened the status of the Company of Guides a few years later, after suppression of the Piedmontese revolution of 1821 and the accession of the more reactionary king Charles-Félix. In August 1822, the commandant of Faucigny received a number of complaints from foreign visitors on Mont Blanc that guides were trying to cheat them. "Nothing would be more scandalous for Our Nation," the commandant wrote, than to see guides "seek to deceive and gouge the said visitors." The reassertion of state authority after the 1821 revolution extended throughout the realm and shaped the new regulations for the Chamonix guides issued in Turin on May 9, 1823. The chief guide was appointed by the syndic of Chamonix, but placed under the vigilant supervision of the intendant, the commandant of Savoy, and the police force, the Royal Carabinieri.[23]

Within this broad framework, the rules regulated the guides and expressed new forms of communal solidarity and sovereignty. For the ascent of Mont Blanc, each traveler was required to hire four guides at 40 livres each. The residents of the nearby village of Argentière protested that the company consisted of Chamonix residents but claimed the exclusive right to lead journeys to the Jardin and the Buet and other destinations that were "on the territory of Argentière." This was to the detriment of the parish of Argentière, "which had as much right as the parish of Chamonix, either by its population, or by the number of its guides, or by their merit and knowledge, or by the meaning and intention to manifest the sovereign, by which each inhabitant of the valley of Chamonix can participate in the advantages of the locality, because those of Argentière bear equally the expenses of the state and the municipality."[24]

The company soon admitted residents of other villages in the valley, but the more significant change was this redefinition of sovereignty as sharing in the fruits of economic development. The assertion of control over the highest glaciers by the Company of Guides was in part an extension into the higher elevations of prior claims to communal pastures on the "middle mountain." As Françoise Loux rightly notes, "this exploitation affirmed symbolically their mastery of a *terroir* [local territory, or sense of place]."[25] In the future, discussions of sovereignty were increasingly cast in terms of residents sharing the benefits from economic exploitation of the mountains. As in earlier decades, state officials envisioned economic benefits within a mercantilist framework. While the rules for the Company of Guides were being drafted, the geologist Joseph-Nicholas Nicollet told the intendant that even if the ostensible goal of the rules for the Company of Guides was to help foreigners, "the real goal will be to keep them longer by provoking their curiosity and then, to call things by their name, to give them the opportunity to spend more money."[26]

State regulation of the guides did not exclude "thinking like a mountain." Consider the stipulation that guides were required to attend Mass before an ascent: "It is forbidden for any guide to undertake a journey on festival days without having first fulfilled religious duties and having heard Holy Mass; the chief-guide is specifically responsible for ensuring the fulfillment of this obligation."[27] Guides had long insisted on hearing Mass before departure and this rule aligned the piety of the guides with the public regulation of morals by the Savoyard state, which in these years defined the first duty of the police of the *Buon Governo* as maintaining devotion to Catholicism.[28] The Hamel accident had taken place on a Sunday, and the regulations ensured that guides were no longer required to continue an ascent against their better judgment and would not have to undertake an ascent at all without the blessing of an even higher authority.

PACCARD SPEAKS OF DISCOVERY

The notoriety of the Hamel accident revived interest in who was first on the summit in 1786. The issue had fallen into desuetude in Chamonix, even as visitors celebrated Balmat as discoverer in terms that had been reserved for William Windham or Saussure. In 1819, for example, William Howard of Baltimore made the ascent with Jeremiah van Rensselaer of New York, and said their curiosity was excited when they "conversed with the guides who had participated in these journeys and among them with Balmat, the Columbus of Chamonix." A few days later, Captain John Undrell of the British Royal Navy climbed the peak with the same guides and instruments borrowed from Dr. Paccard. Undrell published a letter about his ascent only after the Hamel accident and noted that debates about the early ascents were regarded locally as a source of amusement. The guides denied that Marc-Théodore Bourrit had been to the top of Mont Blanc or ever reached a point from which the Mediterranean would be visible: "The whole history is much laughed at by Dr. Paccard and the old guides of Chamonix."[29]

Paccard may have laughed in public, but he remained bitter in private toward Bourrit and Saussure. In 1823, the sixty-six-year-old Paccard responded to a question about the history of the first ascent from Johann-Gottfried Ebel, the Swiss geologist and guidebook author. Paccard claimed he had discovered the route of the first ascent and sent a sketch of the route and the text of the certificate published in Lausanne. He gave this interpretation of Balmat's sworn statement: "He frankly admits the truth before the

Genevan sect had made any effort to disguise it with lies and is irrefutable evidence in court." Paccard thought the certificate was enough "to contradict all they would have one believe on the subject, in making me appear like a criminal for having dared to make the first ascent of Mont Blanc without the participation of those to whom this glory should be reserved." The certificates had provided the means to obtain judicial redress, but Dr. Paccard had chosen another path: "I was told that there was more greatness of soul in preferring to endure insults rather than to inflict harm, that true glory and merit consisted in bearing injuries and not to avenge them."[30]

Climbers had sought Paccard's advice before their own ascent, but he began to take a more public role only after the Hamel affair revived interest in the mountain. In 1802, Paccard gave this advice to potential climbers: "I told them they would be pleased at this type of journey to another world, and they would preserve its memory as the most striking experience in their lives, and at the same time the least dangerous."[31] Infrequent ascents in the 1810s merited only a brief record in his notebook. After the 1820 accident, Paccard wrote letters about new ascents to the *Journal de Savoie* in Chambéry, one of the few newssheets permitted in the region. In 1822, Frederick Clissold of London borrowed instruments from Paccard and delayed his attempt due to the recommendation of "Dr. Paccard, the old guides, and Marie Couttet."[32] A year later, Paccard testified to the ascent by H. H. Jackson, an Englishman, and touted his own success using beer foam to treat a guide's swollen face and puffy eyes. Paccard asserted his discovery of the route in 1786, which then had been less dangerous with lower levels of snowfall, and speculated that a different route was also possible above the Grand Plateau.[33]

A few years later, Paccard reasserted his priority of discovery. In 1825, he wrote to the *Journal de Savoie* to describe the ascent by Dr. Edmund Clark, a London physician, and Captain Markham Sherwill, a wealthy Englishman who had served in the militia but became an antiquarian author, collector of autographs, and host for romantic poets at his home in Fontainebleau, France. Paccard noted that Clark and Sherwill overcame obstacles without incident and compared their instrument readings on the summit with his own observations in the valley: "The steep slope above the Grand Plateau, which Mr. Paccard was the first to indicate as a route in the time of low snow, from the Brévent, was stripped of its snows by an avalanche similar to that which engulfed three guides on August 20, 1820." A few minor details were cut in the copyediting, but his claim to fame was prominent in the lead sentence: "Doctor Michel-Gabriel Paccard who was the first to arrive on the summit of Mont Blanc in 1786."[34]

This was quickly challenged in the *Journal de Savoie* through commentary on a letter that Chevalier A. de la Place had received from Jacques Balmat reporting on the recent ascent. The editors took pleasure in remembering Balmat as

> this estimable man whose courageous enterprises and arduous ascents have been very useful to science and have not been without benefits for our country, by calling the attention of naturalists to our mountains and attracting a crowd of foreign admirers of the great beauties of nature. Jacques Balmat has, in effect, all rights to the honor of discovery of the means to traverse the highest valleys and summits which surround Mont-Blanc and reach to the summit of this colossus, since he was the first to climb to the summit. He later led Messrs. Paccard and Saussure there.

The journal admired the precision and "naïve simplicity" of Balmat's letter and his twelve ascents of Mont Blanc: "This doyen of the guides of Chamonix, at 65 years of age, continues the strenuous exertions of his youth. The services which he has rendered, and the incredible hardships to which he has courageously exposed himself his whole life, are of a nature to inspire a genuine interest in his favor."[35] Balmat's letter was reprinted in France and Britain, and summaries of the exchange were printed in learned journals in Paris and Milan.[36]

This was the last exchange about the ascent during Paccard's lifetime. In certain respects, restoration of the monarchy reclaimed Paccard as a loyal subject of the House of Savoy. A dictionary of Piedmontese physicians, which aimed to recognize those "unjustly neglected or poorly appreciated" in medicine and natural sciences, reserved for Paccard "the glory of the first to touch the summit of Mont Blanc."[37] Yet in other respects, little had changed since the 1780s and 1790s. In the *Journal de Savoie,* Paccard reprised his role as amateur natural philosopher, with records of temperature and air pressure, identification of ornithological and geological specimens, and stale references to 1775 calculations to establish the elevation of Mont Blanc. The journal had greater admiration for Balmat's simple descriptions and his masculine courage, enterprise, and exertions over years of hardship.

The revolutionary upheaval continued to cast its shadow. The *Journal de Savoie* was the mouthpiece for conservative interests in the duchy, and the correspondent who promoted Balmat had been a commander of Savoyard troops and joined the counteroffensive from Piedmont during the revolution.[38] In 1802, Paccard had described the ascent as the most memorable experience in his life, but the decade that followed was difficult for anyone who had been a Jacobin by conviction in the 1790s. Paccard was removed from office during the Napoleonic years, and his enthusiasm for individual sovereignty was curbed still further by the restoration of the monarchy. These institutional pressures should not be underestimated, and help to explain why Paccard developed a reputation for drinking heavily in his later years. After receiving his final communion, Michel-Gabriel Paccard died in Chamonix on the evening of May 21, 1827, and was buried the next day.

In his notebook, Paccard copied his letters to the *Journal de Savoie* and the response containing Balmat's letter. They appear to be the last entries in the notebook in his hand. Other family members added to his list of ascents, recorded births and marriages, and noted a few local events into the 1840s. At the very end of the notebook, now in the Alpine Club Library in London, three jottings appear in Paccard's handwriting. He recorded the elevation of the Col du Talefre inside the back cover, and two fragments on the last page: "The Prince of Sulzbach who married his sister to Charles Emanuel—Mother of King Victor regnant in 1727 came to see the glaciers the same year. Windham and Pococke only came to Chamonix in the month of June 1741 = 14 years after Sulzbach." In this confusing syntax, not intended for publication, Paccard was saying simply this: Windham was not first. Below, Paccard wrote and struck a line through another cryptic comment. This fragment—and its deletion—indicate that Paccard struggled with the limitations on any strong claim of individual autonomy: "A Doctor, who despite the works of Mr. Bourrit, is good, bad, is worth even more than the author. He would bet that closed up with his notes, the author could not have done anything alone."[39]

BALMAT SPEAKS OF GOLD

In the summer of 1834, Jacques Balmat wrote to Dumas to tell him about an ascent of Mont Blanc by two lawyers from Savoy and to thank him for sending the first volume of *Impressions of Swiss Travel*. Balmat asked for the second volume and, if it was not too expensive, F. S. Beudant's two-volume treatise on mineralogy: "By dint of searching, I believe that I have found a gold mine." After receiving these books, Balmat wrote in September to thank Dumas for the work on mineralogy, which "will be very useful to me because I have found, as I said, a vein of gold which should lead me to a mine. When the weather is good, I plan to leave tomorrow for my search."[40]

A crystal hunter in his youth, Balmat searched for gold throughout his later years. Unfortunately, Balmat's interest in gold is too often portrayed as a fool's errand—an atavistic adventure, quixotic quest, or a credulous belief in primitive myths and superstitious legends. Stories of Balmat's "dreams of gold" are usually framed by local legends and folktales about the existence of gold in the mountains.[41] While these are compelling stories—a gold treasure on the Glacier des Bois visible only while Mass is being said during Christmas or the festival of St. John—they should not substitute for an account of Balmat's own motives and agency. The existence of such "legends" has been used to signify his otherness, the possession of primitive mentality that requires no further explanation. Yet it is not his mentality, but the banality and the modernity of his search for gold that deserves to be emphasized. Balmat did not describe his search for gold by reference to such legends, and his interest in gold was not the result of telling tales or being seduced by myths or dreams.

Balmat recorded his search for gold in fragments and notebooks collectively known as the "carnets of Jacques Balmat" at the Musée Alpin in Chamonix. His notes include legible passages and formulas copied from books on mineralogy; references to locations of gold; receipts for purchases, sales, and debts; and indications of his diverse interests and activities as a peasant proprietor, mainly in the 1820s and 1830s. Beyond his prizewinning efforts to breed merino sheep, Balmat harvested the fruits of the soil in the summer and raw materials from the mountains in the winter, including tuff, plaster, and gypsum. In the summer of 1823, for example, Balmat sold 38 quarts of potatoes, and the following winter delivered 108 sleds full of tuff from the mountain of Taconnaz for use in the manufacture of lime.[42]

Many of his mineralogical notes are open to interpretation. "In this book there are only follies," he wrote in one, which is better read as a statement about lack of success than a sign of madness.[43] Suggestions that Balmat dabbled in alchemy also have been greatly exaggerated, as the formulas he copied were from leading chemists, geologists, and natural philosophers who were still negotiating the credibility and institutional boundaries of natural history and "science." This is not to say that no one in the Balmat family looked for portents of gold. His brother, Pierre Dominique Balmat, shared his ambition and pointed out where to find gold in two villages in the Val d'Aosta in such terms in 1814. Maurice Gay makes a distinction between the two brothers: "the prose of Pierre Dominique lets us suppose that he was truly visionary, obsessed with cabalistic signs in the sky and the mountain which, properly interpreted, would allow the discovery of a vein. Jacques uses more serious and more scientific methods after reading Ebel's books on mineralogy."[44]

After the ascent with Saussure, Balmat was sought out by leading savants who visited Chamonix from the 1790s through the 1810s. Although he rarely served as a guide in the 1820s, Balmat traveled broadly, read widely, and took notes avidly, especially on mineralogical treatises. He copied passages by Johann-Gottfried Ebel, the Swiss geologist; made excerpts from Alexandre Brongniart, director of the porcelain works at Sèvres; and took notes on the formulas of Jean-Antoine Chaptal, a chemist and minister of the interior who approved Balmat's commendation for merino sheep. Balmat also picked the brain of younger colleagues who studied natural history in Chamonix, including Michel Carrier, another son of a guide who became a naturalist.

Balmat's notes on the formation of gold in auriferous veins, crystallization, or alluvial deposits were so plentiful that Roger Canac reasonably concluded Balmat's knowledge of practical techniques for the separation of minerals "could be considered fairly complete for the era."[45] The notebooks indicate many places where gold might be found, and Balmat traveled in Savoy, Piedmont, and Switzerland to inspect mines. As late as 1831, Balmat visited gold mines on the Swiss-Piedmont border near Monte Rosa, especially the mine at Macugnaga in the Val d'Anzasca, one of the most productive gold mines in any of the Italian states.[46]

Though Balmat researched many possible locations for gold, he focused his search on Mont Ruan, a peak at the head of the Sixt valley to the north of Chamonix. Jean-François Albanis Beaumont, a Savoyard engineer and naturalist, held the mining rights to the valley under Napoleon and published a prospectus for a foundry and iron mine in 1809. The scheme died when Albanis Beaumont suffered a heart attack in 1811, but it was resuscitated by

Genevans who found iron ore in the valley in 1818. In 1820, Balmat received information about the location of a possible gold mine on Mont Ruan from François Joseph Moccand, *le philosophe,* a bear hunter who earned his nickname for his devotion to mineralogy and the natural sciences. Moccand had been the first mayor of Sixt when Savoy was part of France and guided Albanis Beaumont to the location of mines. Balmat's notebooks record that Moccand told him about a possible gold mine on July 3, 1820: "At the mountain of Prat Ruan, at the spot called the Ficle du Currian there are holes about 30 feet deep. Then there is a very long cavern that could be entered, and then another not as large, and after that another hole less deep in which gold must be found in the rock by scratching in the said bed." On July 9, Balmat interviewed shepherds on the other side of the peak who reported a "reddish mine" at Tenneverge, and he heard from informants at Vallorcine that "a gold mine was taken next to Mont Ruan and is at the second gully and should be reddish stone."[47]

Balmat was patient and waited while others held the mineral rights. On the one hand, the seasonal window was short to look for minerals at the highest elevations, and he was advised to visit before livestock descended to lower pastures. On the other hand, mineral rights were long and often held by others: a Genevan syndicate purchased the right to develop mines in the Sixt valley for ten years in 1824. That enterprise had more success manufacturing wooden screws than searching for ore, and its mining lease expired around the time that Balmat planned his excursions in 1834. A few years later, the mines in the Sixt valley were taken over by a *Compagnie Anglaise* and their experience is instructive. One of the investors, William Phelps Prior, joined the mining company after lawsuits frittered away his family's fortune; after the mines were abandoned, he became an English cleric in Switzerland. The point to emphasize is that all of these other adventurers shared Balmat's hope to make their fortune from mines in the same valley.[48]

Balmat had similar motives as he went into debt to maintain the family farm during the last twenty years of his life. After his brother died in 1817, Jacques Balmat assumed control of all the parcels that had been divided between them and provided support for his sister-in-law and two nephews. The marriage of a son in 1819 and daughter in 1821 added to Balmat's financial burdens. Familial archives in Chamonix document additional debts incurred by Balmat in the 1820s, mostly to relatives and neighbors, and he received assistance from the Company of Guides in 1829. To secure additional loans in 1832, his sons signed an agreement to repay all of his debts after his death. On her deathbed in March 1834, Balmat's wife signed a promissory note to pay an inheritance to their son-in-law, a widower left behind when their daughter died ten years earlier, to support two children.[49]

Thus, in the summer of 1834, the seventy-two-year-old Jacques Balmat had studied the matter and was confident of success when he searched for gold on the cliffs of Mont Ruan. He explored the ledges first by himself and then with a guide named Frasserand, who lowered him with a rope where Balmat thought he found a vein. Balmat reportedly had a specimen tested by a chemist in Geneva that revealed traces of gold. In September, Balmat returned to the same slopes with Louis Pache, an intrepid chamois hunter from Vallorcine. When they reached the same escarpment, however, Pache refused to continue and urged Balmat to turn back. Despite this advice, Balmat "ventured on the narrow ledge, took a few steps, and disappeared," falling 400 feet into a chasm between the rocks and the ice, where he died immediately.[50]

After hearing nothing for several days, Balmat's two sons, Gédéon and Edouard, went looking for Pache, who had returned home alone. Pache appeared worried and embarrassed, but told them he had no idea what happened to their father. He took them to the place where he had last seen Balmat, but they could find nothing during several days of searching. Pache was suspected of murder and arrested in November 1834. He remained silent during the interrogation and was detained for six months at the regional jail. Pache was released only after his wife, the mother of their six children, committed suicide by jumping into a river in March 1835.[51] Although Balmat's body was never found, his funeral was held in Chamonix on *"le jour des Rois,"* the day of Epiphany, in January 1835.[52]

Balmat's death left his family financially as well as emotionally bereft. Within a month of his disappearance, an epidemic took the lives of four of Balmat's grandchildren. Balmat's sons had cosigned his loans and the bills now came due. Their sister's widower sued for his inheritance. The younger son, Edouard, kept a step ahead of the creditors by leaving for the United States in 1838. The elder son, Gédéon, kept the family solvent for several years before liquidating the family estate in 1841. Three buyers paid a total of 5,000 livres for the Balmat properties, but after the repayment of his debts, the sale netted only 118 livres. Gédéon's wife received a modest legacy funded by this repayment of family loans, which enabled the couple and their three children to immigrate to the United States. Although Gé-déon returned several times to work as a seasonal guide, his family settled permanently on a farm in Stark County, Ohio.[53]

The silence surrounding Balmat's death was finally broken in 1853. The syndic of Sixt at the time of the accident, Bernard Biord, explained that two young shepherds on a nearby meadow had watched from a distance as Balmat fell off the cliff by himself. When this was reported to the syndic, he summoned the shepherds and Pache and ordered them not to say anything. A variation of this story told by a guide from Samoëns was that Balmat had died of natural causes on the mountain, and after the syndic verified the death at the scene, he ordered the body dropped into a crevasse and swore everyone to secrecy. In remorse that Balmat had not been given a proper funeral, he later confessed to the *curé* (senior priest) of Sixt and to his successor as syndic.[54] In both versions of the story, the motive for keeping Balmat's final resting place a secret was the same: the syndic was convinced that Balmat had discovered gold and if this became known, other prospectors would follow in his footsteps. As summarized by Alfred Wills, a British mountaineer who built a chalet in the valley in the 1850s: "Mines would be opened, vast quantities of wood would be needed to smelt the ore, the interests of the valley would be sacrificed to the influence of persons who could gain the ear of the authorities at Turin, and their forests would be destroyed to feed the cupidity of strange adventurers."[55]

Both the guide's hopes for gold and the syndic's fears of environmental devastation were confirmed by later events. The gold rushes of California in 1849, Australia in 1851, and many others later in the nineteenth century all confirm the banality of Balmat's dreams of gold. Even though the Sixt valley may have had more pyrite than gold, it would be a profound mistake to view either Balmat's hopes or the syndic's fears as the responses of primitive peasants. In 1860, however, Alfred Wills viewed the syndic's motives as a sign of backwardness: "the dread entertained to the present day by the peasantry of Sixt."[56] On the contrary, the syndic's fears were as "modern" as the mining schemes he opposed, and Balmat's plans for a mine were different in scale rather than in kind from the other mining ventures in the valley. At a greater distance in time, the views expressed by the syndic of Sixt sound almost commonplace, like a conservationist or environmentalist *avant la lettre*. Yet, rather than embrace this anachronism and force Balmat or the syndic into such a procrustean bed, let us recognize the tensions they present to monolithic views of either mining or the peasantry. Consider them alternative modernities. Balmat's search for gold was a search for financial security and personal enfranchisement, an attempt to escape the cycle of debt that his sons left behind only by immigrating to the United States. For Balmat and many others, "gold" represented a variety of widely shared hopes and desires, and a form of subjectivity distinct in many respects from the dreams of individual sovereignty envisioned by the financially secure social climbers whom he and other guides led to the summit.

LADIES FIRST: HENRIETTE D'ANGEVILLE

Marie Henriette d'Angeville de Beaumont was to the manor born and tutored in the cults of nature and love. She was born in 1794, while her father was in prison and a month before her maternal grandfather was executed at the guillotine by a revolutionary tribunal. Two years later, the family returned to her father's ancestral chateau at Lompnès in the Ain region of the Jura Mountains between Geneva and Lyon. Her mother died when she was nine years old, and her father, an enthusiastic admirer of Voltaire, raised her "like a boy, and in the cult of Nature."[57] Henriette read voraciously and copied passages in a notebook from philosophers, novelists, and female authors. She copied passages from Rousseau expressing a preference for the mountains over the plains, and commented "this is in conformity with my taste." Though from a "legitimist" family that supported restoration of the monarchy, she developed several statements of her philosophy, including an apologia about "how I passed from an exaggerated devotion to less orthodox opinions, Catholically speaking."[58] She copied passages by Madames de Genlis, de Staël and d'Épinay about the difficulties faced by female authors and aspired to publish her own book. She had a lively imagination and feared boredom more than anything else. The last remark in her commonplace book foreshadowed higher ambitions: "The hope of conquest is a big step towards victory."[59]

Her brothers went into the military, politics, and agricultural reform, and the youngest, Adolphe, two years Henriette's junior, was her best friend. He entered the navy and served around the world in India, the Philippines, and Indochina, and transported indentured laborers to Guyana. Her notebook copied naval vocabulary and the story of her brother's friend, Jean-Daniel

Coudein, who survived the shipwreck of the Medusa in 1816 and is shown in Géricault's painting of its raft. Adolphe returned to Lompnès to double the value of the estates with agricultural improvements, and is well known for his use of statistics and maps in a study of the French population in 1836.[60] After her father's death in 1827, she received property that she later sold to Adolphe for 25,000 francs and moved to Geneva shortly before Adolphe married in 1832.[61]

Henriette d'Angeville had the idea to ascend Mont Blanc for about ten years and finally resolved to climb the peak in 1838. As she planned her ascent at age forty-two, rain in Geneva and snow on Mont Blanc put her nerves on edge, but she felt a burst of emotion when the weather improved:

> It seemed that I was in exile in Geneva and that my *patrie* [homeland] was on that snowy and golden summit that crowned the mountains. I could not wait to celebrate my engagement, to marry before all Israel and before the brightest sun, and intoxicated by the grand and powerful memories that I will bring back from these days, for the delicious hour during which I will rest on his summit. Oh! When will it come? Truly, these were my thoughts, and reminding myself of them, I feel ready to take pity and excuse the delirium of love in certain exalted natures. It was a monomania of the heart, this passion for Mont Blanc, a monomania of the imagination. What happiness to be in love only in the head, and for a frozen lover! Such curious things we are.[62]

These comments and a kiss from her guide on the summit have led to salacious interpretations that she saw the ascent as the consummation of a sexual relationship.[63] She once privately described her climbing attire as appropriate for the "fiancée of Mont Blanc." On the summit, Joseph-Marie Couttet offered to lift her higher than Mont Blanc and asked to give her a kiss. Even before these events were recounted, contemporary reactions emphasized her gender to denigrate her achievement. According to *Le Fédéral*, a Genevan newspaper: "Our proud Mont Blanc must feel singularly humiliated" at the ascent, an "exploit unheard of in the annals of her sex." The Parisian *Journal des Débats* was more circumspect, noting that the guides boasted of her courage, strength, and presence of mind; after her return, "everyone wanted to see this heroine and the name of d'Angeville is now enshrined alongside those of Saussure and Jacques Balmat" (Figure 14).[64]

Others were less kind: "Eh! What! After Saussure and his barometers, Miss Angeville and her culottes. Oh! Mont Blanc, you're missing only the

Figure 14 Henri Deville, *Henriette d'Angeville dans sa tenue du Mont-Blanc,* ca.1838.
A sketch of Angeville in her climbing gear, one of the many she commissioned for
albums after the ascent.   Acquisition 2007, Conseil Général de la Haute-Savoie.

clowns of the fair."[65] The summit kiss caused comment from Dr. Christian
Müller, a German savant: "It is now an established axiom that ladies who
are coy and prudish in the plain become kind and complying on the top of
Mont Blanc." In a similar vein, a member of the Grenoble academy who
made excursions in Savoy and "*flâneries*" in Vienna wrote: "Miss d'Angeville

is a crazy old woman and an unbearable joker, who never having walked up the steps of a wedding, amused herself by climbing virginally those of Mont Blanc."[66]

Gender difference in titillating commentary by others has obscured her own view of her passion for the mountain. On the eve of her departure, she asked a friend to laugh rather than lecture her: "I have been seized by a beautiful passion for him as the prisoner was for his Picciola, and I expect if not the same result one that has some connection, because I'm going to search for a view of the grand spectacles of nature, for memories powerful enough to occupy me strongly and sustainably during the long retreat that I will make in our mountains between my alpine excursion and the trip to Paris."[67] In X.-B. Saintine's best-selling novel, *Picciola* (1836), a learned French count is imprisoned in a mountain fortress where he sees a flower that has no known botanical name. A guard calls it Picciola and the count lavishes attention on the flower, which gives him insight into the works of God and the love of mankind. The count receives his release, transplants the flower, and marries the daughter of a fellow prisoner. The couple returns to his prison cell where only one piece of his graffiti remains legible: " 'Learning, wit, beauty, youth, fortune, all down here are powerless to give happiness,' to which Teresa added, 'without love.' "[68] Angeville's notebooks repudiated the romantic love found in novels. On Mont Blanc she sought neither a husband nor a consummation, but greater self-knowledge and passion for life. Her motives, she later wrote, were "not the puny fame of being first woman to venture on such a journey that filled me with the ex-hilaration such projects always call forth; rather it was the awareness of the spiritual well-being that would follow. This one memory would counterbal-ance many others less welcome."[69]

After the ascent, Angeville prepared an album that was lavishly illus-trated by Genevan artists. This was a "small luxurious work with views, scenes and portraits," but she was reluctant to divulge details of her journey to Markham Sherwill, as doing so might diminish the market for her book. She would not know if it would be published until after visiting Paris. In the meantime, she spared no expense and spent upwards of 10,000 francs on the illustrations and handwritten calligraphy.[70] Even while claiming to write only for family and friends, she addressed a wider audience: "I am not only a woman but a country-woman to boot, what impertinence to say: here is my book."[71]

"The lion of the fashionable and smart world is currently the famous Miss Angeville, the intrepid traveler who last year climbed Mount Blanc, the first and only woman to have accomplished this dangerous pilgrimage," wrote Delphine de Girardin in *La Presse* in December 1839. "Everyone wants to see her, surround her, and question her," and those in the most distinguished salons, such as Girardin's own, "have had the pleasure of admiring a very fine album carried by Miss Angeville containing the picturesque story of her journey."[72] Delphine de Girardin wrote a column about society, theater, fashion, politics, and literature under the male *nom de plume* Vicomte de Launay, and was the wife of Emile de Girardin, a press baron who increased circulation by cutting prices and adding gossip columns and serial novels to his papers. By 1839, Delphine de Girardin's columns highlighted "celebrity," a novel concept that denoted people who had made a name for themselves rather than inheriting their status and should not be confused with very different notions of celebrity in the twentieth century.[73]

What most earned Girardin's respect was Angeville's demonstration of her individual courage and will, and her column summarized the moment when Angeville was too tired to continue: "Oh, it's impossible, the will is failing, a woman can't expect herself to make such an effort." Angeville asked to sleep and struggled in the cold, "but suddenly a thought of pride revives her. She remembers to look to Chamonix, where a hundred telescopes are trained on Mont Blanc to watch for her arrival; then all her strength returned. She resumes with courage, and soon the inhabitants of the valley saw on top of the Savoyard Caucasus the straw hat of the triumphant pilgrim."[74]

Angeville's account presented the ascent as the triumph of will. On the highest slopes, she asked the guides to promise to take her body to the top if she died before reaching the summit: "My physical powers were abandoning me: I heard without hearing and saw without seeing. And yet I retained one sovereign moral quality: my will, alone capable of galvanizing into action my poor impotent body!"[75] Reanimated, she untied the rope "so that it was alone and unaided that I took the three steps that lay between me and victory. At twenty-five past one, I finally set foot on the summit of Mont Blanc and drove the ferrule of my stick into its flank, as a soldier plants his standard on a captured citadel."[76] Thus, on September 4, 1838, she was lifted in the air by her guides and wrote letters to friends. Before giving the signal for departure, "I inscribed my favorite proverb in the snow, *'Vouloir c'est pouvoir'*"—literally "to will is to do," or more idiomatically, where there's a will there's a way.[77]

This proverb distinguished Angeville from her predecessor, Marie Paradis. Angeville justified her ascent in these terms: "Women sometimes see and feel things very differently from men, and when I went to Mont Blanc it had not been ascended by any woman capable of remembering her impressions."[78] After the ascent, Angeville met Paradis and "her trip, which I never understood, was explained by our conversation." She took a page from Dumas and recounted their conversation in dialogue "in all its simplicity without improving the language or romanticizing the person of this dear old lady." Angeville asked about her motives, exertions, and impressions. Of her motives, Paradis reportedly replied: "Visitors will want to meet you, and they'll pay good money too." Of her exertions: "I was so poorly, no strength in me legs at all, and puffing away, I was like hens when they're over hot." The guides persisted: "they pushes from behind and they pulls from in front, and sometimes they carries me; and in the end they got me there." Of her impressions at the top: "I just remember it was white all around, and black down away below, but that's all." Henriette d'Angeville concluded: "All this is very down to earth, I agree, but at least her account displays both candour and naivety," which were better than the humbug that disguised many pecuniary motives.[79]

Angeville's account of Marie Paradis was less an unvarnished transcript than a kindly representation of a noncontemporaneous contemporary. Her dismissal of Marie Paradis's financial motives is similar to those who disparaged Jacques Balmat's search for gold. Henriette d'Angeville was unstinting in her praise of the guides and porters, but romanticized them as "untainted characters that have become increasingly rare in this civilized world of ours."[80] In his essay on the French population, her brother Adolphe had used economic, anthropological, and "moral" statistics to divide France on a line that ran from St. Malo to Geneva. To the north and east, France was "industrious, rich, and enlightened," where residents paid taxes, ate white bread, and had fewer children out of wedlock.[81] Chamonix was even more backward and underdeveloped since it lay not only south of this line but also to the east across the border with Savoy. She perceived these boundaries and gave thanks that she was born in the "middle station of life" and did not have to work for a living.

Her field notes also included two exchanges with Paradis that she re-placed with other dialogue in the book. In the earlier version, Henriette was surprised to learn that Marie had never married and yet lived with a daughter-in-law. " 'Oh! I have a boy,' said Marie Paradis, 'we had a neighbor and men are such sweet-talkers! He made me believe everything that he wanted, and voila.' Yes, I understand, my dear, I said, laughing." If the earlier account is to be believed, Marie Paradis then blurted out recognition that Angeville's as-cent really should be considered "first." After a few drinks at a guides dinner, Paradis "chatted like a magpie" before saying in a loud voice: "My goodness, this lady took the virginity of Mont Blanc, for I do not count myself: I was dragged, pulled, carried, etc. to the place where she has been all only by the lady's own legs: God! She is strong!"[82]

Henriette d'Angeville added after her signature, "the first woman who made the ascent of Mont Blanc."[83] What did it mean for her to be first? By making the ascent at all, she occupied a transgressive position, a "gender radical" who challenged predominant gender roles.[84] By writing about her motives in contrast to Marie Paradis, Angeville became the "first woman" and reinvented her identity as "a modern individual and subject."[85] But to view her merely as a modern subject is to restate the primacy of the first modern man in more gender-neutral terms. Instead, her summit position represented a historically specific subjectivity, in which reaching the sum-mit meant the acquisition of memories and assertion of will. In 1865, she told Richard Cortambert that she made the ascent "as a tableau for my *musée intérieur* [interior museum] and a memory in my life." She recalled conquering the lethargy of her body with "a faculty of which most people ignore the power: *the force of the will!* . . . It is the victory of soul over the body, of *the other over the beast* (as de Maistre said)."[86]

For long periods, this assertion of will during the history of mountain climbing has been represented or interpreted as the expression of hegemonic masculinity. Perhaps the most important challenge presented by her ascent was not to the "prior" claim of Marie Paradis, but to cultural associations that would equate mountaineering and masculinity, or even the *flâneur* (urban observer or man-about-town) with the male gaze. Angeville's *"musée intérieur"* articulated the position of a *flâneuse* in the mountains, a privileged female observer of others. Her passion to marry Mont Blanc would have seemed unremarkable to contemporaries who wrote of the flâneur, "his passion and profession is to marry the crowd."[87] Angeville's assertion that she was "first" asserted her modernity. The frequent elision of masculinity with modernity or subjectivity more generally has been the consequence of the durable and yet malleable representations of the individual subject as male, as "modern man."[88] Cortambert thought her *musée intérieur* was ingenious, but ignored her comments about the pleasures of high places: "There, no sorrows of life come up with you! We are intoxicated by the sight of the beautiful works of God! . . . The word of another becomes unpleasant to hear, because you want to be alone with yourself, dreaming awake, to be entirely in your impressions, sometimes writing them, or sketching with a pencil the memories that you see, and when finally you must leave these places where one finds such happiness, it is with a sorrow that resembles separating from a friend or from beloved family."[89]

ALBERT SMITH'S PANORAMA OF MONT BLANC

In September 1838, Albert Smith left his medical residency in Paris to visit Chamonix. As a boy in England, he had read about the Hamel accident and knew the route of the ascent by heart. He returned to the London suburbs to join his father's medical practice and gave lectures about Mont Blanc to local literary societies. In 1841, he published an essay on Chamonix to mark the hundredth anniversary "that our illustrious countrymen, Pococke and Windham, first discovered the valley." He soon gave up medicine to become a hack writer, playwright, and a novelist. Smith enjoyed commercial success with a series of "physiologies" and "natural histories" of London social types. In the *Natural History of the Gent* (1847), Smith dissected the social climbers whose "strenuous attempts to ape gentility—a bad style of word, we admit, but one peculiarly adapted to our purpose—are to us more painful than ludicrous."[90]

Smith's satirical journalism found a new target in English travelers abroad and a new venue on the London stage. After the revolutions of 1848, Smith visited the Ottoman Empire to develop a one-man stage show to ridicule "the exaggerated notions entertained in England respecting the beauty, romance, and the grandeur" of Constantinople.[91] Smith's performances combined lectures, music, and panoramic views inserted in a screen onstage. In 1851, Smith returned to Chamonix to gather material for a new show about

Mont Blanc and completed the ascent with three Oxford students. In Chamonix, they were greeted by a crowd, though the London *Times* described the gun salute and ragtag band that welcomed them as creating "a sort of half comical, half triumphal scene." John Ruskin was in Chamonix at the time and was not amused: "There has been a cockney ascent of Mont Blanc, of which I believe you are soon to hear in London."[92]

Albert Smith's Ascent of Mont Blanc opened in March 1852 at the Egyptian Hall, Piccadilly. The stage was reconstructed to look like a Swiss chalet and the walls decorated with artifacts from the Alps and the heraldry of Swiss cantons. Saint Bernard dogs ambled through the hall at intermission. Smith encouraged repeat visits to the show by varying his route to the mountain and inserting fresh references to current events. By the end of 1853, the *Times* wrote that "Pococke and Windham may have first penetrated the wild regions at the base of the monarch of mountains, Balmat and de Saussure may have first achieved the glories of the summit, and some may have followed, as no doubt hundreds will follow, their example; but still to us the mountain belongs, after a sort of fashion, to him who has popularized it among us."[93] Smith earned a fortune from the show, much of it from Mont Blanc merchandise that included polka music, a Snakes and Ladders board game, and lantern slides for a portable peep show (Figure 15), all of which enabled visitors to reproduce Smith's entertainment at home.[94] After two thousand performances and an audience numbered in the hundreds of thousands, Smith closed his "Mont Blanc" show in 1858.

The Mont Blanc entertainment was the culmination of a long series of panoramas, dioramas, and similar entertainments over the previous half century.[95] When Smith first took over the Egyptian Hall, he found that "the accumulated rubbish of Laplanders, Egyptian mummies, overland emigrants to California, Holy Land Bedouins, electro-biologists, and Ojibbeways, had something Augean in its magnitude, and the cellars below formed a perfect mausoleum of dead panoramas."[96] Panoramas put difference on display and intermingled knowledge and power as surely as they combined "entertainment with instruction." The panoramas of the first half of the nineteenth century organized the world around the viewer, but as Bernard Comment has noted, separated them comfortably from it: "a double dream came true—one of totality and possession."[97]

Panoramas attempted to produce subjectivity at the focal point of the panoramic perspective—the individual viewer—but this was not easy to

Figure 15 *Mr. Albert Smith's Ascent of Mont Blanc in Miniature.* These four hand-painted lantern slides (title slide, Smith lecturing, "Coming Down," and the Egyptian Hall) were part of the portable peep show sold at Smith's entertainment, 1855.   Paul Mellon Collection, Yale Center for British Art.

do. Smith wanted to condense the whole panorama visible from the summit into a single glance, but as he gazed in one direction, he thought of territories behind him: "There was too much to see, and yet not enough: I mean, the view was so vast that, whilst every point and valley was a matter of interest, and eagerly scanned, yet the elevation was so great that all detail was lost."[98] The *Times* considered the vicarious experience of Smith's ascent to be more important than an all-encompassing perspective: "He takes his audience with him wherever he goes, but his chief pride, even in landing them safely on the top of the great mountain, is not so much to show them the wonders of the prospect as to make them feel that they have achieved a very difficult and dangerous enterprise, which many have tried unsuccessfully."[99] A press release in 1858 claimed that his success was due to the performative experience of his audience: "Every man or woman, boy or girl, who has visited the metropolis during the past six years, has been able to 'do' the ascent of Mont Blanc by deputy, and to realize it to him (or her) self pretty nearly as if he (or she, as the case may be) had climbed upon the snowy side of that king of European mountains, had crossed his awful ravines, had heard the thunder of his avalanches, and sat upon the summit to enjoy the view."[100]

Smith's audience may have entered the Egyptian Hall hoping to be distracted, but left imagining themselves on the summit. John MacGregor and J. D. H. Browne repeated the ascent and published heroic illustrations in the style of Smith's show.[101] Many others also followed his footsteps to the top of Mont Blanc. In the five years from 1853 to 1858, Mont Blanc was climbed eighty-eight times, nearly twice as many ascents as the entire period from 1786 to 1852. The number of annual visitors to Chamonix had oscillated between three and four thousand after 1830, but exceeded five thousand in 1855 and nine thousand in 1858. The extension of railways slashed the time and expense for journeys to the Alps and this continued after the French annexation of Savoy in 1860. Chamonix welcomed more than twelve thousand visitors in 1865 and tourists spent 1.2 million francs in the upper valley of the Arve in 1867.[102]

Residents of Chamonix celebrated this prosperity and appreciated the mountain as an economic asset. Smith assisted at the dedication of its first climbers' hut in 1853, and the commune of Chamonix built eleven new huts and pavilions in the mountains by 1867. Mountains that had been mined for raw materials were transformed into a new commodity for visiting tourists. Savoyard officials had long hoped that travelers would enrich the province by leaving behind their cold hard cash, but visitors were few and remained heavily regulated. After the influx of visitors in the 1850s, the Chamonix municipal council noted in 1862: "Chamoniards are poor in terms of the fruits of the earth, but if nature has taken with one hand it has given with the other the marvelous horrors which she has interspersed; those pyramids of eternal ice are the source of its riches and well-being."[103]

Albert Smith died in 1860 and as a bohemian journalist, writer of physiologies, and presenter of panoramic entertainments, he lingered on the same threshold that Walter Benjamin identified with the flâneur, "on the threshold of the metropolis and of the middle class," the point where things enter the marketplace as commodities.[104] Smith lampooned the idlers and gents of London who resembled the aesthetic flâneurs of Paris celebrated by Charles Baudelaire. Smith's satires of London society and English tourists abroad were embedded in the social sketches and flâneur journalism of the popular commercial press and panoramic entertainments, and these contexts should not be interpreted too narrowly.[105] Benjamin was surely right to highlight the connection between arcades, panoramas, and social physiologies, as well as men of letters like Alexandre Dumas and feuilleton columnists like Delphine de Girardin who employed the same panoramic perspective and leisurely style as the physiologies.[106]

When was the threshold crossed? These changes were once summarized as the expansion of the middle classes or the bourgeoisie. To be sure, enormous wealth was concentrated in the hands of the middling sort in London and Paris and various provincial cities, yet the very category of "middle classes" appears to be a contingent product of these changes rather than a descriptor of their cause.[107] The expansion of the paraphernalia of gentility including new sports and summer holidays cannot be understood by reference to one nationally bounded and socially stratified group alone. The scramble for social status that Smith satirized in his journalism created the conditions in which social climbers became mountain climbers.

From Dumas to Smith and beyond, climbers have represented themselves as the heroes of their own ascent. For Benjamin, "the hero is the true subject of modernity," but the "modern hero is no hero; he is the portrayer of heroes."[108] Michel Foucault considered the "will to heroize the present" in the Baudelairean aesthetic attitude of modernity as necessarily ironic, and argued that this attitude necessarily led to asceticism and the desire to make one's life a work of art.[109] And yet, this aesthetic attitude is but one among a multitude of modernities rather than "modernity" in the singular. The aesthetic posture is also poorly equipped to illuminate the position of Balmat, Paccard, or the guides who resisted the claims of the curious travelers, or even social climbers such as Henriette d'Angeville and Albert Smith, who aimed to play the sovereign individual and were not interested in playing the role ironically.

Difficulties arise whenever someone is put forward as the boundary figure. Benjamin and others offer the poet Charles Baudelaire for this role. In 1863, Baudelaire approved of artists "looking for that something which we may be allowed to call *modernity;* for no better word presents itself to express the idea in question. . . . Modernity is the ephemeral, the fleeting, the contingent, the half of art whose other half is the eternal and the immutable."[110] In 1855, Théophile Gautier asked whether the word "modernity" even existed in a dictionary, as the idea it expressed was so recent.[111] Examples could be multiplied, but the question is not simply the threshold of enunciation, and the threshold of practice cannot be resolved by playing the parlor game "Who was first?" The middle decades of the nineteenth century were a particularly fertile period for such claims, including Petrarch as the first modern man. Rather than privileging narrow aesthetic or ascetic definitions of "modernity" or similarly cramped economic definitions of the middle classes, it is more productive to see such attitudes and social categories alongside ascents of Mont Blanc as different and divergent responses to a common context and shared threshold—the production of subjectivity amid an expansion of consumption and the commodification of things.

CHAPTER SEVEN

Age of Conquest

"GOLDEN AGE"

Thirty years after Alfred Wills's ascent of the Wetterhorn, it was hailed as the beginning of an epoch, the "golden age" of Alpine mountaineering. In 1887, C. D. Cunningham offered this retrospective judgment: "The 17th of September 1854, the date of the first ascent of the Wetterhorn from Grindelwald, is a red letter day in the history of modern mountaineering—of mountaineering properly so called which is undertaken for its own sake and entirely apart from the performing of some particular feat or from some special scientific object." Few peaks were "conquered" before 1854 "at long and irregular intervals, while Mr. Justice Wills's ascent of the Wetterhorn was the first of a series of expeditions destined to become continuous, and distinctly marked the commencement of systematic mountaineering. Hence it is that the anniversary of this ascent may well be termed the Founder's Day of our craft in its modern guise." The decade before the ascent of the Matterhorn in 1865 "has been called 'the great age of conquest' in the Alps, and it also may well be termed the 'golden age' in the history of mountaineering."[1]

From Cunningham's perspective in the 1880s, the conquest of mountains symbolized the assertion of will in the battle of man against nature. After the Matterhorn, guides looked on "the most inaccessible-looking peaks as a regimental rough rider looks upon an unbroken colt; with full and certain knowledge that human power and patience must eventually master it." A former Scottish military officer, Cunningham shared this hypermasculine outlook. He derided the "vulgarity" of Albert Smith and chose his boundary figure less for what happened in 1854 than for what had happened in the years since then and transformed mountaineers into icons of national virility. By 1887, the Right Honorable Sir Alfred Wills, judge of the High Court of Justice and chairman of the Railway and Canal Commission, was a more attractive figure as the first modern mountaineer.

In the 1850s, however, Wills hoped his record as a climber would help his career as a lawyer. The son of a Birmingham solicitor, Wills thought himself a "nobody" from a provincial, nonconformist family until he had made his name in the mountains. As a Unitarian, Wills was excluded from elite schools and universities that required students to be Anglican. After winning prizes at University College London and studying the law at the Inns of Court, Wills returned to the English Midlands to begin his legal career. He soon turned to the mountains to find relief from insomnia and interrupted his honeymoon to climb the Wetterhorn. Wills hired four guides and en route met two local hunters who carried a fir tree to plant on top. Wills's Chamonix guides were indignant, but allowed the local men to join them as long as "they should not steal from us the distinction of being *the first* to scale that awful peak." In fact, the Wetterhorn had been climbed as early as 1844 and as recently as three months before his ascent. Wills was aware of these ascents when he published *Wandering among the High Alps* (1856), but was content to be regarded at Grindelwald as "first adventurers who had succeeded."[2]

Wills returned to the Alps to find that his ascent and book had made his reputation. In Chamonix, the prince of Wales asked to see his fossils and English grandees were eager to chat with him. A cousin congratulated him: "The name which you were acquiring for general ability would help your progress at the bar."[3] In 1858, Wills made a series of experiments with the Irish physical scientist John Tyndall on the Mer de Glace and summit of Mont Blanc, and they received an exemption from the rotation of Chamonix guides. Wills's lobbying led to a broader change in policy for experienced

Figure 16 *The Club-Room of Zermatt in 1864.* Edward Whymper's composite portrait of Alpine climbers exhibited the easy camaraderie and muscular ethos of the "golden age" of mountaineering in the Alps.   HCL, Widener Library, Swi 685.7.1.

mountaineers and scientists after the Alpine Club also urged the Piedmont-Sardinian government to extend "the regime of individual liberty."[4] Yet Wills complained to friends that Tyndall, a well-known lecturer in London, was getting all the credit even though he had been responsible for the change. From his home in provincial England, Wills wrote in 1859: "Here, I know I am nobody. At Chamonix and in the province of Faucigny, I am somebody."[5]

By 1864, Wills was president of the Alpine Club and at the center of *The Club-Room of Zermatt,* Edward Whymper's portrait of British mountaineers (Figure 16). In the central tableau, Wills stands in a white climbing outfit next to Tyndall, who gestures towards John Ball, an Irish politician with rope over his shoulder and alpenstock in hand. Between them, William Mathews, a Birmingham land agent and surveyor, stands with head cocked and arms akimbo, while E. S. Kennedy, a wealthy gentleman, and T. G. Bonney, a Cambridge geologist, look over his shoulder. The guide, Ulrich Lauener, towers in the background. To the left, Leslie Stephen casually props his leg on the bench as Reginald Macdonald, a Colonial Office clerk, makes a point while straddling his chair. Behind Stephen are clustered a London barrister, Cambridge banker, Rugby schoolmaster, Liverpool lead merchant, and an India Office clerk. To the right, Alpine guides strike poses in front of the hotel. Lucy Walker, the merchant's daughter, and Katharina Seiler, wife of the hotel proprietor, stand by the door. According to Whymper, a wood engraver from the south London borough of Lambeth: "There is a frankness of manner about these strangely-appareled and queer-faced men which does not remind one of drawing-room or city life; and it is good to see—in this club-room of Zermatt—those cold bodies, our too-frigid countrymen, melt together when they are brought into contact."[6]

The men of the Alpine Club embraced manliness and a rugged gentility in its many contemporary forms—wearing beards, *mens sana in corpore sano* (a sound mind in a sound body), muscular Christianity, and athleticism in schools and universities—but if this diverse group shared anything besides a passion for muscularity and mountains, it was a position on the margins of the established Church of England. Wills was a Unitarian and Whymper a Baptist. The merchants and businessmen were frequently Quakers or members of other dissenting sects. Leslie Stephen was raised in an Evangelical household and became an agnostic. John Tyndall was raised in an Irish Protestant family and became an exponent of scientific naturalism. Yet the "crisis of belief" associated with such skepticism came later in the 1860s and 1870s. Very few climbers were Anglo-Catholics, Tory Anglicans, or adherents of the Tractarian or Oxford movements. Instead, many of the clergy from Cambridge and the lawyers from Lincoln's Inn were closely associated with the inclusive, liberal Anglicanism of F. D. Maurice, who preached a theology of unity in the 1840s and led efforts to educate London workingmen in the 1850s.[7]

Indeed, the Alpine Club was proposed in 1857, in correspondence between William Mathews and the Reverend Fenton Hort, a Cambridge theologian and apostle of Maurice. The Christian socialism of Maurice, Charles Kingsley, and their coterie strongly shaped the easy camaraderie and cross-class brotherhood shared by the middle-class British climbers and the peasant guides of the Alps in the 1850s. E. S. Kennedy credited his ascents to the "mutual aid and mutual trust" between climbers and guides. Whymper commemorated this relationship in the *Club-Room at Zermatt* with the inclusion of portraits of the guides Ulrich Lauener, Franz Andermatten, Jean-Joseph Maquignaz, Peter Taugwalder, and Peter Perren.[8]

Even wealthy or well-connected climbers occupied provincial positions in Britain. Take the first two presidents of the Alpine Club. John Ball, an Irish Catholic and liberal politician, had time to become the club's first president in 1858 only because he lost a parliamentary election when Catholic priests campaigned against him in Ireland. Ball opposed papal rule in the Italian states and supported the liberals of the Risorgimento, some of whom became his in-laws after his marriage to the daughter of an Italian naturalist. Ball then devoted himself to natural history and guidebooks to the Alps, which he explored from his wife's estates near foothills in Venetia.[9] The club's second president, Edward Shirley Kennedy, became independently wealthy at age sixteen, when his father, a chief clerk in the Transfer Office at the East India Company, "blew out his brains with a pistol" in 1833. Kennedy published *Thoughts on Being* (1850), a meditation on the infinite in which he cautioned to "gain the top exceeds the power of man."[10] Two years later, he entered Cambridge at age thirty-five, rowed in his college boat at the first Henley regatta, and began climbing in the Alps. In 1855, Kennedy joined an architect and three clergymen from Lincolnshire, Northamptonshire, and Yorkshire to make the first ascent of Mont Blanc without guides. With the Reverend Charles Hudson, an athletic clergyman who had returned from duty as an army chaplain in the Crimean War, Kennedy coauthored a book about their ascent entitled *Where There's a Will There's a Way* (1856).

Climbing became a metaphor for overcoming difficulties in Samuel Smiles's *Self-Help* (1859), and the Alpine Club celebrated a list of first ascents as the "exploration" of the Alps in *Peaks, Passes, and Glaciers,* a series of essays edited by Ball and Kennedy.[11] The hope of making first ascents transformed the boyhood aspirations of Edward Whymper, the Lambeth engraver. At age seventeen, Whymper confessed in his diary to an intense but unfocused ambition: "I should one day turn out to be some great person, be *the* person of *my* day, perhaps Prime Minister, or at least a millionaire."[12] Whymper cut wood engravings for illustrations in works of travel, literature, natural history, and biblical commentary. His contribution to *Peaks, Passes, and Glaciers* claimed that the Dauphiné region of France was unexplored: "Some few travellers from time to time have endeavored to draw attention towards [the Dauphiné], but it remains at the present hour not much better known than the interior of Africa." The region was, Whymper argued, "a perfect mine, full of treasure, and offers a noble field of exploration for travellers—or tourists like myself, whose time and means will not permit them to indulge in more extensive rambles."[13]

British mountaineers saw their climbing as a national endeavor that restored Britain's position in the world. *Blackwood's Edinburgh Magazine* considered it a "national honor" that Alpine peaks and passes had fallen to "islanders" whose countrymen explored Arctic winters and African deserts in a similar spirit. In contrast to France's military ambitions: "Great Britain strives for newer and bloodless laurels, and seeks, according to the Creator's sanction, to assert the supremacy of Man less over his brother than over material Nature."[14] Events from the mid-1850s to the mid-1860s—the Crimean War, Indian Mutiny, Opium Wars, American Civil War, and conflicts in New Zealand and Jamaica—provided the context in which man's conquest of nature elided easily with British conflicts with fellow men.

In 1860, the *London Review* identified the muscularity of natural scientists, Alpine climbers, and Arctic voyagers as new channels of "those energies which had hitherto been expended on war."[15] The *Times* refused to discourage "the true Anglo-Saxon spirit" among English tourists in Switzerland: "It may be a strange and even fantastic direction for heroism to take but we are persuaded that the stuff that won and reconquered India and defended Gibraltar has left its mark on many a peak of the Bernese Oberland and the Pennine Alps."[16] The Boston-based *Universalist Quarterly* wrote the same year: "If 1815 somewhat took the conceit out of the old song of 'Britannia rules the waves,' the old lady of the red-cross shield is, at any rate, in a fair way of asserting her sovereignty over the mountains by the pluck of her muscular sons."[17]

In Britain, some observers identified the founding of the Alpine Club with the crossing of a threshold. *Bentley's Quarterly Review* offered the Alpine Club as an instance that "this world does now and then see something new turn up amongst its inhabitants." The passion for high mountains was a product of "modern times" and "the existence of such a body as the Alpine Club would have been simply incomprehensible at any former period of the world, not so much because the dangers and discomforts of the life of the High Alps would have seemed out of proportion to the rewards, as because these were utterly unintelligible." Among the peoples of northern Europe, "this modern passion has spread so rapidly that we are forced to suppose that its elements must rest deep in their natural character."[18] *Chambers's Journal* claimed that the Alpine Club "affords a very striking example of the pre-eminence of our own countrymen over all others in matters requiring determination, intrepidity, and skill. We doubt whether any other nation but our own will ever boast of such an association."[19]

Such a boast was pure chauvinism, and yet such boasts do serious work. The association of mountaineering with "modern times" is precisely why these years were remembered in Britain as a "golden age" in the 1880s. For more than a century after the period it described—well beyond the 1950s— the "golden age" has remained less a descriptive label for a series of ascents than a formative claim for the modernity of the people who made them. The "golden age" of mountaineering in the Alps commemorated a period when Britannia may have no longer ruled the waves, but British mountaineers still occupied the summit position.

CERVINO/MATTERHORN

The "first" Alpine Club was formed in London, but British climbers never had the peaks to themselves. The Alps were never exclusively a British playground and climbers of many nationalities reasserted their sovereignty over the Alps in the face of external invasion. A popular book on the Alps in 1861 literally and metaphorically illustrated this process with an image of the Swiss flag being planted on an Alpine summit (Figure 17).[20] The Österreichischer Alpenverein (Austrian Alpine Association) was founded in Vienna in 1862. The following year, the Schweizer Alpen Club was organized by climbers from several German-speaking Swiss cities, the Club Alpino Italiano was established at Turin, and the Société des Touristes Savoyards was formed at Chambéry.[21] The invasion to which these clubs responded, however, was not just British. France allied with Piedmont-Sardinia against Austria in 1858–1859, and thousands of people mobilized for war throughout the Alps. In Switzerland, Lieutenant Alexandre Seiler, a Zermatt innkeeper, commanded a garrison from the Valais that was stationed in Geneva and he invited his Genevan friends to visit his hotels and to ascend the Monte Rosa. François Thioly, who had been born in Savoy, embraced the opportunity "to travel to those places where liberty reigns sovereign, especially at this time when the country where one was born has passed into the clutches of a powerful neighbor, an invasive monarchy."[22] Austria's defeat resulted in the French annexation of Savoy and Nice, and Piedmont received

Figure 17 The Alpine Summit in 1861. Residents of the Alps responded to external invasions by English climbers and foreign armies by planting the flag on the summit. Emil Rittmeyer's sketch of the Swiss flag appeared in a popular book by H. A. Berlepsch in German, English, and French.   HCL, Widener Library, Swi 608.57.10.

Lombardy and territories on the Italian peninsula. After Garibaldi's military campaigns, only Venetia and Rome remained separate from the new state of Italy.

European mountaineering clubs were entangled in this reconfiguration of states, sovereignties, and masculinities in the 1860s. Consider the Italian Alpine Club in Turin, which became capital of the unified state when King Vittorio Emanuele II of Piedmont was named king of Italy in 1861. The Italian club was the brainchild of the scientist and politician Quintino Sella, son of a textile manufacturer who transformed Biella into the "Manchester of Piedmont" in the 1830s. Quintino Sella and Felice Giordano studied hydraulic engineering at the University of Turin and the École des Mines in Paris, toured mines and factories, and entered the Royal Corps of Mining Engineers. Sella returned to Turin in the 1850s to teach applied mathematics, research mineralogy, and invent devices to tunnel through the Alps. A lifelong advocate of *mens sana in corpore sano,* Sella began to climb mountains for exercise.[23] Sella served as the Italian finance minister three times before 1873 and employed other mining engineers to reform the state. In Italy after 1860, "thinking like a state" required dealing with the temporal power of the church, and Sella developed an anticlerical reputation for putting the secular capital in Rome and his faith in a universal science.

In 1863, Sella proposed the creation of an Alpine Club in Turin after climbing Monte Viso, a peak visible from Turin at the headwaters of the Po River: "What Italian not entirely insensible to the beauties of nature would not want to conquer this beautiful mountain, whose summit is entirely ours?" Sella noted that the Alpine Club in London was made "for people who spend a few weeks of the year climbing the Alps, our Alps!" Vienna had its own Alpenverein (Alpine Association), and he proposed a similar group for Turin: "It seems to me it wouldn't take much to induce our young people, who were able suddenly to move from the softness of luxury to the life of a soldier, to get to grips with an alpenstock and gain the manly satisfaction of plowing in various directions up the highest peaks in the marvelous Alps, which are the envy of every nation."[24] Later in 1863 he convened a group to discuss the creation of the Italian club and they secretly decided to climb a mountain in honor of the new nation. A few years later, it was reported that "a plan for national vengeance was hatched there. Monte Viso, placed almost at the gates of Turin, had escaped them so it was necessary to take the Cervino by force and win the highest point at any price."

Participants at the meeting later confirmed the existence of such a "conspiracy" to Guido Rey, who cheerfully called it a *vendetta nazionale.*[25]

The Cervino—or the Matterhorn on the German-speaking, Swiss side of the mountain—had become the most prominent unclimbed peak in the Alps. Jean-Antoine Carrel, "the Bersagliere [marksman]," climbed Lion ridge of the Cervino in 1857 with his uncle and the seminary student Amé Gorret, all natives of the French-speaking Valtournache on the Italian side of the peak. Carrel had served in the Bersaglieri, the light-infantry corps of sharpshooters in the Piedmontese army, but resigned to marry and become a hunter and guide. Carrel was recalled to active duty for the war against Austria in 1859 and received a French medal for the Italian campaign.[26] In 1860, the arrival of British climbers in the valley mobilized Carrel for duty once again.

John Tyndall and Edward Whymper tried repeatedly to climb the peak, often with Carrel, and a competition emerged to be first on the mountain. In 1861, Carrel went higher than Tyndall to carve his initials into the rock—"a mark of ownership"—and the next year, Tyndall planted a flag on the top of the southwest buttress, which from that time was called "Pic Tyndall"— another mark of ownership.[27] After scrambling on the peak in 1861, Whymper resolved "to lay siege to the mountain until one or the other of us was vanquished," and he nearly died from falling 200 feet during a solo attempt. Tyndall became convinced that the peak was unclimbable, but Whymper returned again and again.[28] In 1864, Carrel traveled to Biella to meet Quintino Sella, and was later visited by Felice Giordano, the result of which was to plan an Italian ascent of Monte Cervino for the following year.

In 1865, Whymper was pained to learn that Carrel had committed to Giordano, who kept his plans quiet until the last moment. As Giordano wrote to Sella: "I shall go and plant our flag up there that it may be the first. This is essential."[29] Whymper left for Zermatt and joined forces with several Englishmen to create another race for the summit. His new companions included Lord Francis Douglas, the eighteen-year-old younger son of an English aristocrat; Charles Hudson, the muscular clergyman; and Douglas Hadow, a nineteen-year-old novice in the Alps for the first time. The group was completed by Michel Croz, an experienced Chamonix guide, and two Zermatt guides both named Peter Taugwalder, a father and son.

They easily scaled the Swiss ridge and Whymper, Croz, and Hudson untied from the rope to sprint neck and neck to the summit. According to

Whymper, "The world was at our feet, and the Matterhorn was conquered! Hurrah! Not a footstep could be seen." Images of their arrival all depicted Whymper waving his hat heroically. The Italians were mere dots on the ridge below. Whymper continued: "We drove our sticks in and prized away the crags, and soon a torrent of stones poured down the cliffs. There was no mistake about it this time. The Italians turned and fled."[30] The Italians returned a few days later to complete their ascent, but Whymper's triumph was clouded by a disaster on the descent. In a steep pitch, Hadow slipped and fell, knocking over Croz and dragging Hudson and Douglas off their feet. Whymper and the two Taugwalders had an instant to brace themselves before the rope holding them to the falling climbers broke in midair. For a few seconds, Whymper could see his companions sliding on their backs before they disappeared over the cliff and fell 4,000 feet to their deaths. A search party found bits of flesh, fragments of clothes, flattened skulls, and broken limbs. Croz, Hudson, and Hadow were identified by personal items and telltale scars, but the body of Lord Francis Douglas was never found and presumed stuck in a ledge on the cliff.

The "Matterhorn catastrophe" prompted debate about whether alpine climbing had reached a limit point. The most famous attack on the climbers in the London *Times* asked: "Well, this is magnificent. But is it life? Is it duty? Is it common sense? Is it allowable? Is it not wrong? There certainly are limits to audacity." The *Times* stated that the ascent was "utterly incomprehensible," that "there is a point of danger which, if gratuitous, becomes ridiculous, if not disgusting," and advised the Alpine Club to "manage its crusade better" with ropes that did not break.[31] Charles Dickens considered the Matterhorn accident the result of foolhardiness. According to Dickens, the "nonsense" justifying Alpine ascents "becomes ghastly when it implies contempt for and waste of human life—a gift too holy to be played with like a toy, under false pretenses, by bragging vanity." Dickens argued for "a limit which sense and sanity prescribe" when "life is risked for no earthly use whatever."[32]

Anthony Trollope contrasted this critique from "the religious point of view" with his assessment of the Matterhorn catastrophe from the "human point of view." Salvation would not be denied to fallen climbers and the "spirit of enterprise" they exhibited should be encouraged for the sake of England.[33] Others emphasized the moral benefits of danger to strengthen the nation. The *Illustrated London News* opined that mountain climbing contributed to Britain's strength and prosperity: "There would be small philosophy—nay, small knowledge of the world shown in discouraging adventure. It has given us the empire."[34] To the Oxford historian H. B. George, alpine climbing was "ambition translated into physical action," and "essentially a form of that restless energy, that love of action for its own sake, of exploring the earth and subduing it, which has made England the great colonizer of the world, and has led individual Englishmen to penetrate the wildest recesses of every continent."[35]

These arguments persuaded some critics. Even before Whymper published his version of events, the *Times* conceded: "Perhaps it is necessary that there should be an order of men to attempt what no one else will attempt, to show what can be done, and the feats which human courage and endurance can perform." John Ruskin had previously criticized Alpine climbers for looking at the Alps "as soaped poles in a bear-garden, which you set yourselves to climb and slide down again, with 'shrieks of delight.'" After the Matterhorn accident, Ruskin regretted that climbing "excites more vanity than any other athletic skill," but now held that "no blame ought to attach to the Alpine tourist for incurring danger. . . . Some experience of distinct peril, and the acquirements of quick and calm action in its presence, are necessary elements at some period of life, in the formation of manly character."[36]

This pervasive and apparently persuasive rhetoric suggests that it would be misleading to view ascents of the Cervino/Matterhorn as a contrast between nationalist goals of the Italians and the personal ambitions of Whymper.[37] On the contrary, British mountaineers mingled the personal and the political. Charles Kingsley wrote of his Elizabethan protagonist in *Westward Ho!* (1855): "He is a symbol, though he knows it not, of brave young England longing to wing its way out of its island prison to discover and to traffic, to colonize and to civilize."[38] Unlike such fictional adventurers, British mountaineers knew this about themselves quite well. In 1866, Sir Roderick Murchison, doyen of exploration at the Royal Geographical Society, praised Whymper's courage and self-reliance in the Alps and his "bold project of penetrating" the glaciers of Greenland the next year: "This is truly the ne plus ultra of British geographical adventure on the part of an individual!"[39] Whymper's *Scrambles amongst the Alps* (1871) culminated with the ascent of the Matterhorn and surpassed even fictional stories in exemplifying the virtues of British manliness. Whymper concluded with the life lessons of mountaineering beyond physical regeneration and the beauties of the scenery: "We value more highly the development of manliness, and the evolution, under combat with difficulties, of those noble qualities of human nature—courage, patience, endurance, and fortitude."[40]

Italians honored British mountaineers for these qualities and hoped to cultivate them in Italy. After Quintino Sella gave Vittorio Emanuele II a copy of *Scrambles amongst the Alps,* the Italian king made Edward Whymper a knight in the Order of St. Maurice and St. Lazarus in January 1872. Previously, three other British climbers had been named a Cavaliere in this chivalric order of the House of Savoy that dated from the Crusades. William Matthews and Francis Fox Tuckett, a Bristol woolen merchant and archeologist, were made knights in 1865 for first ascents of Monte Viso and peaks in the king's hunting grounds. In 1865, John Ball was knighted for his scientific work and guidebooks and in 1866 he was quietly elevated to officer *(uffiziale)* when he provided Garibaldi a successful plan of attack that the Italian army used to take Fort Ampola during the Austro-Prussian War. Prominent members of the Italian Alpine Club were routinely inducted into *Ordine dei Santi Maurizio e Lazzaro,* and Giordano was made a commander and Sella a grand commander in 1865.[41]

Abbot Amé Gorret, who was inducted into this order for his book on Vittorio Emanuele in the Alps, told an audience of Italian climbers in 1869: "But our mountains, all our highest mountains have been *stolen* by the intrepid sons of indomitable Albion. No, I have said a word that gives me too much pain; I prefer to say that our mountains have been *revealed;* this is the consolation of the present, the hope for the future." Gorret hoped the Italian Alpine Club would become the "patrimony of the masses," bring prosperity to isolated valleys, and provide Italian youth with "exercise, strength, solidity of character, and the pure and solid pleasures which they seek elsewhere in vain," as well as a love of work and "the perseverance and tenacity that distinguishes and elevates the English so high."[42]

The Italian Alpine Club identified the masculinity of mountaineering with nation building and against "modern" civilization. In 1874, Quintino Sella told a congress of Italian alpinists that twenty years earlier the mountains had been investigated by foreigners more than by Italians: "Mountaineering was regarded as an eccentricity, a kind of madness at best given to the British with *spleen*." Alpine climbing inspired a lasting passion and approximately eleven thousand climbers now belonged to the combined Alpine clubs of Europe. "If I am not mistaken," Sella remarked, "mountaineering combats in the physical order the consequences of the too sedentary life to which modern civilization constricts us, as it defends us, on an intellectual and moral level from the pernicious effects of the excessive worship of material interests that have great prominence today."[43] The abbot and geologist Antonio Stoppani included mountaineering and the Cervino in his best-selling natural history of Italy, which echoed a line from Petrarch in its title, *Il bel paese* (the beautiful country): "Italians, taught by the school of the Alpine Club, will become strong and Italy will become a nation of the strong."[44] As summarized by another club official, the Club Alpino Italiano was an expression of patriotism that contributed "to the making of Italy, and the making of Italians."[45]

"Making Italians" was an issue in other states, and Italians were not alone in making ascents to assert citizenship and sovereignty. Why did Edward Whymper keep trying to climb the Matterhorn when so many others turned back? Unlike almost all other members of the Alpine Club, Whymper remained disenfranchised in England, unable to vote until after the second Reform Act of 1867 extended the franchise to the "lower middle classes" and skilled working classes. Alpine clubs were established in the name of new states, "nations" that did not yet exist, and newly democratic regimes. In 1866, Germany was unified under Prussian leadership on the "small Germany" model without Austria, but in 1874 the German and Austrian associations had their *anschluss* (union) as the Deutscher und Österreichischer Alpenverein (German and Austrian Alpine Association), modeling in the mountains a *Großdeutschland* (Greater Germany) that remained aspirational in politics. The Club Alpin Français was established in 1874—only after the fall of Napoleon III, defeat by Prussia, and coinciding with the restoration of popular sovereignty in the French Third Republic.[46] If these alpine clubs were often led by members of the "grand bourgeoisie" such as Sella, membership was open to anyone who paid the membership fee (unlike the British Alpine Club, which had a climbing or literary qualification), and clubs on the continent were more likely to include "lower middle class" climbers such as Whymper.[47] Each club put its own provincial stamp on the masculinity of mountaineering, which was neither British, Italian, Swiss, French, Austrian, nor German, but a "modern sport" that was mutually constituted in a transnational dialogue in the Alps.[48]

FIELDS OF BATTLE AND MONUMENTS TO THE MODERN SPIRIT

Charles Durier commended the victims of the Matterhorn accident for falling to their deaths without crying out, "a stoic death worthy only of a
climber."[49] In the 1870s, Durier, a founding member of the French Alpine
Club, dedicated several monuments to the first ascent of Mont Blanc, which
had been impossible to envision under the Savoyard monarchy or French
Empire of Napoleon III. During previous regimes, monuments in Chamonix were proposed only for visitors. In 1838, an innkeeper and civil engineer
proposed an obelisk to Horace-Bénédict de Saussure engraved with the
names of Marc-Théodore Bourrit, Richard Pococke, William Windham, and
other savants and naturalists. The plan was approved despite objections from
other hotel owners and the obelisk was in transit using corvée labor when
one of the workers died in an accident. In 1840, the municipal council decided that "overloaded with debt and taxes" it would abandon construction
of this "obelisk to the memory of the first people who made the ascent of
Mont Blanc." Later in the year, the obelisk was mysteriously blown up in
the middle of the night and its fragments were used to build the foundation
for an extension to the church and a new hotel, later rechristened Hotel
Imperial after the French annexation of Savoy in 1860.[50]

Even after French annexation, monuments remained problematic in
northern Savoy, where many people would have preferred to join the Swiss
Confederation. Joseph-Agricola Chenal, a Sallanches lawyer who had climbed
Mont Blanc in 1834 and represented the district in the Piedmontese Senate
on the extreme anticlerical Left, led a pro-Helvetic movement opposed to
annexation. A petition in favor of the Savoyard monarchy or union with
Switzerland was signed by 319 people in Chamonix, but went for naught
when the plebiscite on annexation carried by an official margin of 608 to 0,
with one abstention. After annexation, guides planted the French flag on
Mont Blanc while Chenal emigrated and became a naturalized citizen of
Geneva.[51] During the 1860s, the Second Empire promoted tourism in the
Alps by building roads and pavilions in the mountains. It also offered imperial patronage to the Company of Guides and regulated the forests, pastures,
and formerly communal lands. Even as the region was integrated adminis-
tratively into France, national loyalties remained problematic. After the fall
of Napoleon III in 1870, the enthusiasm to defend France against Prussia
coexisted uneasily with a revived secessionist movement that envisioned
northern Savoy joining Switzerland.[52]

The end of the Second Empire elevated Charles Durier into a position to rediscover Jacques Balmat as hero of the first ascent. Durier had studied pharmacy and natural history before becoming a man of letters and entering the Ministry of Justice. In the 1860s, he contributed reviews, news, and a serial novel to *Le Siècle,* a Paris daily opposed to Napoleon III. While his brother, Émile Durier, a lawyer, used the newspaper as a platform to campaign actively for democracy, Charles Durier discovered the mountains and climbed his first peak in 1869. After the Paris revolution of 1870, Émile rose quickly through the ministerial ranks and was named secretary-general in the Ministry of Justice during the German siege of Paris in 1871. Before Émile left office, Charles was promoted to chief of the pensions division, a position he retained for decades while devoting spare time to the history of the Alps. He gave lectures ostensibly intended for the workers of Paris on ascents of Mont Blanc in 1873 and on military crossings of the Alps from Hannibal to Bonaparte in 1874. Durier founded the French Alpine Club with Ernest Cézanne, Adolphe Joanne, and others in 1874 and published his magnum opus, *Le Mont Blanc,* in 1877.[53]

In 1875, the Geological Society of France met at Chamonix and proposed erecting a monument to Balmat during an excursion to the Mer de Glace. At a picnic at the edge of the glacier, Alphonse Favre, a professor at Geneva, recalled the services given to geology by the guides of Chamonix, especially Jacques Balmat. Édouard Jannettaz, the society's president and a mineralogist at the Natural History Museum in Paris, proposed a subscription for "a monument to Jacques Balmat, who, as we know, by dint of energy and daring arrived first at the summit of Mont Blanc." The French Alpine Club and Geological Society shared responsibility for raising the funds for a bronze medallion with a bas-relief portrait of Balmat in profile, executed by the sculptor Justin-Chrysostome Sanson. The medallion was modeled on the Bacler d'Albe print and mounted on a piece of granite taken from the lower section of the Glacier des Bossons. The planners chose this rock since debris at the bottom of the glacier had been near the top during Balmat's lifetime: "It is not impossible that the intrepid guide rested on the stone intended to perpetuate his memory. And some still say that geologists lack imagination!"[54]

The Balmat memorial was dedicated on Sunday, August 11, 1878, after a ceremonial procession of Jannettaz, Durier, prefects, senators, deputies, councilors, the mayor, Balmat's relatives, guides with climbing gear, and the chief guide holding Balmat's baton, followed by bands, schoolchildren, and the rank-and-file members of local and foreign alpine clubs. Windows were bedecked with flags that blended the colors of many nations, and triumphal arches honored Balmat and the geological and alpine societies. When the procession arrived at the monument, located at the bottom of the steps of the church, the curé (senior priest) descended to join them. The band played a zesty rendition of the "Song of the Allobroges," which, according to a Bonneville newspaper, was interrupted with frenetic applause and was the most moving moment of the festival: "This manly and catchy air, already so popular in Savoy before being reflected by the echoes of Mont Blanc, on the day we pay homage to its first conqueror it receives in return the benefit of remaining now *our national anthem.*"[55]

In his remarks, Jannettaz recalled the predilection for Chamonix among generations of geologists: "These men, too great to be ungrateful—de Saussure, [Déodat de] Dolomieu, [Louis] Cordier, [Jean-Baptiste] Elie de Beaumont, [Louis] Agassiz—how often did their books, articles, and remarks give rightful praise to the bravery, experience and dedication of the guides of Chamonix!" He noted that Adolphe Joanne, the president of the French Alpine Club, had lamented the absence of anything at Balmat's birthplace that would recall the name of the guide who blazed the path for Saussure. He also thanked the state officials in attendance: "We could render homage to Balmat in private. Your presence, gentlemen, the official representatives of the country and the brilliance of your personal authority, give this ceremony another character, that of public honors. Who was, then, this man whose glory has become national?"[56]

Jannettaz summarized the portrait of Balmat presented in Durier's book: a child of the mountains who loved its beauties, Balmat spent a night on the snows and discovered a route that brought him to the attention of Dr. Michel-Gabriel Paccard. Without the energy, genius, and experience of Balmat, ignorant of the atmospheric sciences known to Paccard, the ascent would have been impossible. Paccard overcame his fatigue and testified to their victory, and Balmat was celebrated by his contemporaries. But posterity had not respected Balmat's "manly courage" because of his subsequent search for gold. In this endeavor, the geologist thought Balmat "was a pioneer. Had he sensed that the conquest of precious metals, abandoned for several centuries, was going to be the new passion of men?" Jannettaz remarked that the search for gold had been successful in Siberia and the New World: "It would be rash to say that it is unnecessary to search in the Alps, or that the discovery of an ore deposit there would be hopeless. An impartial posterity does not judge an enterprise by its success."[57]

Since Balmat had disappeared in the mountains, the dedication also served as a funerary memorial: "The monument we inaugurate then gives expression to more than our gratitude: it replaces a grave." Jannettaz hoped the monument would bring comfort to those who loved him, and inspire everyone to admire the soul of Balmat, "the soul of a hero" who sacrificed himself for the love of great deeds. After stating, "May our descendants say one day of us that like him we competed for the good of humanity and the glory of the homeland!" Jannettaz made a dramatic gesture: "He extended his hand in the direction of Mont Blanc, pointing to the new field of battle which Jacques Balmat had shown, and the moment he pulled the curtain that still veiled the medallion, by happy coincidence the sun pierced the long-thick clouds and light flooded the ice of the mountain, the valley, and his monument." After the unveiling, Durier paid tribute to the guides and repeated the gesture: "Croz fell on the Cervin, but the soldier who falls on the field of battle falls proud of his destiny, and here is your field of battle (pointing to Mont-Blanc)!"[58]

Durier's other monument to the first ascent, *Le Mont Blanc,* was honored the same year with a prize from the Académie française. In its commendation, the academy noted that "armed with axes, ropes and iron-tipped batons, dressed in velvet and gaiters of chamois, like a *Balmat of Chamonix,* [the book] seizes us, first by force and then willingly, as it is a pleasure to follow his heroic struggle against nature. We are transported all breathless but dazzled to the summit of the young Mont Blanc, more difficult to reach than that of ancient Parnassus and old Helicon."[59] The commendation was a skillful précis of Durier's introduction: Mont Blanc was a "young" mountain, discovered "too late" to be enshrouded in religious and poetic myths because "science" had already seized, climbed, and measured it: "In the absence of the veneration of the faithful and imagination of the poet, it excited the curiosity of the scientist and the ardor of the tourist. It is a mountain for our time—and if the beliefs of antiquity were summarized and personified, so to speak, in the famous mythological summits of Greece and Asia, the modern spirit, if necessary, can find its symbol in the young celebrity of Mont Blanc."[60]

The discovery and ascent of Mont Blanc symbolized for Durier the struggle of man against nature: "The mountain rises in the center of the most populous and most civilized states of the earth; it is indeed the axis around which European civilization has turned and is still turning." Despite Mont Blanc's considerable height and distinctive appearance, no one mentioned it for two thousand years: "The mountain certainly didn't move—it was the spirit of man that moved toward it." The mountain became a fertile field for the physical sciences, and "from another point of view, the discovery of Mont Blanc still appears to us as a symptom of certain modern aspirations. A different social ideal is a different way of understanding and appreciating picturesque beauty."[61] Durier summarized the history of Chamonix and credited Windham and Pococke with discovery of the mountain:

> Without pushing the comparison too far, when Bruce, Levaillant, and Livingstone were given the right to be credited with having discovered some tribe of Central Africa, this tribe was apparently not unknown to neighboring tribes. They paid tribute to Negro chiefs and Arab caravans had come to buy ivory, gold, and ostrich feathers. Other travelers had been to see the Chamonix valley before Windham; this is indisputable. But Windham did something that the others had not done—he talked about it.[62]

Writing in the wake of French defeat in the Franco-Prussian War, German occupation, and the Paris commune, Durier identified mountaineering as the modern equivalent of war. Balmat's body, mind, and will were made to defy the mountain: "Certain men are endowed precisely with the physical qualities demanded by the country which gave them birth: one could say that nature has taken up arms against itself." At the conclusion of his book, Durier contrasted himself to his own noncontemporaneous contemporaries:

> Frankly, and without foolish vanity, when we climb the lofty mountain we believe we are doing something of which our fellow citizens are not capable. We pride ourselves on providing evidence of courage, agility, and composure. That there is danger of an accident from time to time serves to demonstrate this, and it is a necessary point without which our merit would not exist. We have nothing to say in case of defeat. Winning or losing the game, even losing one's life, these are the risks of the game. The ascent of Mont Blanc is combat, the struggle of man against the powers of nature. If we can tame it, to trample the head of Titan under our feet, it is a victory—and if it kills us—it is a good war.[63]

FINGER POINTING

In February 1886, the *Journal de Genève* criticized the design for a monument in honor of Horace-Bénédict de Saussure to be built in Chamonix. Based on a photograph exhibited in Geneva, the memorial featured Saussure and Jacques Balmat with the guide pointing the way to the summit for Saussure. The editor admired the movement, interest, and features of the figures, and the head of the scientist depicted "something more than the banal desire to climb a snow summit." And yet, the editor offered a more serious objection: the grouping "does not correspond, and in our view does harm, to the historical truth. Between these two men, which one indicates with his finger the summit of Mont Blanc: which is the initiator? Is it the scholar, is it the guide? To see the sketch, it seems to be the guide. Now if Balmat was the first to climb the giant of the Alps, it is because the Genevan scholar sought it tirelessly for twelve years; it is because he had pointed a finger to the summit, and ordered him to find the route."[64]

The Saussure monument was the result of a curious time lag. Joseph-Agricola Chenal, the same Sallanches lawyer and former Piedmontese senator who opposed annexation, died on January 27, 1881, and his last will and testament, dictated while suffering from pneumonia at a mountain hut in 1834, left to the commune of Chamonix "4,000 livres of Piedmont" to erect a granite monument "to the memory of M. Bénédict de Saussure, the first to make known my valleys and to give them the rightful celebrity they enjoy." He directed that the funds be paid three years after his death and a monument be erected within the following three years with the inscription: "To Monsieur Bénédict de Saussure, Chamonix Is Grateful."[65]

In August 1883, the president of France issued a decree authorizing Chamonix to accept the gift of 4,000 francs. Simultaneously, the French Alpine Club met at Chamonix and made a carefully choreographed announcement. At the conference dinner, Alexandre Vézian, a geologist, proposed a monument to Saussure: "In this marvelous valley, the cradle of alpinism, we look in vain for a monument, a statue, even a humble stone, consecrated to the memory of the immortal savant who, the first, planted the peaceful and glorious flag of science on the summit of Mont Blanc." The idea was welcomed by Charles Durier, and Senator Xavier Blanc, the club president, committed to erecting a monument during the centenary of Saussure's ascent in 1887.[66]

Fund-raising brought up political considerations. The French Alpine Club appointed an honorary committee headlined by Auguste Daubrée, a geologist and director of the École des Mines, with Charles Durier and Sir Alfred Wills among the geologists and worthies representing alpine clubs in London, Paris, Geneva, Turin, Florence, and Boston, along with the president of the Austrian Tourist Club of Vienna. The Franco-Prussian War influenced the committee's decision to invite the Österreichischer Touristenklub rather than the Deutscher und Österreichischer Alpenverein (DÖAV). The exclusion of the German-Austrian club continued despite repeated offers of cooperation from the merged club—and friendly advice from Swiss mountaineers who noted that fourteen thousand members of the DÖAV could contribute financially to the monument.[67]

The selection committee chose the sculptor, who introduced two figures in his design. Émile Maillot, an attorney at Bonneville and secretary of the Mont Blanc chapter, supervised the committee that included the mayor of Chamonix, the chief guide, two former guides, a banker and naturalist from Chamonix, and another Bonneville lawyer. Proposals were received from sculptors in Geneva, Paris, and Lyon. Sentiment in Chamonix was against anyone from Lyon, and Durier championed the same Parisian sculptor who had executed the Balmat medallion in 1878. Maillot and the selection committee preferred the group submitted by Jean-Jules Salmson, a French-born sculptor who was director of the School of Industrial Arts at Geneva. Salmson strengthened his case before the final vote by sending a photograph of the "Haendel" statue he was then completing for the Paris Opera. In November 1885, Salmson received a contract for 14,000 francs to deliver a "monument, or group of two persons, de Saussure accompanied by his guide (Balmat), who shows him Mont-Blanc."[68]

Durier was irritated that his protégé was passed over, but indignant that "*it is Balmat* who shows Saussure the route which *he had discovered.*" Durier thought Saussure should stand alone, looking at the mountain and holding a telescope to his eye. When questioned about the choice of sculptor, a member of the selection committee told Durier, "We were all seduced by 'the idea of a group that would combine to make a symbol of courage united to science.'" Durier considered this the greatest injustice to Saussure, the man who symbolized the union of courage and science when he left his cabinet to study nature at risk to his life. Durier considered resigning from the honorary committee and asked if the monument violated the terms of Chenal's will or risked lawsuits from heirs or the wrath of Saussure's descendants. Indeed, the monument drew mixed reviews from the scientist's grandsons. Henri de Saussure considered the group an outrage, and Théodore de Saussure told Salmson he had no objections, but would have preferred that Balmat was not there as a matter of principle.[69]

The dispute spilled into the papers with the exhibition of Salmson's design. The *Journal de Genève* maintained that "Saussure is the true hero and the man to whom Chamonix today erects a monument; he is the writer of genius who revealed a new world, and not the intrepid guide who already has a more modest monument in the valley." The artist should reverse their roles: "It should be de Saussure who points with one hand to Mont Blanc, the other on the shoulder of the attentive Balmat, showing him the summit to attain, the route to find." From Chamonix, the naturalist Venance Payot agreed with these objections: "I find it absolutely contrary to common sense that the guide Balmat points his finger to Mont Blanc for Saussure, when the latter offered a prize to reach the summit. Thus it should be Saussure who points to the summit, as if to say: I want to go up there." This would conform to current practice at Chamonix, he argued, in which foreigners ask a guide to make an ascent that they designated in advance.[70]

The sculptor, Jules Salmson, responded that to reverse the roles of Saussure and Balmat violated "the special laws of our art, which produce the real and the agreed at the same time and speak to our eyes with metaphor and metonymy (the part for all)." How could the distinguished Saussure "descend from the heights of contemplative thought to indicate with a vulgar gesture to Balmat, who knew the route to the summit for more than a year while the famous scientist remained ignorant"? Salmson creatively cited prior ascents and noted that Saussure always rendered justice to his predecessors. Returning to aesthetics and the reversal of roles, Salmson thought it would torment the silhouette of the illustrious scholar to show him pointing his arm to Mont Blanc, and "guiding the guide" would be a "mutilation of history and logic." Saussure's raised arm would become "the culminating point of the group, hiding the beautiful head of the scientist like a thin and unfortunate lightning rod and only an unnecessary peg in bad taste. But all this is contrary to the first elements of composition and, if

I yielded to your desire, Mr. Editor, my students would take me in flagrant opposition to the grammar of drawing that I teach them."[71]

Supporters of the statue also pressed for changes. In Chamonix, the mayor wanted alterations in the clothing and an improved resemblance to the historical Saussure and Balmat. Joseph Tairraz interviewed an eighty-two-year-old guide in Chamonix for information about the clothing worn in Balmat's time. The location, pedestal, and inscription for the monument were also debated. Privately, Durier remained irritated, but publicly he simply corrected Salmson's historical details and noted that Saussure was "above all at Chamonix, the shining symbol of courage united to science."[72]

On behalf of the organizing committee, Émile Maillot questioned the artistic competence of Payot, and might not have replied at all but for one word in the editor's acerbic criticism that cast a "dazzling ray of light" on the discussion: "If Balmat, your colleague said, climbed Mont Blanc it is because Saussure himself had pointed a finger to the summit and ORDERED him to find the way. ORDERING him—I read correctly!" Maillot asked if they would permit Balmat such haughty arrogance:

> Balmat was the glorious ancestor of the valiant phalanx of Chamonix guides to whom one could and still can demand energy, courage, loyalty, sacrifice, selflessness, but none of whom—neither Balmat nor his successors—ever stooped to this baseness and servility. Yes, without doubt, Balmat was the humble, modest and devoted collaborator of the great Saussure. He was his collaborator no less intelligent than intrepid, but he was never, to my knowledge, either the Frontin of a Mondor or the servant of a nobleman.

At Chamonix, Maillot continued, "a monument should rise that, in consecrating the imperishable memory of the Genevan scientist, recalls at the same time not merely the memory of Balmat—our theme is much larger—but the expression typical of the Chamonix guide."[73]

The Chamonix guides on the planning committee—Joseph Tairraz, Sylvain Couttet, and Jean Charlet-Stratton—each enjoyed a position of independence consistent with the view that guides were intelligent and intrepid but never servile. Joseph Tairraz was chief guide and had owned a photographic studio in Chamonix since the early 1860s. Sylvain Couttet survived a fatal accident on Mont Blanc in 1866 and was the keeper of two mountain chalets and the proprietor of the Hotel Beau-Site in Chamonix.

The Tairraz and Couttet families had both owned hotels for years. Jean Charlet-Stratton had more humble origins as a shepherd, carpenter, and porter before becoming a guide in 1871, and an independent climber after his marriage to a wealthy Englishwoman. Jean Charlet climbed with Isabella Stratton and Emmeline Lewis Lloyd in 1871, which led to his spending a year as a groom at the Lewis Lloyd manor home in Wales. He continued to climb with Isabella Stratton and named a peak Pointe Isabella in her honor in 1875. Together they made the first winter ascent of Mont Blanc in January 1876, and both took the surname Charlet-Stratton when they married in November 1876. He became a member of the French Alpine Club, served on its examining board for new guides, and began to climb as an "amateur." He perfected a technique to descend vertical cliffs by rappelling with a rope, which was widely adopted. This technique enabled him to ascend solo to a height on the Aiguille Dru in 1877 that Dr. Clinton Thomas Dent considered tantamount to an ascent. Dent, a surgeon and son of a leading British opium trader in China, completed the first official ascent of the Grand Dru a year later. In 1879, Jean Charlet-Stratton returned to make the first ascent of the Petit Dru with Prosper Payot and Frédéric Folliguet, whom he paid for the occasion.[74]

To observers like Charles Durier, these ascents gave fresh evidence of sangfroid and courage by "guides and travelers" in Chamonix. To others, like C. D. Cunningham, the assertiveness of guides called for regulation and showed that Chamonix had declined as a mountaineering center. For Cunningham, the 1880s could not resemble the "golden age," the label he coined for the earlier period of conquest.[75] In Chamonix itself, guides and travelers were seen as equals long before they were put side by side on a pedestal. In his reply to the *Journal de Genève,* Maillot asked rhetorically what crime they had committed: "We are not all scientists, physicists, and geologists." Salmson's simple composition, "faithful to the truth and consistent with history, has beside the great and noble figure of the scientist a humble place for the first climber of Mont Blanc." The criticism had only strengthened their resolve and Maillot offered his thanks "to the eminent artist who has so eloquently translated our thoughts."[76]

The artist himself had second thoughts and revised the sculpture, while the honorary committee defended the inclusion of Balmat. In the pages of *L'Allobroge,* a republican paper in Bonneville, Alfred Wills wrote from London that it was appropriate to include Balmat as someone who possessed all the *montagnard* (mountain dweller) virtues. From Rome, R.-H. Budden viewed the modest place and characteristic physiognomy of the guide as highlighting Saussure's central place in the monument. From Paris, Durier wrote that Saussure, "the first, has the honor of the monument. His calm and dignity and very noble physiognomy contrast with the rough and turbulent figure of Balmat, making him without contest the principal personage. He is the great captain to whom a man of the country shows the path from whence he can surprise the enemy army. Here, for me, is the true expression of the piece."[77]

Maillot and Salmson made modest changes to the sculpture in the shadow of events in overseas France. "Since your last visit, we have worked like negroes," Salmson told Maillot, as he revised the design. In a feuilleton for *L'Allobroge,* Maillot admired the solidarity "above politics" felt by members of alpine clubs across Europe—the mountains and lakes, skies, cascades, and glaciers—"there is all our politics." Each year he awaited good weather to leave behind the French legal discourse for a sunset on the Jungfrau, and he admiringly quoted C. E. Mathews's remarks at a French alpine congress: mountains that once divided now united the people of Europe. Maillot then turned to arrangements for the next meeting in Algeria organized by the Atlas section of the French Alpine Club. After climbers returned from Algeria, Maillot published another article on the Saussure monument with a photograph of the revised design exhibited in Chambéry. Whereas the earlier model placed the two figures on the same level, Saussure now stood head and shoulders above Balmat, who wore a grizzled expression and primitive hat. Balmat pointed to the mountain from behind and below the savant. Even if their roles were not exactly reversed, the power relations between the two figures had shifted dramatically.[78]

Salmson previewed a clay model to the *Journal de Genève* in August 1886. The journal recalled the acrimonious debate about the portrayal of "the two men of such unequal merit." In the most recent incarnation, "the relative importance of the two figures was modified in favor of one who represents genius and intelligence, leaving the other to represent no longer initiative, but audacity and strength, and this is entirely consistent with historical truth." Balmat was full of youthful vigor, and the "rustic simplicity" of his costume with "the coil of ropes thrown over his shoulder and the alpenstock in hand helps to put him in his role." The gesture with the arm

Figure 18 The Saussure and Balmat monument was dedicated in 1887 for the
centenary of Saussure's ascent as a symbol of courage united with science. This image
by the Seeberger brothers, well known as fashion photographers in the early twentieth
century, is a reminder that the monument could teach multiple lessons to its audience.
© Ministère de la Culture/Médiathèque du Patrimoine, Dist. RMN/Art Resource, New York.

showing the summit of the mountain was a mere detail and Saussure was
now the main focus. Saussure's head was "noble, intelligent, joyous even,
the serene joy of a man who will fulfill his dream, the eyes are fixed on the
distant goal. This immobility, which is almost that of ecstasy, contrasts favorably with brusque vivacity of the young mountaineer who explains the
difficulties of the route; these contribute to put each in his place. All this is
very beautiful and very well understood." The journal congratulated Salmson on the work in his atelier and did not regret the debate that had sent
him back to the drawing board. "It will be a better figure still when cast in
bronze and the location in the mountains will provide a magnificent setting
and give the action of the two characters their true meaning" (Figure 18).[79]

COURAGE AND SCIENCE

Chamonix was festooned with triumphal arches for the dedication of the Saussure monument on Sunday, August, 28, 1887. The largest arch welcomed the minister of the republic to the villages and smaller spans carried these slogans: "Liberty, fraternity, equality—Honor to Chenal, first subscriber—To the emulators of De Saussure 1787–1887—To the immortal scientist, we come to render homage—In our city for two days, in our hearts forever—Science has no homeland—Welcome tourists of all nations." The entrance to the Guides Bureau was decorated with "The guides of Chamonix, conquerors of Mont Blanc, who opened the era of climbing." And finally, where the path to Mont Blanc left the village for the mountain, a triumphal arch proclaimed: "Mont Blanc is proud of its conqueror."[80]

Bands, schoolchildren, and the eldest guides of Chamonix marched through these arches at the head of a procession followed by French officials, Saussure's family, delegates from mountaineering clubs, scientific academies, and dignitaries to the town hall and the festival square, henceforward to be known as the "Place de Saussure." Children carrying flags placed bouquets by the statue and Ferdinand Folliquet, the mayor, recalled Chenal's will and the fund-raising efforts of the French Alpine Club before unveiling Salmson's work to cheers and applause: "By putting on a pedestal both the learned de Saussure and the modest guide Balmat, we wanted to honor courage and science at the same time."[81]

After the Marseillaise and Swiss national anthem, Eugène Spuller, the French minister of public instruction, provided the main speech for the dedication. Spuller had been an associate of Léon Gambetta and served in the Chamber of Deputies since 1876.[82] He praised Balmat and Saussure as "the first to place their feet on the summit," and said that the statues represented the union of opposite social strata. Spuller's encomium to their conquest also encapsulated the secular republicanism and critique of religious authority for which he was well known: "Man carries with him something more sublime than the most sublime mountains, and the most inaccessible of finite things must bow before this something that, while not including infinity, has however the idea; that something is reason, this light that over time eventually enlightens for us every dark corner of the universe." In the partnership of Saussure and Balmat, "Science served courage, and courage served science!" Their conquest had nothing in common with antiquity, but resembled Christopher Columbus's discovery of the New World using science and mathematics: "Columbus had faith, as Balmat and Saussure had theirs, in the same degree, faith in their work, the faith which on this occasion was not transported by the mountain, but conquered and enslaved it." The discovery of Mount Blanc could be accomplished only in an epoch when men sought the origins of all things "without any aim other than to discover the truth and disseminate it, apart from and above all prejudices, all beliefs, all superstitions and all terrors. This epoch, gentlemen, was the late eighteenth century, the great century, as we say today in our filial gratitude, we who are children of the French Revolution and who have as a mission to crown, after a century of torment, fever and combat, the glorious and fecund reign of democracy."[83]

Spuller had served on recent commissions of inquiry into workers and agricultural labor, and offered the partnership of Saussure and Balmat as a lesson to ameliorate social conflicts in the present: "This group represents the alliance of intellectual genius and of courage and bodily strength united for the application of an elevated and shared ideal. It also represents the alliance of two classes of society who can do anything when they agree, and are powerless when they are divided and fight." Spuller hoped that the pair would be "a lesson for all, and I would express this wish: that in modern France, in the democracy of our day and in that of the future, there is always this alliance of science and labor, this union of those who know with those who can do, this fusion of intelligences and of classes that would make the homeland so strong, so happy, and so glorious." Spuller closed by offering a kind of secular prayer: "Justice and truth shine upon us, that we have conquered and enslaved the old forces of the past, like Saussure and Balmat conquered and enslaved nature!"[84]

Other speeches celebrated French relations with Geneva and Saussure's priority as "first" explorer or scientist. Charles Durier considered Saussure an honorary Frenchman similar to Jean-Jacques Rousseau, and a representative of scientific academies likened Saussure's family to a "dynasty of knights of the mind." Charles Rabot, a former lawyer who had explored Lapland and the Barents Sea on behalf of the Ministry of Public Instruction, paid homage to Saussure as an explorer: "Mont Blanc at that time was as unknown as Africa at the end of the last century, and the natives had a superstitious fear of it." For his Alpine exploration, Saussure was among "the first travelers," and his methods of observation "produced as significant a revolution in the natural sciences as Descartes had done in the field of philosophy in the seventeenth century." A Genevan pastor considered their glory "human" and pure in its principles and methods. Théodore de Saussure, grandson of the savant, countered the argument that no monument was needed. On the contrary, so many scientists had followed his footsteps that Saussure might be forgotten: "Whatever may be the progress of the geological and meteorological sciences, remember that this man was the founder!" The two figures in the statue represented "the scholar and another man. The latter can be regarded as Balmat, whose fame is inseparable from that of the former; the intention of the sculptor, however, appears to be to represent more than Balmat alone. His figure is a generalized guide of Chamonix; other guides also accompanied Saussure on no less dangerous journeys." Théodore de Saussure thanked the sculptor for his work and the guides of Chamonix "for the invaluable services which their grandfathers showed to my grandfather."[85]

Spuller used the ascent of Mont Blanc as a celebration of republican sovereignty at banquets after dedication of the monument and a new school at Bonneville. Spuller recalled his first visit to Savoy in 1872 with Gambetta, who had faith in the republican mission and was an early member of the French Alpine Club: "He had no doubt that democracy, grouped behind him, would climb the steepest summits and overcome all obstacles to attain the final summit where we would put the Republic as the undisputed sovereign of France." Spuller pointed out that it was during the journey from Chambéry to Grenoble in 1872 that Gambetta had saluted the arrival of "new social strata" that gave political and social significance to the Third Republic. Times had changed from 1872 to 1887, but faith in the republican program remained: "Gentlemen, those who, like me, have remained faithful to the Gambettist tradition cannot abandon these new social strata of which they themselves are the first offspring."[86]

From this visit to Savoy, Spuller took away one word: "It is a very curious word, very characteristic and quite Savoyard, which the guide illustrates— *guide.*" Jacques Balmat demonstrated the value of time and patience and Balmat loved to tell anyone who felt that he was not leading them fast enough to the goal, *"Bien le temps! Bien le temps! Bien le temps!"*—to which the audience reportedly responded with "general hilarity and lively applause." Balmat was right to take his time on Mont Blanc to show that prudence in overcoming obstacles was more important than a passion to reach the goal: "He was a great politician, this guide. Above the desire to do this or that ascent quickly, he put the necessity for time and for reflection." He gained the confidence of his party without leaving anyone behind. Spuller believed a good guide moderates hardships and revives courage to reach the goal, while a bad guide deceives everyone, including himself, about the obstacles: "My fellow citizens, I would counsel republican democracy, of which we here are all its children and servants, to reflect on the maxim of your legendary Jacques Balmat. I would ask her if, from time to time, she does not believe she is pushed a little too much, which requires more than she can give, and hence, she is not made a little breathless on the route to climb."[87]

MEMORY AND FORGETTING

The lessons of the Mont Blanc monument were circulated in the press, taught in schools, and sold as souvenirs. French and Swiss dailies reprinted or summarized Spuller's remarks, with the French daily newspaper *Le Matin* offering this summary: "The necessary alliance of the savant and the worker, the man who thinks and one that executes, in the interest of progress or social peace."[88] This programmatic alliance was consistent with the broader purposes of public education envisioned by Jules Ferry in 1884: "The Republic will be a republic of peasants, or she will not be."[89] Teachers in French schools were advised how to use the dedication of the monument at Chamonix to teach French vocabulary and usage by *L'education nationale* in 1889. Another volume of "anecdotes and lessons" for children in 1893 described the dedication of the statues with potted histories of Saussure and Balmat and endorsed Spuller's plea for the alliance of science and labor.[90]

The most widely circulated account of the ascent as the alliance of courage and science had appeared a decade earlier in *Tour de la France par deux enfants: Devoir et patrie* (1877), a children's book that became one of the best sellers of the Third Republic. This book by G. Bruno, a pseudonym for Augustine Tuillerie Fouillée, a woman of letters, sold more than three million copies from 1877 to 1887 and at least six million copies by 1901. In many rural households, it was said to be one of two books alongside *Lives of the Saints,* and its readership far exceeded sales since it was most often read in school or borrowed from school libraries.[91] *Tour de la France* taught the love of duty and the homeland through the story of two orphans, André and Julien, who toured France in a clockwise direction from their home in Lorraine after the Franco-Prussian War. When they reached the Alps, the images of Mont Blanc, the Mer de Glace, and teams of climbers on the mountain illustrate a chapter on "the love of science and the courage of savants that has done so much for the progress of humanity in our day." The orphans learn about avalanches, glaciers, and methods for ascending by cutting steps in the ice or crossing crevasses with a rope. The orphans summarize what they already knew about the rarity of air at higher elevations, and Mr. Gertal, an adult in the same carriage, described the faster breathing, rapid heartbeat, and burning thirst, as well as the irresistible desire to sleep on the summit of Mont Blanc and the ever-present danger of death.

"'Oh! oh!' said Julien, 'I understand that there are not many people who would risk themselves to that point, but who then ever dared be first to climb Mont Blanc?'" Gertal replied: "It was a bold mountaineer named Jacques Balmat. He went alone the first time, and then helped a great savant named de Saussure to climb it." Saussure made observations on the summit about the rarity of the air and conducted experiments with fire, sound, and the color of the sky. Gertal continued: "All these experiments and many others have been very useful for the progress of science, but how many dangers he had to expose himself to make them! You see, little Julian, the love of science is a beautiful thing for it gave him the courage to risk his life to teach himself and to instruct the others." Savoy was described as a poor region in need of education, even though agricultural labor gave its residents their proverbial strength, agility, and bravery. Progress had been rapid since 1860 because Savoyards understood the importance of education. "You see, little Julien," said Gertal, "it always comes back to education: cultivated minds are like well-tilled land which repays with ample harvest the care it receives."[92]

The orphan's most striking encounter with the mountains came at dawn in a section subtitled "The beauties of nature must raise our thoughts to God." As the snow turns the colors of the rainbow, "a grand festival is prepared between heaven and earth." Instructed to look again, the boys watch the sunrise over Mont Blanc. "'O my God, my God!' said the boy, clasping his little hands, 'It is beautiful!' 'Yes, Julian,' said Mr. Gertal gravely, 'You are right, my child: join your hands at the sight of these marvels. In seeing all the mountains, one after another, leave the night and appear in the light, we are present as if at a new creation. These great works of God remind us of the Father who art in heaven, and that the first moments of the day belong to him.' And all three meditated silently in front of the vast horizon of the Alps, which sparkled now under full rays of the sun, and raising in a single prayer their souls to God."[93]

Shortly after the publication of the first edition of *Tour de la France,* the 1878 dedication of the Balmat medallion in front of the church in Chamonix had explicit religious overtones and the character of a memorial service. Spuller's attempt to give the 1887 dedication of the Saussure and Balmat monument a rather different character, however, was not reinforced by the 191st edition of the *Tour de la France* in 1889, or by subsequent editions for more than a decade. Only in the early twentieth century, when the *Tour de la France* was purged of religious references, did it become common—all too common—to view the book and events such as the dedication of the Saussure and Balmat monument as having a singularly secular and republican cast. But the *Tour de la France* and the Chamonix monuments broadcast more mixed messages including thinking like a mountain.

Prayers were said on Mont Blanc in 1887, a week before the dedication of the Saussure and Balmat monument. A group of four French priests made the ascent and said Mass on the summit. According to *Le Croix,* a Catholic newspaper in Paris, this was the first time that Mass had been said so high.[94] Around the same time, Jacques Balmat's home in the hamlet of Pélerins outside Chamonix received its own modest memorial. For the pilgrims in search of his cabin, the French Alpine Club placed a plaque by the door that read: "Jacques Balmat built this in 1787: *Sit nomen Domini benedictum* [Blessed be the name of the Lord]."[95]

The multiple monuments in Chamonix exhibited more than a few ironies. Not least among these, Michel-Gabriel Paccard, the only ardent Jacobin among the early Mont Blanc climbers, was entirely absent from the proceedings in republican France a century later. By then, his position during the revolution would have been too closely associated with the socialism of the Paris Communards to be incorporated in the republican synthesis articulated by Gambetta, Spuller, Durier, and others. The *Journal de Genève* was among the few reports to mention Dr. Paccard, "a very modest and too often forgotten savant, the author of interesting observations who never published his book."[96] Instead, Spuller appropriated Jacques Balmat, and transformed the devout Catholic and committed royalist into a guide for democracy and a republican politician, the subaltern figure of a paternal alliance of courage and science. Putting Balmat in his place—even if nominally on a pedestal—was an act of subjugation and incorporation into the bourgeois, republican nation, a commemoration simultaneously of memory and forgetting. Spuller and others in 1887 may have desired to "conquer and enslave the old forces of the past," but they were no more successful in this than mountaineers in the Alps were in conquering and enslaving nature.

CHAPTER EIGHT

History Detectives

WHO IS THIS DR. PACCARD?

In "the memorable struggle with the hitherto unknown forces of nature," Charles Edward Mathews wrote in *The Annals of Mont Blanc* in 1898, "the Peasant, the Doctor, and the Philosopher had alike been successful." Chamonix had a handsome medallion commemorating Jacques Balmat and admirable statues of Horace-Bénédict de Saussure and Balmat, but "poor Michel-Gabriel Paccard, the village doctor, lies buried in the ancient churchyard without even a stone to mark the place of his rest." While visitors could gaze at the other memorials, he hoped that "justice may yet be done to the Doctor, and that some similar memorial may keep green the memory of Michel-Gabriel Paccard."[1]

The success of "the Peasant, the Doctor, and the Philosopher" posed a problem for the middle-class climbers in the alpine clubs of Europe a century after the first ascent. They had little in common with Balmat or Saussure and found it difficult to accept that the person most like themselves had occupied a subordinate position. Memorials to Paccard may have aimed to correct an injustice, but also embodied changing representations of modernity, masculinity, and difference in the early twentieth century. Views of the first ascent of Mont Blanc were reshaped by reactions to political revolutions, trade unions, distinctions between professionals and amateurs, assumptions about objectivity, and the changing authority of "men of science." As climbers ventured beyond Europe, climbing with coolies reshaped how they understood the relationship of Balmat and Paccard. Reinterpretations framed as the disenchantment of legends were themselves peculiarly "modern" forms of mythmaking.

In the 1890s, Edward Whymper and Henri de Saussure put Paccard back into circulation in a time knot that entangled sales of a commercial guidebook with the snobbery of a patrician naturalist. Whymper had climbed in the Andes and oversaw the family engraving business until competition from cheap photographic reproductions made his wood engravings redundant. In the 1890s, he turned his entrepreneurial energies to writing guidebooks for Chamonix and Zermatt.[2] To research his Chamonix guide, Whymper looked for Paccard's narrative in libraries, sent a letter to every male resident of Chamonix, and contacted Saussure's descendants.

Henri de Saussure lived in the family's ancestral mansions and was keeper of its archive. The naturalist and agronomist published on subjects ranging from his travels in Mexico to the best methods for slaughtering beef. He read his grandfather's (Horace-Bénédict's) letters in the 1870s, and considered Marc-Théodore Bourrit to be an obsequious flatterer: "one of those jealous characters who cannot accept a superiority, a very common type among the bourgeoisie of old Geneva who could only console themselves for not being the issue of the loins of Jupiter."[3] He compared Bourrit to Genevan revolutionaries in 1846, whom he loathed even more for ending oligarchic rule and establishing universal male suffrage. Four decades later, Saussure still felt the sting of changes that, along with a federal constitution establishing Swiss citizenship, challenged his position of superiority.[4] Irritated that Balmat shared the pedestal with his grandfather in Chamonix, Saussure asked a friend in October 1887 to search back issues of the *Journal de Lausanne* to find the letters from Paccard. Nothing would be more false than to portray Balmat in a leading role, Saussure wrote in the 1890s, and only the "revolutionary ideas of the time" resulted in Balmat being "exalted as a man of the people." Saussure sent the Lausanne certificates to Whymper, who was delighted to find documents that had seemingly disappeared from circulation for a hundred years.[5]

Whymper and Saussure disagreed about whether the Lausanne certificates could be taken at face value. For Saussure, the certificates settled the case. For Whymper, they only raised questions. The unrelenting emphasis on the glorification of Paccard led Whymper to ask if Balmat really knew what he was signing. Saussure and many of Paccard's defenders were born into wealth and privilege, but social position was less important than attitudes toward "difference." Consider Whymper's sympathy for guides and skepticism of Paccard. Whymper invited Jean-Antoine Carrel, his former Matterhorn rival, to join him in the Andes and advised a younger historian to get to the bottom of Paccard: "Slap it well, for I think he was a humbug, and would willingly have taken the bread out of the mouth of le pauvre Balmat."[6] Whymper doubted the reliability of the Lausanne certificates, but he regretted that Paccard had been forgotten:

> Though these curious documents may have answered their purpose at the time of publication, posterity has not estimated Paccard so highly as he might have wished. A monument has been raised in Chamonix to Balmat, and another to De Saussure. Whilst their names are remembered with gratitude, that of the village doctor is well-nigh forgotten; and, if one were to make inquiries about him, it is more than likely that the answer would be, 'Who is this Doctor Paccard?'[7]

ANNALS/*ANNALES* OF MONT BLANC

Charles Edward Mathews set out to answer such questions in *The Annals of Mont Blanc* (1898), which aspired to do for English readers what Durier had done for the French. Mathews, a Birmingham solicitor, civic leader, and former president of the Alpine Club, offered an alternative to Durier's interpretation of mountaineering as the "good war." At the end of his well-researched chronicle of ascents, Mathews reflected that mountaineering only added to "the sum of human happiness." The search for "modern geographical discovery" sent mountaineers to the Andes, Caucasus, and Himalayas, but Mont Blanc retained its appeal. Mont Blanc would never be completely spoiled by tourists or vulgarized by huts: "The tracks of summer are obliterated by the snows of winter, and each new man, each new generation of men, will find in it, as we have found, the same interest and the same charm."[8]

Mathews was dissatisfied with the received wisdom about roles of "the Peasant, the Doctor, and the Philosopher." He admired Saussure, but took offense at the "subjection of Mont Blanc" by scientific observatories. He did not mind the meteorological station built in 1890 by Joseph Vallot, a French mountaineer whose family of engineers and merchants had endowed him with the independent wealth to pursue botany in Senegal and meteorology in the Pyrenees and Alps. Vallot built his observatory below the summit and not visible from Chamonix. This modest profile was almost as impressive as the "great physical strain and constant self-denial" that Vallot endured during three days camped on the summit in 1887.[9]

Mathews was more critical of the summit observatory erected by Dr. Jules Janssen, director of the Paris Observatory. Disabled as a youth, Janssen went to the mountains for research throughout his career. In 1890, Durier climbed Mont Blanc with Janssen literally in tow—dragged in a sled or carried in a chair by the guides. Janssen's wealthy and well-connected patrons raised the funds for a research tower on the summit of Mont Blanc designed by Gustave Eiffel. Since the guides could find no bedrock, only a "prune stone" in the snow, Eiffel's tower was wedged into position on the summit as the triumph of thinking like a state. Visions of French alpine troops conquering the mountain or the white-haired and gray-bearded septuagenarian astronomer on a palanquin were irresistible fodder for the illustrated papers (Figure 19). Janssen returned to the summit several times, the last ascent at age seventy-one.[10] According to Mathews, the Janssen observatory deprived mountaineers of the "mighty panorama," forcing them "to crawl round the building and seek in installments his once unrestricted view. Surely it is time that, in the interests of insulted Nature, some protest should be made against the arbitrary encroachments of misdirected science."[11]

Mathews also had mixed feelings about the guides of his own day. On the one hand, Mathews attributed any of his success as a climber to his Swiss guide, Melchior Anderegg. On the other hand, he detested the Chamonix Company of Guides as "a trades union of the worst sort." The "unfettered guides" of Saussure's time "stand out in the history of Chamonix like

Le Petit Journal

Le Petit Journal
CHAQUE JOUR 5 CENTIMES
Le Supplément illustré
CHAQUE SEMAINE 5 CENTIMES

SUPPLÉMENT ILLUSTRÉ
Huit pages : CINQ centimes

ABONNEMENTS
SEINE ET SEINE-ET-OISE
DÉPARTEMENTS
ÉTRANGER

Douzième année

DIMANCHE 4 AOUT 1901

Numéro 559

LES CHASSEURS ALPINS AU MONT BLANC

Figure 19 The scientific observatory of Dr. Jules Janssen was built on the summit of Mont Blanc in the mid-1890s. The mountain infantry of the French army (the Chasseurs Alpins) claimed the summit position on the cover of *Le Petit Journal, Supplément Illustré,* August 4, 1901.   Beinecke Rare Book and Manuscript Library, Yale University.

peaks above the clouds. Their successors have sadly degenerated." Mathews recounted efforts to regulate the guides from the founding of the company to the most recent rules issued by the French government in the 1890s. In this brief submitted by the Birmingham solicitor, "most regulations are injurious, if not oppressive."[12]

The lawyer identified with the doctor, and Mathews searched across Europe for Paccard's "lost narrative." He placed notices in French, Swiss, and Italian alpine periodicals, and one of his appeals reached Adolphe Balmat, a great-grandson of Dr. Paccard. Mathews bought a notebook started by the doctor for £10 and sold it two years later to the Alpine Club for £8, even though he had higher offers from collectors.[13] The intellectual return on this investment was even more disappointing concerning the first ascent. The notebook included extended commentary about other events, but summarized the first ascent in a sentence: "Our voyage of 8 August 1786 arrived at 6:23—in the evening—left at 6:57, having remained 34 min."

The case of "Paccard v. Balmat" was reviewed by Douglas Freshfield, whose family of solicitors for the Bank of England made its fortune representing slave owners seeking compensation for the abolition of slavery. This family fortune enabled Freshfield to climb in the Alps, Caucasus, and Himalayas and take unpaid positions running the Alpine Club and Royal Geographical Society. Freshfield complemented Mathews for "a fine specimen of the origin and growth of a legend."[14] The *Alpine Journal* likewise viewed the 1786 ascent in terms of social categories circa 1900: "In apportioning the honour we may, perhaps, say, in modern phrase, that Dr. Paccard was the 'Herr,' long desirous of climbing the mountain and keenly interested in devising routes, but needing the help of an efficient guide." Balmat served admirably in this role and "the guide's just honor is surely not diminished by the fact that the 'Herr' who was his comrade in that memorable first ascent was also an enthusiastic and capable mountaineer."[15]

"Some people," Joseph Vallot wrote in 1897, "tormented by the love of *amateurism* taken to its utmost limit, want to argue that Balmat was guide and Paccard the traveler, and only the latter should be named."[16] Vallot heard stories about Balmat from his guides and read the "cahiers de Jacques Balmat" in Chamonix. Balmat had handwriting in the style of a peasant and his search for gold was not without foundation. Precious metals were common in the area and an engineer told Vallot that tests of the Arveryon had yielded positive results for gold. A porter told Vallot his father had exploited an auriferous vein thirty years ago on Mont Blanc that yielded a small gold bar. According to Vallot, "We see that Jacques Balmat was not such a fool as previously thought, and it is possible that one day someone more fortunate will find wealth where he found death." Nevertheless, he read the Lausanne certificates in Whymper's guidebook and conceded that much of the first ascent was legend: "I bow to the truth, when a severe critic has established the reality of facts."[17]

Vallot's sympathy for Balmat stemmed from his rejection of distinctions between amateur and professional and his sympathy for climbers excluded in his own day—guides and women. As an autodidact and "amateur" researcher, Vallot's observatory had been denigrated by "scientists" like Janssen, who were policing the boundaries of an emerging profession. Time was on his side, however, and Vallot was put in charge of both observatories after Janssen's death in 1907. Two years later, the Janssen observatory was abandoned for scrap wood as it slid down the peak. Vallot's attitude toward guides was also radically different from Janssen's. Vallot conscientiously thanked every guide and porter who helped build his station, and his official publication, *Annales de l'observatoire météorologique du Mont-Blanc,* referred to the "guides-conservators" who maintained the facility in terms that resemble coinvestigators.[18] Vallot's wife and daughter assisted in his work and he encouraged them to become active mountaineers.[19] Despite his personal wealth, Vallot's more inclusive attitude toward "difference" enabled him to incorporate rather than exclude Balmat and other guides in his annals of mountaineering. Vallot compared Balmat favorably to the guides of his own day and vigorously defended his snow bivouac.

Alpine archeology unearthed more relics of the first ascent around Chamonix. In 1893, a carving with Jacques Balmat's initials and the date 1786 was found on the mountain with other initials engraved in 1806. A decade later, in 1903, Albert Gex, a schoolteacher from Houches, found two manuscript pages by Jacques Balmat among the notes tucked in an old book bought at a public auction. Mathews and Vallot confirmed its authenticity with varying degrees of reluctance or enthusiasm. Most of this narrative concerned his snow bivouac with a list of ascents that constituted Balmat's own annals of Mont Blanc: "I went twice to the summit of Mont Blanc on 8 August 1786, the third time, on 5 July 1787 by commission from de Saussure with two comrades, the fourth time on 3 August 1787 with Saussure and 18 guides."[20]

HISTORY DETECTIVES

On November 2, 1908, Dr. Heinrich Dübi in Bern posted a letter to Henry Montagnier in Geneva and within the hour received a letter from Montagnier asking him about the same issue—Paccard versus Balmat—their letters had crossed in the mail. They exchanged research agendas and Dübi wrote again a few weeks later to tell Montagnier he hoped to publish,

> but only *after* your publication, a sort of tale how this legend of Paccard's incapacity and Balmat's heroism and prevalent merit began through Bourrit immixing himself in a debate where he was not to play the beau-role, how this legend, after some hesitation in the beginning, grew more and more after the deaths of de Saussure and Paccard, especially by the interview of Alex. Dumas and his *Souvenir de Voyage,* and how it was sanctioned by Durier's book and the monuments at Chamonix, so that nowadays, despite Dr. Paccard's diary and Whymper's publication of the certificates in the *Journal de Lausanne,* it seems nearly indestroyable and I am not sure that even your documents will suffice to deracinate this stupid nonsense out of people's mind. But we must try and do our best.[21]

The two men met in Bern and in Geneva with Whymper, who encouraged the historical detective work of this odd couple.[22] Heinrich Albert Dübi was born in 1848, started climbing in the Alps in 1868, and earned a doctorate and taught ancient languages and history at Bern. He combined these interests with publications on Romans in the Alps, legends about mountain passes, and the history of mountaineering. Dübi edited the Swiss Alpine Club *Jahrbuch* and was a leader in the club when it voted to exclude women from membership for the first time in 1907.[23] Henry Fairbanks Montagnier was born in Cincinnati in 1877, raised in a French-American family in Terre Haute, Indiana, and attended Princeton before dropping out when he came into his inheritance.[24] From 1898, Montagnier lived successively in Belgium, Italy, Spain, India, South America, Geneva, England, Italy, Switzerland, and France. This peripatetic existence was the envy of Guido Rey, an Italian textile industrialist introduced to climbing by his uncle, Quintino Sella. Rey told Montagnier that his only escape from his office in Turin was visiting the Alps or "writing my souvenirs of the mountain life; it seems to me, when I write, to be still there in the freedom and light of the high peaks. In such way I try to forget the slavery of my actual life."[25]

Montagnier visited libraries and archives throughout Europe and tenaciously pursued clues about early Mont Blanc climbers. While in Geneva, he contacted the descendants of Saussure, Bourrit, and others to read their family papers. While living in Hemel Hempstead, England, in 1910, Montagnier searched for traces of Colonel Beaufoy, "the first Britisher who ever ascended an Alpine snow-peak." After finding an obituary, "then I cycled over to the village where he died. The sacristan of the church was positive that 'no gentleman of that name was buried there,'" but Montagnier found a memorial and transcribed the inscription. No one in the village remembered the Beaufoy family until "finally the leading grocer who supplied 'all the local gentry' gave me a clue from which I finally got into touch with Mr. Mark Beaufoy, a grandson of the Colonel."[26] Archivists in Chamonix supplied references to birth, marriage, and death and Paccard's term as mayor. Montagnier interviewed J. P. Cachat, a Chamonix hotelier whose wife was a granddaughter of Dr. Paccard and owned a portrait of the doctor. Cachat recalled a box with Dr. Paccard's letters and manuscripts, but Montagnier's soaring hopes were dashed when "he added that on opening them some fifty years ago he found the contents so damaged by rats that he had destroyed the whole lot."[27]

Their breakthrough came during Dübi's research for a biography of Jakob Samuel Wyttenbach, an eighteenth-century savant and theologian.[28] In the Wyttenbach papers, Dübi found correspondence from Genevan savants as well as Adolf Traugott von Gersdorf, whose eyewitness certificate of the first ascent had been published in Lyon in 1905.[29] These fragments led them to the *Oberlausitzer Gesellschaft der Wissenschaften* in Görlitz, which lent Gersdorf's letter books through interlibrary loan to the Stadtsbibliothek in Bern. Dübi took the lead since Montagnier did not read German and had recently married and had a child. The historian in Bern read the Gersdorf letters with mounting interest in 1910: "I fear I cannot spare to poor Bourrit the castigation he so well earned by his bad behavior against nearly everybody he met in this matter."[30] A Görlitz archivist transcribed parts of Gersdorf's diaries and sent a photograph of the savant's sketch of the first ascent. Dübi was convinced that he now had incontrovertible evidence: "This account and these drawings held together with some phrase in the letter of v. Gersdorf prove absolutely that the Doctor was the 'father of the idea.'"[31]

These historians each wanted to be first with their discoveries. Paccard's narrative remained elusive until Danielle Plan gave Montagnier the materials she had used for a biography of Henri-Albert Gosse that included a copy of Paccard's prospectus tucked into the William Windham and Pierre Martel letters about Chamonix. Montagnier was delighted to confirm Paccard's plans, but reluctantly concluded that it had never been published.[32] Montagnier published a bibliography and article on Paccard's narrative that mentioned Gersdorf's letters, but he never published his own book. He shied away from interpretive questions that could not be solved with bibliographical answers. After Montagnier's commentary on the "lost narrative" appeared in the *Alpine Journal*, Dübi forbade him from further publication: "*you may not give further details out of v. Gersdorf's diary or letter* than those already given in the A.J. The full extract from the diary and the sketch therein are the 'clou' [showpiece] of our publications and I fear that others will profit more than we if either you or I continue to give out parcels of work before the whole."[33]

Henri Ferrand, a Grenoble lawyer and former president of the *Société des Touristes du Dauphiné*, independently researched the same question. Ferrand's long experience in the mountains had taught him the respective worth of guides and travelers: "They certainly arrived almost together, and if Balmat had the most basic pretense of politeness, he would have put himself a step behind allowing his traveler to arrive the first at the summit."[34] Ferrand had more sympathy than Montagnier for Balmat, while still being critical of Bourrit and sympathetic to Paccard. Actually, Ferrand blamed Saussure as much as his "emissary" and "vassal," Bourrit. Saussure wanted to make an ascent that opened the gates of glory: "Under these conditions it was very human to try to overshadow the priority of another man of science. A guide, he does not count: he is an instrument, an employee: he was sent to the discovery, but the ascent is that of the traveler." Ferrand assigned Balmat the preponderant role in physical execution of the ascent,

> because it is generally accepted that the muscles of a peasant, of a chamois hunter, are stronger than an amateur, even a countryman. We were in the habit a few years ago, when there were still virgin peaks, to see projects for ascents elaborated by tourists and their implementation assured by guides who did not claim for themselves a glory eclipsing that of their traveler. But

Balmat wanted to go too far and give the doctor a piteous allure, a state of collapse that the facts themselves contradict.

Ferrand concluded that "the only true author of the discovery of the first route to Mont Blanc, the man of conquest, was Dr. Paccard."[35]

Dübi's book-length treatment, *Paccard wider Balmat, oder Die Entwicklung einer Legende* (1913) attempted to answer the "Balmat-Paccard question" once and for all. The question remained open more than 125 years after the event, "perhaps precisely because so many have worked on this search in modern times." In this respect, Dübi wryly suggested, it resembled the controversy over where Hannibal had crossed the Alps as summarized by Mark Twain: "The researches of many Antiquaries have already thrown much darkness on the subject, and it is probable, if they continue, that we shall soon know nothing at all."[36] The solution must be found now, Dübi argued, "before the last remnant of interest in the pioneers of Mont Blanc is lost in the face of the work of technicians propelled upward with ropes and cableways certain of victory on routes which those with ax and crampons sought in vain to approach the great 'white mountain.'" Dübi was also interested in the development of a historiographical "legend." Besides the satisfaction of conferring honor on

> a long unappreciated man for his epoch-making action, I think it is psychologically not uninteresting to show how the legend of the heroism of Balmat and the weakness of Dr. Paccard gradually developed from modest beginnings, in which prejudice and false testimony turned a simple truth on its head, and by the power of the feuilletons a fantastic construction of the events of 1786 was erected, which was bound to collapse helplessly as soon as the original report of an impartial witness pulled away the foundation.[37]

The scales of justice had been tipped against the doctor too long, and Dübi framed his investigation as a prosecutor giving a deposition in the case of Paccard versus Balmat. Dübi acknowledged his collaboration with Montagnier for the documentary sources on which he rested his case. The book is an exhaustive compendium of quotations and extracts from primary sources in the original French, German, and English, with Dübi's connecting commentary in German. At the end, Dübi hoped that the legend of Balmat and Saussure as the conquerors of Mont Blanc should be buried by the "tribunal of posterity." Paccard had made the ascent in the interests of science and without thought of material reward. Dübi concluded: "We believe we have finally shown also that the modern view of the share of merit of Dr. Paccard and Jacques Balmat in the ascent of Mont Blanc, as depicted in particular in the book of Charles Durier, proves to be quite untenable as soon as one has knowledge of contrasting original sources, the diary of Dr. Paccard and the travel journal of Gersdorf. So let us take leave of our investigation with an expected ruling by the reader in favor of Dr. Paccard."[38]

Despite its erudition, the trilingual format of Dübi's volume proved a substantial obstacle to readers. Almost half the book consisted of quotations in French, and Francophone reviewers thought Ferrand had covered the same ground in much shorter space.[39] Montagnier's Swiss wife read the German sections to him and Ferrand struggled through it with a dictionary, but was disappointed: "The Dübi volume gave me at the same time much pleasure and much boredom. Yes, boredom, even for me, for I could not understand everything that I feel is hidden in its pages in a language unknown to me."[40] Douglas Freshfield's elegant summary of Dübi's key documents in the *Alpine Journal* almost certainly reached a larger audience than the book itself. An English translation was contemplated for a few years, but Dübi had to digest the amount he had invested in publication and nothing came of it after the outbreak of war.[41]

MEMORIALS TO MODERN MOUNTAINEERS

During the First World War, mountaineering in the Alps assumed a quasi-military character, as climbing clubs trained Alpine troops and even research on the history of mountaineering could look like war by other means. In September 1915, Henry Montagnier was expelled from Italy on charges of espionage because he "knew in detail the Maritime Alps and those of Tyrol and all the local fortifications."[42] After a search of his alpine library in San Remo, he was deported to Switzerland and settled in Bern to continue his research for the duration of the war. Montagnier was eventually exonerated, but had to explain his circumstances to the State Department to avoid a presumption of expatriation and loss of U.S. citizenship in 1918.[43] Montagnier then collaborated on smaller projects with Ferrand and on a monumental biography of Saussure with Douglas Freshfield.

The Freshfield and Montagnier book, *Life of Horace Bénédict de Saussure,* appeared in English in 1920 and French in 1924, a portrait of "the true author of our modern passion for Alpine scenery, as well as the first systematic Alpine explorer." The depth of archival research by Montagnier and the breadth of historical context provided by Freshfield combined to paint a portrait of Saussure and of "modern mountaineers" of their own day. Freshfield defined the "modern mountaineer" through comparisons with "primitive" man, a contrast he also developed in books about his own ascents in the Caucasus and India. "In the consciousness of simple peoples," Freshfield wrote, mountains were objects of religious awe or portals to other worlds. He gave examples from the Old Testament, ancient Greece, and the "nations of Farther Asia, the Chinese, Japanese, Tibetans, and Indians." In contrast to primitive peoples, "races further advanced in civilization"— such as the Roman Empire—took a more practical approach. Only in "the third or modern period" did the love of mountains emerge from narrow bounds. Leonardo da Vinci was "a modern" and kindred spirit to Conrad Gessner and Saussure. Swiss naturalists reached learned audiences, but Freshfield argued that neither they nor Jean-Jacques Rousseau could match Saussure as the founder of the cult of mountains.[44]

"Modern mountaineers" in the Alps, Caucasus, Rockies, and Himalayas were similar to Saussure. Freshfield recalled traveling in the Alps through "valleys and villages, many of which, when I first knew them some sixty years ago, had lost comparatively little of the primitive character and charm vividly portrayed in the *Voyages*." Freshfield dismissed rumors that William Windham and Richard Pococke were looking for mines by comparing his own experience: "Modern mountaineers in remote districts have often found themselves subject to similar surmises. When in 1868 English climbers first visited the Caucasus no Russian official could believe that we climbed Kasbek and Elbruz without a commercial or a political purpose, and twenty years later the Prince of Suanetia invited me to develop gold mines under the shadow of Ushba." Saussure had encountered disputes among his guides about the distribution of their loads, "a cause of delay only too familiar to the explorers of the Caucasus and the Himalaya of the present day." The Swiss Alps were not unexplored or uncivilized in the eighteenth century, and their investigation was easy compared to climbing in the Himalayas, Andes, or Rocky Mountains. Freshfield cautioned against judging Saussure "by the standard of modern peak-hunters" and distinguished him from "the average modern mountaineer" because he preferred the certainty of reaching a goal to the "zest of a new and doubtful adventure."[45]

More important, Saussure's panoramic view from the summit was no longer available on Mont Blanc, but Freshfield reassured that "for an equally impressive and suggestive panorama the climber must go to the Caucasus or Sikkim."[46] Put more directly, the Alps offered picturesque prospects, but the uncontested summit position once enjoyed by Saussure was available now only outside Europe on peaks where guides continued to play the subordinate role. Indeed, reassessments of Mont Blanc took place in the shadow of contemporary ascents in the Himalayas, Alaska, and Canadian Rockies. In 1923, for example, General C. G. Bruce tested oxygen equipment for the next British Everest Expedition at Montagnier's Swiss chalet.[47]

The Saussure biography was perhaps the most widely circulated landmark in these historical reassessments of "modern mountaineers." In Switzerland, Montagnier collaborated with Commandant Emile Gaillard, a retired military officer from a family of bankers in Grenoble and Paris, on editions of Saussure's journals, letters, and voyages. In France, Joseph Vallot and his cousin issued a new edition of Durier's *Le Mont-Blanc* that was sympathetic to Paccard. In England, E. H. Stevens, the headmaster of Westminster City School, welded multiple fragments into a coherent narrative written as if from Paccard's point of view in 1787. Stevens had a Ph.D. in physics from Heidelberg and applied a scientist's precision and schoolmaster's didacticism to the reconstruction of this "lost narrative." His gospel according to Paccard put in italics anything "*definitely derived from Paccard* himself" so the reader could see "*all that we know Paccard to have said or written on the subject,* and can neglect the rest at his pleasure."[48] This reconstruction was a remarkable novelization of the work of the history detectives. Stevens also followed Paccard's footsteps around Mont Blanc and found a tablet erected by the French Alpine Club "stating that this was Jacques Balmat's *gîte* [sleeping place], August 7, 1786. Not a word about Dr. Paccard! One might almost think there was a conspiracy among French mountaineers to exalt Balmat at Paccard's expense."[49]

A memorial to Paccard in Chamonix was proposed and funded by two doctors in the American Alpine Club—Dr. William Sargent Ladd of New York, a past president, and Dr. James Monroe Thorington of Philadelphia, the club's secretary. Both had served in the medical or ambulance corps during the Great War and climbed extensively in Canada and Alaska in the 1920s. Thorington proposed a Paccard monument in Chamonix as early as 1928, but the Great Depression discouraged fund-raising, and they offered to pay the costs themselves. They could afford to give generously. Ladd was scion of a family of bankers in Portland, Oregon, whose wealth was immense even by Gilded Age standards—his grandfather's estate was conservatively estimated at $10 million in 1893.[50] Thorington joined the ophthalmology practice his father had founded after the family had made its fortune in Panama. He earned a master of arts degree, as well as a medical degree from the University of Pennsylvania and published exceptionally well-researched essays on alpine maps, Gessner's ascents, American climbers, and physicians on Mont Blanc, as well as a book on Albert Smith.[51] The close connection that he and others felt to the longer history of mountaineering is graphically represented in Thorington's alpine bookplate (Figure 20). He adapted a Tyrolean bookplate from 1593 that showed hunters with alpenstocks and chamois prancing about the rocks. In the revised version, the central oval with a family crest was replaced by a sketch of climbers at a bivouac who raise a glass to toast the predecessors whose names encircle the scene—Petrarch, Gessner, Scheuchzer, Bourrit, Paccard, Saussure, and so on, with the initials of the Alpine Club and American Alpine Club—modern mountaineers all.[52]

The Paccard memorial was approved by the Chamonix authorities in April 1932, and Montagnier hastily made the arrangements so its dedication would coincide with a congress of alpinists in August. Montagnier provided the Bacler d'Albe portrait as a model for the bas-relief bust of Paccard in profile to match the 1878 medallion of Balmat. Of the total cost of $500 (12,500 francs), Thorington and Ladd together paid $300, Montagnier $25, and the Alpine Club £25 (about $90 after the 1931 devaluation of the pound), with the balance coming from "well-known Paccardists" contacted by Montagnier among the Swiss, French, and Italian alpine clubs. The German and Austrian clubs were again excluded and boycotted the Congress. The Susse Frères foundry in Paris recommended the sculptor Paul Silvestre, who designed the bronze plaque for Paccard with space for an inscription. Montagnier and Jean Escarra, the French Alpine Club president and a law professor in Paris, negotiated the dedication, whose last line offered Paccard "grateful homage from the Alpine Clubs."[53]

Figure 20 The Alpine bookplate of J. Monroe Thorington, possibly from the 1920s, adapted a 1593 bookplate from the Tyrol, and placed contemporary climbers within a circle of predecessors from the history of mountaineering.   Henry S. Hall, Jr., American Alpine Club Library.

On Sunday, August 28, 1932, the Paccard medallion was unveiled on the wall of the Chamonix Town Hall. Giovanni Bobba, a retired Turin jurist and former president of the Italian Alpine Club, noted that Paccard had been unjustly "deprived of the halo of glory surrounding Jacques Balmat." Paccard had been a member of the Turin academy of sciences and Bobba announced the discovery of a letter from Paccard at the Biblioteca Civica. Paccard "was an Italian Sardinian at the time of his exploit and that was the reason why Italians were keen to honor him on this day, because he was one of them."[54] Speaking in French, Dübi reflected on his ascents with Chamonix guides and paid tribute to the detective work of Freshfield, Montagnier, and Whymper. The lesson he drew from the first ascent was to be wary of legend and search for the truth: "The truth was on the march and today the Paccard-Balmat controversy is closed: a long struggle ends in a state of affairs where there are no winners or losers, only the convinced."[55] The mayor announced that Chamonix had renamed a recently renovated square *Place Jacques Balmat* and one of the main streets would become *Rue du Docteur Paccard;* a street in Argentière was to be rechristened *Rue Jean Charlet-Straton,* "in honor of the first conqueror of the Dru."[56] At a separate ceremony, those in the Company of Guides were honored as the newest members of the French National Rescue Federation with a plaque listing all of the guides who had died in the mountains. A military governor from Lyon reviewed the assembled alpine troops enrolled at the École de Haute Montagne in Chamonix and warmly praised the work of the guides.

In *La Montagne*, Charles Albert Savine, a Chamonix artist, regretted that Paccard left few traces in the valley. At his funeral, Paccard's name was spoken in a whisper and his tombstone was destroyed while being carved. This destiny had followed him into the grave: "When the old cemetery was abandoned in Chamonix and the graves moved into a new field, some years ago, Dr. Paccard was not found. His ashes are now scattered forever in the land below the bell tower of the old church." Paccard's home had disappeared and its place was taken by a hotel and later a fountain. The medallion was a fitting tribute to the first conqueror of Mont Blanc: "Dr. Paccard has entered into history: the wait was long, the hour of justice has finally come."[57]

NOVEL DEVELOPMENTS

"What matters is not the gold but Balmat's prune-stones," confessed Dan Yack, the narrator of a 1929 novel by Blaise Cendrars. Cendrars, a Swiss-born writer who lost an arm and gained French citizenship while serving in the Great War, framed his modernist novel as a series of cylinders, rather than chapters, representing recordings he made into a Dictaphone. In the fourth cylinder, Dan Yack sees an Englishman whose guide invites him to join their ascent of Mont Blanc. The guide, le Géant, was the great-great-nephew of Jacques Balmat, *dit* le Mont-Blanc, which prompts Yack to record a story told by the guides and porters. When Balmat first reached the summit of Mont Blanc by himself, he had three prunes in his pocket and "buried them in the snow to testify to his exploit." For a century, guides had looked for them without success. During the excavation of the Janssen observatory, workmen uncovered the prune stones, which prompted a battle among the villagers: "Everyone wanted to appropriate these relics, to which the mountaineers attributed talismanic virtues of protection and good luck."[58]

Despite this prophecy, the prune stones fostered vendettas, and calamity seemed to haunt whoever possessed them. The first man to own them was killed stalking chamois. During the next twenty years, he was followed by three brothers who perished on Mont Maudit; Lombard *dit* Jorasse was found hanged in the chapel at Les Tines; and three guides died on the mountain after taking possession of the prune stones: "The guides and porters, who are all superstitious men, lay the blame for these 'misfortunes' at the door of science and that damned scientist who went and set up an observatory on Mont Blanc." In the valley, Janssen was called "The Devil" and women crossed themselves at the mention of his name. Yack's own guide, Marie Coutet, had carried the prune stones in his waistcoat pocket since 1914: "He's a distrustful man, a grimacing savage, the only guide without a license but he knows the mountain like the back of his hand." When the observatory was being built, Coutet carried the heaviest lens of the telescope to the summit and Janssen himself chained Coutet to the lens and the other guides to their cargo. When Coutet reached the summit, "he didn't know how to give vent to his rage and contempt, so he used his ice-axe to cut the word SHIT in gigantic letters in the frozen snow. Then he fell on his knees and passed out." Yack thought Coutet had his revenge on Janssen "by becoming master of Balmat's three prune-stones." However, "less than three weeks ago he was found crushed beneath a pine tree he had just cut down. It was alleged to be an accident. Nobody knows what has become of the three prune-stones. His waistcoat pocket was empty."[59]

The scene ends when Yack refuses the offer to join the ascent by telling the guide he had just come back from there, all alone: "I can still see them decamping, and I laugh out loud in front of my dictaphone, as I laughed on that day." Rather than asking whether the events in Cendrars's novel really happened, it is more productive to inquire what point he was trying to make.[60] Cendrars mocked not only the mountaineers but also the empiricist historians who thought they knew the definitive "Historical Truth." In 1926, Cendrars responded to historical critics of *L'Or* (translated into English as *Sutter's Gold*), his novel about Johann Sutter and the California gold rush. Cendrars's rejection of "Historical Truth" was enmeshed with his simultaneous refusal of the panoramic perspective from the summit: "The Historical Truth is the point of view of Sirius. We can no longer distinguish anything from that height. We must descend, come closer, take a close-up. See. At close quarters. Lean in and look into. Put a finger on. Discover the human. The Historical Truth is death."[61]

Cendrars preferred the messy contradictions of life to the false objectivity of truth. In a scathing tone, Cendrars mocked the "archive rats" nibbling away at documents in dusty piles. The historian, even when recounting events from centuries ago, was always part of the story and is "insufferable or ridiculous so long as he believes himself in sole possession of the Truth." Rivalry between schools and divergent interpretations of a single text rendered the notion of truth problematic. Nevertheless, Cendrars admired the way historians "sort and select, and by grinding to dust and sleight of hand retract certain troublesome documents that fall outside their theories, especially when it comes to a national hero, and it became imperative to cut him down to size, to the size of convention and school lessons since a statue was raised to him."[62] Scholars and academics were no better than the authors of swashbuckling novels in finding the human in life. Before any commemoration as a national hero, "he was above all a human being, that is to say, a breath, a heart, with lung, five senses, one brain, reflexes, a thousand shimmering impressions of timidity and ignorance and helplessness and fear. That is what I want to put a finger on." Novels and films in the 1920s and 1930s sought to bring this Balmat and Paccard to life and considered their efforts to be equal to contemporary historians. The multiple representations of the first ascent by historians, novelists, and filmmakers were all novel forms of modern mythmaking.

Consider *Jacques Balmat du Mont-Blanc* (1929), an award-winning novel by Charles Rochat-Cenise. Born in Switzerland in 1899, Rochat-Cenise was based in Paris as a journalist between the wars and returned to Lausanne in 1939. He was sympathetic to guides, a standpoint summarized in the title of a later book about his native Swiss valley, *Paysans que nous sommes*. Rochat-

Cenise's Mont Blanc novel unfolds from 1775, when four Chamoniards try to climb the peak and the young Balmat dreams of making the ascent himself. Balmat sells crystals to Johann Wolfgang von Goethe and searches for a route to the summit with the goal of being first. In June 1786, Balmat "thought of nothing, his mind was occupied by a single great will," and he promised those who mocked him: " 'I will have it, this white molehill!' " After guides abandon Balmat, he discovers the route. Neither Saussure nor Bourrit would agree to go only with him, so he asks Dr. Paccard. During their ascent, Balmat arrives alone on the summit to raise his arms and cry out his name. Paccard then appears suddenly on the top and only a flashback explains that Balmat had descended to Paccard and pulled him to the summit.[63]

The novel is framed as a reinterpretation of documents in favor of Balmat. In October 1786, Paccard supplies Balmat with wine before asking him to sign a statement, which he refuses when he realizes that Paccard gave himself the leading role: "Ah! How can you write this, write these lies when you know the truth? Sign this! You make me laugh, Doctor!" Paccard agrees to write that they collaborated as brave men and Balmat signs a blank sheet. After publication, Balmat confronts him over the duplicitous certificates and Paccard strikes him with an umbrella. Balmat gets his revenge with another note from the archives when the intendant writes to send his reward and confer a veritable title of nobility. Balmat searches for gold in the Alps and is not discouraged, but shouts, "Bien le temps!" After losing his fortune to swindling bankers, Balmat meets celebrities and disappears while searching for gold: "So often conquered, the mountain this time takes its vengeance."[64]

Rochat-Cenise's novel was praised and criticized in equal measure. "The Mont Blanc novel by Rochat-Cenise is a work of art," declared the *Journal de Genève,* and *Le Petit Dauphinois* in Grenoble awarded it the "Prix des Alpes Française" in 1930. Gaillard warned that the book was amusing, but based on a legend that had been overturned. A Swiss Alpine Club reviewer applauded the book as "one of the finest we have on the history of the mountain. It is a beautiful tribute to a montagnard rendered by an alpinist."[65] Such truth claims in his own club's journal deeply upset Heinrich Dübi, who lamented "it seems to be my fate to fight legends" and offered a point-by-point rebuttal. Dübi enumerated his objections and offered a mock apology: "The reader will excuse the dryness of my deductions in the interest of historical truth." In reply, Charles Pasquine, a French climber, chided Dübi for not giving credit in his own dispute over priority. "In the interest of historical truth," Pasquine wanted to recall that Charles Mathews and Henri Ferrand "were among the first to attempt the rehabilitation of the Chamonix doctor."[66]

PACCARD OR BALMAT, FRIENDS OF NATURE

A more ambitious novel was Karl Ziak's *Paccard oder Balmat? Ein Mont-Blanc Roman* (1930), based on the socialist critique of capitalism and a psychological perspective on the self. Ziak was born in 1902 in Ottakring, a working-class district of Vienna, and came of age when Social Democrats governed "Red Vienna" from 1918. He received his doctorate at the University of Vienna in 1927 and served until 1942 as secretary of the Volksheim, an adult education center. He later became editor for a publishing firm and director of Büchergilde Gutenberg, a populist book club. Ziak was introduced to the mountains by the tourist association Die Naturfreunde, a social democratic hiking club that promoted "social hiking" in contrast to the mountaineering of the German and Austrian Alpine Club.[67]

Ziak wrote historical articles for *Der Naturfreund,* including sociological remarks on the history of mountaineering in 1927: "If real alpinism must be called a phenomenon of modern times, so proletarian climbers—apart from exceptions of course—emerged only in recent decades, indeed perhaps only in the last decade." The development of middle-class mountaineering became possible "only after liberation from the constraints of princes." The English and Swiss became alpine pioneers because the puritanical bourgeoisie in each country achieved early exemptions from princely rule. The ascent of Mont Blanc in 1786, just before the storming of the Bastille, was evidence of "a new class competing for supremacy over Europe at the behest of Saussure, a Swiss professor from Geneva." Yet Ziak thought it remarkable that the ascent was made by Balmat to earn a cash prize: "We see then the wealthy bourgeoisie's early exploitation of the commercially available power of the proletariat in this area, as happened in the factory and in war." Bourgeois mountaineering proceeded from the ascents of great height to imperial conquest of territory ("evident today in efforts to climb Chomolungma") and finally to ascents by routes that promoted the competition preached by liberalism. The proletarian mountaineer sought "not a substitute for political freedom, not competition, not satisfaction of imperialist lust for power, but the spontaneity of a natural life which the city makes impossible for him."[68]

Ziak fictionalized Balmat's snow bivouac for a Vienna mountaineering newspaper and expanded the story into *Paccard oder Balmat* in 1930.[69] Ziak was more interested in "the tragic figure of Paccard" than the adventurous figure of "Jacob Balmat," an inventive storyteller. The young Balmat relocates the biblical story of "Jacob's ladder" to Chamonix, imagines Windham and Pococke as the visit of the Magi to the glaciers, and repeats stories of the cursed mountain and fairies protecting its gold mines. By contrast, Paccard was educated at Geneva and Paris, where he debated ideas of the *philosophes* with classmates. Bourrit waxes lyrical about the wonders of Chamonix and views Paccard as a typical Chamoniard for ignoring them: "If it depended on you, Mont Blanc would be right under your nose for centuries to come, and it would not occur to you to climb it."[70] Paccard decides to climb Mont Blanc out of duty to science and has no doubt the mountain can be climbed: " 'Does not science advance—although slowly—steadily forward, upward? Its progress is unstoppable and it will no more stop short before Mont Blanc than it shrank back from the Cordilleras of South America. Just wait! When the time comes, the men for Mont Blanc will also be found.' And with the calm of one who has learned from the philosophers to feel a part of the universe, in which the life of an individual is only a building block in the work of eternity, he let events come to him and did the duty of his daily life." Paccard was inspired by Bourrit and Saussure's failed attempts to climb the peak, but desired neither fame nor financial reward for himself: "What drives me to the mountains is the desire to know nature."[71]

Ziak presents Paccard and Balmat as alienated from one another. On the night before their ascent, Balmat looked at the sleeping Paccard: "Again, as on several occasions over the past two months, Balmat was aware of the abyss between them. But it was clear to him only now that he hated the doctor in secret, because he was of a different nature. The 'man of science'! Jacob sneered." They approached the summit together with heads bowed against the winds, but everything changed when they reached the top: "From the moment they stepped on the summit and were no longer threatened by danger, any community that still existed between them dissolved. As if they had never done the venture together, each was a separate universe, whose center was Mont Blanc, which their thoughts circled on separate paths."[72]

Balmat and Paccard succeeded in the ascent, but failed in love. Goethe turned down an offer to see gold and crystals by telling Balmat: "I am not eager for such treasures. Gold and precious stones are not the prerequisite for happiness. It is love that makes us rich, the love that we receive, and even more, that we give. Do you still not know that?" Balmat was puzzled by the question, and married Johanna Maria, whom he disappointed more and more: "What he could give her was nothing but the power of sex—and even this was more a transaction than a gift—he could not satisfy the yearning of the soul." According to Ziak, Paccard fell in love with Angelica, a revolutionary firebrand, but initially refused to abandon his patients for politics. After they married, she still worshiped Napoleon and was disappointed by Paccard. Only much later, after his wife demanded that he defend his reputation, did Paccard claim he discovered the route to Mont Blanc by telescope, "but it was with such timid voice, that nobody noticed him and finally he even doubted himself and fell into deeper depression than before."[73]

Ziak collected his historical essays from *Die Naturfreund* in a history of mountaineering that summarized the ascent and referred readers to his "factual novel" for details. Both the novel and the historical survey toned down the "vulgar Marxism" of his earlier sociological essay. In each telling, Ziak asserted its broader relevance. In *Der Mensch und die Berge* (1936), Ziak wrote that "mountaineering is not independent of time and space *(Lebensraum)*; like philosophy and art it is inextricably linked with the overall culture of an epoch." The glory of the first ascent went not to the warrior or merchant, poet or painter, priest or professor, but to a peasant boy from Chamonix: "It is still often the case that gentlemen follow footsteps prepared for them by a peasant's hands." The Balmat-Paccard dispute extended for decades and each had supporters after their deaths. As noted by Ziak, "This is the first example of how the mountains can make rivals of men, and unfortunately, it is not the only one."[74]

The novel asserted a link between the ascent and the French Revolution as an epochal break. In *Paccard oder Balmat,* Paccard was a moderate revolutionary while Balmat hid in the hills with supporters of the monarchy. For Paccard, the revolution drowned out the petty dispute over the first ascent:

For what was the dormant war over the mountain in comparison to the struggle for human rights! And yet when Paccard thought about it, an internal link existed between the conquest of the highest pinnacle of Europe and the storming of the Bastille. It seemed no coincidence that both had happened within the span of a few years. The development of mankind, he thought, manifests itself in different ways. What we have done—that we were not afraid of the spirits of the mountains, not trembling before the violence of the elements—was as much a break with the Middle Ages as the abolition of torture and serfdom: and he remembered the days in Paris when he met Achilles at Bourrit's place, and how they spoke of the freedom of the mountains.[75]

Paccard's humility is the keynote of Ziak's novel, which portrayed him as a "Friend of Nature" *avant la lettre*. He offered this humility as an object lesson for the climbers of his own day, who approached the Alps and Himalayas in search of personal glory. In a deathbed scene, Paccard apologized to his wife for disappointing her: "I could have been a famous man. But, you see, a man cannot go beyond his strength. My fate was to be content with what fell into my lap." He had loved Angelica since they first met, but never would have tried to win her by force. She would not have become his wife if she had not first extended her hand to him. "So it was on the mountains. I always loved them, but I never would have conquered Mont Blanc if fate had not chosen me for it. I know, not everyone is like me and maybe there will be many who still use the sacred heights as the battlefield for their glory. Therefore, I will not chide them, for I do not wish to be chided by them. But, you see, I hope there are also men coming for whom the mountains are nothing but a Fountain of Youth for the soul."[76]

THE ETERNAL DREAM

Loud applause filled the Ufa-Palast am Zoo, Berlin's largest cinema, on November 20, 1934, after the premiere of *Der ewige Traum* (The Eternal Dream) a feature film about the first ascent of Mont Blanc, directed by Dr. Arnold Fanck. This was the latest of Fanck's Bergfilme, a genre featuring skiing and mountaineering that the geologist-turned-filmmaker had popularized during the previous decade. His most successful mountain films introduced a love interest, often with characters played by Leni Reifenstahl and Luis Trenker, who became stars and directors of their own films. After a drama about a rescue mission in Greenland, Fanck had not planned another mountain film until he read Karl Ziak's novel and bought the film rights. Fanck planned a film pitting man versus nature based only on historical facts, yet he reserved the right to use artistic license: "Neither a play nor a film nor a novel can render a historical process precisely in accordance with the former reality. The laws of dramaturgical form alone oppose it."[77]

Fanck rapidly wrote a screenplay at a mountain retreat in 1932, and it was immediately accepted by the producers Gregor Rabinowitsch and Arnold Pressburger for Cine-Allianz. Under the working title of *Das ewige Gold,* Fanck shot the film for eight months in 1933 on location at Mont Blanc in France, the Jungfraujoch in Switzerland, and a studio in Germany. The film crew spent long periods at high altitude and considered the two weeks filming at the Vallot Hut to be torture, calling it "Fancksches Konzentrationslager" (Fanck's concentration camp).[78] The hut had been the focal point of *Storm over Mont Blanc* (1931), Fanck's first sound film, which starred Riefenstahl with Sepp Rist, a Nuremberg policeman who played a meteorologist whose electric lights prompted the Vienna weekly *Der Bergsteiger* to call his character "a modern man of our time."[79] In the new film, Fanck cast Rist as Jacques Balmat and Brigitte Horney as his love interest, Maria.

After the opening credits, the scene is set for *Der ewige Traum,* which had the alternate title *Der König vom Montblanc* (The King of Mont Blanc):

> This film freely describes the history of the first ascent of Mont Blanc. At that time, people still looked up with superstitious fear to the eternal ice of the mountains. Then a farmer from Chamonix—Jacques Balmat, a contemporary of Goethe—overcame his own horror of the spirits of the mountain and, with a fanatical belief in large gold fields at the top, conquered the highest mountain in Europe. With this heroic deed he became the real founder of Alpinism, and ever since many millions owe to him the happiness and freedom felt in mountain climbing.[80]

Dramatis personae are listed as Balmat the boy and man, Maria, Paccard, and the mountain itself, Mont Blanc.

The film enters a modernist *banque d'état* (state bank) and descends to reveal vaults of gold bars. A close-up image of Napoleon on an ingot dissolves into the general on horseback, instructing his troops in the Alps. Napoleon salutes Mont Blanc on the route to Italy and announces, "There we will find glory, gold and power." The young Jacques Balmat asks: "What does the General want?" His father replies, "He wants to be the most powerful man," and tells the boy that the riches of the summit are guarded by spirits. A determined look comes over Jacques Balmat, as the boy's face dissolves into the man. The grown Balmat whispers "gold" and confides his dream of riches to Maria. Guides mock him as a liar and "king of Mont Blanc," which starts a brawl in which Balmat tosses one of them into a cart filled with manure.

A sign above the door of Balmat's home reads: *Das Gold ist die Macht* (Gold is power). At the Mer de Glace, Balmat meets Goethe while Paccard talks to Saussure. Balmat tells Goethe that the mountains have gold, and the poet writes that love is the real gold on a sketch and gives it to Balmat. Saussure announces an award of 1,000 louis d'or to reach the summit. Balmat and Maria look at a crystal and Goethe's sketch, and she has to pull his hair to break his obsession with the peak. They share a moment of intimacy as mists cover the peaks and smoke issues from a chimney. After a comical interlude in which a painter struggles on the Mer de Glace, Paccard climbs with several guides and encounters Balmat. The other guides collapse, but Balmat continues alone. Paccard sketches the avalanche corridor as the "key to Mont Blanc" and descends with the other guides.

Despite wind and snow, Balmat continues until he sees glowing words floating in the air reading "Woe to the One" *(Wehe dem einen)*. Terrified, he finds shelter in a snow cave and sees visions of a cross. Maria prays in a mountain chapel and Balmat is spared. When the weather clears, Balmat sees an avalanche and carves into a rock: "Key to Mt. Blanc. J.B. The liar!" He returns to the village, where he assumes a pose of crucifixion when he finds Maria in the church. Balmat lives with Maria and awaits the harvest and birth of their child, telling Paccard that his farmer's scythe has replaced his climber's ice ax. This domestic bliss is interrupted when a figure standing in the doorway casts the shadow of a cross over their daily bread and tells Balmat that Paccard is planning to climb Mont Blanc with an Englishman. Paccard receives Balmat in his cabinet of natural history and they agree to go together.

During the ascent, Balmat and Paccard show each other the same "key" to Mont Blanc and quickly reach the top. In Chamonix, crowds cheer, bells peal, and children rush to the town square. Hearing the commotion, Maria stumbles to the threshold of the house where she collapses: "Oh, Jacques, the child." On the summit, the climbers hear the celebratory bells interrupted by a death knell. Balmat cries "Maria!" and descends, as villagers batten windows as if from a storm. Jacques finds the crib covered with a shroud and Maria convalescing in bed. As he comforts her, a savant loudly counts gold coins in the next room. Balmat tosses the coins on the floor and kicks the man out. You are my gold he tells Maria, and a close-up of the poet's note reiterates the message: the true gold is love.

A month before the Berlin premiere, the film was screened for Joseph Goebbels, head of the Ministry of Propaganda after the Nazis came to power in 1933. Under the policy of Gleichschaltung, the enforced coordination of cultural life, all films were submitted to censors. Fanck recalled showing the film to Goebbels, who asked bluntly: "Was it necessary to celebrate a French national hero?" Fanck replied: "Balmat was Savoyard, not French, Herr Minister. Savoy was not French until much later. And the fact is the first man to climb Mont Blanc was not German!" Goebbels told him he should have set the film on a German mountain, but Fanck retorted that he made all his mountain films at four thousand meters or more and could not suddenly make a film on the Zugspitze: "I can still see the faces of the SS men standing around, petrified at my daring to contradict."[81] Almost forty years later, when he wanted to distance himself from the Nazi regime, Fanck may have employed the same artistic license he used in his screenplay. Some have wanted to believe Fanck, but lament there were no other witnesses. In fact, Goebbels recorded in his diary that he watched three films on October 21, 1934: the first was good and brisk, the second was rubbish, and "*Ewige Traum,* a marvelous mountain film by Fanck. Then good propaganda films by our department. Many great debates here at home. The whole ministry involved. For me, very instructive."[82]

Der ewige Traum gestured toward National Socialist iconography, but received mixed reviews. The criticism of "gold" was consistent with the Nazi critique of capitalism and the anti-Semitic campaign. Balmat and his scythe matched the "blood and soil" imagery in the same issue of *Völkisher Beobachter,* the official Nazi paper that reviewed the film after its Munich premiere. The review praised the grandeur of the mountain, but criticized its portrayal of fear and superstition. *Reichsfilmblatt,* the organ of cinema owners, agreed that "the fusion of human and spiritual conflicts with the battle for the mountain is not always completely successful in the script."[83] The plot was criticized by *Film-Kurier* in Berlin, *Pour Vous* in Paris, and by *La Stampa* in Turin, which was annoyed at the anachronisms (Goethe and

Napoleon) but admired its pantheism and melodrama. *Lichtbild-Bühne* thought the historic facts, apart from the love story, were reasonably fair, and *Cinemonde* noted "the many controversies surrounding this event and the disputes that opposed Balmat to Doctor Paccard. The recent commemoration of this feat in Chamonix gives additional interest to this grandiose film whose historical value, setting, plot, and interpretation won unqualified approval."[84]

CINEMATIC THRESHOLDS

Der ewige Traum was situated chronologically and politically on a threshold: written in the last year of the Weimar regime, filmed as the National Socialists took office, and released after the Nazi state aggressively regulated the production and distribution of films. Indeed, Nazi rules for the film industry required Cine-Allianz to "Aryanize," and its Jewish producers left Berlin for Paris. When *Rêve éternel, le roi du Mont Blanc*, appeared dubbed in French in 1935, Rabinowitsch and Pressburger were restored to the credits and the film enjoyed two successful runs in Paris.[85] Fanck joined the Reich Film Chamber in 1933, as was required of all German filmmakers, but declined to join the Nazi Party until 1940. His decision to join was not just opportunism, as his letters from that period express a German patriotism, anti-Semitism, admiration for Hitler, and support for the German war effort.[86] Yet the threshold occupied by this film was not merely political, but marked a transitional moment in the assertion of will in mountaineering and modernity.

Consider Fanck's promotional essay, "Who was Jacques Balmat?" Charles Lindbergh's solo flight in 1927 had proved again "that all peoples love a hero, and the urge to hero worship, is deeply rooted in general human attributes" despite the claims of "modern literature" in this "snobbish degenerate age." The same wave of admiration had swept the world in 1786. They knew nothing of modern climbing technology, but Jacques Balmat knew only the goal above his village: "Without all the tools he trusted only one thing—his own power to achieve that goal." The main promotional poster for the film similarly depicted Balmat as a modern man, alone with head bowed ascending through windblown snow (Figure 21). Balmat's motives were "not as idealistic as centuries ago when the Italian poet Petrarch, the first man, climbed a high mountain from the conscious inner urge to be nearer to his

Figure 21 A promotional poster for *Der ewige Traum,* 1934, shows Jacques Balmat struggling against the elements as he ascends Mont Blanc alone. Deutsches Filminstitut DIF e.V., Frankfurt.

God. Still less were there scientific reasons, as there were for Paccard." Instead, Balmat's search for gold on the summit was associated with folktales and then Saussure's reward: "Now real, tangible gold was up there, and nothing more could stop a certain Jacques Balmat from being the first." Fanck hoped the film would show what it meant for a superstitious mountain farmer to overcome the spirits of the mountain and penetrate the eternal ice when even naturalists and travelers recoiled from the mountains. Fanck reiterated that he interpreted his sources freely since it would have been impossible to include the decadelong history of the ascent in a feature-length film.[87]

How should this political threshold be interpreted? The politics of German mountaineering and Bergfilme have been widely debated. The early adoption of anti-Semitic policies by the Deutscher und Österreichischer Alpenverein (DÖAV) has been viewed by some as evidence of Germany's "special path" to the Hitler state.[88] The Great War in the Tyrolean Alps transformed rhetoric about mountaineering as a struggle with nature into a battle between men for the "holy mountain."[89] After the war, some wanted the Alpenverein to become a paramilitary organization to restore the nation's strength and will. Certain club sections had approved anti-Semitic policies to exclude Jews or require Germanic origins as early as the 1890s, and these "Aryan paragraphs" were adopted more widely within the club in 1921. A section for Jewish mountaineers was expelled in 1924. Although the anti-Semitic Right predominated in the DÖAV, German and Austrian mountaineering was not the preserve of one political party before 1933. After taking office, however, the Nazis abolished Die Naturfreunde and incorporated the DÖAV into the state. A Reichssportführer appointed a climber to direct a mountaineering department of the state and sponsor mountaineering expeditions.[90]

As early as the 1940s, German mountaineering and the Weimar Bergfilme were condemned by Sigfried Kracauer as preparation for Hitler's rise to power. Mountaineers were said to be devotees of a cult, the Bergfilme "rooted in a mentality kindred to Nazi spirit," and the success of mountain films indicated a "surge of pro-Nazi tendencies."[91] Since then, such totalizing approaches to "Nazi film" have come under scrutiny, and films before and during Nazi rule appear to be more complex documents capable of contradictory readings. In the most substantial reinterpretation of the Bergfilme, Eric Rentschler noted that mountain films were popular across the political spectrum and indebted to cinematic melodrama, modernist conventions, and romantic landscape painting.[92] The blend of mountains and machines, sentiment and rationality anticipated the Nazi synthesis of romanticism and technology, and the worship of nature was remolded to reflect a reactionary modernism and romantic anticapitalism. In this light, Riefenstahl's *The Blue Light* (1932) is viewed as enacting "the dialectics of enlightenment."[93] One could go further and argue that these films were not "anti-modern" any more than the German idea of Heimat, the "essential modernity" of which has been obscured by the supposed antiquity of a distinctly modern concept that mediated local, provincial, and national categories of citizenship and belonging.[94] Indeed, the Heimatfilme and Bergfilme should be understood not as opposing Heimat or the mountains to modernity but rather as embedding each deeply in the other.[95]

Der ewige Traum entangled self, state, and the mountain, yet too much commentary, following Kracauer's example, remains trapped in outmoded ways of thinking about the Nazi state or narrowly psychoanalytic discourses of the "self." This film has been read as filled with father figures and motherly females with readings of Balmat's snow cave as an escape into the womb or exemplifying sexual frustrations.[96] By contrast, the religious connotations of Fanck's films have gone largely unremarked.[97] Balmat's embrace of love over greed, Maria's prayers, Balmat's crosses, and their devotion after leaving the church embodied the faithfulness of a personalized religion. Fanck and Trenker made films that projected religiosity as a reconciliation of tradition and modernity, but this theme is overlooked in interpretations of the dialectic of enlightenment. When Balmat sees visions of "Woe to the One" as he shivers on the ice, he is confronted with the quotation from Ecclesiastes (4:10) that two are better than one: "But woe to the one, when he falls, and no one else is there to lift him up. Also, if two lie together, they are warm. But how can one be warm alone?"[98]

Fanck examined the legacy of his oeuvre in an essay on "the beginning and end of my Alpine filmmaking" in 1935. His early film *Mountain of Destiny* (1924) had probed first principles: "The will to struggle—one of the basic motives of all mountain-climbing—drove him to ask the heroic question: 'Shall the hill be stronger than I?'" Since then, all his mountain films attempted to answer the question asked by his first wife: "'And what do you see up there?' This was the first great question that my wife from the sea asked the mountain climber. 'Myself' was the equally concise and substantive response she received. But this still did not satisfy her. She asked more in-depth:

'And nothing else?'" Fanck staged the first question and response as a scene in *The Holy Mountain* (1926), and wrote in this essay that the final intertitle of that film also answered the second: "So shone above his holy mountain, the greatest word that stands above the human race: faithfulness!"[99]

For Fanck, *Der ewige Traum* represented the end of the Bergfilme genre and the end of an era of mountaineering:

> The phenomenon of mountaineering in its romantic guise is at an end, and so too the romantic alpine film, which I created and had to create in these 16 years of work. Its last representative—the Jacques Balmat film, *Der ewige Traum*—could no longer have the broad resonance of its predecessors, despite the fact that it was by far the most skillful in terms of the screenplay, casting and design, and also visually surpassed all the wonderful images we had already brought down from the high mountains.

The categorical imperative of duty, the heroic conception of life, the camaraderie of the mountains, and victory of little man over great nature depicted in the *White Hell of Pitz Palü* lived on "in the memories of countless people, almost like a legend," but they could no longer be repeated. "The romantic times of mountaineering are irrevocably over. A new generation now faces the mountain in a completely different frame of mind. Equally enthusiastic, perhaps, and strong willed—but infinitely more prosaic. I would almost say: 'more brash,' because it seems to me that there is less awe before nature among today's generation."[100]

At the very moment that Leni Riefenstahl depicted the Nuremberg rallies as the *Triumph of the Will* (1935), Fanck called this possibility into question in the mountains. Fanck dismissed Riefenstahl's *Blue Light* as "cinematic dilettantism," and his remarks suggest that he did not think much of the climbers who laid siege to the Eiger, Nanga Parbat, or Everest. In 1936, Karl Ziak thought Fanck's film based on his book was "not completely successful," but mountain films had a great future and "this new territory of art is far from exhausted."[101] Trenker made further mountain films in the 1930s, even though Fanck turned his attention elsewhere. The mountain film genre persisted in German films about Himalayan expeditions into the 1950s and beyond.[102] *Der ewige Traum* was less the end of an era than located on a threshold. After the Second World War, amid the slow dissolution of empires, it became problematic to depict mountaineering as the triumph of national or individual will. Problematic, perhaps, but not impossible, and even many years later it remains unclear whether this threshold is one that can ever be fully crossed or put entirely into the past.

In 1950, Karl Ziak reissued his novel under a new title, *Der König des Mont Blanc.* Conscripted into the German army, he survived the Second World War by sheer luck. Ziak wrote a "pastoral chapter" for the Mont Blanc novel while stationed in Austria in the autumn of 1943, and revised other chapters after his release from captivity as a prisoner of war. The new edition brought the novel closer to Fanck's film in certain respects and added material to enrich its historical context. Ziak added a passage to post-war editions of the novel to explain more clearly Paccard's indifference to his own reputation. Paccard had been elected to public office during the revolutionary state and thus stepped "on the first rung of the ladder," which could have elevated him out of his circumstances as village doctor, "but he lacked Achilles's motivation, he lacked Angelika's eyes, he lacked above all the will to power, and the art of making something of himself."[103]

CHAPTER NINE

Almost Together

CEREMONIES OF POSSESSION

"Reading the long accepted myth of Dr. [Michel-Gabriel] Paccard being supported by his companion [Jacques] Balmat to the highest point, after the latter had returned from the top to fetch him," wrote Brigadier Sir John Hunt in the preface to *The First Ascent of Mont Blanc* (1957), "I was reminded of the illustrations of an unconscious Hillary, being dragged hand over hand by the rope, to the summit of Everest by conquering Tenzing (who had no such notion), which adorned the triumphal arches along the road as we returned to Kathmandu four years ago."[1] As Colonel Hunt, he had led the British Mount Everest expedition in which New Zealander Edmund Hillary and Sherpa Tenzing Norgay reached the world's highest summit on May 29, 1953. With some luck and a message in secret code, the expedition relayed news of the ascent to London for publication on June 2, the day of Queen Elizabeth II's coronation.

News of the conquest of Everest gave the crowds waiting in the rain for the coronation parade "a lovely warm feeling inside to think that we, the

British, had got there first."[2] After the Queen's gilded royal coach rolled through archways to and from her coronation at Westminster Abbey, she waved to the crowd from the balcony of Buckingham Palace. "Seldom since Francis Drake brought the Gold Hind to anchor in Plymouth Sound," exulted the London *Times,* "has a British explorer offered to his Sovereign such a tribute of glory as Colonel John Hunt and his men are able to lay at the feet of Queen Elizabeth for her Coronation day."[3] Prime Minister Winston Churchill introduced the Queen's broadcast that evening by telling a worldwide audience: "Let it not be thought that the age of Chivalry belongs in the past. Here at the summit of our worldwide community is a lady." The Queen's remarks drew strength from the living strength and majesty of the Commonwealth and empire, a people "of lands and races different in history and origins but all, by God's Will, united in spirit and in aim."[4]

"A procession in London, another in Central Asia" intoned *The Conquest of Everest* (1953), as the opening scenes of the official expedition film cut from the coronation parade to processions in Nepal that it artfully spliced together. Tenzing was given a place of honor in a state carriage in Kathmandu, while Hunt and Hillary were obscured by flowers. The streets were crowded with people, spanned by banners, and filled with shouts of *Tenzing, Zindabad!* (Long Live Tenzing!). Tenzing was depicted on posters, planting the Nepali flag on top with one hand while dragging Hillary on the rope with the other. The procession ended at the royal palace where Tenzing, Hillary, and Hunt waved to the crowd from the balcony.

The controversies on Everest resembled earlier disputes on Mont Blanc and other peaks. When news of the conquest of Everest was providentially released on coronation morning, some commentators echoed Antoine de Ville's ascent of Mont Inaccessible on behalf of his sovereign. Others viewed the conquest of Everest as elevating Tenzing into the sovereign position. Even if the Everest disputes resembled those on Mont Blanc, the 1953 conundrums were rooted in the revision of sovereignty and masculinity at this particular postcolonial moment at the height of the Cold War. In the aftermath of the ascent, Tenzing, Hillary, and Hunt were appropriated by multiple nations. Parallels between the two ascents created a time knot that inspired alpine historians to rewrite the earlier history. Somewhat paradoxically, Hillary and Tenzing recast the legacy of Paccard and Balmat. Multiple parallels between the two events appeared obvious at the time: proposals to rename the peak, subscriptions to reward the poor guide, and notarized certificates to settle the question of who was first.

Within days of the Everest news, the British government announced
knighthoods for Hillary and Hunt and its intention to honor Tenzing once
his nationality was determined. Tenzing had spent his youth in Nepal, but
lived for twenty years in India. Other proposals to honor the ascent included
postage stamps and renaming the peak. The *Daily Herald*, a conservative,
working-class London newspaper that later became the *Sun*, argued that "all
the Western world" would welcome renaming the peak Mount Elizabeth:
"No race has a better claim to write into the history books a wonderful success story." In India, letter columns debated multiple proposals for mountain eponymy. An Indian newspaper poll went against "Mount Elizabeth" in
favor of "Mount Tenzing" as the new name for Mount Everest, with support
for combinations such as "Tenhillary," "Hillarsing," and "Hilltenhunt."[5]

Tenzing's citizenship was uncertain, but his humble origins were unmis-
takable. The government of Nepal announced that it would honor Tenzing
with an award and a cash prize of 10,000 rupees (about £500), an amount
that dwarfed the average Nepali income of 300 rupees a year.[6] Newspapers
in London and New York reported Tenzing's "dream is to build a house for
his old age," but noted that as sirdar, leader of the porters and high-altitude
Sherpas, he was paid 225 rupees a month (less than £17, or about $48 a
month) plus a daily allowance on the mountain.[7] Newspapers around the
world published stories about Tenzing's ascent from illiterate coolie to the
summit of Everest, the indispensable part played by the Sherpas, and his poverty in Darjeeling. An Indian schoolgirl sent the president of India 25 rupees as a gift for Tenzing and money soon poured in to subscription funds
in India. In Calcutta, the *Statesman* raised 12,000 rupees for a house for
Tenzing and an equal amount for other Sherpas. Tenzing's wife told report-
ers that he earned very little from mountaineering: "I am glad that the world
acclaims him, but that is a poor consolation for his poverty." The *Statesman*
published a photograph of a street in the Sherpa neighborhood in Darjeeling with the caption: "Not fit for heroes—it is to homes like these that some
Sherpa porters return from their mountaineering."[8]

In Nepal, poems were sung, dances performed, and banners unfurled. A
Nepali poet, Dharma Raj Thapa, composed "Hamro Tenzing Sherpa" (Our
Tenzing Sherpa), which was sung in the streets.[9] Tenzing was asked to sign
papers he could not read certifying that he was Nepali, not Indian, and that
he reached the summit before Hillary. Hunt said that Tenzing did not know
what he was signing. Tenzing was put under police protection after he was
threatened with violence unless he signed further statements. At public

ceremonies in Nepal, Hillary was invited to say a few words as "the second man on Everest."[10]

Who was first? Within hours, stories circulated that Tenzing reached the summit before Hillary. The London *Daily Mail* reported the following version from Kathmandu: "Tenzing was the first to reach the summit. Hillary broke down, exhausted, while Tenzing climbed on alone and reached the top. Then Tenzing went back and helped Hillary to reach the peak so that Tenzing got to the top twice." After Hunt said that Hillary led the final assault, the *Evening Post* in Wellington, New Zealand, declared "Hillary first to summit by ten feet."[11] Hunt told a press conference in Kathmandu that Tenzing had limited climbing experience compared to European mountaineers and at no point acted as a guide. Many commentators derided the dispute and viewed the ascent as the result of teamwork. The *Times of India* exhorted its readers to drop the matter: Hillary and Tenzing belonged not to any one country but "to the world and are a glory to the human race."[12] Yet when Tenzing's firsthand account of the climb was published in Italy a year later, it received a familiar title: *Gli eroi del Chomolungma* (The King of Mount Everest).[13]

Banner headlines in Britain placed the Queen in the summit position, while street banners in Nepal put Tenzing on top. In Kathmandu, Hillary, Tenzing, and Hunt held another kind of "summit," a diplomatic meeting in the office of the prime minister of Nepal with the British ambassador to negotiate notarized statements. Three official statements were released, one by Hillary, another by Tenzing, and a joint statement signed by both men. All three statements reported that the two men took turns in the lead and Hillary took photographs at the top of Tenzing holding the flags of Great Britain, Nepal, the United Nations, and India. While the statements varied in minor details, they all used precisely the same phrase to describe the moment of arrival: "We reached the summit almost together."[14]

ALTERED STATES

The contentious reception of the Everest expedition in 1953 was the result of a redefinition of sovereignty that had extended over the first half of the twentieth century. An ascent envisioned before 1914 to represent British authority in India and launched in the 1920s when the British Empire had

reached its widest extent, succeeded only in the 1950s amid the disman-
tling of the empire and the beginning of the Cold War. In 1921, the British
received permission to climb Everest from Tibet in exchange for weapons for
use in military conflicts with China. The earliest British Everest expeditions
were on a grand scale and commanded by army officers who employed military logistics and siege tactics. The imperial context was inscribed in memorials to George Mallory and Andrew Irvine after 1924, and resembled
the nationalist discourses of redemptive mountaineering in other parts of
Europe between the wars. Nationalist rhetoric soared to new heights in
1933 during a British airplane flight over Everest sponsored by right-wing
ideologues with links to British fascists.[15] Many British climbers were uncomfortable with these politics and experimented with Himalayan expeditions on a smaller scale between the wars that succeeded in reaching the
summits of Kamet and Nanda Devi.

The independence and partition of Repeated failures transformed ascents of Everest or Nanga Parbat into
matters of "national importance." Even so, the imperialist or nationalist
rhetoric has often obscured the extent to which Himalayan expeditions were
always cross-cultural collaborations of British or Germans with Indians,
Sikkimese, Bhotias, Sherpas, and Tibetans. The deaths on Everest of seven
Sherpas in 1922 and of Mallory and Irvine in 1924, and on Nanga Parbat
of ten Germans and Sherpas in 1934 and sixteen more in 1937 consolidated
heroic masculinities among Sherpas as well as Europeans. During his boyhood at the foot of Everest in Nepal, Tenzing heard firsthand accounts of
these expeditions from the porters, and the sacrifices on Nanga Parbat
made a deep impression: "Even though I had not yet been on a mountain,
such a story made me, too, proud to be a Sherpa."[16]

The independence and partition of India in 1947 and the revolution in
China in 1949 combined to close Tibet and open Nepal to mountaineering
expeditions. In 1950, a French team visited Nepal and scaled Annapurna,
the first 8,000-meter peak to be climbed. The jubilant reaction to the ascent in France and Maurice Herzog's harrowing narration of the descent in
a best-selling book became a source of national pride in France and was
widely celebrated.[17] Nepal gave permission to the British to climb Everest in
1951, but they made little progress during a leisurely "reconnaissance" led
by Eric Shipton, a former tea planter in Kenya. Nepal did not distinguish
between a "reconnaissance" and a serious ascent, and gave permission for
Everest in 1952 to Swiss diplomats in Delhi. After the British hastily made

their own request, the Nepali government asked if the two proposals could be combined for a joint Anglo-Swiss attempt.

The tepid British response to the Nepali proposal for a joint expedition exemplifies divergent conceptions of sovereignty. Everest organizers in London wanted an "all-British" team for 1952, and would only consider a joint expedition if Eric Shipton were named the overall leader. The Swiss proposed joint leadership of a joint expedition, but refused to accept sole British command. Shipton was amenable to joint leadership, but the Everest organizing committee flatly refused. The British Foreign Office encouraged a joint expedition and was disappointed at the committee's recalcitrance, which exhibited the assumptions of an earlier era of imperial dominance.[18] Divergent responses to a joint expedition did not represent a contrast between "western" and "south Asian" conceptions of sovereignty, but rather the disjuncture between the unitary sovereignty held by the British organizing committee and the layered or shared sovereignty articulated by Nepali officials, Swiss climbers, and British diplomats. Indeed, the double sovereignty shared by federal and cantonal authorities in Switzerland had a long history within the Swiss Confederation.[19] The Swiss team on Everest in 1952 put this shared sovereignty into practice by promoting Tenzing to a full member of the climbing team, and he nearly reached the summit with Raymond Lambert, a Swiss guide from Geneva.

The British organizing committee replaced Shipton with Colonel Hunt for his organizational abilities and the team succeeded as a result of developments funded by the British "warfare state."[20] Hunt developed a systematic plan for logistics of the summit "assault" using his background as a member of Field Marshall Montgomery's wartime planning staff. The lessons of Anglo-American wartime and postwar research on high-altitude aircraft pilots were also applied to mountaineering. "Operation Everest" at the U.S. Naval School of Aviation Medicine tested high-altitude acclimatization in a pressure chamber in Florida in 1946, and Dr. Griffith Pugh researched high-altitude physiology at British laboratories and during state-funded fieldwork in the Himalayas.[21] One of the climbers, Tom Bourdillon, developed his own oxygen apparatus for Everest during his day job as a rocket scientist at the Ministry of Supply.[22] The British state paid the salaries for most climbers, the War Office provided rations at cost, free transport to the Himalayas, and loans that became gifts of clothing, supplies, and oxygen equipment. *The Conquest of Everest* film paid tribute to these efforts in

scenes showing climbers testing equipment and themselves at the RAF Institute of Aviation Medicine at Farnborough.

The application on Everest of wartime logistics, planning, and physiology were peace dividends, deferred compensation for investments by the
British and U.S. governments in fighting the Second World War and the
Cold War. Together, they enabled the 1953 expedition to provide Hillary
and Tenzing adequate supplies of oxygen, food, and fluid at their highest
camps. Previously, Everest climbers had failed to advance very far in the
"thin air" of the mountain's highest slopes. Put another way, the states altered by the postwar military-industrial-scientific complex provided the resources that enabled the 1953 climbers to ameliorate the risks of an altered
state of consciousness in the "death zone" on Everest.

The flags fluttering from Tenzing's ice ax on Everest also signified the
competing sovereignty of nation-states whose relations had been dramatically altered by Indian independence. Colonial regimes in the British Empire had created states without citizenship. After 1947, the newly independent states of south Asia automatically classified every inhabitant as a citizen.
Nepal was not a "formal" colony only because the British were content to
let hereditary Rana prime ministers govern this "little kingdom" in the
Himalayas in exchange for control of Nepal's foreign policy. Independent
India inherited the mantle of unitary sovereignty from the British and this
unique role in Nepal. The Indian government brokered a Nepali compro-
mise that ended the rule of the Ranas and restored King Tribhuvan to the
throne. In 1953, Nepali nationalism intensified after India sent a military
mission into Nepal in response to an aborted coup by the Rana-dominated
military. Some of these Indian troops were stationed at Namche Bazar during the Everest expedition, and they relayed a coded radio message to Kathmandu that (unknown to them) announced the successful ascent.

In a postcolonial system of sovereign states, singular citizenship was the
corollary of unitary sovereignty, and this produced differential awards for
the climbers. The Treasury office in charge of the British honors system was
considering Tenzing for a British Empire Medal (BEM)—the so-called
working-class medal—the day before the coronation. Three days later, after
the ascent had been announced, Tenzing's nationality remained unclear, but
the George Medal was quietly designated as the most suitable award.[23] Left-
leaning papers complained after this news was leaked. The *Manchester
Guardian* inquired, "Would it not be wiser, since Hillary and he stood on

the summit side by side, to honor them in the same way?" Churchill dodged the issue during the prime minister's question time, which led the *News Chronicle* to remark: "As Sir Winston Churchill observed during the war, medals not only glitter: they sometimes cast shadows. This medal, by discriminating between white man and brown, casts a particularly unpleasant shadow."[24]

Postcolonial sovereignties forestalled a title for Tenzing and forced a knighthood on Hillary. The Indian constitution abolished titles and prohibited Indian citizens from accepting any from foreign states. The prime minister, Jawaharlal Nehru, agreed to special medals in India for Tenzing and Hillary and had no objection to the George Medal for Tenzing: "This is not a title and in the circumstances I think we should raise no objection. We may consider this a special case."[25] Tenzing was a resident in India and on its electoral rolls, and therefore classified as a citizen. This position required the rejection of British honors as symbols of British domination. Hillary's position was paradoxically similar. New Zealand's distinctive nationalism featured the embrace rather than rejection of British imperial ties. Returning from Everest, Hillary received a letter addressed to Sir Edmund Hillary, KBE (Knight of the British Empire): "It should have been a great moment, but instead I was aghast . . . I had never really approved of titles and couldn't imagine myself possessing one." The prime minister of New Zealand, Sidney Holland, had insisted on a KBE for Hillary and already accepted it on his behalf during the coronation celebrations. Hillary felt he had no choice and was "miserable rather than pleased."[26] As a serving military officer, Colonel Hunt was ineligible for a KBE and the War Office recommended a knight bachelor rather than the parallel military order. By the arcane hierarchies of the British honors system, Hunt's knighthood thus ranked lower than Hillary's. This caused the *Daily Herald* to reject the suggestion that Tenzing should be considered for an honorary KBE: "His award would then be equal to Hillary's: and surpass Col. Hunt's. Would that be just?"[27]

Tenzing said he was "born in the womb of Nepal but raised in the lap of India," and struggled with the exclusive claims of singular sovereignty. This predicament was typical for Sherpas who migrated across national boundaries in search of seasonal labor. Only years later, after Tenzing's death, was his birthplace identified as a village on the northern, Tibetan side of Everest. Needless to say, this did not make him in any sense Tibetan. Tenzing told *Life* magazine after the ascent: "For me Indian Nepali same. I am Nepali but I think I also Indian. We should all be same—Hillary, myself, Indian, Nepali, everybody."[28] Rather than self-identification by statehood, Tenzing vacillated between identification with where he lived or worked. These more primordial categories of belonging represented a form of existential resistance to statist classification by citizenship. Tenzing had no problem carrying multiple national flags to the summit (Figure 22), but after the ascent he would be asked to choose only one.

MAKING TENZINGS

King Tribhuvan awarded Tenzing the Nepal Tara, Star of Nepal, the highest decoration not reserved for royalty, and the prime minister gave Hillary and Hunt the Gorkha Dakshina Bahu, Order of the Gurkha Right Hand, First Class. These awards combined British and Nepali models of the nation-state and mirrored the hierarchical honors already announced in Britain. The queen of Nepal gave Tenzing 10,000 rupees, and Tenzing, Hillary, and Hunt each received *khukhris,* "the famous curved Gorkha knife," in sheaths encrusted with jewels. Such awards reinforced the place of the monarchy at the apex of the Nepalese polity, claimed Tenzing as Nepali rather than Indian, and symbolized the new Nepal in contrast to the old Rana regime. As the Bombay newspaper, *Bharat Jyoti,* reported from Kathmandu: "Sherpa Tenzing's victory is like a new star in the firmament which revives the hope of the people and reassures them that God creates not only Ranas but also Tenzings. Tenzing is a challenge to these feudal lords."[29]

The old and new regimes in Nepal competed to claim Tenzing. An early proposal to rename Everest "Tenzing Peak" had come from a leader of Gorkha Parishad, a party representing the rump of the Ranas. He called Tenzing "the bravest among the brave and the real conqueror of Everest," and said that the peak should be renamed after "the great Gorkha who climbed it."[30] This language attempted to reclaim martial traditions of the Gurkhas and newer languages of Nepali nationalism. In the nineteenth century, the Gurkha soldiers recruited in Nepal by the British came to represent the exemplary martial tradition and masculinity of Nepal. During the 1930s and 1940s, Nepalis living in India also developed two cultural elements of their nationalism that undergirded their opposition to the Rana regime: the use of the Nepali language and new histories that emphasized *bir* (brave) national

Figure 22 Tenzing Norgay (center) prepares to tie the flags of India, Nepal, and Britain to his ice ax before his ascent with Edmund Hillary of Mount Everest in 1953. He also carried the flag of the United Nations. At the summit, he left the string of four flags on the snow.   Royal Geographical Society.

traditions.[31] The singer Navin Bardewa adapted these in his Nepali song in Tenzing's honor: "Bir Tenzing themro biswa la gaudhachaa jai gan" (Brave Tenzing, the World Is Singing for You).[32]

The Cold War led British observers to blame Communists for the controversy, but Nepali politics were characterized much more by factional diversity and Nepali-Indian antagonism. John Hunt reported that Tenzing "appears to have been 'got at' by local politicians—we are pretty certain the Communist party is behind it."[33] In the fluid context of Nepali politics at the time, however, every political party celebrated Tenzing. As the climbers returned to Kathmandu, negotiations for yet another coalition government came to a halt to welcome Tenzing. As a Sherpa, a religious and ethnic minority, Tenzing was a potent symbol of the Nepali nation. At a large public ceremony in the middle of Kathmandu, Tenzing was given illuminated addresses, presents, bags, and medals. Prime Minister M. P. Koirala told the audience that "the Nepalese nation is, of course, proud of Tenzing, proud that we have in our midst today a son of Nepal who has justified the existence of the highest summit of the world on Nepalese soil by climbing to its peak and planting our national flag there."[34] Amid Nepal's continuing efforts to define a post-Rana polity, Koirala was saying that Tenzing's ascent had justified the existence of Nepal.

After flying to Calcutta, Tenzing declared that he was glad to be back in his "own province," and John Hunt said he felt "as if I have come back home." Hunt had been born in India and served in the Indian police near Calcutta in the 1930s. Calcutta's civic celebration focused on Tenzing as a citizen of India and brother from West Bengal. Rabindranath Mitra, a Bengali friend of Tenzing's in Darjeeling who had given him the Indian flag to take to the summit, suggested to the state and national governments that they use the occasion to create a mountaineering school. The governor of West Bengal, B. C. Roy, announced that he would establish a mountaineering school in Darjeeling under Tenzing's leadership.

The mountaineering institute reappropriated the Himalayas for India and contested British representations of the "effeminate" Bengali. Since the mid-nineteenth century, British officials had viewed Bengali men as lazy and effeminate, an image they extended to India's educated, middle-class elite. Some Indian intellectuals promoted a culture of athleticism to demonstrate their virility, and others accentuated competing models of indigenous masculinity, of which Gandhian nationalism is perhaps the best known and most important. B. C. Roy announced the school by telling the youth of Bengal that mountaineering "helped to mold character and instill self-confidence, discipline, initiative, and determination."[35] Nehru praised the ascent of Everest "because that is the way nations grow. That is the way communities become strong and great—not by soft living; not by soft thinking, not by soft talk." In another speech, Nehru noted that "recently an Indian and a foreigner climbed Mount Everest," and this was considered "a feat of great daring because it was a symbol of the courage of a human being and if there is such courage in our nation, we shall climb mountains higher than the Everest."[36]

These encomiums to the virtues of mountaineering would have sounded familiar to the founders of the Club Alpino Italiano (CAI) and other alpine clubs in Europe. While this rhetoric has the ring of a derivative discourse, it would be a mistake to view the Himalayan Mountaineering Institute (HMI), or Indian reactions to the ascent of Everest more generally, merely as examples of "first in Europe, then elsewhere." When Nehru opened HMI in November 1954, he thanked Swiss mountaineers for help in training "Indian Sherpas," but denied that Europeans had greater experience and knowledge than climbers in India. "The Himalayan range," he said in Hindi at the opening, "was India's oldest friend. In learning to climb the mountains no disrespect was intended to them. Rather it was in love and affection that such ventures were undertaken."[37] Quintino Sella and the founders of the CAI had promoted mountaineering in Italy to "make Italians." Nehru and the leaders of independent India had something more distinctive in mind than merely "making Indians." Nehru gave Tenzing the following charge as the first field director of the Himalayan Mountaineering Institute: "Now you will make a thousand Tenzings."[38]

When the climbers arrived at the airport in New Delhi in July 1953, John Hunt waved the Indian flag from Tenzing's ice ax. The crowd roared its approval, broke through the police barriers, and swept Tenzing down the tarmac before the police rescued him. In ceremonies at Rashtrapati Bhavan, the president of India, Rajendra Prasad, presented the climbers with medals depicting Mount Everest on one side and the Asoka Lion on the other, with the Sanskrit inscription *Sahase Shri Prativa* (Adventure Is Glory). In announcing these awards, the Indian government was careful to note that "these are special medals and do not mark the commencement of a special order."[39] Prasad warmly praised teamwork on Everest and hoped that this "spirit of enterprise and adventure" will guide people "in making the greater and higher conquest of the human spirit, which will enable all of us to live in peace, to help each other in time of need and to live as members of one family."[40]

Appeals for unity served multiple purposes. In India, the call for unity countered communal rivalry and separatism, especially in Kashmir. Internationally, this cooperation and comradeship assuaged Nepali resentment and appealed to a wider audience in the nonaligned movement. Nehru's correspondence disparaged the controversy over Tenzing's nationality and who was first—"neither could have done so without the help of the other"—and warned that nationalist celebrations of Tenzing could lead people to think Indians suffered from "some kind of inferiority complex."[41] For Nehru, Everest and the Himalayas represented the unity and integration of India—"an integrated, united nation—not a regimented nation, not a uniform nation. We want to preserve the magnificent variety of India."[42]

The ascent of Everest also recuperated Indian practices of paternalism and protection. On public occasions, Tenzing stood literally draped in Nehru's own jacket. "Since I had hardly any clothes of my own," Tenzing recalled, "he opened his closets and began giving me his. He gave me coats, trousers, shirts, everything—because we are the same size they all fitted perfectly."[43] Nehru did not give Tenzing a white Congress Party hat and advised him to stay out of politics. By this gesture, Nehru became Tenzing's patron and the gifts cementing this relationship were examples of Indian practices of "protection." Nehru worried that the "uncontrolled adulation" thrust on Tenzing "might well spoil him and make him unfit for any great work in the future."[44]

Tenzing's poverty before the ascent was an important symbol of his incorporation into the prosperous "new" India on his return. In addition to the fund sponsored by the *Statesman,* groups in India gave Tenzing a radio, gramophone, electric stove, wristwatches, pieces of gold, 180 square yards of land, and a Gandhi cap; Tenzing's wife received a sewing machine.[45] At the Gandhi grounds in Delhi, Hunt was given a replica of the Asoka Pillar, while Hillary and Tenzing received models of Mount Everest, with another 2,000 rupees for Tenzing. A few days later at the National Stadium in New Delhi, Tenzing was given 5,000 rupees in National Savings Certificates and he announced: "None of us could have climbed to the summit of Everest alone. Our success was due to our team spirit!" The climbers laid wreaths at the samadhi of Mahatma Gandhi at Rajghat. Before leaving India, the London *Times* estimated that Tenzing had been given nearly 100,000 rupees (about £7,500 at the time).[46]

At each of these events, the climbers themselves rarely spoke. When interviewed at the Nepali Embassy in New Delhi, the *Times of India* noted that "Tenzing showed extreme reluctance to speak."[47] Tenzing appeared several times on All India Radio, when interviewers asked how he had felt on the summit. From Calcutta, Tenzing said that "all the hills and mounts round about looked like gods and goddesses to us and the plains below appeared so many broken pieces of habitation." In a broadcast on the Children's Hour, Tenzing replied, "Just as when one meets a well-loved friend after a long absence there is little that can be put into words, so he felt when he reached the top in his seventh attempt."[48] To many observers, Tenzing's humility, inarticulacy, and subalternity were the very qualities that made him a hero in India. As he left for London, the *Times of India* reported that Tenzing became "the cynosure of admiration" because "he was the 'underdog' in the minds of the Indian people. That feeling, and the fact that Tenzing has borne with humility, detachment, and a sense of gratitude all the adoration that has been bestowed on him, have served to make a national hero of him."[49]

MAKING UNITY

Colonel Hunt waved the Union Jack from his ice ax when the Everest climbers arrived at London airport. "The whole Commonwealth," said Brigadier Anthony Head, the secretary of state for war, "is moved, and is proud of your great achievement." The climbers received a rousing welcome from family and friends. "Everest Heroes Home," a Pathé newsreel of the event, contained little overtly "political" narration. Hunt paid tribute to his predecessors, Hillary emphasized that he and Tenzing had climbed roped together as a unit, and Tenzing was translated as saying he was very happy on the summit. Nevertheless, with Hunt waving the flag and the minister of war glad-handing the climbers, the scene in London was as political as those before it. On the tarmac, Hunt and Tenzing each waved the British flag from an ice ax, incorporating them into the Commonwealth. In radio interviews, Hunt said he was delighted that Hillary and Tenzing "representing, in a sense, members of the Commonwealth, had been successful in getting to the top. It was only right and proper."[50]

Yet Hillary's antipodean accent and Tenzing's foreign language in newsreels and radio broadcasts were auditory reminders of their marginality in Britain. Hillary went from the airport to stay at his sister's house near Norwich. As part of the diaspora of British settler colonies, Hillary was white but not quite British when he returned to London and occupied the ambivalent position of a colonial in the metropolis. Tenzing stayed at the Indian Services Club and also gave interviews for newspapers, radio, and television. Some newspaper coverage portrayed Tenzing as the exotic "other" in a world beyond his ken, but his own "voice" could still be heard. When asked if he was "thrilled" at seeing the sights of London, Tenzing replied, "I have spent all my life in the mountains and the hills have taught me calm."[51]

Hunt's return to Llanfair-Waterdine, a Shropshire village near the border of Wales, celebrated a Welsh/British identity that troubled a unitary British nationalism. Hunt waved the British flag from his ice ax as he stood in a cart towed by twenty local farmers up a hill to his house: "There was a bonfire, supper party, barbecue, speeches, the mayor, the county council, chairman of the county councilors, all very local, but all the more moving."[52] Hunt had already announced that he had flown the Welsh flag at camps on Everest. When a Welsh nationalist party read a message from Hunt at a rally, the War Office reminded him of his pledge to remain nonpartisan while in the military. Hunt replied that he had merely expressed "my sympathy with the preservation of the culture and traditions of Wales."[53] To the British state, however, gestures of Welsh solidarity could threaten the myth of a United Kingdom.

On July 16, 1953, the British government paid tribute to the Everest climbers at a previously scheduled garden party at Buckingham Palace attended by eight thousand people in a pelting rain. In the downpour, the climbers jostled with debutantes and dignitaries for limited dry space as the band played a soggy rendition of Handel's Water Music. After Queen Elizabeth II made a brief appearance outdoors, the climbers were ushered into a drawing room in the palace. The Queen touched Hunt and Hillary lightly on the shoulders with a sword and bestowed the George Medal on Tenzing. That evening, Prince Philip presided at a small state dinner—for "Men Only"—after which wives and other guests joined them for a large state reception at Lancaster House.[54]

British honors had set an example for other nations, but the ceremonies in Nepal and India also created awkward precedents in London. Since Tenzing had been given money in Nepal and India, British diplomats were concerned that Tenzing and his wife might expect to receive gold coins from Queen Elizabeth. A Civil List Pension for Tenzing had already been rejected, and the Foreign Office recommended against a purse for his wife. Both, it was argued, would devalue the George Medal: "It is not the practice to make monetary awards to foreign recipients of British honors, much less to their wives. To add money to honors would imply that the latter are not by themselves an adequate recognition."[55]

This was an issue of some importance, since to question the honors system was to question traditions of British nationalism. By the mid-twentieth century, Britain's peculiar, monarchical form of nationalism had extended beyond the multinational boundaries of England, Scotland, Wales, and Northern Ireland to embrace an even more diverse, multiethnic empire, and the honors system proliferated to an unprecedented degree.[56] The rationale for empire had oscillated between narratives that emphasized military conquest, monarchy, and manly character and parallel narratives of empire as exporting liberty, self-government, and economic development. The coincidence of coronation and conquest reinforced the complementarity of these traditions with monarchy and masculinity. Prince Philip's stag party evoked this tradition, as did a female admirer in Britain who wrote to the team on Coronation Day: "It is fitting that your team should symbolise for us the vigor, vitality, and high endeavor of manhood, as the Queen symbolises the sweetness, grace and dutiful service of a woman."[57]

When Hillary and George Lowe, his fellow New Zealander on Everest, returned to Auckland, New Zealand, they were greeted with "the same lack of reserve usually kept for triumphant All Black teams," that is, the national rugby squad. Hillary and Lowe left the plane and strode through an archway of ice axes held by members of the New Zealand Alpine Club. At a civic reception, Hillary said, "We felt more nervous walking up the stairs here than we did on Everest itself." The mayor gave Hillary a chair in the shape of Everest, and said he had brought luster and renown to his place of birth: "In other words it is 'our' Hillary who has climbed to the top of Everest." The New Zealand minister of defense added that Hillary and Lowe "represent a truly New Zealand effort—two North Islanders who went to the South Island for their training."[58]

Indeed, for many New Zealanders, Hillary became the icon for a New Zealand identity that replaced the affinity they felt for Britain. Hillary recalled his first visit to Britain in 1950: "As a citizen of a new country with little history I felt I was being accepted back into the ancestral fold—it gave me an astonishingly warm feeling. In those days, like most of my fellow citizens, I was British first and a New Zealander second—it is only in recent years that we have been thrust firmly out of the family nest."[59] If imperialism had been a form of nationalism in the nineteenth century, a distinctive New Zealand identity developed in the twentieth century. Military sacrifices during the two world wars, successful rugby tours, and Hillary's ascent of Everest each contributed to the consolidation of a nationalism that supplemented and then supplanted their loyalties as British or Commonwealth subjects. By the 1950s, the distinctive toughness, versatility, and "mateship" of the "Kiwi bloke" were civilized and subdued by new models of the "family man."[60] Like previous Kiwi heroes, Hillary and Lowe had been tough, resourceful, and self-confident on the mountain and were quiet, modest, and well behaved off it. The appearance of Hillary's apiary in newspaper photographs testified to his rural roots in the pioneer tradition, and he conformed to the more recent stereotype by announcing his engagement to a childhood sweetheart only a few days after his return, and they were soon married.

The state reception by the New Zealand Parliament emphasized Hillary and Lowe's distinctiveness as New Zealand men. The prime minister praised "two of the greatest New Zealanders the country had produced"; the leader of the opposition lauded them for "the most superlative modesty that could ever be achieved by human beings."[61] Hillary and Lowe were modest, plainspoken blokes, but the link between masculinity and national identity was reaffirmed in yet another way—by the official exclusion of women from the state reception. Although local mountaineering clubs had suggested women for the invitation list, the organizers crossed them out and women had to gate-crash the event. Afterward, the climber Mavis Davison complained that their exclusion suggested either a "lack of appreciation of the widespread interest in mountaineering in this country," or "prejudice or acceptance of prehistoric or antediluvian concepts as to the place of women in the community."[62]

New Zealand's commemoration of Everest was based on exclusion and an appropriation. New Zealand's gift to Tenzing was a volume of news clippings and telegrams with photographs of the New Zealand Alps. Embossed in gold on the cover was "the outline of a Maori chieftain, with two huia feathers—a sign of rank—in his head-dress, and holding a taiaha, one of the main fighting weapons of the Maori."[63] One of the Maori members of Parliament, E. T. Tirikatene, ridiculed the gift. He wondered what Tenzing would make of newspaper clippings in English, which he could not read, and found a parallel with his own status as a New Zealand citizen: "Although I am a citizen of the Dominion I am not permitted to speak in Parliament the Maori language, my own language, because the majority of members have not taken the trouble to acquaint themselves with that tongue."[64]

At the end of 1953, Queen Elizabeth II visited New Zealand during her postcoronation tour of the empire and Commonwealth and delivered her Christmas Day address from Auckland. The radio broadcast was preceded by "The Queen's Journey," a program conveying pledges of loyalty from around the globe. After a Maori Haka dance and greetings from Sydney, the program jumped "to Britain, to the homeland, cradle of pioneers, discoverers and creators of the Commonwealth." For an hour, tributes poured in from British territories and former colonies until the narrator announced: "We have girdled the earth and flashed from pole to pole." The highlights of the year were the coronation, peace in Korea, and the conquest of Everest. The Queen's journey was renewing the Commonwealth: "This is a great pyramid of unity, a mountain massive as Everest, a peak still clouded by the future challenges to all men of goodwill and courage."[65] Edmund Hillary, at his sister's home in Norfolk, sent the final greeting to the Queen, then in his hometown, before "God Save the Queen" introduced her address.

Although Queen Elizabeth II did not feel like her namesake, she identified at least one "resemblance between her age and mine." England during the reign of Elizabeth was "great in spirit and well-endowed with men who were ready to encompass the earth." While her forebears had founded an empire, in the Commonwealth, "the United Kingdom was an equal partner with many other proud and independent nations. And she is leading other still backward territories forward for the same goal." Unlike previous empires, she concluded, the Commonwealth was built on "the highest qualities of the spirit of man: friendship, loyalty, and the desire for freedom and peace. To that new conception of an equal partnership of nations and races I shall give myself heart and soul, every day of my life."[66] The Queen did

not mention Everest or the partnership of Hillary and Tenzing, the unspo-
ken subtext of her entire speech. The Queen's speech, like many of Nehru's
speeches from the same period, did not have to mention the ascent of Everest because the Himalayas had become great pyramids of unity.

EVEREST TO MONT BLANC

Thomas Graham Brown and Gavin de Beer were among the worthies of the
Alpine Club and Royal Society invited to the British state reception for the
British Everest expedition. The day after the reception, they jointly wrote to
the Alpine Club to propose a book about the first ascent of Mont Blanc to
mark the centenary of the club and the bicentenary of the birth of Paccard.[67]
John Hunt's preface drew parallels between the two ascents and imagined
the feelings of excitement in 1786:

> To the educated people in Europe, it was probably not less stirring than the
> climbing of Everest to the wider public in 1953. In terms of human endeavor,
> it was, perhaps, greater, in that no comparable challenge had ever been sur-
> mounted. Indeed the heights were surrounded in popular belief with all
> manner of superstitions; I would compare the spirit which carried Paccard
> and Balmat to the top of Mont Blanc with that which fired Vasco da Gama,
> who dared to risk sailing over the brink of the world's edge to reach the
> fabulous continent of India.

The *Times Literary Supplement* regretted that the stories about Paccard,
"unlike the efforts of the Indian Press over Everest, they were not foiled by the
probity of the other person concerned." The book was an act of justice by
the "men of the class Dr. Paccard revered from afar, scientists, Fellows of the
Royal Society that honored [Horace-Bénédict de] Saussure and passed
the village doctor by."[68]

The First Ascent of Mont Blanc was framed not only by parallels between
Everest and Mont Blanc but also by contemporary attitudes toward masculinity, men of science, and "Western civilization." De Beer identified with
the earlier cosmopolitan republic of letters and became fluent in French and
German while growing up in Paris as the son of a journalist. He taught zool-
ogy and embryology at Oxford and London and worked on military intelligence and propaganda during the Second World War. De Beer then led

scientific societies and served as director of the Natural History Museum throughout the 1950s. The example of earlier polymath savants made him skeptical of the dichotomous "two cultures" debate, and "it occurred to me to wonder whether science itself, in my hands, might contribute to the humanities."[69] He became an expert on the manuscripts of Charles Darwin and earlier "men of science." A clue in the Joseph Banks papers launched a five-year quest that eventually located Paccard's original barometrical observations on Mont Blanc in the British Museum.[70] He obtained copies of Saussure's journals from Geneva and of Gersdorf's diaries from Görlitz and wrote a chapter on Paccard's scientific observations as well as the historical appendices. Graham Brown wrote the other chapters reconstructing the ascent and the debates about who was first.

Graham Brown identified closely with Paccard as a medical doctor and a climber who claimed priority of discovery. The son of a prominent Edinburgh physician, Graham Brown became a doctor, researched neurophysiology, and served in the medical corps in the Great War. In 1920 he became director of the Cardiff Institute for Physiology, but soon devoted himself to mountain climbing after 1926.[71] He dated his interest in Mont Blanc from "a rainy afternoon early in life when my governess read aloud a popular account of Mademoiselle d'Angeville's ascent." The guides lifted her in the air so she could boast she was higher than Mont Blanc, and "this took my fancy, and some friends and I mimicked the event on Arthur's Seat to make similar boasts."[72] In 1927 and 1928, Graham Brown and Frank Smythe made first ascents of new routes on the Brenva face of Mont Blanc and disputed who had chosen the routes. Graham Brown attended the dedication of the Paccard memorial in 1932, and made additional first ascents on Mont Blanc in 1933 and Mount Foraker in Alaska in 1934. He also joined an Anglo-American team to Nanda Devi in 1936. Throughout this period, Graham Brown sniped at Smythe and got the last word in *Brenva* (1944), a book that asserted his own priority of discovery.[73]

In *Brenva*, Graham Brown wrestled with the definition of discovery. After making a "direct" ascent of a peak in the Lake District via a gully, Graham Brown daydreamed about doing so on the Brenva ridge of Mont Blanc, which he had read about in a novel. When he asked himself, "Might a direct Brenva route be made to Mont Blanc?" it was "with the asking of this question the history of these Brenva climbs really begins." Graham

Brown considered climbing for its own sake the chief motive in "pure mountaineering" and dismissed the "romantic or poetic fantasies [that] are likely to suggest themselves as substitutes for the good climbing."[74]

After vindication for himself, Graham Brown turned to Paccard. In notes from the 1940s, Graham Brown criticized British mountaineers for an attitude of "appeasement" between the wars and viewed with disdain any attitude of awe, mysticism, or pilgrimage in mountains: "The idea that great mountains are inhabited by 'demons' or 'spirits' is natural to primitive man, and it is correspondingly widespread," but the persistence of such legends "seems to call for a cause." The only explanation he could discern was "lack of enterprise or actual timidity" of those who professed such beliefs: "These 'legends' of demons and danger are the *leveling* devices of small men." In contrast, "The British attitude should be—'stand up to the mountain like a man.'" According to Graham Brown, Paccard was a man of courage, Balmat was strong but motivated by gain, Marc-Théodore Bourrit was jealous, and Saussure shrank from controversy: "his friends would probably have called him an appeaser if the word had been in use."[75]

In 1947, Graham Brown viewed the ascent of Mont Blanc as a symbol of partnership, adventure, and teamwork: "The fact of the partnership proves that each was necessary for the other. Mont Blanc was therefore conquered by a team of two men, and the mountaineering achievement of any party is a joint affair which has been brought to success by team work. Extreme individualism is out of place on such occasions." Each member of a climbing pair should share the credit. Paccard and Balmat shared the sense of adventure that stemmed from reliance on two people and the possibility of defeat: "That, in fact, is the essence of teamwork in mountaineering, and Mont Blanc was conquered by the Paccard-Balmat team."[76]

When *The First Ascent of Mont Blanc* appeared a decade later in 1957, this once-generous tone had changed markedly. Instead, Graham Brown and de Beer credited Paccard with discovery of the route, leadership of the climb, and he alone was "the prime cause of the first ascent of Mont Blanc." Paccard's ascent "with a single porter" was motivated by "a kind of local patriotism—the wish to establish beyond dispute the supremacy of Mont Blanc amongst the mountains of Europe." The doctor was ambitious for the mountain rather than himself. Graham Brown insisted that Paccard was first on the summit: "Which of them was the actual first to step on the very highest bit of snow is of course a trivial matter; but the truth of it is important as a disproof of the lie that Dr. Paccard collapsed and had to lean upon the aid of his porter."[77]

Paccard "discovered" the route just as Graham Brown had done on the Brenva face—when he thought of the very idea: "The treading of previously untrodden ground is not in all cases a measure of discovery, because discovery implies that something hidden or unknown, but not necessarily material, is brought to light. Discovery in climbing is the solution of a problem, which may sometimes be solved before the climb and settled by the ascent." Paccard had to free himself from the "evil spell" cast by other routes and "trust his own judgment." The question of priority between climbers was "distasteful," but the issue had been raised in Balmat's favor and cast in bronze in Jean-Jules Salmson's statues: "What was hidden from everyone but Dr. Paccard was a quality and not a material form, the quality of practicality and accessibility—the fact (or probability) that the Passage could be climbed."[78]

Despite its erudition and authoritative appendices, *The First Ascent of Mont Blanc* is a curious combination of empiricism and speculation so tendentious in its criticism of anyone other than Paccard as to raise questions of bad faith. The narrative declared Balmat's snow bivouac "an invention" and frequently described the guide as "shaken" by the doctor's displays of bravery during the ascent: "It may have been here that Balmat first faltered, perhaps shaken by his recent discovery that Dr. Paccard meant to penetrate the untrodden regions ahead." "When Paccard directed him, as he must have done, to bear away to the left. . . . This may perhaps have shaken him again. . . . Balmat, perhaps again faltering." When observers in the valley watched the two men arrive together at the top, Balmat "had to run to reach the summit *nearly* at the same time as the doctor (our italics). In other words, Dr. Paccard was the first actually to attain the summit, if perhaps just by a short neck; this is important only because of Balmat's later inventions."[79]

WHAT IS A FACT?

Where earlier historians faulted Bourrit, Graham Brown and de Beer reserved their harshest criticism for Saussure as an unethical "man of science." In their view, he was motivated by a selfish ambition to make observations rather than the arduous ascent. Graham Brown pictured Saussure as "shaken" and in fear of becoming "a laughing-stock" when he received a letter from Paccard in 1785. He "learned with surprise, disappointment and alarm that he had been anticipated, a year before, by a village doctor, unknown to the world but also a man of science." In Graham Brown and de Beer's triptych of climbers, Paccard cared only for knowledge, Saussure only for glory, and Balmat only for financial reward. Paccard did not make any contribution to knowledge with the first ascent, but Saussure's lack of understanding of "lesser mortals" was unforgivable and showed a lack of moral courage: "Any decent man of science in the professor's position" would have invited the younger colleague to join him, and it was his duty "as an impartial man of science" to ascertain facts and defend the truth. "As a man of science, Professor de Saussure had a conscience: facts are facts, and there is a curious flavor of half-truth, which suggests another delicate balance" in his treatment of Paccard.[80]

What is a "fact" and what is a "man of science"? At almost the same time that Graham Brown and de Beer were writing about Mont Blanc, sociologists and historians of science were reconceptualizing facts and the structure of scientific discoveries. In 1957, Robert K. Merton noted that the frequency of disputes over scientific discovery could not be explained by simultaneous discoveries or by egotistical and disputatious personalities. Such explanations could not account for the frequent involvement of third parties, bystanders with no direct personal stake who took up the cudgels of battle to express "their great moral indignation over the outrage being perpetrated upon their candidate."[81] National chauvinism played its part, but the disputes had more to do with a desire for individual recognition and institutional rewards for originality.

Merton distinguished this approach from earlier historians of science who saw themselves as guardians of posthumous fame. In the 1930s, George Sarton described his task in these terms: "As the historian is expected to determine not only the relative truth of scientific ideas at different chronological stages, but also their relative novelty, he is irresistibly led to the fixation of *first* events. 'So-and-so was the first to do this-or-that.'" Novelty was a matter of interpretation, but it was "the historian's sacred duty" to celebrate heroic individuals: "The heroic scientist adds to the grandeur and beauty of every man's existence."[82] A century earlier, the physicist François Arago had revived the "water controversy" between Henry Cavendish and

James Watt by dismissing suggestions that experiments by two men *"about the same time"* could ever be *"the whole truth." "'About the same time' proves nothing;* questions as to priority may depend on weeks, on days, on hours, on minutes."[83]

Since the mid-twentieth century, wider communities of scholars have recast facts and discoveries. For Thomas S. Kuhn, discovery could not be localized to a particular time and place but was an extended episode with recurring structures. Under normal conditions, scientific communities accommodated anomalies within existing "paradigms" of thought. Some adaptations were not incremental but transformational and resulted in the adoption of a new paradigm by a scientific community. In Kuhn's influential *The Structure of Scientific Revolutions* (1962), a scientific "fact" depended on the judgment of a community rather than the eye of the individual discoverer as beholder: "Until the scientist has learned to see nature in a different way—the new fact is not quite scientific at all."[84]

This paradigm was influenced by the work of the Polish-Jewish immunologist Ludwik Fleck, whose *The Genesis and Development of a Scientific Fact* was published in German in 1935 and in English in 1979. Fleck held that scientific facts were the result of a "thought style" *(Denkstil)* developed within a "thought collective" *(Denkkollektiv),* a community of people who discussed particular topics. He considered it fundamentally an error to take a "symbolic epistemological subject, known as 'human spirit,' 'human mind,' 'research worker' or simply 'man'" as absolute and unchanging in every epoch. As thought styles changed, so did definitions of facts. Fleck paid more attention than Kuhn to the sites where knowledge was produced and practices of laboratory life could explain developments that otherwise appeared dependent on accident or individual inspiration. According to Fleck, "many workers carried out these experiments almost simultaneously, but the *actual authorship is due to the collective, the practice of cooperation and teamwork."*[85]

Kuhn transformed concepts that in their formulation by Fleck remained politically and epistemologically unspeakable during the Cold War.[86] While it is still possible for historians to focus on developments internal to scientific communities and write histories of science with the politics left out, wider communities of scholars over the last fifty years have examined the myriad ways in which science has a history with politics embedded into its very structures of knowledge. For many years, Kuhn's paradigm has remained more influential than Fleck's epistemological critique, in large part because it was consistent with narratives that scientific revolutions were constitutive elements of modernity and Western civilization.

Gavin de Beer was ambivalent about priority but passionate about knitting together British culture, scientific revolutions, and Western civilization. He equated Charles Darwin's theory of evolution by means of natural selection with earlier paradigm shifts of Copernicus and Newton and presided over a congress to mark the Darwin-Wallace centenary, the anniversary of their simultaneous publication, in 1958. De Beer believed that natural selection was still at work in society and his collected essays were the reflections of a Social Darwinian. His 1959 Boyle lecture at Oxford compared lineages to climbers levering themselves up a cliff and regretted that the mechanisms of natural selection in ancient Sparta were no longer at work in contemporary Britain: "In our welfare state, on the other hand, everything is done to shield the individual from the effects of natural selection as far as possible, so that however unfortunate the mental or physical condition of the individual may be, he is within limits assured of a basic standard of living and may even suffer little handicap in producing a family and perpetuating his genetic factors in the population."[87]

De Beer located the culture and "civilization" of the Western world at the apex of evolutionary development: "This becomes apparent when Western culture is compared with a really different culture, such as that of India, which is difficult for Westerners to grasp." In this instance, "it would certainly be legitimate to speak of two cultures." De Beer reflected on John Tyndall's research on the greenhouse effect in the nineteenth century and feared the effects of natural selection during a period of climate change: if world temperatures rose, "the human race best adapted to heat is the Negro," but if temperatures fell, "the human race best adapted to withstand extreme cold is the Mongolian." In either case, a looming Malthusian crisis and "danger of the population bomb" demonstrated the inadequacy of religion: "If there is a deep cleavage between streams of Western culture, it is between theology and the rest." Earlier atheists and skeptics in the Alps were among his favorite research topics. De Beer professed a faith in the orderliness of the universe and a reverence for an ideal of objective truth and the heroes of the Western tradition.[88]

The first ascent of Mount Everest changed the "facts" of the first ascent of Mont Blanc. The politics of knowledge in the 1950s provided the warrant for Graham Brown and de Beer to deny a position of prominence to anyone beside Paccard. In 1958, Graham Brown wished as an act of symbolism and justice that someone would place a statue of Dr. Paccard between Mont Blanc and the statue of Saussure and Balmat to block their view.[89] De Beer contended that Isaac Newton's adage that he saw further because he stood on the shoulders of giants could never be the standpoint for inferiors. If Newton saw further, "it was not only by standing on the shoulders of giants, but by having ideas, imagination and inspiration of his own that enabled him to make use of his privileged position. After all, a pygmy raised even to the summit of Everest would see only with the eyes and mind of a pygmy, which means that shoulders are all very well, but men of genius can see vast horizons because they are who they are."[90]

The First Ascent of Mont Blanc was a literary monument to block the view of Balmat and Saussure—and of Tenzing. It remains an invaluable record of documentation and research. As the knot entangling empire, nation, masculinity, and Western civilization has frayed, however, its interpretation of the ascent of Mont Blanc is no longer satisfying or convincing. Rather than understanding Graham Brown and de Beer's work as simply in error or superseded by a new paradigm, consider the terms that Ludwik Fleck used to characterize the existence and revision of knowledge. It remains a salutary lesson in scholarly humility: "It is altogether unwise to proclaim any such stylized viewpoint, acknowledged and used to advantage by an entire thought collective, as *'truth or error.'* Some views advanced knowledge and gave satisfaction. These were overtaken not because they were wrong but because thought develops. Nor will our opinions last forever, because there is probably no end to possible development of knowledge."[91]

SUMMIT OFFERINGS

On August 8, 1953, the same day that Hillary arrived in Auckland, Tenzing returned to Darjeeling. He told fifteen thousand people in the market square: "As one faggot does not make a fire, so the credit for the conquest of Everest is not mine alone but that of the whole team." He then visited the Sherpa Buddhist monastery, where "small lighted tapers flickered in front of the image of Buddha as Tenzing and his family bowed low before the altar."[92] Tenzing told *Life* magazine after the ascent that he had often looked at Chomolungma (Mount Everest) as a boy: "Then I sit think what lamas at Tengboche say. They say Buddha god live there on top and they make worship to mountain. I have feeling for climbing to top and making worship more close to Buddha god. Not same feeling like English Sahibs who say want 'conquer' mountain. I feel more making pilgrimage."[93] In many interviews, Tenzing recalled that his first thought at the summit of Everest was gratitude to God that he had succeeded. He remembered previous climbers especially from the Swiss expedition. He then buried an offering to the god of the mountain—biscuits, candy, a small pencil. Tenzing covered these gifts with snow and said a prayer of thanks to the Goddess Mother of the World, "I am grateful, Chomolungma."[94]

When Hillary stepped on the summit, he later said he felt relief, astonishment, and satisfaction, "a satisfaction less vociferous but more powerful than I had ever felt on a mountaintop before." He extended his arm to shake hands "in good Anglo-Saxon fashion," but Tenzing threw his arms around him and they hugged each other with thumps on the back. Hillary took photographs of Tenzing and in each direction as proof of their ascent. He checked the oxygen equipment and ate a bar of mint cake. Griffith Pugh had insisted that they drink as much fluid as possible the night before, so "we arrived on top with full bladders." Hillary used the break to urinate on the summit. They descended after fifteen minutes on top. As they neared the South Col, Hillary gave the news to George Lowe in the slang of a Kiwi bloke: "Well, George, we knocked the bastard off!"[95]

In September 1953, Reuters reported that "along with Sherpa Tenzing's gifts of sweets to the mountain gods, Sir Edmund Hillary left a small fibre crucifix at the summit of Mount Everest."[96] Hillary saw Tenzing burying his offerings and remembered that he had in his pocket an envelope with a two-inch-long crucifix: "I shoved it in the snow next to Tenzing's gifts." Hunt had given Hillary the envelope and crucifix that an English Roman Catholic priest had asked him to take to the top. No one on the expedition was Catholic. Asked why this news had not been made public earlier, Hillary told a reporter that he only put an envelope in the snow, and it would be up to Hunt to say what was in it: "It didn't matter to me at all; I have no religious beliefs."[97] Before the expedition, Father Martin Haigh, a monk at the Benedictine abbey of Ampleforth, asked Hunt to take the crucifix "as a symbol of God's eventual triumph and the rededication of the world to his service." Years later, Hunt recalled his initial reaction—"I groaned, honestly"—but agreed because it was small and he considered himself a "humanist" and "ecumenical Christian" who believed profoundly in the message of love in the Christian Gospels. Hunt replied that it would be a privilege to carry the cross and asked for the team to be remembered in prayers.[98]

When they returned to London, Father Haigh was ecstatic to learn that the small crucifix from his own rosary, blessed by Pope Pius XII, had been placed on the summit of the world. Haigh told Hunt that their ascent would appear in history books and in "another history, the real history, far more fundamental and far greater, which at the moment we can only glimpse with the eyes of faith and which God alone knows fully." Haigh also implored Hillary to release the news: "Tenzing and yourself, the representative of the East and the West, fulfilled a far deeper mission than the mere conquest of a mountain. You reached the summit of the world and, as was only right, you both left there your offerings."[99] Haigh sent copies of this correspondence to the Vatican, and the papal secretary responded warmly and enclosed medallions for the climbers.

Hunt returned to the image of the summit offerings to answer the question, "Why climb mountains?" In July 1953, a female Chinese student from Malaya had posed this question on *London Calling Asia,* a BBC radio program. Hunt was left dissatisfied both by his own response about "a strictly non-material end" and the moderator's quip that Mallory had said the same thing with "because it's there."[100] Upon further review, Hunt wrote in 1954: "It is not sufficient to reply, 'Because it is there'; the climbs are symbols of man's conquest of himself and man's smallness in relation to his environment—God's creation." Hunt was struck by the image of "the Westerner and the Asian upon the summit of the world," each of whom "left a token on the peak, something symbolic of his belief in the aid of a Higher Power." In an article for Rotarians, whose motto was "Service above Self," Hunt said that the point of climbing mountains was "comradeship, regardless of race or creed, forged by the hardships and dangers." The ascent would not be considered worthwhile until it had inspired international cooperation: "If men, striving in unity and strengthened in spirit, can attain such a goal as Everest, then we can likewise solve other problems, less lofty but more pressing, in this sorely troubled world."[101]

At the height of the Cold War, the summit position remained political. In 1960, a Chinese team that climbed the northern side of the mountain

left its own summit offerings, a bust of Chairman Mao Zedong and the flag
of the People's Republic. The expedition leader, Shih Chan-Chun, attributed their success to the teachings of Mao, the support of hundreds of millions of countrymen, and the experience of Soviet mountaineers. They
owed their success to "the fidelity of our mountaineers to the Communist
Party and the people, their confidence in the victory of the revolutionary
cause, their collective spirit of solidarity, friendship and brotherhood which
they had displayed to the fullest extent, their noble quality and communist
style of sacrificing the self for the honor of the collective."[102]

Multiple versions of "thinking like a state" dominated the Everest expeditions of the mid-twentieth century. Nationalisms and internationalisms
that competed with one another to appropriate ascents of Mount Everest,
Mont Blanc, and other peaks have shared much in common. "Making Tenzings" was not limited to postcolonial nation-states. The renegotiation of
sovereignty in Geneva and Piedmont-Savoy, revolutionary and Napoleonic
France, imperial Britain and France, unified Italy and Germany, the French
Third Republic, the Weimar Republic and Third Reich, and postcolonial
states after the Second World War all created categories of difference, marginality, and exclusion with corresponding efforts at inclusion and appropriation of their respective Tenzings or Balmats. The production of "Tenzings" was as integral to the making of commonwealths, Catholicism, or
Communism as it was to the imagining of national communities in Britain, Nepal, India, or New Zealand. If "making up people" describes the
creation of individual subjects by state classification, then "making Tenzings" represents the simultaneous production of subalternity and difference
that accompanies thinking like a state. Making people and making Tenzings occur almost together in a world of multiple and shared modernities.

Tenzing's autobiography, *Tiger of the Snows,* made news in 1955 by announcing that "Hillary stepped on the top first. And I stepped up after
him."[103] This confession is framed by a series of elaborate disclaimers that
the question did not matter to him and he only answered out of concern for
the "truth" and the prestige of Everest itself. The book gave fulsome expression to Tenzing's gratitude to God on the summit, but its enumeration of
causes was clearly the result of a multilingual dialogue among Tenzing's
collaborators on the book. Even so, Tenzing articulated much the same
position without translators or ghostwriters. Consider an interview he gave
in London in Hindi without Hillary and Hunt, in which the interviewer,

A. Hasan, said he would ask the same question as earlier interviews because "either you didn't answer it properly or you couldn't answer it properly. When you reached the summit, how did you feel?" Tenzing: "When I reached the summit, I felt good." Hasan: "Felt good?" Tenzing: "Yes, felt good. Because we had attempted this climb six times earlier. This was the seventh time. The fact that we made it, this was the grace of God. Second, we had planned the climb from the north face and I looked down the mountaintop from that side. I saw the Rongbuk Monastery, et cetera, and Tibet. I saw all. I cannot exactly say I saw such and such landmark specifically, but I saw all." Tenzing saw "all," but did not attempt to encompass a panoramic perspective or assert a position of autonomy. Efforts by others to "make Tenzings" should not obscure the position that Tenzing made for himself but shared with many others: "With the grace of god, with the blessings of the whole world, with the blessings of my brothers and sisters, I was successful."[104]

Tenzing's role at the Himalayan Mountaineering Institute continued to entangle him in Indian politics for many years. After his death in 1986, the funeral procession to the site of his cremation on the HMI grounds stretched for a mile and was the largest Darjeeling had ever seen. A tomb and statue commemorate Tenzing as "the first man" to climb Everest "with Edmund Hillary." The life-size statue of Tenzing depicts him not making his summit offerings, but on a rock pedestal in the iconic pose of Tenzing in the summit position above a sea of clouds, holding aloft flags, and trampling the mountain underfoot. On a road in Darjeeling, a larger-than-life statue of Tenzing gives this pose an even more militant interpretation, as Tenzing charges forward, brandishing his ice ax. In both renditions, the metal flags on the statue hang stiffly in the air, unbending to any breeze, frozen forever in time.

CHAPTER TEN

Bodies of Ice

FROZEN TRANSCRIPTS

Body parts protruding from a crevasse in the Glacier des Bossons caught the eye of Ambroise Simond in 1861. Distinctively colored hair identified the fragments of flesh as the mortal remains of guides in the Hamel accident. The 1820 avalanche had buried three guides high on the mountain, but the movement of the ice deposited their broken remains 3,000 meters below, near the valley floor. The inquest inventory included two skulls, tufts of hair, a jaw with teeth, arms, hands, legs, ribs, vertebrae, and "many other anatomical fragments more or less crushed, but all recognized and labeled as human remains." A survivor of the accident, Joseph-Marie Couttet, then seventy-two years old, identified and grasped the severed hand of Pierre Balmat and exclaimed, "I never dared to believe that before leaving this world I would be allowed again to shake the hand of one of those fine comrades, the hand of my good friend Balmat!"[1]

On the glacier, the frozen flesh had been odorless. In the inquest room in Chamonix a few hours later, a cooked leg of lamb rescued from the glacier began to thaw, decompose, and emit a nauseous smell. A wine cork was so well preserved in the deep freeze that it was said its vintage could be identified by sniffing its distinctive bouquet. For several years, some of the debris was exhibited at Chamonix, Annecy, Paris, and London. The human remains were buried respectfully in the village cemetery, but the grave had to be reopened several times, as the glacier released more relics from the ice, a process repeated in Chamonix and other parts of the Alps.

A century later in 1961, a historian and glaciologist clambered over the glaciers in search of different kinds of relics. Emmanuel Le Roy Ladurie and Jean Corbel were looking for bits of wood rather than pounds of flesh. The discovery that tree trunks in glaciers in Switzerland and Alaska had been dated with dendrochronology and carbon testing inspired them to search the glaciers of Mont Blanc. After inspecting all of the tongues of ice that once reached the valley, "one of us finally located on the edge of the Taconnaz glacier, some remains of tree trunks completely stripped of their bark and firmly caught under a lateral moraine."[2] The samples of wood were difficult to extract, but carbon testing dated the fragments embedded in the ice between 1630 and 1680.

This search of the glacier exhibited Le Roy Ladurie's profound disagreement with Marc Bloch's famous description of the historian's craft: "The good historian resembles the ogre in the legend. Wherever he smells human flesh, there he knows he will find his prey." A nice phrase, thought Le Roy Ladurie, but too narrow for the true scientific spirit. In the 1940s, Bloch viewed man, or rather men, as the true object of study for the historian. For Bloch, a history of volcanic eruptions might be of interest to geologists, but it was of no concern to historians: "Man's actions are the most complex in the animal kingdom, because man stands upon nature's summit."[3] By the 1960s, however, Le Roy Ladurie rejected Bloch's anthropophagous ogre and argued that the historian should be interested in nature for its own sake: "The time has gone by when Greek philosophers and physicists spoke of man as 'the center of the universe' and 'the measure of all things.'" Le Roy Ladurie placed glaciers at the center of his investigation because they were the great "accumulators of climate" and "to talk about glaciers is the same thing as talking about climate."[4]

Reconstructing an archive of climatic fluctuation required clambering over the ice and combing through articles in dusty and esoteric journals "or the unobtainable yearbook of some Teutonic Alpine club."[5] The most reliable glacial records had been created by thinking like a state. To reduce the risk of catastrophic flooding at the beginning of the twentieth century, Paul Mougin, an inspector for the French Ministry of Agriculture's division of water and forests, made a detailed survey of the glaciers of Savoy, and other government geographers and archivists searched for additional historical records.[6] Mougin was responsible for reforestation and hydraulic engineering to contain rivers, and his photographic and topographic surveys were more detailed than previous studies of the oscillation of the glaciers by Chamonix naturalists. Movement of the glaciers was measured in 1816 by Jean-Michel Cachat *dit le Géant* on behalf of Genevan naturalists. Twentieth-century archivists found numerous requests to reduce payments of the tithe because of the advance of the glaciers by at least 1580. Around 1600, one hamlet near Chamonix was destroyed and another abandoned due to encroachment of the ice. Seventeenth-century prelates visited periodically to offer blessings to halt glacial advance. Mougin viewed eighteenth-century prints and cadastral maps to compare depictions of the glaciers with their current positions. The villagers of Montquarts erected a cross at the end of the Glacier des Bossons in 1818, and its location was still well known in 1904, which permitted more precise estimates of glacial retreat. The greatest concern at the turn of the twentieth century was the return of the deadly glaciers. If disputes over "feudal" dues created records of advancing glaciers and colder temperatures in the seventeenth and eighteenth centuries, a wider variety of sources documented the recession of the glaciers amid warmer temperatures after the 1850s.

What was the connection between climate and human history? In the 1960s, Le Roy Ladurie criticized the "naïve anthropocentrism" of earlier historians of climate who exaggerated the connection between events in natural history (rainfall or glaciers) with human history (migration or economic crises). He viewed the impact of climate on humans as slight and perhaps negligible over the *longue durée* (long term). Before writing an ecological history "with a human face," it was necessary to reconstruct "a pure climatic history free of any anthropocentric preoccupation or presupposition." By rejecting anthropocentric prejudices, the "fictionalized history of climate can become scientific history of climate, just as alchemy eventually turned into chemistry."[7] At almost the same time, the Cambridge geographer Jean Grove studied the advance and retreat of the glaciers in the Alps, Scandinavia, and other parts of the world. Since the 1960s, a wider community of scholars confirmed the existence of the "Little Ice Age," a cooler period with advancing glaciers from about 1550 to 1850, though specific dates and definitions have varied.[8] Glaciologists have returned to the historical records and artistic representations of Chamonix to develop "high-resolution" indices of the glaciers of Mont Blanc over the last five hundred to one thousand years.[9]

More broadly, researchers using ice core samples have extended these timescales back into the deep past of paleoclimatology. On Mont Blanc, Michel-Gabriel Paccard noted that the layers of snow were "so distinct that they are not from the same year," and Mark Beaufoy provided a more detailed observation in 1787: "At this place I had an opportunity of measuring the height of the snow which had fallen the preceding winter and which was distinguished by its superior whiteness from that of the former year. I found it to be five feet. The snow of each particular year appeared as a separate stratum. That which was more than a twelvemonth old was perfect ice, while that of the last winter was fast approaching to a similar state."[10] As these porous layers of snow settled and froze, they preserved microscopic air bubbles as a frozen transcript of past atmospheric and climatic conditions. In recent years, the gas and chemical compounds and organic matter trapped in these annual layers of ice have been analyzed to provide data for the history of climate. The ice core samples extracted from glaciers on equatorial peaks document the last 10,000 to 40,000 years, Greenland's ice sheets provide an archive of the last 100,000 to 200,000 years, and glaciers in Antarctica and the Qinghai-Tibetan Plateau have preserved the annals of 500,000 to 800,000 years of climate.[11] These natural archives demonstrate that global temperatures have varied cyclically over very long periods of time in the deep past. Shifts in the earth's orbit appear to have created cyclical swings within a wide but well-defined range of temperatures. No consensus exists to explain the hundreds of smaller fluctuations in temperature over shorter periods of time within this recurring pattern. However, there is near unanimity among investigators that the accelerated warming observed in global temperatures over the last half century is outside the range of historical variability.[12]

After writing about peasants and the people without history, Le Roy Ladurie aspired in his earliest works about climate to write a "history without people."[13] By the early 2000s, however, he compared human histories and climate histories in multiple volumes.[14] The heat wave of 2003 closed

Mont Blanc to climbing on some routes before the end of the summer and inspired a wider audience to take an interest in this work. With coinvestigators, Le Roy Ladurie identified a number of shorter fluctuations, each lasting about thirty years or less. Curiously, in this more recent work, each of these fluctuations were anthropomorphized and named after a kind of patron saint of the era: eighteenth-century fluctuations, for example, were named after Saint-Simon (1702–1717), Montesquieu (1718–1746), Choiseul (1747–1774), and Lavoisier (1775–1799). Yet no earlier period was as severe as the most recent "Promethean fluctuation (1988–2010)," when warming accelerated rapidly. Following the conclusions of the Intergovernmental Panel on Climate Change (IPCC), Le Roy Ladurie and other observers associated this rise in global temperatures with increasing levels of carbon dioxide and greenhouse gases in the atmosphere.[15] By 2011, Le Roy Ladurie remained skeptical that climate alone could explain a global crisis in the seventeenth century—"it is missing the Pope"—but the hypothesis raised questions about the future: "Will the accumulation of heat during the twenty-first or twenty-second centuries play a role similar to that of the accumulation of cold in the age of Louis XIV and other Eurasian monarchs, now in terms of more frequent disasters?"[16]

CHAMONIX BICENTENNIAL, 1986

When Jacques Balmat and Michel-Gabriel Paccard reached the summit of Mont Blanc on August 8, 1986, their arrival was filmed for French television. Two guides dressed in period costume left Chamonix the previous day, slept at the bivouac site, and followed the route of the first ascent. The mountain was still dangerous: in the previous week, twelve people died and another thirty-three were injured on the Mont Blanc massif. On the morning of the anniversary, a commemorative postage stamp was issued on the summit and the bishop of Annecy said a Mass for mountaineers in Chamonix. A folkloric festival recreated a peasant village with traditional crafts at Pèlerins, the birthplace of Jacques Balmat. Three French television stations were competing to make the first live broadcast from the summit, which led *Le Figaro* to remark: "Mont Blanc appears to have become a field of battle for broadcasters." The summit was enveloped in clouds on the day of the anniversary. When the Balmat and Paccard reenactors arrived on top that afternoon, they were not visible from below and barely could be seen by cameras that followed their progress on foot. The clouds and storm canceled most helicopter rides to the summit for dignitaries, as well as the first live broadcast from "the roof of Europe." The French television station Antenne 2 had planned for this eventuality, and preempted live pictures by showing footage that had been filmed days earlier of "Balmat and Paccard" reaching the summit in sunshine.[17]

"Balmat and Paccard" seemed to be everywhere in the valley. Four pairs of guides played the two protagonists in costume from one end of the festivities to the other. One pair was welcomed back to the village of Bossons and another returned to the center of Chamonix, "while their 'namesakes' continued to the summit for the shooting of a film."[18] After a parade, the inauguration of a statue to Paccard included the usual suspects—prefects, senators, deputies, and counselors as well as civil, military, and religious officials and representatives from mountaineering clubs. The government of Prime Minister Jacques Chirac was represented by a minister for local affairs and an advisor for youth and sports. It was rumored that the president of France, François Mitterrand, would make a flying visit, including a helicopter ride to the summit, but bad weather canceled the journey. The national figures did not make speeches. Instead, the mayor of Chamonix, Michel Charlet, thanked the dignitaries and the bicentennial committee and paid tribute to Dr. Paccard: "Like him, let us turn our gaze to the heights, to larger horizons, to the vastness of space."[19] A thousand balloons were released into the air. A choir in traditional costumes sang a new hymn to Mont Blanc with lyrics from Saint-Preux, a character in Jean-Jacques Rousseau's *Julie*. As a band played the Savoyard anthem "Les Allobroges," "Balmat and Paccard" pulled an oversized French flag off the statue to reveal a seated Michel-Gabriel Paccard. *Le Dauphiné Libéré* reported: "Together they entered history for the second time and it was together that this first *cordée sans corde* [roped partners without a rope] entered into legend." It had taken two centuries "for public opinion to put Paccard on the pedestal he deserved and now his bronze gaze turns ironically toward Mont Blanc and forever away from oblivion."[20]

The highlight of the festivities was supposed to be a sound and light show in the evening. Music played as the guide and writer Roger Frison-Roche read about the ascent. Before the inclement weather intervened, nine hundred people were to be stationed on nearby mountains to light fires on ten summits as well as on the route of the first ascent. The route was still marked by torches that could be glimpsed through the clouds, but the fireworks display did not reach its full potential—illuminating the summit with rockets designed by NASA, culminating in a "magisterial bomb" said to be visible from Geneva or Lyon in good weather. Mist and clouds covered the summit and limited the view even in the valley.[21]

The French postal service issued its commemorative stamp on top of Mont Blanc. The stamp's design reversed Balmat's profile so that the Bacler d'Albe busts of Balmat and Paccard no longer faced each other but now rubbed shoulders looking at the mountain and a barometer. Switzerland had already minted a banknote honoring Horace-Bénédict de Saussure in the 1970s. On the morning of the anniversary, a dozen French postal officials ascended Mont Blanc with professional climbers from the Association Sportive des Postes, Télégraphes et Téléphones (ASPTT), a sporting federation founded by postal workers, to issue philatelic souvenirs on the summit and symbolize its slogan, *La Poste bouge* (the Post Office moves). To add to the stunt, they threw a few letters into a crevasse near the top of the mountain for delivery sometime in the future when that part of the glacier reached the valley.[22]

Two days later, Genevan citizens tried to organize a human chain along the 93 kilometers of roads linking Geneva and Chamonix. The chain of people holding hands was intended to symbolize fraternity and peace and recognize the role of Saussure. At least 100,000 people were needed, but the chain had many "missing links" when fewer than 20,000 participated. Larger cities enjoyed a convivial atmosphere, especially closer to Geneva, and the links held fast across the Swiss-French border under the watchful eyes of customs agents.[23]

Some questioned the "circus" atmosphere in Chamonix, but many took a longer view of the historical controversy. *Le Monde* noted that "the bicentennial celebrations are the occasion for the 'rehabilitation' of the doctor." Paccard may now "rest in peace," wrote *L'Humanité*, because "the quarrel is well and truly buried."[24] According to *Neue Zürcher Zeitung*, the controversy had remained alive even though Paccard's role "had long been proven, not least by British Alpine historians and other studies," including a Swiss researcher who recently found a letter from Paccard.[25] Alexandre Dumas was widely blamed for the "growth of the legend" in the nineteenth century. In the twentieth century, as summarized by the *Los Angeles Times*, historians "concluded that Paccard did reach the top of the summit on his own strength that day 200 years ago, probably a step ahead of Balmat." That was certainly the view of Thomas Graham Brown and Gavin de Beer during the postcolonial controversies over Edmund Hillary and Tenzing Norgay in the 1950s. But Paccard was emphatically not considered "first" by everyone in Chamonix, where elevating Paccard did not require diminishing Balmat. Instead, both were celebrated as native sons and citizens of France. The French bicentennial rehabilitated Paccard to celebrate Mont Blanc as a symbol of civic and national unity. "The mountain once again," wrote *Le Dauphiné Libéré,* "instead of separating men, brought them together."[26]

A television docudrama re-created the first ascent as a joint achievement for French television. *Les Inconnus du Mont-Blanc,* written and directed by Denis Ducroz, a Chamonix guide and filmmaker, opened with Balmat returning from his snow bivouac and the announcement of Saussure's reward. Shortly afterward, a priest blesses a cross erected by villagers at the end of a glacier. Paccard has treated Balmat's daughter for an illness and after some hesitation, they consent to climb together after Balmat agrees to accept Saussure's reward as payment. From the sleeping place, Balmat goes on alone and reaches fantastic crevasses, but returns to carve his initials into the rock. They discuss the route, which Paccard identifies on a map in his notebook. Nearing the summit, the two men race to the top and collapse together as their two alpenstocks remain planted side by side on the summit. Balmat's wife rushes out of the house, and the film closes with an aerial shot above the summit as the climbers descend. A scrolling postscript announces that "alpinism had been invented," Paccard became mayor, and Balmat disappeared in the mountains.[27]

The Paccard statue tried to use modern materials to represent the doctor as a modern man. The Chamonix municipal council chose Jean-Loup Bouvier and André Sandel as sculptors in February 1986, and selected a design with Paccard seated on a rock rather than standing in other poses. A bicentennial subscription was opened to pay the cost of 300,000 francs. To meet this tight budget and short timetable, a bronze figure was rejected in favor of an "epoxy resin mixed with bronze powder on a base of cement that seems modern, economical, fast to use, ideal." However, this modern material could not withstand the severe winter in Chamonix, and less than six months later the statue was eroding and exfoliating: "flaking patches of paint, large holes on the right foot, the hat, with many cracks and fissures."[28] The defective statue was removed and a bronze statue of Paccard cast on the same model was unveiled on July 27, 1991.

On its elevated granite base, the seated Paccard sits erect holding a wooden alpenstock and gazing toward Mont Blanc. A knapsack and hat rest at his feet and a sheath holding scientific instruments is strapped across his back. The statue is positioned so that Paccard looks down the river Arve and over the shoulders of Balmat and Saussure, whose statues had been erected a century before. The knapsack and hat at the feet of Paccard and Saussure are almost the same and establish the doctor's credentials as a "man of science." The 1887 and 1986 statues are themselves frozen transcripts of contemporary representations of masculinity and sovereignty. If the Balmat-Saussure group had represented the alliance of courage and science in the interest of social peace in the late nineteenth century, the solitary Paccard embodied the myth of an autonomous individual forged by the politics of difference from the eighteenth to the twentieth centuries. Today, the Paccard statue is a favorite place for the children of Chamonix to scramble on its base and even climb onto its shoulders (Figure 23). The great irony is that the sovereign individual autonomy exemplified by such a solitary figure did not exist in Paccard's time and still does not in ours. Truth be told, to say that either Paccard or Balmat was "first" when they climbed the peak together really does require the growth of a legend.

THE POPE ON MONTE BIANCO

The bicentennial celebrations on the Italian side of Monte Bianco had a very different character. On August 8, 1986, Courmayeur held its own Mass for mountaineers, ribbon-cutting ceremony, parade with folk costumes, balloons, fireworks, and a variety show. The focal point at 6:23 p.m. was the ringing of church bells and the singing of "Happy Birthday Monte Bianco." The opening ceremony was for the *via ferrata del bicentenario al Monte Chétif*, a path to a panoramic summit above the village occupied by a 13-meter-high statue of the Virgin Mary. The day before, a group of mountaineers including Reinhold Messner, Chris Bonington, and the leader of an Italian parliamentary group, Amici della Montagna, held a press conference to criticize both a planned superhighway in the valley and Chamonix's excessive celebrations. The Chamonix events contributed to "an image of Mont Blanc de-cultured, trivialized, reduced to the role of 'picturesque' backdrop to a sound and light show that does not exalt but rather ridicules two hundred years of struggle, conquest, drama, dreams."[29] More sympathetic

Figure 23 Standing on Shoulders: The Paccard Statue in Chamonix, 2011.
© Peter H. Hansen.

commentators in Italy viewed the French rehabilitation of Paccard as reaf-
firming "with a certain nationalistic pride the existence of a presumed mo-
nopoly on the history of mountaineering. So the celebration has a national
character." In contrast, Courmayeur's celebrations aimed not to emulate

Chamonix, but "above all to revive the image of a well-equipped modern tourist resort 'despite some past mistakes.'"[30]

The Italian celebrations reached their peak a month later with the arrival of Pope John Paul II in the Val d'Aosta on September 7, 1986.The anniversary of the first ascent provided the occasion for the pope to articulate a critique of "modern man" and appeal for a return to the Christian roots of European civilization "from the highest pulpit in Europe."[31] At the *Scuola Militare Alpina* in Aosta, John Paul II began the day by challenging the cadets to apply the lessons of the mountains to life: "In a permissive society like ours, it is necessary to recover some of those virtues that we could call Alpine," including discipline, loyalty, solidarity, constancy, and sacrifice. The pope then flew by military helicopter to the foot of Mont Blanc. His pastoral advice to the citizens of Courmayeur was to promote tourism based on Christian values. The goal of tourist development should never be exclusively economic advantage, but also to promote hospitality, ecological education, and spiritual growth. An avid skier, Karol Wojtyła praised mountain sports for enhancing physical capacities and contributing "to the formation of the human person" by opening him or her up to the beauties of creation, the values of friendship, and the spirit of cooperation, "required especially in ascents with ropes." The pope explained to the clergy of the region that his visit commemorated "the conquest of Mont Blanc" two hundred years earlier by Paccard and Balmat, who already had been celebrated in France and Italy and by the international community: "The Church wants to participate in this commemoration, wanting to walk alongside men in their enterprises and encourage their ideals."[32]

After ceremonies in Courmayeur, a military helicopter transported the pope to the Brenva glacier of Mont Blanc. Plans to fly the papal helicopter to the summit were altered by bad weather. Instead, the helicopter landed on an "X" cleared in the snows at 3,500 meters for a brief walkabout: "Even on the ice of Mont Blanc, which also could hide dangers, the Pope did not heed protocol." When he deviated from the well-trodden snow and headed away from the summit, he was brought back to the helicopter, which quickly took off for the next destination. Observers reported the "bewildered images of the happy man (of Karol Wojtyła, not the Pope), who leaves almost astonished and smiling his footprints on the eternal snows of Mont Blanc."[33] Later in the day, John Paul II earned applause when he thanked the pilots who "conducted me if not to the top of Mont Blanc, at least close to Mont Blanc, very close. And, certainly, one should not go to the top of

Mont Blanc by helicopter. On foot yes, by helicopter, no. We could have and should have gone on the glacier to contemplate the grandeur of the peak, and thank God for giving me this privilege today."[34]

After visiting the glaciers, the pope's next destination was the summit of Mont Chétif above Courmayeur. A short ascent protected by iron railings led from a helicopter landing pad to the summit with its massive statue of the Madonna Regina Pacis, erected in 1946. Below this statue, he delivered remarks based on Psalms 90:2—"Before the mountains were born and the earth brought forth, from everlasting to everlasting you are God." In every age, humanity viewed the mountains as privileged places to experience God: "The mountain silences the chaotic din of the city and the silence of boundless spaces dominates: a silence in which man is given to hear more distinctly the inner echo of the voice of God." From the perspective of the summit, "how evocative it is to look at the world from on high, and to contemplate this magnificent panorama, taking it all in with a single glance!" Yet this perspective cannot be sustained. The eye never ceases to admire and the heart keeps climbing higher, echoing the call of the liturgy to lift up your hearts. However, "modern man" (*l'uomo contemporaneo*) followed the opposite principle and turned to "the things of the earth in a materialistic vision of life." Petrarchan echoes were followed by an injunction to acknowledge a dignity above and beyond the self, "the traces of the living God, not only impressed on these majestic beauties of nature, but above all in your immortal spirit!" Over the centuries, man had tried to climb inaccessible peaks including Mont Blanc and only two centuries ago, "two brave mountaineers succeeded in setting foot for the first time on the summit of this mighty mountain covered in snow and ice."[35]

"We are here to celebrate this historic event, in which we admire the confirmation of the fundamental charge to dominate the earth, that God has entrusted to man since the dawn of time, and that the Bible has faithfully recorded already in its first pages." The meaning of the first ascent of Mont Blanc had aroused great interest, at that time and even today. The pope then echoed Charles Durier's nineteenth-century history of the mountain: "The highest peak of Mont Blanc, located geographically at the center of the continent, Europe has always seen as a source of pride, a symbol of itself. The celebration of the bicentennial of this courageous ascent thus offers, in a sense, the occasion to reflect on the profound unity that binds together the nations of Europe."[36] This appeal to European unity was more than merely a gesture of solidarity in a continent still divided by walls, but a plea to reverse the process that had provincialized Christianity as the sovereign subject of Europe and of history.

This papal mountain of European unity was rooted in the heritage of the Christian faith. "From the top of this Alpine proscenium, which allows the eye to range over the territories of three different countries," Pope John Paul II called for "Europe" to return to its Christian values, reconstruct itself, and regain its progress toward "authentic civilization." In the shadow of a Marian statue and on the eve of the festival of the Nativity of the Blessed Virgin, his intercessory prayer asked that "Europeans of today obtain a keen sense of those indestructible values that imposed on the Europe of yesterday the admiration of the world, by promoting progress towards prestigious goals of culture and of welfare." After recent terrorist attacks at Karachi and Istanbul, he called for the intercession of the "Queen of Peace" so that "love prevails over hate to guarantee finally a peaceful and fraternal human coexistence."[37]

Four years later, in July 1990, John Paul II finally completed his ascent of Mont Blanc. He retreated for his annual vacation to a Salesian Center in the Val d'Aosta, where he could see Mont Blanc from his window. Before this break, he was so exhausted it was rumored that the Vicar of Christ might resign the papacy. Yet on the day that Poland and the soon-to-be-reunified Germany confirmed that the Oder and the Neisse Rivers would remain their permanent boundary, John Paul II flew to the mountain. As his helicopter hovered over the summit making the sign of the cross in the air, the pope prayed for a continent "united and at peace." The helicopter then landed below the highest point on the Col Major and the pope walked up to the less-frequented Italian summit of Monte Bianco with a guide. He spent about twenty minutes in contemplation, prayed for fallen mountaineers, and sang a Te Deum.[38]

Afterward, his ascent was celebrated and disparaged as a symbol of papal sovereignty. The theologian and essayist Sergio Quinzio thought the pope's gesture of the cross above the summit was a symbol that spoke louder than words: "John Paul II is Slavic, and in conformity with his culture is a man capable of experiencing visions and symbols, much more than we are capable of doing, we men of the modern West." The future growth of the church depended on less developed countries, and his "Slavic" awareness of myths and symbols enabled him to "mediate between East and West, and between North and South." "On the roof of a Europe fraught with contradictions between the ideal and the real, the Pope climbs as if onto a throne: back, at least in the language of symbols, as the universal sovereign, as it was in the Middle Ages." This was too much for Domenico Del Rio, Vatican analyst for *La Repubblica* and papal biographer, who lamented that a pope could never take a banal vacation or enjoy the mountains without mentioning the creator of the universe: "Wojtyła traced a great blessing on the new Europe exiting from the upheavals of East. A pope at that altitude, with white vestments in front of white snowfields, must be celebrated immediately. He was the sovereign of a new Europe on the path to unification that appeared on the eternal snows. Medieval visions were exhumed that came straight out of *Dictatus papae* and the pontiff of the two swords." The metamorphosis was remarkable: one day he ascended tired and ready to abdicate the throne of St. Peter, and "after descending he was Emperor, keeper of the spiritual and temporal power over the old continent."[39]

John Paul II's summit position on Mont Blanc inevitably entangled thinking like a mountain with assertions of thinking like a state. Yet hyperbolic rhetoric comparing his position to the throne of a universal monarch merely served as a reminder that he was a head of state without a state beyond the confines of Vatican City. His ideal of a united Christian "Europe" also had not existed for some time, if ever. But then, "secularization" also had never been as complete as its advocates were convinced or its critics feared. In an interview at the end of his vacation, the pope identified his apostolic blessing of Mont Blanc with the threshold of a "new experiment" that followed a "painful and humiliating" experiment for fifty years in Eastern Europe. He pontificated that gods and spirits were not just present in Europe's past and the non-European present, but provided the resources for Europe's present and the hope for the world's future. "Nature is our mother," declared the pope as an analogy for the return to beauty and the resources of nature: "These resources are certainly of a physical and visual order, but at the same time spiritual. And nature, although it is a physical thing, a material thing, it speaks simultaneously with its spiritual language. It does not know it is 'speaking,' because it has no consciousness, but we know it."[40]

ANTHROPOCENE

The retreat of mountain glaciers was the crucial evidence of "the Anthropocene, the new 'man-made' geologic epoch we are living in," according to a working group assembled by the Pontifical Academy of Sciences in 2011. At almost the same time, a group of Nobel laureates released a memorandum on sustainability that urged "humans are now the most significant driver of global change, propelling the planet into a new geological epoch, the Anthropocene." These manifestos adopted the unitary voice of *ex cathedra* pronouncements. Geological societies held multivocal conferences devoted to the Anthropocene in 2011, and the Royal Society published a theme issue of *Philosophical Transactions* devoted to research "consistent with the suggestion that an epoch-scale boundary has been crossed within the last two centuries." Although each intervention called for additional research, all were convinced that a threshold had been crossed: modern man was no longer in the ascendant, but now occupied the summit position on earth. The Nobel laureates looked in the mirror and saw the first modern men: "We are the first generation with the insight of the new global risks facing humanity."[41]

The Anthropocene is a slogan that wants to declare itself an epoch. Around the year 2000, the Dutch chemist Paul Crutzen asserted that we no longer lived in the Holocene, the name for the epoch since the last global glaciation, about twelve thousand years ago. Crutzen had received a Nobel Prize for research on ozone depletion and argued that rising levels of carbon dioxide archived in glaciers since the late eighteenth century were caused by anthropogenic emissions and marked the beginning of a new human-dominated, geological epoch, the Anthropocene. Crutzen selected James Watt for his invention of the steam engine in 1784 as the exemplary boundary figure who inaugurated the epoch. The environmental changes over the last two centuries may require "internationally accepted, large-scale geo-engineering projects, for instance to 'optimize' climate."[42]

Who was first? Since geological societies determine the nomenclature used in the official Geological Time Scale, the search is on to find a sedimentary stratum or geological layer on the earth's surface that marks the boundary of the epoch. Needless to say, it is a challenge to find a geological layer for such a recent and brief period of time. Moreover, before the "Anthropocene" could be recognized officially as a geological epoch, three separate professional organizations would have to agree that it meets technical criteria for geological periodization.[43] The choice of names for older layers such as Cambrian, Jurassic, Pleistocene, and so forth were highly contested and imprinted with the imperial politics that prevailed when they were chosen.[44] The *New York Times* was impressed by the multiple pronounce-ments of the Anthropocene in 2011, but noted that such labels are usually applied in retrospect and historical eras tend to have "fuzzy" edges: no one awoke in Florence in the 1300s and said, "Today the Renaissance begins!"[45]

When did the Anthropocene begin? To some critics, it was far too soon to identify a new stratigraphic layer: let's talk in ten thousand years. Others argue that humans began to change the earth's climate five thousand to eight thousand years ago, with the introduction of agriculture and defores-tation.[46] To its advocates, however, the Anthropocene defines the epoch in which we are living, so it is not merely descriptive of existing strata but pre-dictive of atmospheric, biological, geological, and oceanic changes still to be measured in the future. Investigators have put forward a variety of bound-ary figures—or "golden spikes" in the geological vernacular—usually dated between 1750 and 1950. The team that provided the historical context for the Anthropocene in *Philosophical Transactions* settled on three stages: 1800 as an arbitrary date to signify the Industrial Revolution, stage two for the "great acceleration" of the global economy after 1950, and stage three with the awareness of human impact circa 2000.[47]

Rather than searching for a boundary figure or stratigraphic layer, the Anthropocene would be better understood as yet another alternative mo-dernity, a deeply ambivalent assertion of human sovereignty at this particu-lar postcolonial moment. It is far from the "first" declaration of its kind.[48] Consider, by comparison, the manner in which colonization, the world wars, and the Cold War defined previous labels announcing the same epoch—Anthropozoic, Psychozoic, Anthropogene/Anthropocene, and Ho-locene. Despite exaggerated claims that the "Holocene" was adopted by everyone by 1833, 1885, or 1900, there was no consensus in the nineteenth century or the first half of the twentieth century about what to call the most recent geological epoch. Or, to put the matter succinctly but uninspir-ingly, the consensus was to call it "Recent." In the 1830s, Charles Lyell proposed "Recent" to describe the postglacial present, and geologists em-ployed "Recent, modern, historic or actual" with precious few references to the Holocene for at least fifty years after the Holocene was coined by the French paleontologist and zoologist Paul Gervais around 1860.[49] Instead, Lyell defined man's relationship to nature not with a name but by analogy with colonial expansion and the imposition of European sovereignty: "The greater part of the inhabited planet remains still as insensible to our presence, as before any isle or continent was appointed to be our residence."[50]

Anthropozoic was proposed in the mid-nineteenth century to assert human sovereignty over the natural world by divine decree. An English congregational minister, Thomas W. Jenkyn, may have coined this neologism in geological lessons for the *Popular Educator* in 1854: "All the recent rocks, called in our last lesson Post-Pleistocene, might have been called Anthropozoic, that is, human-life rocks." Reverend Samuel Haughton's *Manual of Geology* (1865) defined the Anthropozoic as the "epoch in which we live." The Dublin geology professor argued that archaeologists and geologists had proven that "the termination of the reign of Mammals on the globe was mainly due to the creation of the race of Man, who is endowed with faculties which enable him to destroy with ease all rival races, however superior to him in the brute qualities of size and strength." Once again, sovereignty over races in all senses of the term was sanctioned by a higher power: "Man is the direct product of the creative power of God, and governs the other creatures by His express decree."[51]

Italian priest, geologist, and mountaineer Antonio Stoppani's endorsement of Anthropozoic is often cited by advocates of the Anthropocene as a worthy predecessor, without reference to its context in a broader eschatology. In the 1870s, Stoppani argued that many would be scandalized by giving so much importance to the human era because it was so short in geological history. Some of those who would be scandalized "proclaim man tertiary and in the sovereign creature of the universe only recognize the ignoble trace of an ancient primate." The importance of an epoch did not depend on its length or duration. Man was the elemental force that separated old from new to create universal history. Stoppani noted that the Common Era based on the Christian calendar had been adopted as a convention by all nations to mark the beginning of universal time:

This occurred when the world resounded with the great word, when the Christian yeast was introduced within the dough of ancient pagan societies, the new element par excellence, the food that replaced former servitude with liberty, darkness with the light, and the fall and degeneration with resurgence *(risorgimento)* and the true progress of humanity. It is precisely in this sense that I do not hesitate to proclaim the era Anthropozoic. The creation

of man is the introduction of a new element in nature, a force wholly unknown to ancient worlds.

Then, infusing the language of the flaneur with the chaste piety of a priest,
Stoppani asserted that the "marriage" of old and new had rendered the material world the "spouse" of intellectual and moral principles: "a new telluric
force, which by its power and universality faints not in the face of the major
forces of the earth."[52]
Later in the 1870s, Joseph Le Conte proposed Psychozoic to name "the
age of man." The Recent epoch was "dignified by the appearance of man as
the dominant agent of change, and therefore well entitled to the name Psychozoic sometimes given it." A geology professor, mountaineer in Yosemite,
and a founder of the Sierra Club, Le Conte had previously defined the ascent of man in lectures on religion and science: "Completed individuality—
separation from the all-pervading forces of Nature—this is the distinctive
characteristic of man." Natural history was defined by the ascent of this
self-conscious, individual man, and human history "struggles upward and
attains Divinity in Christ."[53] The importance of man in Le Conte's geological periodization was due not merely to his "transcendent dignity" but also
to his capacity to "modify the whole fauna and flora of the earth. With the
establishment of his supremacy the reign of man commenced."[54]
The Anthropocene, Noösphere, and Holocene were then promoted by
different research communities in the shadow of world wars, revolution, and
the Cold War. "Anthropogenic" had entered the lexicon via post-Darwinian
debates over anthropogenesis, the generation or evolution of man. After
theosophists adopted anthropogenesis to signify the synthesis of science
and religion, British geologists shunned similar words in their periodization
and turned to Holocene, although it was not universally adopted in other
countries. In 1922, the Russian geologist Aleksei Petrovich Pavlov proposed
that the longer Quaternary period be renamed the anthropogenic period or
"Anthropocene" and this was taken up in the Soviet Union and still circu-
lates in Russia.[55] His colleague, Vladimir I. Vernadsky, recalled that his
outlook changed radically after the First World War and the Bolshevik
Revolution: "An historical phenomenon of such power may and should be
examined as a part of a single great terrestrial *geological* process, and not
merely as an *historical* process." Where historians had viewed man as autonomous individuals moving freely about the planet, Vernadsky argued

that in the biosphere, "no living organism exists on earth in a state of freedom. All organisms are connected indissolubly and uninterruptedly." Writing during the Second World War, Vernadsky was inspired by the evolution of human intelligence represented by Psychozoic and Anthropocene and settled on "Noösphere" to signify the age when man became a geological force. "In the twentieth century," he wrote, "man, for the first time in the history of the earth, knew and embraced the whole biosphere, completing the geographic map of the planet earth, and colonized its whole surface. *Mankind became a single totality in the life of the Earth.*"[56] During the Cold War, Soviet scientists continued to use "Anthropogenic system (period) or Anthropocene" in geological periodization, including at a U.S. conference in 1965. The American Commission on Stratigraphic Nomenclature then recommended in 1967 that "Holocene" officially be sanctioned to replace "Recent" as the uniform label for this geological epoch.[57]

The Anthropozoic, Psychozoic, Anthropogene, and Anthropocene are not the same, but they share more than etymological roots. Each declaration of the new age of man has been entangled in a broader time knot, often called "modernity" in other domains. It has been suggested that humanity's collective agency as a geological force challenges historical convention: "Anthropogenic explanations for climate change spell the collapse of the age-old humanist distinction between natural history and human history."[58] This needs to be qualified. Advocates of the Anthropozoic and earlier periodization also viewed man as the dominant agent, a geological force that collapsed distinctions between natural and human histories. However, the telos of their periodization was providential revelation or future utopia, usually Christian in the nineteenth century and occasionally Bolshevik in the twentieth century.

In the early twenty-first century, the more restrained but convincing claim is that global shifts summarized under the slogan of Anthropocene are "highly plausible."[59] Yet as with earlier claims for periodization, ardent advocates of the Anthropocene make "strong" claims on behalf of its explanatory power, and they would like it to be something more than a metaphor. The climatologist Will Steffen and colleagues view the Anthropocene and "planetary boundaries" as a unifying theory that integrates biodiversity, climate change, population growth, ocean acidification, freshwater, land use, and atmospheric pollution. These authors claim that the Anthropocene challenges notions of progress, neoclassical economics, and the place of humanity in the natural world, and that its revolutionary impact will equal Charles Darwin's theory of evolution.[60] Such muscular claims for the Anthropocene are almost invariably coupled with calls for human intervention to change the climate in the name of "geoengineering" or "planetary boundaries."

Who decides? The telos of the "strong" version of the Anthropocene is not stratigraphic layers but the summit position, a periodization that revives the sovereignty of "modern man" by another name. Ironically, arguments for intervention in the name of geoengineering secularize and universalize the biblical charge for human mastery over the earth. Visions of global governance resuscitate the universal sovereign, with papal infallibility replaced by scientific certainty, a prospect that has been characterized more as "Orwellian nightmare" than apostolic blessing.[61] Techno-scientists will decide the exception, which resurrects the legal grounds for suspension of the rule of law during colonial regimes.[62] Criticism of the growth of India, China, and other developing nations in such scenarios also raise questions about whether the "strong" Anthropocene is an expression of imperial nostalgia.[63] Historians of science note that "climate discourse" has often served as a framing device for other issues and can be deployed to naturalize "matters of social concern into matters of natural fact."[64] It is too soon to say whether research and development for geoengineering will promote business as usual or become another way of saying "not yet" to the non-Europe.[65]

The Anthropocene periodization requires revisiting the issue of nominalism, put aside in Chapter 3. Does it matter whether a mass of rock and snow is called *les glacières, Mont Maudit,* or Mont Blanc? Recall Ian Hacking's distinction between the static consequences of naming things and the dynamic nominalism of labeling people. Rocks reputedly are indifferent, but people adjust in complex ways to the labels they are given. The assumption of a static nominalism in nature was founded on assumptions of human autonomy from nature. When humanity collectively becomes a geological agent, can what we call mountains have dynamic effects? Mountains may look immutable, but, as any geologist will tell you, they are not. If what "we" call mountains or nature changes how we interact with the wider world, then a formerly static nominalism could become dynamic.

If "modernity" were called "Anthropocene," would that change how "we" act within it? The Anthropocene encourages thinking beyond the autonomous self, but it tends to promote high-modernist schemes to improve

climatic conditions, thinking like a state on steroids. Put another way, perhaps the most prominent dynamic effect of promoting the "Anthropocene"
has been to spur investment in geoengineering. Many advocates of the Anthropocene prefer "mitigation" to geoengineering and view the epoch as a call
for shared responsibility: "We accept our duty to one another and to the
stewardship of a planet blessed with the gift of life."[66] "Man and the biosphere" played a similar role as a metaphor for fifty years. In the biosphere,
man and nature were indissolubly connected, but neither was sovereign. In
the Anthropocene, man is the sole sovereign of the vale. We live *in* the biosphere but *during* the Anthropocene, and those prepositions define very different relations to the natural world. "We" might change how we live in order
to change the conditions where we live; but to change a period of time—let's
just change the name. It is not clear that a new name for the epoch would
have the effect of convincing people that the autonomy of modern man at
the summit of nature should be re-envisioned, that sovereignty could be
shared, or that we are all on the same belay.

The duration of an epoch and the panoramic perspective of humanity
are too broad to be encompassed. Dipesh Chakrabarty intriguingly suggests
that the universals created by awareness of climate change surpass the limits of historical understanding: "Climate change poses for us a question of a
human collectivity, an us, pointing to a figure of the universal that escapes
our capacity to experience the world."[67] These universals escape us because
they conceal peculiarity and difference, the standpoints through which we
actually experience the world. The Anthropocene offers the view from
above the summit, indeed a view from above the earth. But this becomes an
unattainable limit point since the world of multiple, diverse, but ultimately
shared modernities resists incorporation into the singular and universal
perspective of "modern man."

People do care about the glaciers, however. According to an eighteenth-
century pen, "Glaciers are masses of Ice accumulated upon the Declivities
between Mountains."[68] Glaciers also occupy the declivities between the
universal and the particular. Located in this intermediary position, glaciers
help to integrate the multiple levels of global knowledge and local meaning
in a changing climate.[69] As they advance and retreat, the instability of the
glaciers clears a space for thinking like a mountain. Humans have left detailed accounts of visiting the glaciers of the Alps for at least a thousand
years, but "we" have lived among the mountains for well more than five

thousand years. In some traditions, glaciers speak, or at least they can be heard, and narratives of "endangered glaciers" have a long history.[70] Glaciers are not silent, but make noise as they move. Perhaps that is why the scientists and mountaineers who convened at the Vatican examined "the fate of the mountain glaciers in the Anthropocene"—not the fate of humanity in general—because the glaciers so often serve as symbols of something else, whether a timeless nature outside of history, a set of broader resources, or thinking like a mountain.

Such thinking is not excluded from the Anthropocene because it is native to modern science. Some of the ice core climatologists who extended climate histories into the deep past frequently describe how they approach the glaciers, mountains, and local cultures with respect. "One thing a driller always has to ask is for forgiveness from the mountain for taking the ice," says Bruce Koci, a high-altitude ice core driller, "If you don't, it won't part with it very easily." In an interview on Kilimanjaro, the climatologist Lonnie Thompson reflected on the connections between mountains and religious traditions around the world: "Mountains are interesting places. . . . There are a lot of words in the world of science and everyday affairs, but words don't work on mountains; you have to experience them."[71]

The declivities accumulate histories as well as glaciers. On a good day in the summer, hundreds of people may reach the top of Mont Blanc, but many thousands will visit the valley of the Mer de Glace. Crystals and minerals from the area are displayed in an exhibit that is cut like a mine shaft into the mountain. The eighteenth-century Temple of Nature and nineteenth-century Grand Hotel still stand on the ridge at Montenvers. The early twentieth-century train station is thronged with tourists and climbers who arrive on the funicular railway from Chamonix. A scenic path is dotted with plaques bearing quotations from literary visitors or monuments describing the history of *Les rendez-vous du Montenvers*. Cable cars descend from the station toward the glacier, but stop well above its current level. A path continues the descent to the glacier with signs indicating the level of the ice in 1980, 1990, 2000, and 2005. At the base of the cliff, the path enters a grotto that is cut into the ice and contains exhibits and curiosities. Inside the glacier, you can smell the ice, hear the rush of water, and feel cold drops of a melting glacier dripping on your head. The Anthropocene may be good to think with, but a glacier you can touch in the flesh.

LIVING ON THRESHOLDS

"Good lord, it's a man!" exclaimed a married couple from Nuremberg, Germany, when they saw a body lying facedown, head and naked torso exposed above the ice in the gully of an Alpine glacier on the border of Austria and Italy.[72] Erika and Helmut Simon had taken a shortcut off the main path near the Hauslabjoch pass when they found the corpse on September 19, 1991. They snapped a photo and informed the keeper of the nearby Similaun Refuge, a mountain hut, about the body of a dead climber or skier. Mountaineers Reinhold Messner and Hans Kammerlander read the news while training nearby and visited the scene two days later. From the shriveled skin, Messner estimated that the body must be at least four hundred years old. The boundary between Austria and Italy was indistinct on the pass, so the case was taken up by the Austrian gendarmerie. Forensic investigators arrived with Austrian state television but without equipment to extricate the body from the ice. Meltwater had refrozen so they had to chisel at the ice with borrowed ski poles and ice axes. The corpse and fragments of clothing and tools were shoved into a coffin and taken by helicopter and hearse to Innsbruck, where an archeologist immediately identified the find as more than four thousand years old. Archeologists urgently returned to the site, and radiocarbon testing confirmed that the well-preserved mummy was 5,300 years old, a Neolithic man in the ice.

The discovery was a sensation, and raised many questions. The most pressing: was he "Austrian" or "Italian"? Surveyors soon determined that his grave was 92.6 meters inside Italy. Fractious negotiations over national possession eventually led to an agreement to return the "glacier mummy" to the autonomous Italian province of South Tyrol within a few years. On January 16, 1998, under heavy security, the iceman was shipped in a refrigerated truck over the Brenner Pass from Innsbruck to Bolzano, where he came to rest in a new South Tyrol Museum of Archaeology. The mummy inspired many popular nicknames, including Similaun man, Hauslabjoch man, Tisenjoch man, Homo tirolensis, Hibernatus, Frozen Fritz, and most frequently Ötzi, after the area of the Tyrolean Alps where he was found. In his bilingual homeland, his official name became *Der Mann aus dem Eis/L'Uomo venuto dal ghiaccio*—the man from the ice, or simply the iceman.[73]

More important, people wanted to know who he was. Between forty and fifty years old, he stood 5 feet, 2 inches tall, was short and stocky in build, and weighed between 110 and 135 pounds. He had brown hair and was born in what is now the South Tyrol. Beyond vital statistics, there was little agreement initially about whether he was a shepherd or hunter, leader or outcast, shaman or prospector, farmer or trader. Early theories read like adventure novels and claimed that he froze to death during a blizzard after being chased from his village.[74] In 2001, researchers found an arrowhead lodged in his shoulder and determined five years later that the wound had severed an artery that almost certainly caused him to bleed to death.[75] Traces of blood from four different people were found on his knife and other possessions. However, interpretations of his place of death have varied widely: it was alternately the place he collapsed after his wounds, the scene of a summary execution, or the site of a ritual burial.[76] Inevitably, but anachronistically, some even contend that the iceman was the first mountaineer or the first victim of a mountaineering accident.[77]

The medical history and genetic predispositions of the iceman are better known than for most living people. When he was diagnosed with osteoarthritis, the millennia between his age and ours seemed to vanish: "It's really not much different from modern man," said one doctor, "there are just very impressive similarities."[78] Dental exams showed that he had periodontal disease and cavities. His equipment and diet were well-adapted for frequent journeys in the mountains and he ate ibex meat for his last meal. The iceman's entire genome was mapped, revealing that he had brown eyes and Type O blood. He was lactose intolerant, at high risk for coronary disease, and the earliest known carrier of Lyme disease. It is thought that he did not have any direct descendants himself. His genetic profile is most similar to populations living in southern Corsica, northern Sardinia, and the Caucasus Mountains, and certain genetic markers indicate that he may share a common ancestor with about one in ten people in Italy.[79]

With new research appearing each year, it may seem surprising that for almost twenty years a central question remained: "Who discovered the iceman first?" When the corpse became a celebrity, Erika and Helmut Simon, caretakers in Nuremberg, enjoyed the honor of being Ötzi's discoverers. They appeared on German, Italian, and British television and were interviewed by journalists from Russia, China, and France. After the mummy was transferred to Bolzano, however, the Simons suffered a series of indignities. The official exhibit referred to them as explorers but not discoverers, and they were not invited to the opening but had to pay for a ticket. The South

Tyrolean state offered a premium of 5,100 euros if they would renounce any further claim. Helmut Simon was furious at the offer of "hush money" to relinquish his claim as "discoverer" and filed suit in Bolzano in 1998. If recognized as Ötzi's official discoverer, the financial rewards were potentially much higher. A 1939 Italian law provided a finder's fee worth 25 percent of the value of recovered property. With its new museum and booming sales of merchandise, Ötzi's value was now considerable. The South Tyrolean state maintained that a discoverer is only a discoverer when searching for something intentionally and the Simons had stumbled across Ötzi by accident. At trial, the state maintained that if they had been searching for a glacier mummy on purpose, then that would have been an unauthorized expedition—either way, they were not entitled to any reward.[80]

In January 2003, Helmut Simon, now retired from his caretaker position, testified about the humiliation he endured: "I feel as though I'm being defamed."[81] His lawyer demanded "moral reparation" and said that his clients would be happy if a plaque went up in the museum with their names. They admitted it was about money as well as honor. Ötzi's value was difficult to determine—"It's not a simple coin collection," Simon said. The mummy had been insured for €1.5 million during transit in 1998, and museum admission fees now totaled more than €2.5 million annually. The arguments offered by both sides were considered bizarre by many observers. A journalist for *Dolomiten,* a German-language paper in Bolzano, explained that the province was afraid of setting a costly precedent: "Our glaciers are melting. In the coming years a lot will come to the surface."[82]

In November 2003, the provincial court in Bolzano ruled that Helmut Simon and Erika Simon were the official discoverers of the glacier mummy. The court condemned the Bolzano provincial governor for contesting the case and ordered the state to pay all legal costs. Simon's lawyer was pleased at the decision and insisted that his clients were primarily interested in the satisfaction of formal recognition. The financial settlement would be determined by mediators and depended on the value of the iceman. South Tyrol offered €50,000, while the Simons demanded €250,000.[83] Two years later, the case took another bizarre turn when two women came forward to say that they were the real discoverers. A Swiss woman claimed that she was with the Simons when they found the body and had spit on it, so her DNA would be found on the corpse. A Slovenian actress said that she had seen the body while filming a television commercial in the area in 1991. Both claims were dismissed, but the *Ötzi-Streit* continued.

Helmut Simon was ecstatic at being named the discoverer. He printed "Discoverer of Ötzi" on business cards, wore a badge with the title wherever he went in the Alps, and said Ötzi was like a third son.[84] Simon was figuratively and literally born again: that year he became a Lutheran for the first time and was baptized by immersion. He went with a film crew to see both the discovery site and Ötzi at the museum for a documentary entitled *De ontdekking van Helmut Simon* (The Discovery of Helmut Simon) made by an evangelical television network in the Netherlands. "The circumstances, how we discovered Ötzi, was such an unbelievable chain of coincidences, that it was clear to me that my life was guided by a kind of divine providence," he told an interviewer in October 2004: "God helped me find Ötzi. Ötzi helped me find God."[85] Weeks later, Helmut Simon disappeared while climbing alone on Gamskarkogel peak in the Salzburg Alps. Heavy snow hindered the rescue efforts for a week, and he was found at the bottom of a ravine. Apparently, he had slipped on a hunter's trail and fallen 150 meters to the stream below. His corpse was lying facedown under a sheet of snow and ice.[86]

Was this the revenge of the mummy? Was there an Ötzi curse? Had he identified so strongly with Ötzi that he sought to meet the same fate? It remains a mystery. The curse was widely debated since a number of people associated with the iceman had died prematurely.[87] As for Helmut Simon, some commentators suggested that his curse was less the mummy's than the desire to win immortality. "Being a discoverer is like being the author of an important invention," said one of his lawyers. "It becomes your identity."[88]

The litigation over discovery of the iceman finally ended in 2010, when South Tyrol agreed to pay the estate of Helmut Simon €175,000 to cover both the finder's fee and legal expenses. The province had to pay another €48,000 for its own lawyer's bills. "At last there is peace surrounding the discovery of Ötzi," said the governor of South Tyrol as he presented a ceremonial check made out to Helmut Simon.[89] For the twentieth anniversary in 2011, Erika Simon was welcomed to the festivities that reunited again the community of mountaineers, police, coroners, judges, politicians, and journalists who had all participated collectively in the discovery of "Ötzi." In an interview, she recalled the motivations of her husband: "He always said, I don't give a hoot about the money. But we want to be recognized as the discoverers. We did not want it to have to end in a trial."[90]

A photograph taken by the Austrian police of the man they found in the ice (Figure 24) has superficial resemblances to the *Rückenfigur,* literally "back

Figure 24 Rückenfigur: The Iceman/Der Mann aus dem Eis/L'Uomo venuto dal ghiaccio, 1991. Austrian Police.

figure," the person viewed from behind that ornaments the landscape in many romantic paintings. The viewer of this photograph knows they have arrived very late, long after this person in the ice has passed into death. The back of the man in the ice does not invite the viewer into the frame, encourage the projection of the self, or embellish a panoramic point of view. The snapshot captures isolation from, rather than identification with, the man in the ice, but the Rückenfiguren of romantic landscape painting were also equivocal in that regard.[91] Only after the corpse was hacked out of the glacier did it become the iceman. Only after the mummy was placed on its back, faceup, eye sockets peering at the viewer in innumerable photographs, did the iceman become Ötzi. This is a man, the man with aching knees, bad teeth, and wrinkled flesh that Helmut Simon identified with, not a generic Rückenfigur. He went to court to prove that he was the discoverer not of an iceman, but of Ötzi.

At the South Tyrol Museum of Archaeology in Bolzano, both the iceman and Ötzi are on display. The man from the ice is kept in a refrigerated

cell with sophisticated climate controls to preserve the mummy indefi-
nitely. A small opening provides a window into his tomb, where visitors
may look at the mummy from the side as he lies on his back. Original artifacts found with the body are displayed nearby. Ötzi also stands in life-size
models similar to those in a wax museum. An earlier model depicted him
bundled in his warmest gear, covered with thick beard, straw cloak, and
fur hat, a hunter placing one foot higher than the other as if he were looking over a sea of clouds. That figure was retired to make way for a naturalistic model based on the latest research for the twentieth anniversary of his
discovery—Ötzi 2.0.[92] In the new model, the fit, muscular, and bare-chested
Ötzi has a grizzled face and piercing gaze, caught in midstride as he glances
to his left, greeting visitors at the entrance of the museum. According to the
museum director, "It gives our history a face, in the truest sense of the word."
An exhibition sponsor agreed: "Now we can finally look him in the eyes
and recognise, to our amazement, that he is really one of us!"[93]

The iceman stood at a threshold in his time and so do "we," with Ötzi,
in ours. In many obvious ways, these thresholds are not the same. Whatever "modern man" may be remains unstable and however sovereignty may
be defined—between man and nature or between men—also remains unsettled. The iceman was not the "first modern man," though he was unmis-
takably one of "us" in ways that test the limits of our historical understanding. From the longer perspective of "deep history," to view anyone as first
would be to "privilege the moment of beginning, not the process of becoming that precedes it and unfolds within it."[94] Yet even the seemingly descriptive label for the iceman as an "anatomically modern human" puts a
distance between him and us, shorthand for anatomically yes, but in other
ways no. Indeed, representations of Ötzi as our contemporary negotiate the
limits about what we can know about the remote past or how to figure the
universal category of humanity. Whether or not any one of us shares certain genomic markers with the iceman/Ötzi, we are all entangled with him
and with one another. The verticality of the mountains locates us in a continuum of past and present and future. If we envision ourselves in a summit
position on the uppermost layer, it can only be briefly, for a moment both
ephemeral and evanescent. A descent will soon follow. In this longer continuum of time, we can never step on the same mountain twice. We are
always on that belay. Tying on a rope is not the beginning of this knot of
time. And the ties that bind do not end with "Off belay!" "Belay off!"

Abbreviations

ACL	Alpine Club Library Archives, London
ADHS	Archives départementales de la Haute Savoie, Annecy
AJ	*Alpine Journal*
AN	Archives nationales, Paris
ASTO	Archivio di Stato di Torino
BGE	Bibliothèque de Genève
BL	British Library, London
BLNSA	British Library, National Sound Archives, London
BnF	Bibliothèque nationale de France, Paris
CAF	Club Alpin Français
CAI	Club Alpino Italiano
CC	*Correspondance Complète de Jean-Jacques Rousseau*
DÖAV	Deutscher und Österreichischer Alpenverein
Dübi	Heinrich Dübi, *Paccard wider Balmat: Oder, Die Entwicklung einer Legende* (Bern, 1913)

EE   Everest Expedition

FAMB   Thomas Graham Brown and Gavin de Beer, *The First Ascent of Mont Blanc*
            (Oxford, 1957)

HCL   Harvard College Library

HMI   Himalayan Mountaineering Institute

IPCC   Intergovernmental Panel on Climate Change

NARA   National Archives and Records Administration, College Park

NLS   National Library of Scotland, Edinburgh

NYPL   New York Public Library

OC   *Oeuvres complètes*

RGS   Royal Geographical Society

SAC   Schweizer Alpen Club

TNA   The National Archives, Kew

Notes

For additional resources related to this book, including bibliography and illustrations, see http://digitalcommons.wpi.edu/summits/.

I. BEGINNINGS

1. John Ball, *Peaks, Passes and Glaciers* (London, 1859), 488; nineteenth-century dictionaries and encyclopedias record exclusively nautical definitions of "belay."

2. For pitons, see Kerwin Lee Klein, "A Vertical World: The Eastern Alps and Modern Mountaineering," *Journal of Historical Sociology* 24 (2011): 519–548; for references to the search for belaying pins, see works by W. P. Haskett Smith and Owen Glynne Jones in the 1890s.

3. Joseph E. Taylor III, *Pilgrims of the Vertical: Yosemite Rock Climbers and Nature at Risk* (Cambridge, MA, 2010); Maurice Isserman and Stewart Weaver, *Fallen Giants: A History of Himalayan Mountaineering from the Age of Empire to the Age of Extremes* (New Haven, CT, 2008); for the postwar guide to belaying, see Richard M. Leonard and Arnold Wexler, "Belaying the Leader," *Sierra Club Bulletin* 31 (December 1946): 68–90.

4. Leslie Stephen, *The Playground of Europe* (London, 1871), 312.

5. Ibid., 1, 75, 317–318.

6. Leslie Stephen, "Alpine Climbing," *St. Pauls*, January 1868, 470, and *British Sports and Pastimes*, ed. Anthony Trollope (London, 1868), 257.

7. *AJ* 3 (1867): 203; "The Alps in the Last Century," *Fraser's Magazine*, August 1870, 173; Stephen, *Playground of Europe*, 17.

8. C. E. Mathews, *Annals of Mont Blanc* (London, 1898), 6; Francis Gribble, *The Early Mountaineers* (London, 1899), 14, 79–81; on Whymper's slide show in the 1890s, see Peter Berg, *Whymper's Scrambles with a Camera: A Victorian Magic Lantern Show* (London, 2011), 4–5, 122.

9. Fergus Fleming, *Killing Dragons: The Conquest of the Alps* (London, 2000); cf. Robert Macfarlane, *Mountains of the Mind* (London, 2003).

10. Stephen, *Playground of Europe*, 45.

11. Ibid., 20, 47, 66–67, 304; *AJ* 3 (1867): 200.

12. John Ruskin, *Modern Painters* (London, 1856), vol. IV, 325–393; for discussion of Ruskin's vulnerable eye, see Ann C. Colley, *Victorians in the Mountains: Sinking the Sublime* (Burlington, VT, 2010).

13. Marjorie Hope Nicolson, *Mountain Gloom and Mountain Glory: The Development of the Aesthetics of the Infinite* (New York, 1959), 3; Andrea Walton, " 'Scholar,' 'Lady,' 'Best Man in the English Department'? Recalling the Career of Marjorie Hope Nicolson," *History of Education Quarterly* 40, no. 2 (2000): 169–200.

14. Philippe Joutard, *L'invention du mont Blanc* (Paris, 1986); Yves Ballu, *Le Mont Blanc* (Paris, 1986); Roger Canac, *Jacques Balmat, dit Mont-Blanc* (Paris, 1986); Walt Unsworth, *Savage Snows: The Story of Mont Blanc* (London, 1986); *Découverte et sentiment de la montagne* (Annecy, 1986); *Imaginaires de la haute montagne* (Grenoble, 1987).

15. Peter H. Hansen, "Albert Smith, the Alpine Club, and the Invention of Mountaineering in Mid-Victorian Britain," *Journal of British Studies* 34 (1995): 300–324; Peter Bayers, *Imperial Ascent: Mountaineering, Masculinity and Empire* (Boulder, CO, 2003); Reuben Ellis, *Vertical Margins: Mountaineering and the Landscape of Neoimperialism* (Madison, WI, 2001); Jim Ring, *How the English Made the Alps* (London, 2000).

16. See the forum on historiographical turns in the *American Historical Review* 117 (2012): 698–813, and related discussion in Bruno Latour, "The Recall of Modernity: Anthropological Approaches," *Cultural Studies Review* 13 (2007): 11–30.

17. Talal Asad, *Formations of the Secular: Christianity, Islam and Modernity* (Stanford, 2003); Charles Taylor, *A Secular Age* (Cambridge, MA, 2007).

18. Compare the emphasis on the sacredness of nature in Simon Schama, *Landscape and Memory* (New York, 1995), 18, with Martin Scharfe, *Berg-Sucht: Eine Kulturgeschichte des frühen Alpinismus* (Vienna, 2008), 21, the most original recent history of mountaineering, in which religious doubt domesticates mountains; or Nicolas Giudici, *La Philosophie du Mont Blanc* (Paris, 2000), which reproduces the narrative of disenchantment. The treatment of summit crosses by Schama and Scharfe could not be more different.

19. Francesco Petrarca, "Familiares IV, 1," my translation. Unless otherwise stated, all translations are my own.

20. Ibid. Cf. Francesco Petrarca, *Rerum Familiarium Libri, I-VIII*, trans. Aldo S. Bernardo (Albany, 1975), 172–180.

21. Werner Handschin, *Francesco Petrarca als Gestalt der Historiographie* (Basel, 1964); Hannah Gray in *Speculum* 41 (1966): 539; Wallace K. Ferguson, *The Renaissance in Historical Thought: Five Centuries of Interpretation* (Boston, 1948).

22. Edward Gibbon, *The Decline and Fall of the Roman Empire*, chap. 66.

23. Jacob Burckhardt, *The Civilisation of the Renaissance in Italy*, trans. S. G. C. Middlemore (New York, 2000), 219.

24. Jacob Burckhardt, *The Greeks and Greek Civilization*, trans. Sheila Stern (New York, 1998), 7.

25. Edward Said, *Beginnings: Intention and Method* (New York, 1975), 5.

26. Ibid., 32.

27. Hans Blumenberg, *The Legitimacy of the Modern Age* (Cambridge, MA, 1983), 138, 468.

28. Ibid., 341–342, 470.

29. Theodor E. Mommsen, "Petrarch's Conception of the 'Dark Ages,'" *Speculum* 17 (1942): 226–242; Ferguson, *Renaissance in Historical Thought*, 21, 23, 106; Hans Ulrich Gumbrecht, "A History of the Concept 'Modern,'" in *Making Sense in Life and Literature* (Minneapolis, 1992), 83; and Hans Robert Jauss, "Modernity and Literary Tradition," *Critical Inquiry* 31 (2005): 341–342.

30. Reinhart Koselleck, *Futures Past: On the Semantics of Historical Time* (Cambridge, MA, 1985), 233, 235.

31. Dipesh Chakrabarty, *Provincializing Europe: Postcolonial Thought and Historical Difference* (Princeton, 2000), 6–7, 27, 109–112; Koselleck, *Futures Past*, 247–249.

32. Kathleen Davis, *Periodization and Sovereignty: How Ideas of Feudalism and Secularization Govern the Politics of Time* (Philadelphia, 2008), 20.

33. Chakrabarty, *Provincializing Europe*, 74.

34. Michel-Rolph Trouillot, *Global Transformations: Anthropology and the Modern World* (New York, 2003), 43.

35. Bruce Knauft, *Critically Modern: Alternatives, Alterities, Anthropologies* (Bloomington, IN, 2002); Timothy Mitchell, *Questions of Modernity* (Minneapolis, 2000).

36. Lynn M. Thomas, "Modernity's Failings, Political Claims and Intermediate Concepts," *American Historical Review* 116 (2011): 727–740, esp. 737.

37. Jean Bethke Elshtain, *Sovereignty: God, State and Self* (New York, 2008).

38. Burckhardt, *Civilisation of the Renaissance in Italy*, 3, 100, 219–221; Ernest Renan, *Averroès et l'averroïsme* (1852), in *Oeuvres Complètes* (Paris, 1947), vol. III, 252–259; Georg Voigt, *Wiederbelebung des classischen Alterthums oder das erste Jahrhundert des Humanismus* (Berlin, 1893 [1859]), vol. I, 129–130.

39. Lionel Gossman, *Basel in the Age of Burckhardt: A Study in Unseasonable Ideas* (Chicago, 2000); John R. Hinde, *Jacob Burckhardt and the Crisis of Modernity* (Montreal, 2000).

40. Quoted in Jan Goldstein, *The Post-Revolutionary Self: Politics and Psyche in France, 1750–1850* (Cambridge, MA, 2005), 157–158.

41. François Guizot, *Histoire de la civilization en Europe* (Paris, 1859), 213; Goldstein, *Post-Revolutionary Self,* 228–232, and passim.

42. Lucien Febvre, "*Civilisation:* Evolution of a Word and a Group of Ideas," *A New Kind of History* (London, 1971), 247; Tzvetan Todorov, *On Human Diversity* (Cambridge, MA, 1993), 90–170; Bruce Mazlish, *Civilization and Its Contents* (Stanford, 2004), 49–72.

43. BnF, Département des Manuscrits, Division occidentale, Latin 6802, fol. 143v; Pierre de Nolhac, *Pétrarque et l'humanisme,* rev. ed. (Paris, 1907), vol. II, 268; the attribution of the sketch is much debated, though it is frequently assigned to Giovanni Boccaccio and the inscription to Petrarch. See Maurizio Fiorilla, *Marginalia figurati nei codici di Petrarca* (Florence, 2005), 52–58; J. B. Trapp, "Petrarchan Places: An Essay in the Iconography of Commemoration," *Journal of the Warburg and Courtauld Institutes* 69 (2006): 3–4.

44. Gilbert Allardyce, "The Rise and Fall of the Western Civilization Course," *American Historical Review* 87 (1982): 695–725; Daniel A. Segal, " 'Western Civ' and the Staging of History in American Higher Education," *American Historical Review* 105 (2000): 770–805.

45. Ernst Cassirer, *Individual and the Cosmos in Renaissance Philosophy* (Philadelphia, 1963), 142, 144.

46. Riccardo Fubini, "Renaissance Historian: The Career of Hans Baron," *Journal of Modern History* 64 (1992): 558; Lionel Gossman, "Jacob Burckhardt: Cold War Liberal?" *Journal of Modern History* 74 (2002): 538–572; Anthony Molho, "The Italian Renaissance, Made in the USA," in *Imagined Histories: American Historians Interpret the Past,* ed. Anthony Molho and Gordon Wood (Princeton, 1998), esp. 279–280.

47. Nicolson, *Mountain Gloom and Mountain Glory,* 49–50.

48. Morris Bishop, *Petrarch and His World* (Bloomington, IN, 1963), 104.

49. Giuseppe Billanovich, "Petrarca e il Ventoso," *Italia Medioevale e Umanistica* 9 (1966): 389–401; Vittorio Rossi, "Sulla formazione delle raccolte epistolari petrarchesche," *Annali della cattedra petrarchesca* 3 (1932): 68–73; and editions of Petrarch's familiar letters.

50. Robert M. Durling, "The Ascent of Mt. Ventoux and the Crisis of Allegory," *Italian Quarterly* 18 (1974): 16–17, 22; for the prestidigitator, see Francisco Rico, *Vida u obra de Petrarca* (Chapel Hill, NC, 1974), 349; Hans Baron, *From Petrarch to Leonardo Bruni* (Chicago, 1968), 17–21, and *Petrarch's Secretum* (Cambridge, MA, 1985), 196–202.

51. Thomas Greene, *The Light in Troy: Imitation and Discovery in Renaissance Poetry* (New Haven, CT, 1982), 104.

52. Nicholas Mann, *Petrarch* (Oxford, 1984); Lyell Asher, "Petrarch at the Peak of Fame," *PMLA* 108 (1993): 1051; Craig Kallendorf, "The Historical Petrarch," *American Historical Review* 101 (1996): 130–141.

53. Giuseppe Mazzotta, *The Worlds of Petrarch* (Durham, NC, 1993), 3, 6, 98.

54. William J. Bouwsma, "The Renaissance and the Drama of Western History," *American Historical Review* 84 (1979): 1–15.

55. John Jeffries Martin, *Myths of Renaissance Individualism* (New York, 2004); Patrick Coleman, Jayne Lewis, and Jill Kowalik, eds., *Representations of the Self from the Renaissance to Romanticism* (Cambridge, 2000), 1–15; Roy Porter, ed., *Rewriting the Self: Histories from the Renaissance to the Present* (London, 1997), 17–28.

56. *Observer*, February 8, 2004.

57. Mark Bevir, *The Logic of the History of Ideas* (Cambridge, 1999), 121–123, 140–143.

58. Translation from Gossman, *Basel in the Age of Burckhardt*, 310.

59. Serge Briffaud, "Visions de la montagne et imaginaire politique: L'ascension de 1492 au Mont-Aiguille et ses traces dans la mémoire collective (1492–1834)," *Le Monde alpin et rhodanien* 16 (1988): 39–95; Gaston Letonnelier, "Nouvelles recherches sur Antoine de Ville et la première ascension du mont Aiguille," in *Dix ans d'activité de la Société des Tourists du Dauphiné* (Grenoble, 1940), 121–151.

60. François Rabelais, *Le Quart Livre des faicts et dicts Heroïques du bon Pantagruel* (Paris, 1552), 119.

61. Denis de Salvaing de Boissieu, *Septem miracula Delphinatus* (Grenoble, 1656), 53–85; *Annuaire Société des touristes du Dauphiné*, (1879), vol. VI, 101–110; trans. in Gribble, *Early Mountaineers;* W. A. B. Coolidge, *Josias Simler et les Origines de l'Alpinisme jusqu'en 1600* (Grenoble, 1904); Letonnelier, "Nouvelles recherches."

62. Claude-François Menestrier, *Le sept miracles de Dauphiné* (Grenoble, 1701), 6. The title *Supereminet invius* (It Rises Above or Towers Over, Inaccessible) is loosely translated as Mont Inaccessible.

63. *Mémoires de littérature tirés des registres de l'Académie royale* 6 (1729): 761.

64. Coolidge, *Josias Simler et les Origines de l'Alpinisme*, xxvi, xxxi–xxxv.

65. W. A. B. Coolidge, "Was ist eine 'Erste Besteigung'?" *Österreichischen Alpen-Zeitung*, May 26, 1893, offprint, 4–6; Coolidge, *Josias Simler et les Origines de l'Alpinisme*, xxii, xxxiv.

66. Letonnelier, "Nouvelles recherches," 128.

67. Ca. 1492 in Paris, wages were 2.5 sous a day over an average work year of 250 days; Robert C. Allen, "The Great Divergence in European Wages and Prices from the Middle Ages to the First World War," *Explorations in Economic History* 38 (2001), 411–447, and Micheline Baulant, "Le salaire des ouvriers du bâtiment à Paris de 1400 à 1726," *Annales. Histoire, Sciences Sociales* 26 (1971), 463–483.

68. James C. Scott, *Seeing like a State: How Certain Schemes to Improve the Human Condition Have Failed* (New Haven, CT, 1998).

69. Lauren Benton, *A Search for Sovereignty: Law and Geography in European Empires, 1400–1900* (Cambridge, 2010); Patricia Seed, *Ceremonies of Possession in Europe's Conquest of the New World, 1492–1640* (Cambridge, 1995).

70. Jack Lesage, *"Pour l'amour du nom du Roy," Le mont Aiguille* (Grenoble, 1992); Philippe Bourdeau et al., *Le mont Aiguille et son Double* (Grenoble, 1992).

71. Fernand Braudel, *The Mediterranean and the Mediterranean World in the Age of Philip II* (New York, 1972), vol. I, 25, 29, 33–34, 44.

72. Aldo Leopold, *A Sand County Almanac* (Oxford, 1949), 129–133; Susan L. Flader, *Thinking like a Mountain: Aldo Leopold and the Evolution of an Ecological Attitude toward Deer, Wolves, and Forests* (Madison, WI, 1994).

73. Wolves were prominent metaphors for World War II Resistance movements; see Peter H. Hansen, "Returning Upland: Provincializing Europe and the Anthropocene on Mont Ventoux" (unpublished essay); and Marco Armiero, *A Rugged Nation: Mountains and the Making of Modern Italy* (Cambridge, 2011), 16–20, 165.

74. Robert A. Orsi, *Between Heaven and Earth: The Religious Worlds People Make and the Scholars Who Study Them* (Princeton, 2005). Jon Mathieu, *The Third Dimension: A Comparative History of Mountains in the Modern Era* (Cambridge, 2011) productively combines material factors and the sacred and "religious" dimensions here associated with thinking like a mountain.

75. Leslie Stephen, *The Playground of Europe,* new ed. (London, 1894), 260–262; *Cornhill Magazine,* October 1873; and, for related discussion, see Kevin A. Morrison, "Embodiment and Modernity: Ruskin, Stephen, Merleau-Ponty, and the Alps," *Comparative Literature Studies* 46 (2009): 498–511, and Catherine W. Hollis, *Leslie Stephen as a Mountaineer: 'Where Does Mont Blanc End, and Where Do I Begin'* (London, 2010).

76. Stephen, *Playground of Europe,* 1894 ed., 277–278, echoing Tennyson's poem, "Tithonus."

77. Gustaf Sobin, *Luminous Debris: Reflecting on Vestige in Provence and Languedoc* (Berkeley, 1999), 5–6, 189–190.

2. DISCOVERY OF THE GLACIÈRES

1. Quoted in Emmanuel Le Roy Ladurie, *Times of Feast, Times of Famine: A History of Climate since the Year 1000* (New York, 1971), 133–134.

2. Gaston Letonnelier, "Documents relatifs aux variations des glaciers dans les Alpes Françaises," *Bulletin de la Section de Géographie* 28 (1913): 288, is one of many transcriptions from the ADHS.

3. Peter Burke, "How to Become a Counter-Reformation Saint," in *Religion and Society in Early Modern Europe, 1500–1800,* ed. Karspar von Greyerz (London, 1984), 45–55.

4. Laura Aliprandi and Georgio Aliprandi, *La découverte du Mont-Blanc par les cartographes, 1515–1925* (Ivrea, It., 2000), 30, 43.

5. BL, Add. MSS 22998, fol. 129, p. 241; Richard Pococke journals, Letter LXI, June 12–26, 1741.

6. William Windham and Peter Martel, *An Account of the Glacières or Ice Alps in Savoy, in Two Letters* (London, 1744), 1, 4–5; for variations, see Théophile Dufour, *William Windham et Pierre Martel, Relations de leurs deux voyages aux glaciers de Chamonix (1741–1742)* (Geneva, 1879); and A. V. Carozzi and J. K. Newman, *Horace-Bénédict de Saussure: Forerunner in Glaciology* (Geneva, 1995), 5–28.

7. Windham and Martel, *Account of the Glacières,* 10–12.

8. Ibid., 13–14, 22; Margarida Archinard, "A propos de l'alidade de Pierre-Guillaume Martel," *Genava* 37 (1989): 43–57.

9. J. G. Ebel, *Manuel du Voyageur en Suisse* (Zurich, 1805), vol. 2, 228.

10. Markham Sherwill, *A Brief Historical Sketch of the Valley of Chamouni* (Paris, 1832), 12.

11. Ibid., 34.

12. Lorraine Daston and Katherine Park, *Wonders and the Order of Nature, 1150–1750* (New York, 1998); Neil Kenny, *The Uses of Curiosity in Early Modern France and Germany* (Oxford, 2004); R. J. W. Evans and Alexander Marr, *Curiosity and Wonder from the Renaissance to the Enlightenment* (Aldershot, 2006).

13. Simon Schaffer, "Making Up Discovery," in *Dimensions of Creativity* (Cambridge, MA, 1994), 13–51.

14. Simon Schaffer, "Scientific Discoveries and the End of Natural Philosophy," *Social Studies of Science* 16 (1986): 387; Steven Shapin and Simon Schaffer, *Leviathan and the Air Pump* (Princeton, 1985); and Schaffer, "Making Up Discovery."

15. J. J. Thillet, *Chamonix, une vallée, des hommes* (St. Gervais, 1978), 57; André Perrin, *Le Prieuré de Chamonix: Historie de la vallée et du Prieuré de Chamonix du Xe au XVIIIe siècle* (Chambéry, 1887), 158–163.

16. Michèle Mestrallet, *Les étrangers et les mines savoyardes au XVIIIe siècle: La Compagnie Anglaise, 1740–1771* (Chambéry, 1965), 10–11, 13, 20–22; Francois Coutin, *Histoire de la Collegiale de Sallanches* (Montmélian, 1996), 55–60; Jean Nicolas, *La Savoie au 18e siècle: Noblesse et bourgeoisie* (Paris, 1978), vol. II, 818.

17. Kenny, *Uses of Curiosity,* 225–226.

18. Quoted in Nicolas, *La Savoie,* vol. II, 948.

19. Ibid., 554–558; Christopher Storrs, ed., *The Fiscal-Military State in Eighteenth-Century Europe* (Burlington, VT, 2009), 201–235.

20. Geoffrey Symcox, *Victor Amadeus II: Absolutism in the Savoyard State, 1675–1730* (Berkeley, 1983), 7.

21. Windham and Martel, *Account of the Glacières,* 17; Nicolas, *La Savoie,* vol. I, 121–135; Roger J. P. Kain and Elizabeth Baigent, *The Cadastral Map in the Service to the State: A History of Property Mapping* (Chicago, 1992), 213–217.

22. Aliprandi and Aliprandi, *La découverte du Mont-Blanc,* 56–57.

23. Lin Chao, "Zhum langma de faxian yu mingcheng" [Chomolungma: Its discovery and name], *Beijing Daxue xuebao: Renwen kexue* 4 (1958): 143–163, esp. 146–147. Many thanks to Gray Tuttle for help with translation.

24. Laura Hostetler, *Qing Colonial Enterprise: Ethnography and Cartography in Early Modern China* (Chicago, 2001), 22; Peter C. Perdue, *China Marches West: The Qing Conquest of Central Asia* (Cambridge, MA, 2005), 454; Mathew Edney, *Mapping an Empire: The Geographical Construction of British India, 1765–1843* (Chicago, 1997); David Buisseret, ed., *Monarchs, Ministers, and Maps: The Emergence of Cartography as a Tool of Government in Early Modern Europe* (Chicago, 1992).

25. David Gugerli, "Politics on the Topographer's Table: The Helvetic Triangulation of Cartography, Politics and Representation," in *Inscribing Science: Scientific Texts and the Materiality of Communication,* ed. Timothy Lenoir (Stanford, 1998), 94.

26. Sherwill, *Brief Historical Sketch,* 34.

27. *Annuaire du CAF* 8 (1893): 468, 479, and BnF MSS Fr. 14657.

28. Marc-Théodore Bourrit, *A Relation of a Journey to the Glaciers in the Dutchy* [*sic*] *of Savoy* (Norwich, 1775), 105. William Coxe, *Sketches of the Natural, Civil, and Political State of Swisserland* (London, 1779), 288.

29. ACL, B10, Henri Ferrand to H. F. Montagnier, October 29, 1916. Henri Ferrand, "La Pierre des Anglais," *Bulletin de la Société de statistique, des sciences naturelles et des arts industriels du département de l'Isère* (1918): 115–126.

30. Gaston Letonnelier, "De l'identification du nom de lieu 'Rupes Alba,'" *Revue Savoisienne* 54 (1913): 243–246.

31. Jean-André Deluc, *Recherches sur les modifications de l'atmosphere* (Geneva, 1772), vol. 2, 328, cf. 228; emphasis in original.

32. Horace-Bénédict de Saussure, *Voyages dans les Alpes* (Geneva, 1786), vol. II, 144.

33. Bourrit, *Relation of a Journey,* 8–9; in the original, "rude relations" was *récit bizarre.*

34. Conrad Gessner, *De raris et admirandis herbis* (Zurich, 1555); translation modified from Brian W. Ogilvie, *The Science of Describing: Natural History in Renaissance Europe* (Chicago, 2006), 113, and Conrad Gessner, *On the Admiration of Mountains* (San Francisco, 1937), 30, 34.

35. Ogilvie, *Science of Describing,* passim; Laurent Pinon, "Conrad Gessner and the Historical Depth of Renaissance Natural History," in *Historia: Empiricism and Erudition in Early Modern Europe,* ed. Gianna Pomanta and Nancy G. Siraisi (Cambridge, MA, 2005), 242–267.

36. W. A. B. Coolidge, *Josias Simler et les origines de l'alpinisme jusqu'en 1600* (Grenoble, 1904).

37. Johann Aicholz to Joachim Camerarius II in July and September 1582; University Library of Erlangen, Trew Collection: Aichholtz nos. 18–19. Many thanks to Tilmann Walter for this reference.

38. Robert W. Scribner, "The Reformation, Popular Magic, and the 'Disenchantment of the World,'" *Journal of Interdisciplinary History* 23, no. 3 (1993): 475–494.

39. Johann Jakob Scheuchzer, *Ouresiphoites Helveticus, sive Itinera Alpina tria* (London, 1708), for this version of the title.

40. Alix Cooper, *Inventing the Indigenous: Local Knowledge and Natural History in Early Modern Europe* (Cambridge, 2007), 138–139; Martin J. S. Rudwick, *Scenes from Deep Time: Early Pictorial Representations of the Prehistoric World* (Chicago, 1992), 4–26.

41. This follows Michael Kempe, "Sermons in Stone: Johann Jacob Scheuchzer's Concept of the Book of Nature and the Physics of the Bible," in *The Book of Nature in Early Modern and Modern History,* ed. Klaas van Berkel and Arjo Vanderjagt (Leuven, 2006), 111–119; and Michael Kempe, *Wissenschaft, Theologie, Aufklärung: Johann Jakob Scheuchzer (1672–1733) und die Sintfluttheorie* (Epfendorf, 2003).

42. Cooper, *Inventing the Indigenous,* 136.

43. Ibid., 131–166.

44. Johann Jakob Scheuchzer, *Ouresiphoites Helveticus, sive Itinera per Helvetiae alpines regiones* (Leyden, 1723), vol. I, preface, unpaginated. For the 1690s, see Cooper, *Inventing the Indigenous,* 135.

45. Quoted in Cooper, *Inventing the Indigenous,* 158.

46. Scheuchzer, *Ouresiphoites Helveticus* (1723 ed.), vol. III, 366–397.

47. Johann Jakob Scheuchzer, *Jobi physica sacra, oder Hiobs Natur-Wissenschaft* (Zurich, 1721), 259. Many thanks to David Dollenmayer for this translation.

48. Lorraine Daston and Katherine Park, *Wonders and the Order of Nature, 1150–1750* (New York, 1998), 192, 204, 349; cf. Claude Reichler, *La découverte des Alpes et la question du paysage* (Paris, 2002), 81–108.

49. Michael Kempe, "Noah's Flood: The Genesis Story and Natural Disasters in Early Modern Times," *Environment and History* 9 (2003): 163.

50. Ibid., 162–165.

51. Charlotte Klonk, "Science, Art, and the Representation of the Natural World," in *The Cambridge History of Science, vol. 4, Eighteenth-Century Science,* ed. Roy Porter (Cambridge, 2003), 593–599, esp. 597.

52. Marjorie Hope Nicolson, *Mountain Gloom and Mountain Glory* (New York, 1959), develops this theme, focusing on Burnet.

53. Scheuchzer, *Ouresiphoites Helveticus* (1723 ed.), vol. III, 399.

54. Quoted in Anke te Heesen, *The World in a Box: The Story of an Eighteenth-Century Picture Encyclopedia* (Chicago, 2002), 185.

55. Albrecht von Haller, *Premier Voyage dans les Alpes et autres texts, 1729–1732* (Geneva, 2008), 46–47.

56. Albrecht von Haller, *The Alps,* trans. Stanley Mason (Dübendorf, 1987), 45, 63.

57. Trans. adapted from Chenxi Tang, *The Geographic Imagination of Modernity: Geography, Literature, and Philosophy in German Romanticism* (Stanford, 2008), 62; cf. Haller, *The Alps,* 65.

58. Tang, *Geographic Imagination,* 62–66, affirms the "Newtonian eyes" that Marjorie Hope Nicolson identified from the 1720s in *Newton Demands the Muse: Newton's* Opticks *and the Eighteenth Century Poets* (New York, 1946), 25, 43.

59. Tang, *Geographic Imagination,* 66.

60. Jean Starobinski, "The Idea of Nostalgia," *Diogenes* 14 (1966): 88–89; Kempe, *Wissenschaft, Theologie, Aufklärung,* 282–311.

61. Daston and Park, *Wonders and the Order of Nature,* 350; Lisbet Koerner, *Linnaeus: Nature and Nation* (Cambridge, MA, 1999), 25–26.

62. Otto Sonntag, ed., *The Correspondence between Albrecht von Haller and Horace-Bénédict de Saussure* (Bern, 1990), 33.

63. Claudia Schweizer, "Scheuchzer, von Haller and de Luc: Geological World-Views and Religious Backgrounds in Opposition or Collaboration?" in *Geology and Religion: A History of Harmony and Hostility,* ed. M. Kölbl-Ebert (London, 2009), 95–101.

64. *The Poems of Baron Haller,* trans. Mrs. Howorth (London, 1794), 36–50.

65. Daston and Park, *Wonders and the Order of Nature,* 208.

66. Rousseau to Moultou, February 14, 1769, in *CC* (Oxford, 1980), vol. 37, 57; and Maurizio Viroli, *Jean-Jacques Rousseau and the 'Well Ordered Society'* (Cambridge, 2003), 15 and passim.

67. Jean-Jacques Rousseau, *Emile,* trans. Allan Bloom (New York, 1979), 277, 307; Jean Starobinski, *Transparency and Obstruction,* trans. Arthur Goldhammer (Chicago, 1988).

68. Arthur M. Melzer, "The Origin of the Counter-Enlightenment: Rousseau and the New Religion of Sincerity," *American Political Science Review* 90, no. 2 (1996): 344–360.

69. Jean-Jacques Rousseau, *Julie, or the New Héloïse* (Hanover, NH, 1997), 497; Jean-Jacques Rousseau, *OC,* vol. II, 607.

70. Rousseau, *Julie, or the New Héloïse,* 3; cf. 11–16.

71. Ibid., 63–65, 344.

72. Ibid., 424, 428.

73. Robert Darnton, *The Great Cat Massacres and Other Episodes in French Cultural History* (New York, 1984), 232.

74. Richard Whatmore, "Rousseau's Readers," *History of European Ideas* 27 (2001): 317–331.

75. Rousseau, *Julie, or the New Héloïse,* 428, 439, 462; *OC,* vol. II, 523, 537, 563.

76. Micheli du Crest to Johann Jacob Huber, March 9, 1754, Universitätsbibliotek, Basel, Mscr. L II 7, fol. 40–41.

77. Martin Rickenbacher, "Das Alpenpanorama von Micheli du Crest: Frucht eines Versuches zur Vermessung der Schweiz im Jahre 1754," *Cartographica*

Helvetica 11–12 (1995): 21–34; Barbara Roth-Lochner and Livio Fornara, eds., *Jacques-Barthélemy Micheli du Crest 1690–1766: Homme des Lumières* (Geneva, 1995), 151–165; Pirmin Meier, *Die Einsamkeit des Staatsgefangenen Micheli du Crest: Eine Geschichte von Frieheit, Physik und Demokratie* (Zurich, 1999), 204–276.

78. Roth-Lochner and Fornara, *Jacques-Barthélemy Micheli du Crest*, 133–137; Hasok Chang, *Inventing Temperature: Measurement and Scientific Progress* (Oxford, 2004), 10, 61.

79. See Gugerli, "Politics on the Topographer's Table," 97, for a discussion of political implications of this transparency.

80. Richard Whatmore, *Against War and Empire: Geneva, Britain, and France in the Eighteenth Century* (New Haven, CT, 2012); Helena Rosenblatt, *Rousseau and Geneva: From the First Discourse to the Social Contract 1749–1762* (Cambridge, 1997); Linda Kirk, "Genevan Republicanism," in *Republicanism, Liberty, and Commercial Society, 1649–1776*, ed. David Wootton (Stanford, 1994), 279–309.

81. Micheli du Crest, *Discours en forme de lettres sur le gouvernement de Genève (1735)*, ed. K. Goodwin, G. Poisson, G. Silvestrini, and R. Whatmore (Geneva, 2011), 82; Rosenblatt, *Rousseau and Geneva*, 144, emphasis in original; Roth-Lochner and Fornara, *Jacques-Barthélemy Micheli du Crest*, 141–146.

82. Richard Whatmore, "Rousseau and the Représentants: The Politics of the *Lettres Ecrites de la Montagne*," *Modern Intellectual History* 3, no. 3 (2006): 398–399; Douglas G. Creighton, *Jacques-François Deluc of Geneva and His Friendship with Jean-Jacques Rousseau* (University, MS, 1982), 12–35.

83. Douglas Freshfield, *The Life of Horace Bénédict de Saussure* (London, 1920), 47–49; René Sigrist, ed., *H.-B. de Saussure (1740–1799): Un regard sur la terre* (Geneva, 2001), 395–408, 453–485; Pierre Bourrit, *Marc-Theodore Bourrit 1739–1819* (Geneva, 1989), 30–35, 53; Marita Hübner, *Jean-André Deluc (1727–1817), Protestantische Kultur und moderne Naturforschung* (Göttingen, 2009), 33–44; J. L. Heilbron and René Sigrist, eds., *Jean-André Deluc: Historian of Man and Earth* (Geneva, 2011).

84. Deluc, *Recherches*, vol. I, 185–186.

85. Deluc to Rousseau, January 20, 1755; Rousseau to Deluc, December 28, 1754; *CC* vol. 3, 78–79, 94; see also 326–328.

86. Maurice Cranston, *The Solitary Self: Jean-Jacques Rousseau in Exile and Adversity* (Chicago, 1997), 76.

87. Jean-Jacques Rousseau, *Letter to Beaumont, Letters Written from the Mountain, and Related Writings* (Hanover, 2001), 233–234, 260–261; *OC* 3: 809; Whatmore, *Against War and Empire,* chap. 3.

88. Saussure to Haller, December 28, 1765 (for Rousseau); February 28, 1764, et seq. (for Voltaire); Sonntag, *Correspondence,* 178–180.

89. See Carozzi and Newman, *Horace-Benedict de Saussure,* 53, for the Latin and English.

90. Peter Gay, *Voltaire's Politics: The Poet as Realist* (New Haven, CT, 1988), 214; Peter Gay, *The Party of Humanity* (New York, 1964), 55–96; and articles by J.-D. Candaux in Raymond Trousson et al., eds., *Dictionnaire Voltaire* (Paris, 1994), 88–94.

91. Andre Gür, "La Négociation de l'édit du 11 Mars 1768 d'après le journal de Jean-André Deluc et la correspondance de Gédéon Turrettini," *Schweizerische Zeitschrift Für Geschichte* 17 (1967): 166–217.

92. Saussure to Haller, October 25, 1766, and May 13, 1767; Sonntag, *Correspondence,* 301, 357.

93. Bourrit, *Marc-Théodore Bourrit,* 51.

94. Bourrit to Auzière, 1766, quoted in Jane Ceitac, *L'affaire de natifs et Voltaire: Un aspect de la carrière humanitaire du patriarche de Ferney* (Geneva, 1956), 74–75.

95. Émilie Cherbuliez, *Mémoires de Isaac Cornuaud sur Genève et la Révolution de 1770 à 1795* (Geneva, 1912), 63–64; Bourrit, *Marc-Théodore Bourrit,* 52–53. See Bourrit's direct appeal: University of Maryland Archives, Savoy Collection, Acc. 72–279, box 6, M. T. Bourrit to J. A. Deluc, October 24, 1767.

96. Jean-Pierre Bérenger, *Le Natif, ou lettres de Theodore et d'Annette* (Geneva, 1767), 5, 46, 63.

97. *Le Citoyen ou suite des lettres de Theodore et d'Annette* (Geneva, 1767), 2, 10, 13, 35.

98. *Le Natif à Mr. César J . . . ou conclusion des lettres de Théodore et d'Annette* (Geneva, 1767), 4, 28, 30–31.

99. Gür, "La Négociation de l'édit du 11 Mars 1768," 206; Kirk, "Genevan Republicanism," 296.

100. Charles Dardier, *Ésaïe Gasc, citoyen de Genève* (Paris, 1876), 67–68; Emile Rivoire, *Bibliographie Historique de Geneve* (Geneva, 1935), vol. III, 351 (re: 1216) for Bourrit's political songs in January 1770.

101. Deluc, *Recherches,* vol. II, 298.

102. Ibid., 310.

103. Ibid., 313.

104. Ibid., 322; Bourrit, *Relation of a Journey,* 201.

105. Bourrit, *Relation of a Journey,* 203–204, 216–217; Deluc, *Recherches,* 227–230, 324, 329.

106. Christoph Hoffmann, "The Ruin of a Book: Jean André Deluc's *Recherches sur les modifications de l'atmosphère* (1772)," *MLN* 118 (2003): 586–602, esp. 588.

107. Heilbron and Sigrist, *Jean-André Deluc;* Martin S. J. Rudwick, *Bursting the Limits of Time: the Reconstruction of Geohistory in the Age of Revolutions* (Chicago, 2005), 150–158.

108. See BGE, Ms. fr. 9143, env. 15–16, for the exchange; see ACL, C144 for the itinerary/guide.

109. Marc-Théodore Bourrit, *Description des aspects du Mont-Blanc* (Lausanne, 1776), 123.

110. Ibid., 138, 142.

111. Charles Bourrit, *Notice Biographique sur Mr. Marc-Théodore Bourrit* (Geneva, 1836), 5; and *Biographie universelle, ancienne et moderne* (1843), vol. 5, 332.

112. Bourrit to Louis XVI, July 13, 1780; BGE Ms. fr. 9143, env. 10, 21, 22.

113. Freshfield, *Life of Horace Bénédict de Saussure,* 131.

114. Ibid., 94.

115. Ibid.; Albert V. Carozzi, *Horace-Bénédict de Saussure (1740–1799): Un pionnier des scienes de la terre* (Geneva, 2005), 44–173.

116. Saussure, *Voyages dans les Alpes,* vol. I, xiii; Freshfield, *Life of Horace Bénédict Saussure,* 291.

117. Freshfield, *Life of Horace Bénédict Saussure,* 162.

118. *CC,* vol. I, 2, 206.

119. Horace-Bénédict Saussure, *Projet de réforme pour le Collège de Geneve* (Geneva, 1774), 1–2; trans. in Freshfield, *Life of Horace Bénédict Saussure,* 314; cf. Charles Magnin and Marco Marcacci, "Le projet de réforme du Collège (1774): Entre instruction publique, politique et économie," in *H.-B. de Saussure (1740–1799),* ed. René Sigrist, 409–429.

120. Freshfield, *Life of Horace Bénédict Saussure,* 315; BGE Arch. Saussure 107/1–3.

121. Jean-Daniel Candaux and René Sigrist, "Saussure et la Société des Arts," in *H.-B. de Saussure (1740–1799),* ed. René Sigrist, 431–451.

122. Saussure, *Voyages dans les Alpes,* vol. I, iv; trans. adapted from Freshfield, *Life of Horace Bénédict Saussure,* 287.

123. Saussure, *Voyages dans les Alpes,* vol. I, 473.

124. Ibid., 496–497. For Saussure's sketch in 1776, see BGE Arch. Saussure 119/1; reproduced in Carozzi, *Horace-Bénédict de Saussure,* 144.

125. Rousseau, *Julie, or the New Héloïse,* 403; *OC,* 491; Jean Starobinski, *The Living Eye,* trans. Arthur Goldhammer (Cambridge, MA, 1989).

126. Oliver Fatio, "La spirtualité de Saussure," in *H.-B. de Saussure (1740–1799),* ed. René Sigrist, 487–499.

127. Horace-Bénédict de Saussure, *Eclaircissemens sur le Projet de Réforme pour le Collège de Geneve* (Geneva, 1774), 6, emphasis in original.

3. ASCENT AND ENFRANCHISEMENT

1. *FAMB*; Alfonso Bernardi, *Il Monte Bianco: Dalle esplorazione alla conquista (1091–1786)* (Bologna, 1965); and Philippe Joutard, *L'invention du Mont Blanc* (Paris, 1986).

2. Marc-Théodore Bourrit, *Nouvelle Description des glacières de Savoye* (Lausanne, 1785), 159.

3. Marc-Théodore Bourrit, *Description des aspects du Mont-Blanc* (Geneva, 1776), 147–156; Bourrit, *Nouvelle Description,* 159–167; *FAMB,* 76–81, 395.

4. Horace-Bénédict de Saussure, *Voyages dans les Alpes* (1786), vol. II, 550.

5. Jean Nicolas, "La fin du régime seigneurial en Savoie (1771–1792)," in *L'abolition de la feodalité dans le monde occidentale* (Paris, 1971), vol. I, 28; Geoffrey Symcox, *Victor Amadeus II* (London, 1983), 33; Max Bruchet, *L'abolition des droits seigneurial en Savoie (1761–1793)* (Annecy, 1908), 55–74.

6. Bruchet, *L'abolition des droits seigneurial,* lxiv–lxvi, lxxi–lxxvi; Jean Nicolas, *La Savoie au 18e siècle* (Paris, 1978), vol. II, 641–642.

7. Jerome Blum, *The End of the Old Order in Rural Europe* (Princeton, 1978), 20, 33–38.

8. Bruchet, *L'abolition des droits seigneurial,* xxiv–xxv; Nicolas, *La Savoie,* vol. I, 32–34.

9. Bruchet, *L'abolition des droits seigneurial,* lx. Nicolas, *La Savoie,* vol. II, 632–636.

10. On Joseph Paccard's election, see André Perrin, *Le prieuré de Chamonix: Histoire de la vallée et du prieuré de Chamonix de Xe au XVIIIe siècle* (Chambéry, 1887), 202; on Nollet, see Saussure, *Voyages,* vol. 2, 56; and on notaries, see Nicolas, *La Savoie,* vol. I, 72–84.

11. François Coutin, *Histoire de la Collégiale de Sallanches* (Montmélian, 1996 [1941]), 203–204; and Max Bruchet, *Inventaire sommaire des Archives départementales antérieures à 1790, Haute-Savoie* (Annecy, 1904), 294–295. For the 1749 petition, see ADHS, E depot Chamonix DD 2.

12. Coutin, *Histoire de la Collégiale de Sallanches,* 205, cf. 191; and Bruchet, *Inventaire sommaire,* 294.

13. Bruchet, *L'abolition des droits seigneurial,* liv, 567, 566–586; Perrin, *Le prieuré de Chamonix,* 201–202; Bruchet, *Inventaire sommaire,* 294; R. Couvert du Crest, *Une vallée insolite: Chamonix, le Mont Blanc, la Savoie; histoire des origines à 1860* (Annecy, 1971), vol. II, 40–41.

14. Bruchet, *L'abolition des droits seigneurial,* 456, "statistique"; xxxii–xl, for emigration.

15. Ian Hacking, "Making Up People," in *Reconstructing Individualism: Autonomy, Individuality, and the Self in Western Thought,* ed. T. C. Heller, M. Sosna, and D. E. Wellbery (Stanford, 1986), 222–236; Ian Hacking, *Historical Ontology* (Cambridge, MA, 2004), 99–114.

16. Hacking, "Making Up People," 228.

17. Ian Hacking, *The Social Construction of What?* (Cambridge, MA, 1999), 186–205.

18. Max Bruchet, *La Savoie d'après les Anciens Voyageurs* (Annecy, 1908), 280.

19. John Moore, *A View of Society and Manners in France, Switzerland, and Germany,* 2 vols. (London, 1779), vol. I, 201.

20. Thomas Blaikie, *Diary of a Scotch Gardener at the French Court at the End of the Eighteenth Century* (London, 1931), 75.

21. See Archives de Chamonix, Amis du Vieux Chamonix, geneanet.org, familysearch.org for the Chamonix registers; Biblioteca Nazionale Universitaria di Torino for degrees; Jh-M. Lavanchy, *Le Diocèse de Genève (Partie de Savoie) Pendant la Révolution Française* (Annecy, 1894), vol. II, 613, for Pierre-Joseph's appointments.

22. See Symcox, *Victor Amadeus II,* 217–222; Marina Roggero, "State and Education in Eighteenth-Century Italy: The School System in Turin," *Paedagogica Historica* 36 (2000): 539–569.

23. Blaikie, *Diary of a Scotch Gardener,* 47–82; Henry F. Montagnier, "Thomas Blaikie and Michel-Gabriel Paccard," *AJ* 45 (1933): 2–34.

24. Bernardi, *Monte Bianco,* 235–240; Luciano Ratto, "Michel Gabriel Paccard: Un 'quasi torinese' per primo sulla vetta del Bianco," *Scàndere* XLIX–LI (1997/99): 139–140. Paccard's theses are at the Biblioteca Nazionale Universitaria di Torino.

25. Agnese Visconti, "The Naturalistic Explorations of the Milanese Barnabite Ermenegildo Pini (1739–1825)," *Proceedings of the California Academy of Sciences,* 4 ser., 59, supp. I, no. 4 (2008), 51–63.

26. Paccard to Pini, January 4, 1779, Biblioteca Civica Centrale, Turin, Collezione Nomis di Cossilla, mazzo 29; reproduced many times: *La Montagne,* 4th ser., vol. 1 (1933): 20–21, 102–103; *AJ* 46 (1934): 12–13; Giovanni Bobba, "Lo studente torinese Gabriele Paccard e il Padre Ermenegildo Pini," estratto *Montagna* (Torino, 1935), 10–11.

27. BL, Egerton MSS 2002, fol. 36; Thomas Bowdler to John Strange, September 7, 1779.

28. Louis Seylaz, "Relations du pays de Vaud avec Chamonix à la fin du 18e siècle," *Die Alpen* 32 (1956): 141–142; Ferdinand Jaïn, *Choix de lettres et documents tirés de papiers de famille* (Morges, 1882), 94–95; *FAMB,* 89–91; emphasis in original.

29. Paccard to Jaïn, September 22, 1779, in Seylaz, "Relations du pays de Vaud avec Chamonix," 141–142.

30. ACL, F11.7, Paccard to Bourrit, September 3, 1782.

31. *Observations sur la physique sur l'histoire naturelle et sur les arts* 18, part 2 (September 1781): 184–192, commonly known as *Journal de physique.*

32. Paccard's consultation is reproduced in Couvert du Crest, *Une vallée insolite,* vol. II, plates 117–130, and discussed in Nicolas, *La Savoie,* vol. II, 1019.

33. Carl Egger, *Michel-Gabriel Paccard und der Montblanc* (Basel, 1943), 8.

34. Bourrit, *Nouvelle Description,* vol. III, 292.

35. Paccard to Jaïn, November 29, 1783, quoted in Seylaz, "Relations du pays de Vaud avec Chamonix," 144.

36. For Paccard's election, see Ratto, "Michel Gabriel Paccard," 140–141; *Mémoires de l'Académie royale des sciences* (Turin, 1790), cxlvii; Vincenzo Ferrone,

"The Accademia Reale delle Scienze: Cultural Sociability and Men of Letters in Turin of the Enlightenment under Vittorio Amedeo III," *Journal of Modern History* 70 (1998): 519–560.

37. Douglas William Freshfield, *The Life of Horace Benedict de Saussure* (London, 1920), 201.

38. Société d'histoire et d'archéologie de Genève, *Histoire de Genève des origines à 1798* (Geneva, 1954), 466–468; and for the text, see Danielle Plan, "Un Genevois d'autrefois: Henri-Albert Gosse (1753–1816)," in *Bulletin de L'Institut National Genevois* 39 (1909): II–VIII (Annexe II).

39. Otto Karmin, *Sir Francis d'Ivernois* (Geneva, 1920), 55.

40. Franco Venturi, *"'Ubi Libertas, Ibi Patria': The Genevan Revolution of 1782*," in *The End of the Old Regime in Europe, 1776–1789* (Princeton, 1991), vol. II, 461–462; Richard Whatmore, *Against War and Empire: Geneva, Britain, and France in the Eighteenth Century* (New Haven, CT, 2012), chap. 5.

41. Bourrit to Hennin, n.d., and Hennin to Bourrit, April 20, 1780; BGE, Ms. fr. 9143, env. 9.

42. Société d'histoire et d'archéologie de Genève, *Histoire de Genève*, 459–468.

43. Venturi, *"'Ubi Libertas, Ibi Patria,'"* 464; Linda Kirk, "Try It on the Dog: Revolution in Geneva," in *1789: The Long and Short of It*, ed. David Williams (Sheffield, 1991), 44–45; Freshfield, *Life of Horace Benedict de Saussure*, 333.

44. Karmin, *Sir Francis d'Ivernois*, 75; Francois d'Ivernois, *Tableau historique et politique des deux dernières révolutions* (London, 1789), vol. II, 30. For Deluc and rebuttals, see Emile Rivoire, *Bibliographie historique de Genève au XVIIIme siècle* (Geneva, 1897), 346–355; Deluc's brother, Guillaume-Antoine, had become a *Constitutionnaire;* Deluc's political views and continued disputes with Saussure are summarized in his letters to Marc-Auguste Pictet, *Correspondance–sciences et techniques,* ed. René Sigrist (Geneva, 1998), vol. II, 204–239.

45. Pierre Bourrit, *Marc-Théodore Bourrit 1739–1819: Une histoire des Natifs de Genève* (Geneva, 1989), 72.

46. Bourrit to Clavière, August 12, 1781; Clavière to Bourrit, February 15, 1782; BGE Ms. fr. 9142, env. 10; Bourrit, *Marc-Théodore Bourrit,* 77–79; Édouard Chapuisat, *Figures et choses d'autrefois* (Paris, 1920), 26, 32–35.

47. Rivoire, *Bibliographie historique,* 371. Édouard Chapuisat, *La prise d'armes de 1782 à Genève* (Geneva, 1932), 14.

48. Freshfield, *Life of Horace Benedict de Saussure,* 335.

49. J.-D. Candaux, "La Révolution Genevoise de 1782: Un état de la question," in *Études sur le XVIIIe siècle,* vol. VII, ed. R. Mortier and H. Hasquin (Brussels, 1980), and Venturi, *"'Ubi Libertas, Ibi Patria,'"* were the best accounts before Whatmore, *Against War and Empire,* chaps. 1, 5, which appeared as this book went to press.

50. Karmin, *Sir Francis d'Ivernois,* 89–90; Richard Whatmore, "'Neither Masters nor Slaves': Small States and Empire in the Long Eighteenth Century," *Proceedings of the British Academy* 155 (2009): 53–81.

51. Karmin, *Sir Francis d'Ivernois,* 90–97.

52. Chapuisat, *La prise d'armes,* 76; and Chapuisat, *Figures et choses d'autrefois,* 36–37.

53. Chapuisat, *La prise d'armes,* 90.

54. Freshfield, *Life of Horace Benedict de Saussure,* 336–338; Chapuisat, *La prise d'armes,* 98–101.

55. Freshfield, *Life of Horace Benedict de Saussure,* 340; Chapuisat, *La prise d'armes,* 131, 137. Karmin, *Sir Francis d'Ivernois,* 100; John Hardman and Munro Price, eds., *Louis XVI and the Comte de Vergennes: Correspondence 1774–1787* (Oxford, 1998), 308; William Coxe, *Travels in Switzerland* (London, 1789), vol. 2, 348–384.

56. Richard Whatmore and James Livesey, "Étienne Clavière, Jacques-Pierre Brissot et les foundations intellectuelles de la politique des girondins," *Annales historiques de la Révolution française,* no. 321 (2000): 1–26; J. Benetruy, *L'Atelier de Mirabeau: Quatre proscrits genevois dans la Tourmente Révolutionnaire* (Geneva, 1962); Marc Neuenschwander, "Les Troubles de 1782 à Genève et le temps de l'émigration," *Bulletin de la Société d'histoire et d'archéologie de Genève* 19 (1989): 127–188.

57. Venturi, *"'Ubi Libertas, Ibi Patria,'"* 472–473.

58. François d'Ivernois, *Tableau historique et politique des révolutions de Genève dans le dix-huitième siécle* (Geneva, 1782).

59. Jacques-Pierre Brissot, *Le Philadelphien à Genève ou Lettres d'un Américain sur la dernière révolution de Genève* (Dublin, 1783), 68; Whatmore and Livesey, "Étienne Clavière, Jacques-Pierre Brissot"; Richard Whatmore, "'L'amité de grands Etats est leur plus sûr appui,' The Small State Dilemma in Genevan Political Economy, 1762–1798," *Schweizerische Zeitschrift für Geschichte* 50 (2000): 353–371.

60. See Dror Wahrman, *The Making of the Modern Self: Identity and Culture in Eighteenth Century England* (New Haven, CT, 2004), for the role of the American Revolution in such changes.

61. James Livesey, *Making Democracy in the French Revolution* (Cambridge, MA, 2001), 30.

62. Venturi, *"'Ubi Libertas, Ibi Patria,'"* 469–470.

63. Plan, "Un Genevois d'autrefois," 109, and Annexe II.

64. Saussure, *Voyages,* vol. II, 552–553; *FAMB,* 97.

65. *FAMB,* 98.

66. Bourrit to Saussure, September 20, 1783, in *AJ* 24 (1909): 420–423; Dübi, 274–276; *FAMB,* 99–101, 345–346.

67. Paccard's notebook, 3–12, in *FAMB,* 342–344. *Pierre à Bérenger* received the name before 1779.

68. Paccard's notebook, 15, in *FAMB,* 344.

69. Bourrit, "Account of the Discovery of the White Hill, or Mont Blanc, in the Alps," *Scots Magazine* 47, January 1785, 31.

70. *Scots Magazine,* January 1785; *London Magazine,* February 1785; *Edinburgh Magazine,* March 1785; *Connecticut Courant,* September 12, 1785.

71. Bourrit, *Nouvelle Description,* 108, 307–308.

72. *Le journal des sçavans* (September 1785): 631; *Journal de physique* 27 (August 1785): 157–158.

73. "Fragment d'une Lettre," *Nouveau journal de littérature et de politique de l'Europe, et surtout de la Suisse* 2 (October 15, 1784): 278.

74. *FAMB,* 123, 350–351.

75. Saussure, *Voyages,* vol. 2, 562.

76. Saussure to Prince de Ligne, September 26, 1785, BGE Arch. Saussure 6/2 (I/1–2); Freshfield, *Life of Horace Benedict de Saussure,* 207; also *FAMB,* 126; and Saussure, *Voyages,* vol. 2, 571. For the cost of Saussure's expedition, see Paccard's notebook, 43, in *FAMB,* 353.

77. Pierre Bourrit to Saussure, September 23, 1785, and Saussure draft replies to Marc-Théodore Bourrit and Pierre Bourrit; BGE Arch. Saussure 3/11, 258–263; Freshfield, *Life of Horace Benedict de Saussure,* 203–205.

78. Paccard notebook, 41, in *FAMB,* 352. Charles Edward Mathews, *Annals of Mont Blanc* (London, 1900), 47–49; and E. H. Stevens, "Paccard's Lost Narrative," *AJ* 41 (1929): 119–122, include translations of Paccard's notebook, but the transcription in *FAMB* is more reliable, and the source on which I base my translations.

79. Paccard to Saussure, September 25, 1785; BGE Arch. Saussure 9/17 (L338–339); *FAMB,* 405–406; Dübi, 38–39.

80. Saussure to Prince de Ligne, September 26, 1785; and Prince de Ligne to Saussure, October 23, 1785, in BGE Arch. Saussure 6/2 (223/5), trans. from Freshfield, *Life of Horace Benedict de Saussure,* 206–209; see also David Ripoll, "L'iconographie des *Voyages dans les Alpes,*" in *H.-B. de Saussure (1740–1799),* ed. René Sigrist (Geneva, 2001), 323.

81. Saussure, *Voyages* (Neuchatel, 1796), vol. 4, 139.

82. Pierre Balmat to Saussure, June 9, 1786, in H.-B. Saussure, *Le Mont-Blanc et le Col du Géant,* ed. E. Gaillard and Henry-F. Montagnier (Lyon, 1927), 81; cf. *FAMB,* 384.

83. Paccard notebook, 47, in *FAMB,* 354, 141–147.

84. A. Gex, "Un Autographe de Jacques Balmat, premier ascensionniste du Mont-Blanc," *Revue Savoisienne* 43 (1902): 294; see also *Annuaire du CAF* 29 (1902): 554.

85. Saussure, *Voyages,* vol. 4, 140.

86. See Maurice Gay and Marie-France Balmat, *Les Pellarins: Village natal de Jacques Balmat dit Mont-Blanc* (Chamonix, 1986), 128–138, for his family. Les Bots is sometimes spelled des Baux. For lessons, see Alexandre Dumas, *Impressions de voyage: Suisse,* vol. III, nouvelle éd., in *OC* (Paris, 1869), 275.

87. Michel Carrier, *Notice biographique de Jacques Balmat dit le Mont Blanc* (Geneva, 1854), 5; Gay and Balmat, *Les Pellarins,* 137, lists the property.

88. Gay and Balmat, *Les Pellarins,* 140–142, 163; also ADHS, 1 J 2315.

89. Saussure, *Voyages,* vol. 2, 34.

90. Carrier, *Notice biographique,* 7–8; cf. *FAMB,* 304; H. Dübi, "La contro-verse Paccard-Balmat," *Die Alpen* 6 (1930): 347–356.

91. *Juvenile Miscellany* (1842): 162, based on an interview in 1819 or 1820.

92. A guinea equaled 1 louis d'or (or 24 livres) and the prize was 48 livres. Saussure had paid the guides 6 francs (livres) a day in 1785 and reported that the finest chamois was worth 12 francs (*Voyages,* vol. II, 152). For ordinary journeys, guides were paid 4 livres per day (Bourrit, *Nouvelle Description,* 65). A decade later, Johann-Gottfried Ebel reported 4 or 5 francs per day (Ebel, *Instructions pour un voyageur qui se propose de parcourir la Suisse* [Basel, 1795], vol. II, 63). Near the Grimsel, William Coxe reported that a hunter could get 1 guinea for a good chamois skin (Coxe, *Travels in Switzerland: In a Series of Letters to William Melmoth* [London, 1789], vol. I, 343). For a similar estimate, see E. H. Stevens, "Paccard's Lost Narrative," *AJ* 42 (1930): 167.

93. Bourrit, *Nouvelle Description,* 56.

94. Saussure, *Voyages,* vol. II, 145–148.

95. Ibid., 152; Saussure's description of the hunter was widely reprinted.

96. Sherry B. Ortner, *Life and Death on Mt. Everest: Sherpas and Himalayan Mountaineering* (Princeton, 1999), 162.

97. Cf. Jeremy Bernstein, *Ascent: The Invention of Mountain Climbing and Its Practice,* rev. ed. (New York, 1989), chap. 1; and Robert Macfarlane, *Mountains of the Mind* (New York, 2003), 71.

98. Carrier, *Notice biographique,* 8.

99. Thomas Raffles, *Letters, during a Tour through Some Parts of France, Savoy, Switzerland, Germany, and the Netherlands: In the Summer of 1817* (New York, 1818), 213; also William Howard in *Analetic Magazine,* 1820, 378; Coxe, *Travels in Switzerland,* vol. I, 384. Balmat said Paccard invited him days after his bivouac: Gex, "Un Autographe de Jacques Balmat," 554.

100. Jérôme Lalande, "Voyage au Mont Blanc," *Magasin Encyclopédique* 4 (1796): 443.

101. ADHS, E depot Chamonix DD 3/14.

102. Ibid., 3/27. Emphasis in the original.

103. Ibid.

104. Perrin, *Le prieuré de Chamonix,* 205; Bruchet, *L'abolition des droits seigneurial,* 568; Couvert du Crest, *Une vallée insolite,* vol. II, 41–42. For August 9, see Coutin, *Histoire de la Collégiale de Sallanches,* 189.

4. WHO WAS FIRST?

1. "Document sur l'Ascension au Mont Blanc par Dr. Paccard et J. Balmat," *Revue Alpine* 11 (1905): 90–91; Dübi, 52–53.

2. J. B. D'Espine to Corte [Court], August 15, 1786; ASTO, Corte. Materie politiche per rapporto all'estero. Lettere ministri, Ginevra, mazzo 12 inventariato; printed in Pietro Crivellaro, "Nuovi documenti sulla prima ascensione al Monte Bianco dall'Archivio di Corte di Torino (1786–1788)," *Bulletin de la Société académique religieuse et scientifique de l'ancien duché d'Aoste,* n.s. 11 (2010): 153.

3. Adolf Traugott von Gersdorf's diary, August 10, 1786; *FAMB,* transcription p. 380, translation pp. 162–163; a facsimile for August 1786 is in NLS, Acc. 4338, no. 163 (5). The original is in the Oberlausitzische Bibliothek der Wissenschaften, Görlitz, Germany; a new transcription of Gerdorf's notes on his travels in Switzerland in 1786 is in preparation at Zurich.

4. Charles Bonnet's letters in August and September 1786; see Dübi, 55–56, 68–70; and *AJ* 26 (1912): 42.

5. Horace-Bénédict de Saussure's 1786 journal: transcription *FAMB,* 386–388, cf. 170–173. The younger brother, Jean-Marie Paccard, received a law degree at Turin in 1786, and had followed his father as secretary of Chamonix by 1793. See his thesis at the Biblioteca Nazionale Universitaria di Torino and Paul Guichonnet, *Les monts en feu: La guerre en Faucigny, 1793* (Annecy, 1994), 156–157.

6. *Affiches de Dauphiné,* September 8, 1786; thanks to Jerry Lovatt for this reference, and the NYPL, Rare Books Division. See *AJ* 30 (1916): 116–118; *AJ* 26 (1912): 41; Dübi, 54–56; *FAMB,* 181–183; Marc-Auguste Pictet, *Correspondance–sciences et techniques,* ed. René Sigrist (Geneva, 1998), vol. II, 490.

7. *L'Année littéraire* 6 (August 29, 1786): 72; *Affiches de Dauphiné,* September 8, 1786; for Jean-Pierre Blanchard's ascents, see *Affiches de Dauphiné,* June 30, 1786, and Blanchard in a "temple de mémoire" in Frankfurt, *Journal de Paris,* March 3, 1786.

8. BL, Add. MSS 35057, fol. 59, Cumberland to Banks, August 24, 1786; and Add. MSS 8096, fol. 437, "Observations Sur le Mont Blanc le 7 et 8 Août 1786 Conquis par le Dr Paccard." Both are reproduced in *FAMB,* 49, 53, and Gavin de Beer and Max H. Hey, "The First Ascent of Mont Blanc," *Notes and Records of the Royal Society of London* 11, no. 2 (1955): 236–255.

9. BL, Add. MSS 33272, Blagden to Banks, October 5, 1786; and de Beer and Hey, "First Ascent of Mont Blanc."

10. Reprinted in *FAMB,* 408–413; Dübi, 72, 241–244; Henry F. Montagnier, "Dr. Paccard's Lost Narrative: A Note," *AJ* 26 (1912): 36–52.

11. Marc-Théodore Bourrit, *Lettre de M. Bourrit sur le premier voyages fait au sommet du Mont-Blanc, le 8 Août 1786, dernier,* reproduced in Dübi, 58–67, 245–257.

12. See *Mercure de France* and *Journal politique de Bruxelles* (November 4, 1786); *FAMB,* 190–196; Dübi, 58–67.

13. BGE Arch. Saussure 3/11, Bourrit to Saussure, October 11 and 13, 1786; Saussure to Bourrit, October 19, 1786; *FAMB,* 196, 209, 415–418; emphasis in

original. Bourrit and Jean-Pierre Bérenger were longtime friends, but not in-laws until their children married in 1795.

14. Gersdorf and Carl Andreas von Meyer, November 23, 1786, introduction to the edition of Bourrit published in Görlitz, and reproduced in Dübi, 73–74, 241–257.

15. *Journal politique de Bruxelles* (September 30, 1787): 235; *Lausizische monatsschrift* (March 1798): 142; and the Gersdorf-Bourrit correspondence in Dübi, 107–125.

16. Jean-François Garnier d'Alonzier to Giambattista Fontana di Cravanzana, December 14, 1786; ASTO, Sezioni riunite, Azienda generate Finanze, seconda archiviazione, capo 73, vol. 24; copy in ADHS 1 C 3 (30), fols. 48–54; and Augusta Lange, "1786: L'intendente del Faucigny invia alla Corte di Torino una *Note des voyageurs de distinction qui ont été visiter les Glacières de Chamonix depuis l'an 1746*," *Société académique, religieuse et scientifique de l'Ancien Duché d'Aoste*, nouv. Sér. XI (2010): 113–133.

17. ASTO, Sezioni riunite, Finanze, seconda archiviazione, capo 73, vol. 24; Lange, "1786," 123.

18. Cravanzana to Garnier d'Alonzier, December 20, 1786; ASTO, Sezioni riunite, Finanze, seconda archiviazione, capo 54; Lettere dell'Ufficio Generate a vari uffici, vol. 227, Registre de Savoie.

19. J. B. D'Espine to Corte, October 13, 1786; ASTO, Corte. Materie politiche per rapporto all'estero. Lettere ministri, Ginevra, mazzo 12 inventariato; and Crivellaro, "Nuovi documenti," 153–155.

20. ADHS, 1 C 3 (30), fol. 5; Lange, "1786," 125–131; Augusta Lange, "Exorcismes et tourisme au XVIIe et XVIIIe siècles dans la vallée de Chamonix et au Mont-Blanc," Archives départementales Savoie, Chambéry, J267; G. Letonnelier, "Une liste de touristes dans la vallée de Chamonix en 1788," *Revue Savoisienne* 54 (1913): 187–190; and the list in ADHS 2 F 55.

21. Cravanzana to Garnier d'Alonzier, February 5, 1787; ASTO, Sezioni riunite, Finanze, seconda archiviazione, capo 73, vol. 24; and Lange, "1786," 123.

22. ADHS, 1 C 3 (29), fol. 20 (ref. 39).

23. Ibid., fol. 49 (ref. 82).

24. For the earlier claim, see Charles Durier, *Le Mont-Blanc* (Paris, 1877), 125; for the search, see Lange, "1786," and Crivellaro, "Nuovi documenti."

25. *Journal de Lausanne,* May 12, 1787; *FAMB,* 419–420. "Le contour que je fis, me retarda un peu, & je fus obligé de courir, pour être presque aussi-tôt que lui à la dite cîme." The certificate was dated October 18, 1786. Translations have varied and some remove the tone of a legal document in the original.

26. See Miriam Nicoli, *Apporter les lumières au plus grand nombre: medicine et physique dans le* Journal de Lausanne *(1786–1792)* (Lausanne, 2006); the journal was not a "newspaper."

27. *Journal de Lausanne,* February 24, 1787; Dübi, 76–77; *FAMB,* 214.

28. *Journal de Lausanne,* March 10 and 17, 1787; Dübi, 77–79; *FAMB,* 214–217; emphasis in original.

29. *Journal de Lausanne,* May 12, 1787; Dübi, 80–81; *FAMB,* 217, 419–420.

30. Dr. Michel-Gabriel Paccard to Gersdorf, May 31, 1787, and Gersdorf to Paccard, July 15, 1787; Dübi, 118–119.

31. *Journal de Lausanne,* July 21, 1787; Dübi, 85–86; *FAMB,* 227–228, 421.

32. See *FAMB,* 220–235, 427–431, for discussion of the 1803 memorandum of Henri-Albert Gosse and a transcript of Gédéon Balmat to Auguste le Pileur, January 26, 1839, which recounts the incident.

33. Dübi, 87; *FAMB,* 229–238; Bourrit to Saussure, October 13, 1786; BGE Arch. Saussure 3/11 (249).

34. Horace-Bénédict de Saussure, *Journal de l'ascension du Mont-Blanc,* ed. Anne Fauche and Samuel Cordier (Chamonix, 2007), 80, 84–85, 93, 96.

35. Horace-Bénédict de Saussure, *Voyages dans les Alpes* (1796), vol. IV, 145, 161–162; Saussure, *Relation abrégée d'un voyage à la cime du Mont-Blanc, en Août 1787* (Geneva, 1787), 12.

36. Saussure, *Voyages,* vol. IV, 175; Saussure, *Relation abrégée,* 15.

37. Saussure, *Journal de l'ascension du Mont-Blanc,* 136–137.

38. Garnier d'Alonzier to Corte di Bonvicino, August 6, 1787; ADHS 1 C 3/30, fols. 102–103 (ref. 59); ASTO, Corte, Lettere di particolari, G, mazzo 11; and Lange, "1786," 132.

39. *Journal de Genève* (August 11 and 18, 1787); *Journal de Paris* (August 31, September 1, 4–5, 1787); also Martin J. S. Rudwick, *Bursting the Limits of Time: The Reconstruction of Geohistory in the Age of Revolution* (Chicago, 2005), 15–22.

40. For Beaufoy, see ACL, C12; and *Annals of Philosophy* 9 (February 1817): 97–103.

41. *Journal politique de Bruxelles* (September 30, 1787): 235. This may refer to a Mr. Bolton, who offered a reward of 300 livres in 1786; Coutterand to Saussure, September 9, 1786; BGE Arch. Saussure 9/17 (L337).

42. *Mélanges, extraits des manuscrits de Mme. Necker* (Paris, 1798), vol. II, 180–181.

43. Jean-Étienne-François Marignié, *Hommage à Mr De Saussure sur son ascension et ses expériences physiques au sommet du Mont Blanc* (Geneva, 1787).

44. *Journal de Lausanne,* August 25, 1787; *L'Année littéraire* 6 (September 18, 1787): 348–351; *Nouvelles de la Républiques des lettres et des arts* 8 (September 19, 1787): 359–360; *Journal encyclopedique ou Universel* 7 (October 1787): 89–91; *L'Esprit des Journaux* (December 1787): 251–253.

45. Étienne-Salomon Reybaz, *Epître à Messieurs Balmat et Pacard sur leur ascension au Mont Blanc le 8 Août 1786 au sujet de l'Hommage à Mr De Saussure par Mr Marignié au mois d'août 1787. Cui-que suum* (Geneva, 1787).

46. The Jason and Hercules passages were reproduced in Jérôme Lalande, "Voyage au Mont Blanc," *Magasin Encyclopédique* 4 (1796): 446–447; and many accounts in the nineteenth century.

47. *Scène dialoguée entre Balmat et l'auteur de l'Hommage à l'occasion de l'Epitre d'un anonyme à MM Pacard et Balmat ayant pour épigraphe: Cuique suum. Chacun sa part; voici la vôtre* (Geneva, 1787).

48. *Hommage à Mr De Saussure sur sa glorieuse ascension au sommet du Mont Blanc. Par le petit domicilié de l'hôtel de Patience le 18 du mois d'Auguste et la cent et vingt neuvième lune de sa captivité* (Geneva, 1787); this was signed by de Coponnex and written after Marignié and Reybaz.

49. Marie-Christine Vellozzi et al., *Mont-Blanc: Conquête de l'Imaginaire: Collection Paul Payot* (Montmélian, 2002), 368–369.

50. *Claudian,* trans. Maurice Platnauer (London, 1922), vol. II, 148–149.

51. Jules Cochon, "Michel Paccard et Jacques Balmat, Deux portraits Savoyards du XVIIIe siècle," *Mémoires et documents publiés par la Société savoisienne d'histoire et d'archéologie* 46 (1908): 1–18.

52. *Claudian,* vol. II, 129, 146, 153.

53. Harold Parker, *The Cult of Antiquity and the French Revolutionaries* (Chicago, 1937).

54. *Mercure de France,* suppl. no. 17, May 9, 1789, 10.

55. *Journal de Lausanne,* September 1, 1787. Lydie Touret, "Charles-François Exchaquet (1746–1792) et les Plans en Relief du Mont-Blanc," *Annals of Science* 46 (1989): 1–20; cf. C. A. Crommelin, "L'ascension du Mont-Blanc par H. B. De Saussure en 1787 et un relief du Mont-Blanc en 1790," *Tijdschrift van het Koninklijk Nederlandsch Aardrijkskundig Genootschap* 66 (1949): 327–331.

56. BGE Arch. Saussure 67/15, folder brouillons de 1790; David Ripoll, "L'iconographie des *Voyages dans les Alpes,*" in *H.-B. de Saussure (1740–1799),* ed. René Sigrist (Geneva, 2001), 323; Douglas Freshfield, *The Life of Horace Bénédict de Saussure* (London, 1920), 260. For the images, see Vellozzi, *Mont-Blanc: Conquête de l'Imaginaire,* 52–55, 370.

57. Immanuel Kant, "An Answer to the Question: What Is Enlightenment?" in *What Is Enlightenment? Eighteenth-Century Answers and Twentieth Century Questions,* ed. James Schmidt (Berkeley, 1996), 58–64.

58. Immanuel Kant, *Critique of the Power of Judgment,* trans. Paul Guyer and Eric Matthews (Cambridge, 2000), 144–147.

59. Ibid., 148, 158. Cf. Saussure, *Voyages,* vol. II, 181.

60. Saussure, *Voyages,* vol. IV, 175.

61. Quare religio pedibus subiecta vicissim opteritur, nos exaequat victoria caelo. Lucretius, *De rerum natura,* 1.78–79.

62. Immanuel Kant, *Physische Geographie* (Mainz, 1802), vol. 2, 59. For his use of Lucretius, see Immanuel Kant, *Theoretical Philosophy after 1781,* ed. H. L Allison

and P. L. Heath (Cambridge, 2002), 443; essays by James I. Porter and Eric Baker in *The Cambridge Companion to Lucretius,* ed. Stuart Gillespie and Philip R. Hardie (Cambridge, 2007), 167–184, 274–288; and Stephen Greenblatt, *The Swerve: How the World Became Modern* (New York, 2011).

63. See *Journal de Paris* (October 11, 1787); *Nouvelles de la Republique des letters et des arts* (October 24, 1787), etc.

64. Daniel Chaubet, ed., *Les Carnets de Cachat Le Géant: Mémoires de Jean-Michel Cachat de "Le Géant," Guide de Monsieur de Saussure, Paysan de la vallée de Chamonix* (Montmélian, 2000), 113. For the certificates, see Freshfield, *Life of Horace Bénédict de Saussure,* 246; on the name, see Saussure, *Voyages,* vol. IV, 219.

65. Maurice Gay and Marie-France Balmat, *Les Pellarins: Village natal de Jacques Balmat dit Mont-Blanc* (Chamonix, 1986), 143.

66. Registre du Conseil, December 17, 1787, quoted in Pierre Bourrit, *Marc-Théodore Bourrit, 1739–1819: Une histoire des Natifs de Genève* (Geneva, 1989), 131

67. Miriam C. Meijer, "The Fifth Ascent of Mont Blanc from the Diaries and Letters of A. G. Camper (1759–1820)," *AJ* 105 (2000): 177–189, based on manuscripts at Amsterdam and Groningen.

68. Loubier to Gersdorf, May 12, 1792; Balmat to Gersdorf, August 9, 1792; and later correspondence, including Jakob Samuel Wyttenbach to Gersdorf, February 22, 1793; Dübi, 120–125.

69. Frederick Matthisson, *Letters Written from Various Parts of the Continent, between the Years 1785 and 1794,* trans. Anne Plumptre (London, 1799), 130.

70. Philippe Joutard, *L'invention du Mont Blanc* (Paris, 1986), 185–186.

71. Freshfield, *Life of Horace Bénédict de Saussure,* 351.

72. *Journal de Lausanne,* March 15, 1788; Dübi, 127.

5. TEMPLE OF NATURE

1. Charles-Louis Huguet de Sémonville to Bourrit, July 10, 1793, in Marc-Théodore Bourrit, *Description des cols, ou passages des Alpes* (Geneva, 1803), vol. II, 174–180, esp. 177–178.

2. Michel de Certeau, *Heterologies: Discourse on the Other* (Minneapolis, 1986), 189; and Certeau, *The Practice of Everyday Life* (Berkeley, 1984), 61.

3. Roger Chartier, *On the Edge of the Cliff: History, Language, and Practices,* trans. Lydia G. Cochrane (Baltimore, 1997), 1; William H. Sewell Jr., "Language and Practice in Cultural History: Backing Away from the Edge of the Cliff," *French Historical Studies* 21, no. 2 (1998): 241–254; Sewell, *The Logics of History* (Chicago, 2005).

4. James K. Chandler, *England in 1819: The Politics of Literary Culture and the Case of Romantic Historicism* (Chicago, 1998), 156; Talal Asad, "The Concept of

Cultural Translation in British Social Anthropology," in *Writing Culture: The Poetics and Ethics of Ethnography*, ed. James Clifford and George E. Marcus (Berkeley, 1986), 141; Asad, *Formations of the Secular*, 13–14.

5. Percy Bysshe Shelley, "On Life," in *Complete Works of Percy Bysshe Shelley*, ed. Roger Ingpen and William Peck (London, 1929), vol. VI, 196.

6. Jean Nicolas, *La Savoie au 18e siècle* (Paris, 1978), vol. II, 1121; Nicolas, *La Révolution Française dans les Alpes, Dauphiné et Savoie, 1789–1799* (Toulouse, 1989), 45–103.

7. Nicolas, *Révolution Française dans les Alpes*, 71, 152.

8. *Le premier cri de la Savoie vers liberté* (Chambéry, 1791), 3, 6, 25–28.

9. Nicolas, *La Savoie*, vol. II, 1121.

10. Joseph Dessaix, *Histoire de la réunion de la Savoie à la France en 1792* (Chambéry, 1857), 160, 196–197.

11. Jean-Marie Clément Berthet quoted in Nicolas, *Révolution Française dans les Alpes*, 164; *Vivre en Révolution, La Savoie 1792–1799* (Chambery, 1989), 219.

12. Nicolas, *Révolution Française dans les Alpes*, 168.

13. ADHS, 4 L 100/2; Dübi, 150; and AN: AF III 449/2653, for Paccard as ex-commissaire municipal, 1 prairial an V (May 20, 1797).

14. Nicolas, *Révolution Française dans les Alpes*, 178; Corinne Townley and Christian Sorrel, eds., *La Savoie, la France et la Révolution: Repères et échoes, 1789–1799* (Chambéry, 1989), 157.

15. Quoted in Christian Sorrel in *Vivre en Revolution, La Savoie 1792–1799*, 167.

16. Nicolas, *Révolution Française dans les Alpes*, 196–198; Albert Mermoud, *Mémoire du Mont-Blanc d'antan: La vie dans la vallée de Montjoie* (Aoste, 2001), 224–226, 252–265.

17. Quoted in Paul Guichonnet, *Les monts en feu: La guerre en Faucigny, 1793* (Annecy, 1994), 226.

18. Max Bruchet, "Une fête Républicaine à Sallanches en 1792," *Revue Savoisienne* 47 (1906): 50–52.

19. Nicolas, *La Révolution Française dans les Alpes*, 209; Guichonnet, *Les monts en feu*, 257.

20. François Descostes in *Mémoires de l'Académie des sciences, belles-lettres et arts de Savoie* (1903), 4th ser., vol. X, 328–329, 522–523; Abbé Desnoues in *Annales religieuses du diocèse d'Orleans* 29 (1899): 567.

21. ADHS 4 L 100/30; Guichonnet, *Les monts en feu*, 266. Jean-François Albanis Beaumont, *Description des Alpes grecques et cottiennes, ou tableau historique et statistique de la Savoie* (Paris, 1802), vol. 1, pt. 2, 210.

22. Guichonnet, *Les monts en feu*, 156–157.

23. De Maistre to Vignet des Etoles, September 3, 1795, in Jean-Louis Darcel, ed., "Les lettres de Joseph de Maistre," *Revue des études maistriennes* 10 (1986–1987): 130.

24. Nicolas, *La Révolution Française dans les Alpes,* 219. Maurice Besson, "Le contre revolution dans le Haut-Faucigny," *La revue Savoisienne* 798 (1938): 22; J.-M. Lavorel, *Cluses et le Faucigny: Étude historique* (Annecy, 1888), vol. 1, 49–54.

25. Nicolas, *La Révolution Française dans les Alpes,* 223.

26. Ranajit Guha, "The Prose of Counter-Insurgency," in *Selected Subaltern Studies,* ed. Ranajit Guha and Gayatri Chakravorty Spivak (New York, 1988), 78.

27. Darrin McMahon, *Enemies of Enlightenment: The French Counter-Enlightenment and the Making of Modernity* (Oxford, 2001), passim, esp. 75–77, 196–197.

28. Henri Baud, ed., *Le diocèse de Genève-Annecy* (Paris, 1985), 184.

29. Paul Payot, *Au royaume du Mont Blanc* (Montmélian, 1996), 66; and J.-J. Thillet, *Chamonix: une vallée, des hommes* (Saint-Gervais, 1978), 172. On Couttet, see *AJ* 32 (1918): 16–19, 37.

30. Nicolas, *La Révolution Française dans les Alpes,* 213; Townley and Sorrel, *La Savoie, la France et la Révolution,* 22; Clovis Grosset, *Histoire de Megève pendant la rèvolution Française* (Annecy, 1869), 122.

31. Mary Ashburn Miller, *A Natural History of Revolution: Violence and Nature in the French Revolutionary Imagination, 1789–1794* (Ithaca, NY, 2011); Mona Ozouf, *Festivals of the French Revolution* (Cambridge, MA, 1988); Monique Mosser, "Le temple et la montagne: Généalogie d'un décor de fête Révolutionnaire," *Revue de l'Art* 83 (1989): 21–35; James A. Leith, *Space and Revolution: Projects for Monuments, Squares, and Public Buildings in France 1789–1799* (Montreal, 1991).

32. F.-A. Aulard, *Le culte de la raison et le culte de l'être suprême (1793–1794)* (Paris, 1892), 53–55.

33. Mona Ozouf, "Montagnards," in *Critical Dictionary of the French Revolution,* ed. François Furet and Mona Ozouf (Cambridge, MA, 1989), 381; Miller, *Natural History of Revolution,* chaps. 4–5.

34. Abbé Orsaz, "Monographie de Servoz," in *Mémoires et documents publiés par l'Académie salésienne* 17 (1894): 169–170.

35. Jean-Michel Cachat, *Les Carnets de Cachat le Géant* (Montmélian, 2000), 158, 189–190. On removal of bells in Chamonix, see ADHS 4 L 100/12–15.

36. Mermoud, *Mémoire du Mont-Blanc d'antan,* 283; Townley and Sorrel, *La Savoie, la France et la Révolution,* 246–256; Ozouf, *Festivals,* 134–135, 249, 260; Leith, *Space and Revolution,* 261–263.

37. Douglas Freshfield, *The Life of Horace Bénédict de Saussure* (London, 1920), 357.

38. Eric Golay, *Quand le peuple devint roi: Mouvement populaire, politique et révolution a Genève de 1789 à 1794* (Geneva, 2001).

39. Eric Golay, "Un paratonnere pour l'arbre de la liberté: Horace-Bénédict de Saussure sous la Révolution," in *Les plis du temps,* ed. Albert Carozzi et al. (Geneva, 1998), 155–199.

40. Barbara Roth-Lochner, "Comment Saussure perdit sa fortune," in *H.-B. de Saussure (1740–1799),* ed. René Sigrist (Geneva, 2001), 478–484.

41. Golay, *Quand le peuple devint roi,* 493.

42. *Correspondance de Grenus et Desonnaz; ou, État politique et moral de la république de Genève* (Geneva, 1794), vol. I, 65–66; cf. Freshfield, *Life of Horace Bénédict de Saussure,* 366–367.

43. Freshfield, *Life of Horace Bénédict de Saussure,* 380.

44. On these events, see Golay, *Quand le people devint roi;* on the burning, see J. Jullien, *Histoire de Genève racontée aux jeunes genevois* (Geneva, 1863), 412.

45. ADHS, 4 L 100/24.

46. Frédéric Barbey, *Félix Desportes et l'annexion de Gèneve à la France, 1794–1799* (Paris, 1916), 39; Henri Ferrand and Henry Montagnier, "Le temple de la nature: Son histoire et sa restauration," *La montagne* 20 (1924): 344–346; Henri Ferrand, "Le temple de la nature," *Comité des travaux historiques et scientifiques: Bulletin de la Section de géographie* 38 (1923): 19–32.

47. ACL, B7, Chamonix resolution, 10 Floréal Year III (April 29, 1795); Ferrand and Montagnier, "Le temple de la nature," 340–341.

48. J. G. Lemaistre, *Travels after the Peace of Amiens* (London, 1806), 52; *Magasin Encyclopédique* (1796): 438.

49. Cachat, *Carnets de Cachat le Géant,* 160–161.

50. Bourrit, *Description des cols,* 48–49, 79, 106–107.

51. ACL, B33, Pontécoulant to Couteran, 20 Brumaire Year XII (November 11, 1802); Ferrand and Montagnier, "Le temple de la nature," 344–346.

52. *Letters from Switzerland and France* (London, 1821), 43; Philippe-Xavier Leschevin, *Voyage à Genève et dans la vallée de Chamonix* (Paris, 1812), 265–266.

53. Charles-Julien Chênedollé, *Oeuvres completes de Charles Chênedollé,* new ed. (Paris, 1864), 231–232.

54. Trans. in *The Collected Works of Samuel Taylor Coleridge,* ed. Carl Woodring (Princeton, 1990), vol. 14, app. H, 21–22.

55. *Collected Works of Samuel Taylor Coleridge,* vol. 16, no. 2, ed. J. C. C. Mays, 922–933.

56. Keith G. Thomas, "Coleridge, Wordsworth and the New Historicism: 'Chamouny; The Hour before Sunrise, a Hymn' and Book 6 of *The Prelude,*" *Studies in Romanticism* 33, no. 1 (1994): 81–117.

57. E. S. Shaffer, "Coleridge's Swiss Voice: Friederike Brun and the Vale of Chamouni," in *Essays in Memory of Michael Parkinson and Janine Dakyns,* ed. Christopher Smith (Norwich, 1996), 67–76.

58. Charles-Julien Chênedollé, *Le génie de l'homme,* in *Oeuvres complètes,* 40–53.

59. François-René Chateaubriand, *Voyage au Mont-Blanc,* ed. Gabriel Faure (Grenoble, 1920), 21–23.

60. Chateaubriand to Staël, September 7, 1805, in François-René Chateaubriand, *Correspondance générale* (Paris, 1977), vol. I, 368.

61. Chateaubriand, *Voyage au Mont Blanc,* 37–40.

62. Ernest de Selincourt, ed., *The Early Letters of William and Dorothy Wordsworth (1787–1805)* (Oxford, 1935), 32–33.

63. Geoffrey H. Hartman, *Wordsworth's Poetry, 1787–1814* (New Haven, CT, 1964), 102.

64. William Wordsworth, *Descriptive Sketches,* ed. Eric Birdsall (Ithaca, NY, 1984), 102–106.

65. William Wordsworth, *The Prelude, 1799, 1805, 1850,* ed. Jonathan Wordsworth, M. H. Abrams, and Stephen Gill (New York, 1979), 208–219; Simon Brainbridge, "Romantic Writers and Mountaineering," *Romanticism* 18 (2012): 1–15.

66. Alan Liu, *Wordsworth: The Sense of History* (Stanford, 1989), 14–18, and Howard Erskine-Hill, *Poetry of Opposition and Revolution: Dryden to Wordsworth* (Oxford, 1996), 212–222.

67. Liu, *Wordsworth,* 21.

68. Jean-Francois Albanis Beaumont, *Description des Alpes grecques et cottiennes, ou tableau historique et statistique de la Savoie* (Paris, 1802), vol. II, 82–83, 89–90.

69. Meyer Howard Abrams, *Natural Supernaturalism: Tradition and Revolution in Romantic Literature* (New York, 1973), 453.

70. Wordsworth, Abrams, and Gill, *The Prelude, 1799, 1805, 1850,* 214.

71. Cachat, *Carnets de Cachat le Géant,* 162; Francois Coutin, *Histoire de la Collégiale de Sallanches* (Montmélian, 2000), 211, 241–242.

72. Dübi, 150–151; Cachat, *Carnets de Cachat le Géant,* 222.

73. For the petitions, see ADHS E Depot Chamonix N 1/6, 8, 13; for his "epizooties" mission, see ADHS E Depot Chamonix F3; for the purchases, see *Bibliothèque britannique* 7 (1802): 351; and Balmat to Pictet, April 7, 1805, in Marc-Auguste Pictet, *Correspondance–sciences et techniques,* ed. René Sigrist (Geneva, 1998), vol. II, 86–87.

74. *Mémoires d'agriculture, d'économie rurales et domestique, publiés par la Société de la départment de la Seine* 12 (1809): 128–130; cf. 14 (1811): 99; *Magasin encyclopédique* 2 (1809): 377.

75. Georgette Ducrest, *Mémoires sur l'impératrice Joséphine, ses contemporains, la cour de Navarre et de la Malmaison* (Paris, 1828), 134–135. On the biography, see ACL F 11/9, Gosse to Jacques Balmat Mont Blanc, January 3, 1803; Dübi, 147–149; and Danielle Plan, "Un Genevois d'autrefois, Henri-Albert Gosse," in *Bulletin de l'Institut National Genevois* 39 (1909): 455, lxxix–lxxxii.

76. Maurice Gay and Marie-France Balmat, *Les Pellarins: Village natal de Jacques Balmat dit Mont-Blanc* (Chamonix, 1986), 144–145; *Revue Alpine* 3 (1897): 167.

77. *Revue Savoisienne* 43 (1902): 294–295.

78. See John Auldjo, *Narrative of an Ascent to the Summit of Mont Blanc* (London, 1828), 114, among many accounts in the 1820s.

79. *Philosophical Magazine,* May 1831, 328–330; *Arcana of Science and Art* 5 (1832): 193–195.

80. Suzanne Desan, *Reclaiming the Sacred: Lay Religion and Popular Politics in Revolutionary France* (Ithaca, NY, 1990), 16–17; and Alain Corbin, *Village Bells* (New York, 1998), 32–43.

81. Marianne Klemun, *"Mit Madame Sonne konferieren": Die Großglockner-Expeditionen 1799 und 1800* (Klagenfurt, 2000), 153. For other summit crosses, see Martin Scharfe, *Berg-Sucht: Eine Kulturgeschichte des Frühen Alpinismus 1750–1850* (Vienna, 2007), passim.

82. Ozouf, *Festivals,* 261.

83. Gabriel Lory, *Voyage pittoresque aux glaciers de Chamouni* (Paris, 1815); Samuel Birmann, *Souvenirs de la vallée de Chamonix* (Basel, 1826).

84. Reprinted in Mary Paillon, "Au Mont Blanc en 1808," *Revue Alpine* 2 (1896): 114.

85. Ducrest, *Mémoires sur l'impératrice Joséphine,* vol. I, 134.

86. Ibid., 133–134.

87. Henriette d'Angeville, *My Ascent of Mont Blanc* (London, 1987), 102–104.

88. Alexandre Dumas, *Impressions de voyage Suisse* (Paris, 1834), 281–283.

89. Paul Tugler, "Marie Paradis 'La Paradisa' 1er femme au Mont-Blanc le 14 juillet 1808," in *La femme dans la société savoyarde,* ed. Marthe Dompnier and Pierre Dompnier (Saint-Jean-de-Maurienne, 1993), 241–244.

90. J. Burlet, *Le culte de dieu, de la sainte Vierge et des saints en Savoie avant la Revolution* (Chambéry, 1922), 58, 62, 291; Caroline Bellot, *Les chapelles et les oratoires du pays du Mont-Blanc* (Université de Savoie, 1998); Archives départementales de Savoie, Chambéry, J 1602.

91. André Perrin, *Le Prieuré de Chamonix: Histoire de la vallée et du prieuré de Chamonix de Xe au XVIIIe siècle* (Chambéry, 1887), 220; Arnold van Gennep, *La Savoie* (Voreppe, 1991), 282–283.

92. Denise Z. Davidson, "Women at Napoleonic Festivals: Gender and the Public Sphere during the First Empire," *French History* 16 (2002): 299–322, esp. 315.

93. Dumas, *Impressions du Voyage Suisse,* 296; Charles Durier, *Le Mont-Blanc* (Paris, 1877), 200.

94. Natalie Zemon Davis, *Society and Culture in Early Modern France* (Stanford, 1975), 143.

95. Paillon, "Au Mont Blanc en 1808," 115; and *Revue Savoisienne* 29 (1888): 323–324.

96. Cécile Ottogalli-Mazzacavallo, *Femmes et Alpinisme: Un genre de compromis 1874–1919* (Paris, 2006), 38–39.

97. Conservatoire d'art et d'histoire de la Haute-Savoie, *Découverte et sentiment de la montagne, 1740–1840* (Annecy, 1986), 89.

98. Gennep, *La Savoie,* 254, 256; Sudhir Hazareesingh, *The Saint-Napoléon: Celebrations of Sovereignty in Nineteenth-Century France* (Cambridge, MA, 2004).

99. Alan Liu, *Local Transcendence: Essays on Postmodern Historicism and the Database* (Chicago, 2008), 129–130.

100. Shahid Amin, *Event, Metaphor, Memory: Chauri, Chaura, 1922–1992* (Berkeley, 1995), 196.

101. Dumas, *Impressions de voyage Suisse,* 287.

102. Charles Étienne François Moulinié, *Promenades philosophique et religieuse aux environs du Mont-Blanc* (Geneva, 1817), 183, 280.

103. Percy Shelley and Mary Shelley, *History of a Six Weeks' Tour through a Part of France, Switzerland, Germany and Holland* (London, 1817), 151–152.

104. Ibid., 164, 167.

105. Ingpen and Peck, *Complete Works of Percy Bysshe Shelley,* vol. VI, 138–139; Mary Shelley, *The Journals of Mary Shelley, 1814–1844* (Oxford, 1987), 116–118.

106. Geoffrey Matthews and Kelvin Everest, eds., *The Poems of Shelley* (New York, 1989), vol. I, 532–549.

107. Gavin de Beer, *On Shelley* (Oxford, 1938), 35–54; and Gavin de Beer "An Atheist in the Alps," *Keats-Shelley Memorial Association Bulletin* 9 (1958): 1–15.

108. Frances Ferguson, "Shelley's *Mont Blanc:* What the Mountain Said," in *Romanticism and Language,* ed. Arden Reed (London, 1984), 202–214.

109. Geoffrey Hartman, "Gods, Ghosts and Shelley's 'Atheos,' " *Literature and Theology* 24 (2010): 8, 15. Robert M. Ryan, *The Romantic Reformation: Religious Politics in English Literature, 1789–1824* (Cambridge, 1997), 200–202.

110. Christopher Hitt, "Shelley's Unwriting of Mont Blanc," *Texas Studies in Literature and Language* 47 (2005): 140, 145, offers a stimulating reading.

111. Ranajit Guha, *Dominance without Hegemony: History and Power in Colonial India* (Cambridge, MA, 1997), 78.

112. Ingpen and Peck, *Complete Works of Percy Bysshe Shelley,* vol. VII, 113.

113. Shelley and Shelley, *History of a Six Weeks' Tour,* 162–163, 170–171.

114. Robert Brinkley, "Spaces between Words: Writing *Mont Blanc,*" in *Romantic Revisions,* ed. Robert Brinkley and Keith Hanley (Cambridge, 1992), 243–267.

115. With apologies to Harold Bloom, *Shelley's Mythmaking* (New Haven, CT, 1959), 30. For endemic ghosts, see Richard Holmes, *Shelley: The Pursuit* (New York, 1974), 113.

116. Cf. Cian Duffy, *Shelley and the Revolutionary Sublime* (Cambridge, 2005), 220; and Nigel Leask, "Mont Blanc's Mysterious Voice: Shelley and Huttonian Earth Science," in *The Third Culture: Literature and* Science, ed. Elinor S. Shaffer (Berlin, 1998), 188–193.

117. Duffy, *Shelley and the Revolutionary Sublime,* 119.

118. Susan J. Wolfson, "Byron's Ghosting Authority," *ELH* 76 (2009): 763–792.

119. Mary Shelley, *Frankenstein; or, The Modern Prometheus: The 1818 Text,* ed. Marilyn Butler (London, 1993), 75, 78–82, 196.

120. Anne K. Mellor, *Mary Shelley: Her Life, Her Fiction, Her Monsters* (New York, 1988), 95–106.

121. Ryan, *Romantic Reformation,* 179–192.

122. Kari Lokke, "The Last Man," in *Cambridge Companion to Mary Shelley,* ed. Esther H. Schor (Cambridge, 2004), 116–118.

123. Liu, *Wordsworth,* 20.

124. Wolfson, "Bryon's Ghosting Authority," 771.

125. Mary Shelley, *Frankenstein* (London, 1831), 79–81.

126. Jane Nardin, "A Meeting on the Mer de Glace: Frankenstein and the History of Alpine Mountaineering," *Women's Writing* 6 (1999): 447.

127. John Ruskin, *Sesame and Lilies* (1865), in *Works of John Ruskin,* ed. E. T. Cook and Alexander Wedderburn (London, 1905), vol. 18, 89.

128. For a similar perspective, see Jon Mathieu, "The Sacralization of Mountains in Europe during the Modern Age," *Mountain Research and Development* 26, no. 4 (November 2006): 343–349; and McMahon, *Enemies of Enlightenment,* 14–15, 197–200.

129. Ferrand and Montagnier, "Temple de la nature," 346; Robert Avezou, *Le tourisme dans la vallée de Chamonix au siècle dernier* (Annecy, 1933), 21–23.

130. Durier, *Le Mont-Blanc,* 163.

131. Maison de Saint-Gervais, "Saint-Gervais Mont-Blanc: La montagne à l'état pur. Une commune s'engage dans une opération de sensibilisation environnementale d'envergure. Communiqué de presse N°2. De bonnes attitudes à toutes les altitudes," April 30, 2004.

6. SOCIAL CLIMBERS

1. Alexandre Dumas, *Impressions de voyage Suisse,* new ed. (Paris, 1868), vol. I, 1–4; and Dumas, *Mes mémoires* (Paris, 1863), vol. X, 47–48.

2. Dumas, *Impressions de voyage Suisse,* vol. I, 115.

3. Ibid., 128, 130; *Revue des deux mondes* 1 (1833): 565–566.

4. Dumas, *Mes mémoires,* vol. X, 57–58.

5. Alexandre Dumas, "Comment je devins auteur dramatique," *Revue des deux mondes* 4 (1833): 617.

6. Claude Schopp, *Alexandre Dumas: Genius of Life* (New York, 1988), 220.

7. Charles Durier, *Le Mont-Blanc* (Paris, 1897), 106; Venance Payot, *Guide-itinéraire au Mont-Blanc et dans les vallées comprises entre les deux Saint-Bernard et le Lac de Genève,* 2nd ed. (Geneva, 1869), 166–180.

8. Georgette Ducrest, *Mémoires sur l'impératrice Joséphine* (Paris, 1828), vol. I, 176.

9. Sherry B. Ortner, *Life and Death on Mt. Everest* (Princeton, 1999), 86.

10. Michel de Certeau, *Heterologies: Discourse on the Other* (Minneapolis, 1986), 153.

11. Dumas, *Impressions de voyage Suisse,* vol. I, 137, 143.

12. Edmund Clark and Markham Sherwill in *New Monthly Magazine* 16 (1826): 595–597; and Stephen d'Arve, *Les Fastes du Mont Blanc* (Paris, 1876), 63.

13. Dorothy Galton, "Iosif Khristianovich Hamel (1788–1861)," *Slavonic and East European Review* 44 (1966): 473–474; Hamel's obituary in *Zapiski Imperatorskoĭ akademīi nauk* 3 (1863): 189–198; Elisabeth Simons and Oswald Oelz, *Kopfweh-berge: Eine Geschichte der Höhenmedizin* (Zurich, 2001), 52–58; and Simons and Oelz, "Mont Blanc with Oxygen: The First Rotters," *High Altitude Medicine & Biology* 2 (2001): 545–549.

14. Joseph Hamel in *Bibliothèque universelle des sciences, belles-lettres, et arts,* n.s. 14 (1820): 317–320; Joseph Hamel, *Beschreibung zweyer Reisen auf den Montblanc unternommen in August 1820* (Vienna, 1821); Joseph Dornford, "Mont Blanc," *New Monthly Magazine* 1 (1821): 511–516.

15. *Bibliothèque universelle* (1820): 319–320; *New Monthly Magazine* (1821): 508.

16. Paccard's notebook in *FAMB*, 359.

17. Dumas, *Impressions de voyage Suisse,* 146–147; Venance Payot, *Oscillations des quatre grands glaciers de la vallée de Chamonix* (Geneva, 1879), 195; Stephen d'Arve, *Les fastes du Mont Blanc,* 62.

18. Dumas, *Impressions de voyage Suisse,* 147; Durier, *Le Mont-Blanc* (1877), 411.

19. *Journal de Savoie,* February 2, 1821, 42.

20. d'Arve, *Les fastes du Mont Blanc,* 64.

21. *Le Moniteur Universel,* October 28, 1820; *Journal de Savoie,* September 22, 1820; *Feuille d'Avis de Genève,* August 26, 1820; Hamel, *Beschreibung zweyer Reisen auf den Montblanc,* 22.

22. Quoted in Françoise Loux, "Le regard des premieres guides de Chamonix sur la haute montagne," *Le Monde alpin et rhodanien* 16 (1988): 187–195.

23. Daniel Chaubet, *Histoire de la compagnie des guides de Chamonix* (Mont-mélian, 1994), 15, 21–24; René Simond, "La compagnie des guides de Chamonix et son organisation socio-professionnelle durant les premières années des son exis-tence," in *La sociabilité des Savoyards* (Chambéry, 1982), 317–325.

24. Quoted in Loux, "Le regard des premieres guides de Chamonix," 188.

25. Ibid., 189, 193–194.

26. Quoted in Paul-Louis Rousset, *Memoires d'en haut: Histoire des guides de montagne des alpes Françaises* (Meylan, 1988), 101.

27. Chaubet, *Histoire de la compagnie des guides de Chamonix,* 144, art. 34.

28. Michael Broers, "Sexual Politics and Political Ideology under the Savoyard Monarchy, 1814–1821," *English Historical Review* 114 (1999): 607–635.

29. William Howard in *Analetic Magazine* 1 (1820): 382; John Undrell in *Annals of Philosophy* 1 (May 1821): 379.

30. Paccard to Ebel, February 12, 1823, Staatsarchiv des Kantons Zürich, B IX 214, n. 121; for a partial transcript see Josef Auf der Maur, "La première ascension du Mont Blanc en 1786: Découverte récente d'une lettre du premier vanqueur du sommet, le Dr. M. G. Paccard," *Les Alpes / Le Alpi / Las Alps / Die Alpen* 61 (1985): 28–36, esp. 34; the parallel version in *Die Alpen* is entirely in German.

31. Paccard to Alexis Bouvard, copy in Paccard's notebook, *FAMB,* 356.

32. Frederick Clissold, *Narrative of an Ascent to the Summit of Mont Blanc Aug 18th 1822* (London, 1823), 6, 8. For Paccard on Clissold, see *Journal de Savoie,* September 6, 1822, 340.

33. *Journal de Savoie,* September 19, 1823, 352; and October 3, 1823, 377–378; Paccard notebook, *FAMB,* 340.

34. *Journal de Savoie,* September 16, 1825, 787–788; Paccard notebook, *FAMB,* 362–363.

35. *Journal de Savoie,* September 30, 1825, 811–812.

36. Ibid., October 14, 1825, 825; *Mirror of Literature, Amusement, and Instruction* (October 15, 1825): 259; *Bulletin des sciences géographiques, etc: Économie publique; voyages* 5 (1825): 263–265; *Bulletin des sciences mathématiques, astronomiques, physiques et chimiques* 6 (1825): 264; *Annali universali di statistica, economia pubblica, storia, viaggi e commercio* 8 (1826): 97–100.

37. Giovanni Giacomo Bonino, *Biografia medica piemontese* (Turin, 1824), vol. I, v, 472–473.

38. Corinne Townley and Christian Sorrel, eds., *La Savoie, La France et la Révolution: Repères et échoes, 1789–1799* (Chambéry, 1989), 38; François Descostes, *Joseph de Maistre pendant la révolution* (Tours, 1895), 141.

39. ACL, C71; *FAMB,* 366.

40. *Revue des deux mondes* 6 (1836): 59–60; and Dumas, *Impressions de Voyage Suisse,* vol. III, 274–281.

41. Roger Canac, *Jacques Balmat dit Mont-Blanc* (Grenoble, 1986), 51; Hubert Ducroz, "Jacques Balmat et le mythe de l'or à Sixt (Haute-Savoie)," in *Imaginaires de la haute montagnes* (Grenoble, 1987), 53–68.

42. Musée Alpin (Alpine Museum), Chamonix; see Hubert Ducroz, "Jacques Balmat et le mythe de l'or à Sixt (Haute Savoie)"; Roger Canac, *L'or des cristalliers* (Paris, 1980), 34–42; Canac, *Jacques Balmat,* 51–60; J. Vallot, "Jacques Balmat d'après ses papiers," *Revue Alpine* 3 (1897): 165–176; and *La Revue du Mont Blanc,* July 20, 1898.

43. Canac, *L'or des cristalliers,* 42.

44. Maurice Gay and Marie-France Balmat, *Les Pellarins: Village natal de Jacques Balmat dit Mont-Blanc* (Chamonix, 1986), 147.

45. Canac, *L'or des cristalliers,* 38.

46. Canac, *Jacques Balmat,* 55. Cf. Alexandre Brongniart, *Traité élémentaire de minéralogie* (Paris, 1807), vol. II, 344. For his travels, see Gay and Balmat, *Les Pellarins,* 147.

47. See Ducroz, "Jacques Balmat et le mythe de l'or à Sixt (Haute-Savoie)," 60–62, especially for Moccand; Canac, *L'or des cristalliers,* 38; Paul Mougin, *Les Torrents de Savoie* (Grenoble, 1914), 153; Vallot, "Jacques Balmat d'après ses papiers," 170–171.

48. Ducroz, "Jacques Balmat et le mythe de l'or à Sixt (Haute-Savoie)," 54–55; Mougin, *Les Torrents de Savoie,* 153–154; *Annales de la Chambre royale d'agriculture et de commerce* 4 (1858): 31; *Churchman,* February 7, 1885, 146.

49. Gay and Balmat, *Les Pellarins,* 146–150; Canac, *Jacques Balmat,* 58; Rousset, *Mémoires d'en haut,* 107. Some copies are in ADHS, 1 J 2315; ACL, C9, has documents on his debts in 1828–1829.

50. Michel Carrier, *Notice biographique de Jacques Balmat dit le Mont Blanc* (Geneva, 1854), 18; Alfred Wills, *The Eagle's Nest in the Valley of Sixt* (London 1860), 39; Durier, *Le Mont-Blanc,* 118.

51. Gay and Balmat, *Les Pellarins,* 148; Durier, *Le Mont-Blanc,* 132.

52. Jean-Michel Cachat, *Les carnets de Cachat le Géant* (Chambery, 2000), 148.

53. See Gay and Balmat, *Les Pellarins,* 148–151, for discussion of these finances based on familial archives in Chamonix. The 1860 U.S. Census identifies Gideon and Edward living in Nimishillen Township, Ohio.

54. Ducroz, "Jacques Balmat et le mythe de l'or," 63.

55. Carrier, *Notice biographique de Jacques Balmat,* 18; Wills, *Eagle's Nest,* 37–46; Ducroz, "Jacques Balmat et le mythe de l'or à Sixt (Haute-Savoie)," 62.

56. Wills, *Eagles Nest,* 46.

57. Quoted in Colette Cosnier, *Henriette d'Angeville: La dame du Mont-Blanc* (Chamonix, 2006), 28. See also Émile Gaillard, *Une Ascension romantique en 1838: Henriette d'Angeville au Mont Blanc* (Chambery, 1947), 11–13.

58. Quoted in Cosnier, *Henriette d'Angeville,* 28–34, 39–44.

59. BGE, MSS, suppl. 925.

60. Emmanuel Le Roy Ladurie, "Un Theoricien du developpement: Adolphe d'Angeville," in *Territoire de l'historien* (Paris, 1973), 349–392.

61. Gaillard, *Une Ascension romantique,* 25.

62. Cosnier, *Henriette d'Angeville,* 106–107; and Gaillard, *Une Ascension romantique,* 42; *Revue Alpine* 6 (1900): 65–80, 97–122.

63. Simon Schama, *Landscape and Memory* (New York, 1995), 497–498.

64. *Le Fédéral,* September 11, 1838; *Journal des Débats,* September 12, 1838.

65. Quoted in John Grand-Carteret, *La Montagne à travers les ages* (Paris, 1904), vol. II, 228.

66. *New Monthly Magazine* 60 (1840): 387–391; Lohis Hermenous, *Excursions, ou, quelques journées de mes vacances* (Grenoble, 1846), quoted in Yves Ballu, *Les alpinistes* (Paris, 1984), 46.

67. Angeville to Louis Augerd, August 30, 1838, reprinted in Gaillard, *Une Ascension romantique,* 153.

68. X.-B. Saintine, *Picciola* (Brussels, 1836), 236.

69. Henriette d'Angeville, *My Ascent of Mont Blanc* (London, 1992), 38.

70. Paul Guichonnet, "Une Bugiste célèbre: Henriette d'Angeville," *Bugey,* no. 80 (1993): 200.

71. d'Angeville, *My Ascent of Mont Blanc,* xxiii.

72. *La Presse,* December 21, 1839; Madame Émile de Girardin, *Lettres parisiennes* (Paris, 1843), 417–422.

73. Lenard R. Berlanstein, "Historicizing and Gendering Celebrity Culture: Famous Women in Nineteenth-Century France," *Journal of Women's History* 16 (2004): 68–70.

74. *La Presse,* December 21, 1839; and Girardin, *Lettres parisiennes,* 421–422.

75. d'Angeville, *My Ascent of Mont Blanc,* 74; Henriette d'Angeville, *Mon excursion au Mont-Blanc* (Paris, 1987), 131.

76. d'Angeville, *My Ascent of Mont Blanc,* 76.

77. Ibid., 82

78. Ibid., xxi.

79. Ibid., 101–104, 130.

80. Ibid., 29.

81. Adolphe d'Angeville, *Essai sur la statistique de la population Francaise* (Bourg, 1836), 125; see also Le Roy Ladurie, "Un Theoricien du developpement."

82. Quoted in Cosnier, *Henriette d'Angeville,* 140–141, 143.

83. University of Maryland Archives, Savoy Collection, Acc. 72–279, box 6, Henriette d'Angeville to Madame Panckoucke, October 12, 1839.

84. See Cécile Ottogalli-Mazzacavallo, *Femmes et alpinisme: Un genre de compromis, 1874–1919* (Paris, 2006), 42–54; and for "gender radicals," see Ortner, *Life and Death on Mt. Everest,* 217; and Sherry Ortner, *Making Gender: The Politics and Erotics of Culture* (Boston, 1996).

85. See also Tanja Wirz, "Wer ist die Braut des Montblanc?" in *Die Alpen! Les Alpes!* ed. Jon Mathieu and Simona Boscani Leoni (Bern, 2005), 267–277; and Tanja Wirz, *Gipfelstürmerinnen: Eine Geschlechtergeschichte des Alpinismus in der Schweiz 1840–1940* (Baden, 2007), 32–39.

86. Angeville to Cortambert, March 12, 1865, emphasis in original; quoted in Cosnier, *Henriette d'Angeville,* 9, 290; and Richard Cortambert, *Les illustres voyageuses* (Paris, 1866), 78–99.

87. Charles Baudelaire, "Le peintre de la vie moderne," in *Le Figaro,* November 26, 1863; cf. "épouser la foule" as "become one flesh with the crowd" in Charles

Baudelaire, *The Painter of Modern Life and Other Essays*, trans. Jonathan Mayne (London, 1964), 9.

88. See Aruna D'Souza and Tom McDonough, eds., *The Invisible Flâneuse? Gender, Public Space, and Visual Culture in Nineteenth-Century Paris* (Manchester, 2006); and Rita Felski, *The Gender of Modernity* (Cambridge, MA, 1995).

89. Cosnier, *Henriette d'Angeville*, 290–291.

90. *Bentley's Miscellany* 10 (1841): 576–580; Albert Smith, *The Natural History of the Gent* (London, 1847), 2–3, 16, 22–23, 57–58; the best biography is still J. Monroe Thorington, *Mont Blanc Sideshow: The Life and Times of Albert Smith* (Philadelphia, 1934).

91. BL, Add. MS 35027, fol. 122.

92. *Times* (London), August 20, 1851; E. T. Cook and A. Wedderburn, eds., *The Works of John Ruskin* (London, 1909), vol. 36, 117–118.

93. *Illustrated London News*, March 20, April 10, and December 25, 1852, and December 10, 1853; *Punch*, June 25, 1853; *Times* (London), December 6, 1853.

94. *Mr. Albert Smith's Ascent of Mont Blanc in Miniature* (London, 1855), Yale Center for British Art, Paul Mellon Collection.

95. Richard D. Altick, *The Shows of London* (Cambridge, 1978); Ralph Hyde, ed., *Panoramania* (London, 1988); Stephan Oettermann, *The Panorama* (New York, 1997); Bernard Comment, *Panorama* (London, 1999).

96. *Times* (London), September 18, 1854.

97. Comment, *Panorama*, 19.

98. Albert Smith, *The Story of Mont Blanc* (London, 1853), 202.

99. *Times* (London), November 30, 1852.

100. BL, Add. MS 35027, fol. 122.

101. John MacGregor, *The Ascent of Mont Blanc* (London, 1855), with views by George Baxter; J. D. H. Browne, *Ten Scenes in the Last Ascent of Mont Blanc* (London, 1853).

102. Jean Miège, "La vie touristique en Savoie," *Revue de géographie alpine* 21 (1933): 763, 767, 771, 776.

103. Quoted in Bernard Debarbieu, "Chamonix vers 1860: Strategies d'appropriation de la haute montagne," *Le Monde alpin et rhodanien* 16 (1988): 198–200.

104. Walter Benjamin, "Paris, the Capital of the Nineteenth Century," in *Arcades Project*, trans. Howard Eiland and Kevin McLaughlin (Cambridge, MA, 1999), 10, 13.

105. Mary Gluck, *Popular Bohemia: Modernism and Urban Culture in Nineteenth-Century Paris* (Cambridge, MA, 2005); Martina Lauster, *Sketches of the Nineteenth Century: European Journalism and Its Physiologies, 1830–50* (New York, 2007).

106. Walter Benjamin, "The Paris of the Second Empire in Baudelaire," in *Selected Writings, vol. 4: 1938–1940,* ed. Howard Eiland and Michael W. Jennings (Cambridge, MA, 2003), 19.

107. For example, see Dror Wahrman, *Imagining the Middle Class: The Political Representation of Class in Britain* (Cambridge, 1995); and Sarah Maza, *The Myth of the French Bourgeoisie: An Essay on the Social Imaginary, 1750–1850* (Cambridge, MA, 2003).

108. Benjamin, "Paris of the Second Empire in Baudelaire," 44, 60.

109. Michel Foucault, "What Is Enlightenment?" in *Essential Foucault: Selections from Essential Works of Foucault, 1954–1984,* ed. Paul Rabinow and Nikolas Rose (New York, 2003), 49–51.

110. Baudelaire, "Le peintre de la vie moderne," cf. the trans. in Baudelaire, *The Painter of Modern Life and Other Essays,* trans. Mayne, 13–14.

111. *Moniteur Universel,* May 25, 1855; Théophile Gautier, *Les beaux-arts en Europe: 1855* (Paris, 1855), vol. I, 19.

7. AGE OF CONQUEST

1. C. D. Cunningham and W. de W. Abney, *The Pioneers of the Alps* (London, 1887), 1, 23.

2. Alfred Wills, *Wandering among the High Alps* (London, 1856), 270–271, 273, 290–297, 312–313; emphasis in the original.

3. BL, Add. MSS 603084, fol. 108, John Ryall to Alfred Wills; for "English grandees," see ACL, B38, fols. 48, 91, 98, Alfred Wills to Lucy Wills in September 1857.

4. John Ball to Marquis d'Azeglio, 1858, ACL, AC3S1, fols. 1–10.

5. St. Andrews University Library, Forbes 1859/33; Alfred Wills to J. D. Forbes, April 11, 1859.

6. Edward Whymper, *Scrambles amongst the Alps in 1860–69* (London, 1873), 110. For a key, see the 1893 edition, 423.

7. Jeremy Morris, *F. D. Maurice and the Crisis of Christian Authority* (Oxford, 2005); Seth Koven, *Slumming: Sexual and Social Politics in Victorian London* (Princeton, 2004), 231–235; Christopher Oldstone-Moore, "The Beard Movement in Victorian Britain," *Victorian Studies* 48 (2005) 7–34; J. A. Mangan, *Athleticism and the Victorian and Edwardian Public Schools* (Cambridge, 1981).

8. E. S. Kennedy, ed., *Peaks, Passes and Glaciers* (London, 1862), 183.

9. On Ball and other members of the Alpine Club, see A. L. Mumm, *The Alpine Club Register* (London, 1923); and *Oxford Dictionary of National Biography* (Oxford, 2004).

10. E. S. Kennedy, *Thoughts on Being* (London, 1850), v, 2; on his father's death, see *Cabinet Annual Register* (London, 1834), 399–400.

11. *Peaks, Passes and Glaciers,* appeared in London, edited by Ball in 1859 and by Kennedy in 1862. Cf. Felix Driver, *Geography Militant: Cultures of Exploration and Empire* (Oxford, 2001); Dane Kennedy, *The Last Blank Spaces: Exploring Africa and Australia* (Cambridge, MA, 2013).

12. Ian Smith, ed., *The Apprenticeship of a Mountaineer: Edward Whymper's London Diary* (London, 2008), 87, 120, 139; emphasis in original.

13. Whymper in Kennedy, *Peaks, Passes, and Glaciers,* vol. II, 224.

14. *Blackwood's Edinburgh Magazine,* October 1859, 470.

15. *London Review,* September 15 1860.

16. *Times* (London), August 29, 1860.

17. *Universalist Quarterly and General Review* 17 (April 1860): 182.

18. *Bentley's Quarterly Review* 2 (October 1859): 214–215.

19. *Chambers's Journal* (July 23, 1859): 63.

20. H. A. Berlepsch, *Die Alpen, in Natur- und Lebens-Bildern* (Leipzig, 1861); English translation by Leslie Stephen in 1861, a French edition in 1868, and at least five German editions from 1861 to 1885.

21. Olivier Hoibian, ed., *L'invention de l'alpinisme: La montagne et l'affirmation de la bourgeoisie cultivée (1786–1914)* (Paris, 2008); Claudio Ambrosi and Michael Wedekind, eds., *L'invenzione di un cosmo borghese: Valori socali e simboli culturali dell'alpinismo nei secoli XIX e XX* (Trento, 2000); and studies by Rainer Amstädter, Dagmar Günther, Tanja Wirz, Anneliese Gidl, and Alessandro Pastore.

22. François Thioly, *Voyage en Suisse et ascension du Mont-Rose 1860* (Geneva, 1860), 3–4.

23. Guido Quazza, *L'utopia di Quintino Sella: La politica della scienza* (Turin, 1992), 178; Giorgio V. Dal Piaz, "Felice Giordano and the Geology of the Matterhorn," *Atti della Accademia delle Scienze di Torino* 130 (1996): 163–179.

24. *Una salita al Monviso* (Turin, 1863), 4, 60–61; Guido Quazza and Marisa Quazza, eds., *Epistolario di Quintino Sella* (Rome, 1980), vol. I, 466–481; and the original in Museo Nazionale della Montagna, Turin.

25. *Bullettino del Club Alpino Italiano* 3 (1868): 45; Guido Rey, *Il monte Cervino* (Milan, 1904), 120; Guido Rey, *The Matterhorn,* trans. J. E. C. Eaton (London, 1907), 126, 311.

26. For J.-A. Carrel, see *Dizionario Biografico degli Italiani* (Rome, 1973), vol. 20, 725–730.

27. Rey, *Matterhorn,* 119; on Pic Tyndall, see *Bullettino del Club Alpino Italiano* 3 (1868): 61.

28. Whymper, *Scrambles,* 95, 103.

29. Giordano to Sella, July 11, 1865, in Rey, *Matterhorn,* 136.

30. Whymper, *Scrambles,* 389, 391.

31. *Times* (London), July 27, 1865. More generally, see the documentation in Alan Lyall, *The First Descent of the Matterhorn: A Bibliographical Guide to the 1865 Accident and Its Aftermath* (Llandysul, 1997).

32. *All the Year Round,* August 19 and September 2, 1865.

33. Anthony Trollope, *Travelling Sketches* (London, 1866), 84–97.

34. *Illustrated London News* 47 (July 29, 1865): 82.

35. H. B. George, *The Oberland and Its Glaciers* (London, 1866), 196–197.

36. *Times* (London), August 5, 1865; E. T. Cook and A. Wedderburn, eds., *The Works of John Ruskin* (London, 1905), vol. 18, 21, 89–90.

37. Stefano Morosini, *Sulle vette della patria: Politica, guerra e nazione nel Club alpino italiano (1863–1922)* (Milan, 2009), 49.

38. Charles Kingsley, *Westward Ho!* (Cambridge, 1855), 18.

39. *Journal of the RGS* 36 (1866): cxc.

40. Whymper, *Scrambles,* 407.

41. *Elenco alfabetico dei decorati dell'ordine dei SS. Maurizio e Lazzaro* (Turin, 1870), 12, 84, 112, 165, 179, edition for 1861–1869; and (Turin, 1873), 24, edition for 1870–1872; *AJ* 2 (1865): 91; *AJ* 5 (1872): 375. On Ball and Garibadi, see *Proceedings of the RGS* 12 (1890) 108; *Bollettino della Società geografica italiana,* ser. 3, vol. 3 (1890): 338.

42. *Bollettino del Club Alpino Italiano* 4 (1869): 333–335; emphasis in original; Amé Gorret, *Victor-Emmanuel sur les Alpes* (Turin, 1878).

43. *Discorsi parlamentari di Quintino Sella* (Rome, 1887), vol. 1, 599, 603, 614; emphasis in original.

44. Antonio Stoppani, *Il bel paese* (Milan, 1876), 25.

45. *Revista Mensile di CAI* 8 (1889): 287.

46. Yann Drouet, "The 'CAF' at the Borders: Geopolitical and Military Stakes in the Creation of the French Alpine Club," *International Journal of the History of Sport* 22, no. 1 (2005): 59–69; Tait S. Keller, "The Eternal Mountains—Eternal Germany: The Alpine Association and the Ideology of Alpinism, 1909–1939," (Ph.D. diss., Georgetown University, 2006).

47. Hoibian, ed., *L'invention de l'alpinisme*; Michael Wedekind and Claudio Ambrosi, eds., *Alla conquista dell'immaginario: L'alpinismo come proiezione di modelli culturali e sociali borghesi tra Otto e Novecento* (Treviso, 2007).

48. See also Jonathan Westaway, "The German Community in Manchester, Middle-Class Culture and the Development of Mountaineering in Britain, c. 1850–1914," *English Historical Review* 124 (2009): 571–604.

49. Charles Durier, *Le Mont-Blanc* (Paris, 1877), 472.

50. Archives Municipales de Chamonix, 1D11, February 29, 1840, quoted in Gilbert Gardes, *Histoire Monumentale des Deux Savoies* (Lyon, 1996), 192; Paul Payot, *Au Royaume du Mont Blanc* (Paris, 1950), 85–86; Stephen d'Arve, *Fastes du Mont Blanc* (Geneva, 1876), xxv–xxviii.

51. *Manifeste et déclaration de la Savoie du Nord* (Geneva, 1860), 120–124; Sarah Wambaugh, *A Monograph on Plebiscites: With a Collection of Official Documents* (New York, 1920), 552–554, 600; Guy Gavard, *Histoire d'Annemasse et des communes voisines: Les relations avec Genève de l'époque romaine à l'an 2000* (Montmelian, 2006), 205, 209–211; Joëlle Paccalet-Dartigue and Christine Boymond-Lassere, *1860: La vallée de Chamonix et l'Annexion* (Chamonix, 2010).

52. Paul Guichonnet, *Nouvelle encyclopédie de la Haute-Savoie* (Montmélian, 2007), 25–26. For the 1860s, see Bernard Debarbieux, *Chamonix-Mont-Blanc: Les coulisses de l'aménagement* (Grenoble, 1990); Tamara L. Whited, *Forests and Peasant Politics in Modern France* (New Haven, CT, 2000).

53. Charles Durier, *Le Mont-Blanc* (Paris, 1877); Durier, *Histoire du Mont-Blanc: Conférences faites a Paris les 23 et 30 Mai 1873 a la salle du Boulevard des Capucines* (Paris, 1873); for biographical details, see *Annuaire du CAF* 26 (1899): xiii–xx.

54. *Bulletin de la Société géologique de France,* 3rd ser., 3 (1875): 792; *Annuaire du CAF* 2 (1875): 691–692. On Sanson, see E. Bénézit, *Dictionnaire critique et documentaire des Peintres, Sculpteurs, Dessinateurs et Graveurs,* new ed. (Paris, 1976), vol. 9, 281.

55. *L'Allobroge* (Bonneville), August 25, 1878; emphasis in original.

56. Ibid., August 18, 1878; *Bulletin de la Société géologique de France,* 3rd ser., vol. 6 (1878): 644–649.

57. *L'Allobroge,* August 18, 1878; *Bulletin de la Société géologique de France,* 3rd ser., vol. 6 (1878): 649–651.

58. *L'Allobroge,* August 18 and 25, 1878; *Bulletin de la Société géologique de France,* 3rd ser., vol. 6 (1878): 651.

59. *Recueil des discours, rapports et pièces diverses lus dans les séances publiques et particulières de l'Académie française, 1870–1879,* part 2 (Paris, 1880), 679.

60. Durier, *Le Mont-Blanc,* 1–2.

61. Ibid., 3–5.

62. Ibid., 66.

63. Ibid., 112, 473–474.

64. *Journal de Genève,* February 4, 1886.

65. Ibid., March 30, 1881, and May 23, 1885; Louis Bouvier, *De Saussure: Sa vie, ses voyages et ses observations dans les Alpes* (Geneva, 1877), 9–10; Archives Municipales de Chamonix, 1D25, July 5, 1885.

66. *Journal de Genève,* May 23, 1885; *Revista Alpina Italiana* 2 (October 31, 1883): 113.

67. ADHS 89 J 42, letters to Émile Maillot from Alfred Pictet, October 17 and 27, 1885, and Eduard Richter, November 26, 1885.

68. ADHS 89 J 42, for the contract, November 27, 1885, and correspondence.

69. ADHS 89 J 42, Durier to Maillot, December 2–18, 1885; ADHS 89 J 43, T. de Saussure to Salmson, January 24, 1886; emphasis in original.

70. *Journal de Genève,* February 4 and 11, 1886.

71. Ibid., February 11, 1886.

72. ADHS 89 J 42, letters from Tairraz, February 10, 1886; Durier, February 17, 1886; *Journal de Genève,* February 16, 1886.

73. *Journal de Genève,* February 17, 1886; see also ADHS 89 J 43.

74. On Charlet-Stratton, see *Annuaire du CAF* 4 (1877): 136–141; *AJ* 9 (1879): 186–187.

75. Compare Durier, *Le Mont-Blanc,* 2nd ed. (Paris, 1880), 171; and Cunningham in *AJ* 11 (1884): 459–471.

76. *Journal de Genève,* February 17, 1886.

77. *L'Allobroge,* March 21, 1886; see also ADHS 89 J 43, letters from Durier, March 2 and 10, 1886.

78. ADHS 89 J 43, Salmson, April 17, 1886; *L'Allobroge,* May 2 and 9, 1886.

79. *Journal de Genève,* August 17, 1886; *L'Allobroge,* August 29, 1886.

80. "Saussure-Denkmal," *Mitteilungen DÖAV* 13 (September 15, 1887): 225.

81. *Schweizer Alpen-Zeitung* 5 (1887): 218–219; *Journal de Genève,* August 31, 1887.

82. See Nathalie Bayon, *Eugène Spuller (1835–1896): Itinéraire d'un républicain entre Gambetta et le ralliement* (Villneuve-d'Ascq, 2006).

83. Eugène Spuller, *Au Ministère de l'Instruction Publique, 1887: Discours, allocutions, circulaires* (Paris, 1888), 140–146; for his edited draft, see ADHS 1 M 128.

84. Spuller, *Au Ministère de l'Instruction Publique,* 146–147.

85. *Schweizer Alpen-Zeitung* 5 (1887): 224–227; *Journal de Genève,* August 30 and 31, 1887.

86. Spuller, *Au Ministère de l'Instruction Publique,* 149–150, 171; see also ADHS 1 M 128.

87. Spuller, *Au Ministère de l'Instruction Publique,* 172–174.

88. *Le Matin,* August 29, 1887, widely reprinted in French and Swiss papers.

89. Quoted in Jean-François Chanet, *L'Ecole républicaine et les petites patries* (Paris, 1996), 27.

90. *Journal de Débats,* August 27 and September 1, 1887; *L'education nationale,* December 1, 1889, 762–763; P. de Sandt, *Anecdotes et leçons pour mes petits-enfants* (Rouen, 1893), 7–18.

91. Jacques Ozouf and Mona Ozouf, "*Le Tour de France par deux enfants:* The Little Red Book of the Republic," in *Realms of Memory: The Construction of the French Past,* vol. II, ed. Pierre Nora and Lawrence Kritzman, trans. A. Goldhammer (New York, 1997), 125.

92. G. Bruno, *Tour de la France par deux enfants* (Paris, 1877), 87–93.

93. Ibid., 84, 86–87.

94. *Le Croix,* August 20, 1887.

95. Maurice Gay and Marie-France Balmat, *Les Pellarins: Village natal de Jacques Balmat dit Mont-Blanc* (Chamonix, 1986), 143; *Le Figaro,* August 31, 1887.

96. *Journal de Genève,* August 31, 1887.

8. HISTORY DETECTIVES

1. C. E. Mathews, *The Annals of Mont Blanc* (London, 1898), 89–90, 107.

2. Ian Smith, *Shadow of the Matterhorn: The Life of Edward Whymper* (Hiddersley, 2011), 234–262.

3. BGE, Arch. Saussure 3/11/195, note dated 1881; and *FAMB,* 431–432; Maurice Bedot, *Henri de Saussure* (Geneva, 1906).

4. Oliver Zimmer, *A Contested Nation: History, Memory and Nationalism in Switzerland, 1761–1891* (Cambridge, 2003), chap. 4–5.

5. BGE, Arch. Saussure 49, Henri de Saussure's dossier on the case of Balmat-Paccard-Bourrit.

6. BL, Add. MSS 63112, fol. 89, 66, Whymper to Montagnier, October 8, 1909.

7. Edward Whymper, *Chamonix and the Range of Mont Blanc: A Guide* (London, 1896), 27.

8. Mathews, *Annals of Mont Blanc,* 281–285.

9. Ibid., 270; Robert Vivian, *L'Épopée Vallot au Mont Blanc* (Paris, 1986).

10. Stéphane Le Gars and David Aubin, "The Elusive Placelessness of the Mont-Blanc Observatory (1893–1909): The Social Underpinnings of High-Altitude Observation," *Science in Context* 22, no. 3 (2009): 509–531; Françoise Launay, *The Astronomer Jules Janssen: A Globetrotter of Celestial Physics* (New York, 2012).

11. Mathews, *Annals of Mont Blanc,* 273.

12. Ibid., 252–253, 260.

13. *FAMB,* 339; ACL, B65.

14. Douglas W. Freshfield, "Paccard v. Balmat," *AJ* 19 (1899): 341–349. Freshfield's wealth at death was £147,610, among the highest in the Alpine Club. See the *Oxford Dictionary of National Biography* (Oxford, 2004).

15. *AJ* 19 (1899): 374.

16. Joseph Vallot, "Jacques Balmat d'après ses papiers," *Revue Alpine* 3 (1897): 171–172; emphasis in original; *La Revue du Mont Blanc,* July 20, 1898.

17. Vallot, "Jacques Balmat d'après ses papiers," 171–172.

18. *Annales de l'Observatoire météorologique du Mont-Blanc* 1 (1893): v; Vivian, *L'Épopée Vallot au Mont Blanc,* 69–70.

19. See, especially, Cecile Ottogalli-Mazzacavallo, *Femmes et alpinisme: Un genre de compromis, 1874–1919* (Paris, 2006).

20. "Un Autographe de Jacques Balmat, Premier ascensionniste du Mont-Blanc," *Revue Savoisienne* 43 (1902): 293–297; also *Annuaire du CAF* 29 (1902): 552–557; *AJ* 21 (1903): 408–409.

21. ACL, B28, Dübi to Montagnier, November 28, 1908; emphasis in original; the letter was in English. See also Dübi, 7.

22. BL, Add. MSS 63112, fol. 63, 85, Whymper to Montagnier, November 22, 1908, September 28, 1909.

23. See Tanja Wirz, *Gipfelstürmerinnen: Eine Geschlechtergeschichte des Alpinismus in der Schweiz 1840–1940* (Baden, 2007), 158–168, and passim.

24. *AJ* 45 (1933): 349–355; *American AJ* 6 (1934): 234, and 6 (1947): 376–379; *Die Alpen* 39 (1963):132–133.

25. ACL, B29, Rey to Montagnier, November 17, 1905.

26. ACL, F11.21a, Montagnier notes on Mark Beaufoy; see also ACL, B29; Montagnier to Beaufoy, August 9, 1910; Montagnier to Thorington, September 28, 1928; J. Monroe Thorington Collection, WC005, box 17, folder 2, Department of Rare Books and Special Collections, Princeton University Library.

27. Henry F. Montagnier, "Paccard's Lost Narrative: A Note," *AJ* 26 (1912): 41; also *AJ* 42 (1930): 95.

28. ACL, B28, Dübi to Montagnier, December 24, 1908.

29. *Revue Alpine* 11 (1905): 90–91; ACL, Emil Fontaine to Whymper, January 17, 1905.

30. ACL, B28, Dübi to Montagnier, November 30, 1910; see also October 2 and November 15, 18, and 28, 1910.

31. Ibid., October 14, 1911.

32. Montagnier, "Paccard's Lost Narrative," 36–52; *Journal de Genève,* April 22, 1912.

33. ACL, B28, Dübi to Montagnier, June 15, 1912; emphasis in original.

34. ACL, B10, Ferrand to Montagnier, May 20, 1911, also June 19 and November 24, 1911. See Anne Féron, "Variété alpine: L'épopée d'un avocat grenoblois," *Revue de Géographie Alpine* 79 (1991): 57–69.

35. Henri Ferrand, "Une revision d'un vieux procès: Paccard contre Balmat," *La Montagne* 9 (1912): 457–478.

36. Quoted in Dübi, 1.

37. Ibid., 2.

38. Ibid., 4, 231.

39. *La Montagne* 9 (1913): 113; *Bibliothèque universelle et revue Suisse* 70 (1913): 420; *Annales de Géographie* 23 (1914): 19, issue bibl; for a compilation of documents in France, see AN: 262 Mi 1.

40. ACL, B10, Ferrand to Montagnier, May 16, 1913.

41. See *AJ* 30 (1916): 118; ACL, B28, Dübi to Montagnier, February 16, 1913, January 10, 1916. For Freshfield's summary, see *AJ* 27 (1913): 202–209.

42. *La Stampa,* September 29 and 30, 1915; *New York Times,* October 1, 1915, and August 24, 1918; *Gazette de Lausanne,* August 22, 1918.

43. NARA; Passport Applications, January 2, 1906–March 31, 1925; ARC Identifier 583830/MLR Number A1 534; NARA Series: M1490; Roll #478, Certificate 7538.

44. Douglas W. Freshfield with Henry F. Montagnier, *The Life of Horace Benedict de Saussure* (London, 1920), vii, 8–9, 22–23.

45. Ibid., vii, 35–36, 63, 147, 159, 226, 280–285.

46. Ibid., 233.

47. *New York Times,* August 10, 1923.

48. E. H. Stevens, "Dr. Paccard's 'Lost Narrative,' an Attempted Reconstruction," *AJ* 41 (1929): 98–156, esp. 105–106; *AJ* 42 (1930): 94–96, 165–184; emphasis in original.

49. *AJ* 42 (1930): 182.

50. On the younger Ladd, see *American AJ* (1959): 263–264; on his grandfather's estate, see *Morning Oregonian,* January 7, 1893.

51. For Thorington, see *American AJ* (1990): 337–338; and *AJ* (1991–1992): 293–294.

52. Examples are at the Henry S. Hall, Jr., American Alpine Club Library, and other libraries. His model was the 1593 bookplate of Christoph Zuppacher, reproduced in Alfred Steinitzer, *Der Alpinismus in bildern* (Munich, 1913), 470, or 2nd ed., 1924, 479.

53. See letters to Thorington during 1928–1932 from Montagnier, Jean Escarra, Sydney Spencer, and E. L. Strutt in the J. Monroe Thorington Collection, WC005, box 11, folder 54, and box 17, folder 2, Rare Books and Special Collections, Princeton University Library.

54. *Le Temps,* September 1, 1932, quoting Bobba; *Le Petit Dauphinois,* August 29, 1932; *La Stampa,* August 29, 1932; see also Giovanni Bobba, "Lo studente torinese Gabriele Paccard e il Padre Ermenegildo Pini," estratto *Montagna* (Torino, 1935), 6–7.

55. Heinrich Dübi, "A propos de la question Paccard-Balmat," *Die Alpen* 15 (1939): 439–440, his remarks at the 1932 inauguration.

56. *Le Petit Dauphinois,* August 29, 1932; *AJ* 44 (1932): 340–341.

57. *La Montagne,* 4th ser., vol. 1 (1933): 4–10, 21, 102–103.

58. Blaise Cendrars, *The Confessions of Dan Yack,* trans. Nina Roots (London, 2002), 45.

59. Ibid., 46.

60. For comparisons, see Dominique Abry-Deffayet, "Blaise Cendrars et les pruneaux de Jacques Balmat: Fiction ou réalité?" in *Imaginaires de la haute montagne,* Documents d'ethnologie régionale, n. 9 (Grenoble, 1987), 69–72.

61. Blaise Cendrars, "Touchez du doigt," in *John Paul Jones ou l'Ambition* (Montpellier, 1989), 23–25.

62. Ibid., 27–32.

63. Charles Rochat-Cenise, *Jacques Balmat du Mont Blanc* (Paris, 1929), 68, 89, 134, 140. Rochat-Cenise, *Paysans que nous sommes: Chroniques de la Vallée de Joux* (Geneva, 1953).

64. Rochat-Cenise, *Jacques Balmat du Mont Blanc,* 147, 154, 189.

65. *Journal de Genève,* November 21, 1929; *Revue des Lectures* 18 (September 1930): 1028; Gaillard in *Le Correspondant* 317 (1929): 629; *La Montagne,* 3rd ser., vol. 2 (1930): 274; *Die Alpen* 5 (1929): 251.

66. Heinrich Dübi, "La controverse Paccard-Balmat," *Die Alpen, Les Alpes, Le Alpi* 6 (1930): 347–356; reply by Charles Pasquine in *Die Alpen* 7 (1931): 178–180.

67. John Alexander Williams, *Turning to Nature in Germany: Hiking, Nudism, and Conservation, 1900–1940* (Stanford, 2007), 67–104; Dagmar Günther, *Wandern*

und Sozialismus: Zur Geschichte des Touristenvereins "Die Naturfreunde" im Kaiserreich und in der Weimarer Republik (Hamburg, 2003).

68. Karl Ziak, "Soziologische Bemerkungen zur Geschichte des Alpinismus," *Der Naturfreund* (1927): 212–213.

69. *Allgemeine Bergsteiger-Zeitung,* September 21, 1928; afterword to Karl Ziak, *Der König des Mont Blanc* (Vienna, 1980), 279–280.

70. Karl Ziak, *Paccard oder Balmat? Ein Mont-Blanc roman* (Vienna, 1930), 9, 37.

71. Ibid., 93–95, 149.

72. Ibid., 155, 159, 163.

73. Ibid., 66, 88, 213, 242–243.

74. Karl Ziak, *Der Mensch und die Berge* (Vienna, 1936), 5, 48–50, 202.

75. Ziak, *Paccard oder Balmat?,* 224–225.

76. Ibid., 259.

77. Arnold Fanck, *Er führte Regie mit Gletschern Stürmen und Lawinen: Ein Filmpionier erzählt* (Munich, 1973), 317–318.

78. Jan-Christopher Horak, ed., *Berge, Licht und Traum: Dr. Arnold Fanck und der deutsche Bergfilm* (Munich, 1997), 43. On the filming, see Fanck, *Er führte Regie,* 317–320; and Pierre Leprohon, *Le cinéma et la montagne* (Paris, 1944), 67.

79. *Der Bergsteiger,* February 1931, reprinted in Horak, *Berge, Licht und Traum,* 214.

80. *Der ewige Traum, der König vom Mont Blanc;* I have viewed copies of the Deutsche Kinemathek, Berlin, and Museo Nazionale della Montagna, Turin.

81. Fanck, *Er führte Regie,* 321–322; Matthias Fanck, *Arnold Fanck: Bergfilme und bergbilder 1909–1939* (Zurich, 2009), 135.

82. Elke Fröhlich, ed., *Die Tagebücher von Joseph Goebbels,* Bd. 3/1 (Munich, 2005), 123; on the ministry, see Eric Rentschler, *The Ministry of Illusion: Nazi Cinema and Its Afterlife* (Cambridge, MA, 1996).

83. *Völkisher Beobachter* (Munich edition), April 3, 1934; *Reichsfilmblatt,* November 24, 1934.

84. *Film-Kurier,* November 22, 1934; *LichtBild-Bühne,* November 22, 1934; *La Stampa,* November 24, 1934; *Pour Vous,* April 4, 1935; *Cinemonde,* April 4, 1935; *Cine-miroir,* November 23, 1934–January 4, 1935, serialized the story in its own fictionalization.

85. Gerald Koll, "Pas de deux mit DuBarry: Pressburgers Produktionen über die Französische Revolution," in *Alliierte für den Film: Arnold Pressburger, Gregor Rabinowitsch und die Cine-Allianz,* ed. Jan Distelmeyer (Munich, 2004), 92. For *Rêve éternel,* see Archives françaises du film du Centre national du cinéma, Paris, and Cinémathèque française, Paris.

86. Horak, *Berge, Licht, und Traum,* 55–56, 58–59.

87. "Wer war Jacques Balmat? Dr. Arnold Fanck über den Bezwinger des Mont Blanc," *Film-Kurier,* November 20, 1934.

88. Helmuth Zebhauser, *Alpinismus im Hitlerstaat* (Munich, 1997); Rainer Amstädter, *Der Alpinismus: Kultur, Organisation, Politik* (Vienna, 1996).

89. Tait Keller, "The Mountains Roar: The Alps during the Great War," *Environmental History* 14 (2009): 253–274; Marco Armiero, "Nationalizing the Mountains: Natural and Political Landscapes in World War I," in *Nature and History in Modern Italy,* ed. Marco Armiero and Marcus Hall (Athens, OH, 2010), 231–250; Marco Armiero, *A Rugged Nation* (Cambridge, 2011); George Mosse, *Fallen Soldiers: Reshaping the Memory of the World Wars* (Oxford, 1990), 114–119.

90. Zebhauser, *Alpinismus im Hitlerstaat;* Maurice Isserman and Stewart Weaver, *Fallen Giants: A History of Himalayan Mountaineering from the Age of Empire to the Age of Extremes* (New Haven, CT, 2010), 132 ff.; Lee Wallace Holt, "Mountains, Mountaineering and Modernity: A Cultural History of German and Austrian Mountaineering, 1900–1945" (Ph.D. diss., University of Texas at Austin, 2008).

91. Siegfried Kracauer, *From Caligari to Hitler* (Princeton, 1947), 111–112, 257–258.

92. Eric Rentschler, "Mountains and Modernity: Relocating the Bergfilm," *New German Critique* 51 (1990): 137–161.

93. Rentschler, *Ministry of Illusion,* 38, 43–44.

94. Celia Applegate, *A Nation of Provincials: The German Idea of Heimat* (Berkeley, 1990), 8–9; Alon Confino, *The Nation as a Local Metaphor: Württemberg, Imperial Germany, and National Memory, 1871–1918* (Chapel Hill, 1997), 118–124, 156; Johannes von Moltke, *No Place like Home: Locations of Heimat in German Cinema* (Berkeley, 2005).

95. Moltke, *No Place like Home,* 15–16, 24; Guinevere Narraway, "Modernity and the Politics of Place in Luis Trenker's *Der verlorene Sohn,*" in *Culture, Creativity and Environment: New Environmental Criticism,* ed. Fiona Becket and Terry Gifford (Amsterdam, 2007), 215–231.

96. Ben Gabel, "Der ewige Traum," *Film und Kritik* 1 (June 1992): 48; Horak, *Berge, Licht und Traum,* 51, 55, 67, 79.

97. For a welcome exception, see Moltke, *No Place like Home,* 47.

98. This melds German versions of Fanck's time and current English renditions. For the German context, see Jonathan Sheehan, *The Enlightenment Bible: Translation, Scholarship, Culture* (Princeton, 2005).

99. Arnold Fanck, "Anfang und Ende meines alpinen Filmschaffens," *Deutsche Alpenzeitung* 30, no. 5 (May 1935); reprinted in *Berges-schönheit* (Munich, 1939), 133–139, and Horak, *Berge, Licht, und Traum,* 173–180.

100. Horak, *Berge, Licht, und Traum,* 179.

101. Ziak, *Der Mensch und die Berge,* 205.

102. See Moltke, *No Place like Home;* Harald Höbusch, "Rescuing German Alpine Tradition: Nanga Parbat and Its Visual Afterlife," *Journal of Sport History* 29

(2002): 49–76; Stefan König, Hans-Jürgen Panitz, and Michael Wachtler, *Bergfilm: Dramen, Trick und Abenteuer* (Munich, 2001); and many catalogs from the Museo Nazionale della Montagna.

103. Karl Ziak, *Der König des Mont Blanc* (Vienna, 1950), 4, 239, and (Vienna, 1980), 237, 280.

9. ALMOST TOGETHER

1. John Hunt's preface, *FAMB*, v–vi.

2. RGS Archives, EE 89, J. Maltby to J. Hunt, October 12, 1953. Some material in this chapter appeared in a different form in Peter H. Hansen, "Confetti of Empire: the Conquest of Everest in Nepal, India, Britain and New Zealand," *Comparative Studies in Society and History* 42 (2000): 307–332.

3. *Times* (London), June 2, 1953.

4. BLNSA, 1CD0126380, Queen's Coronation Day Speech; *Times* (London), June 2, 1953.

5. *New York Herald Tribune,* June 15, 1953; *Daily Herald,* June 3, 1953; *Times of India,* June 4–18, 1963.

6. *Times* (London), June 8, 1953.

7. *News Chronicle* and *New York Herald Tribune,* June 3, 1953; cf. Tenzing Norgay with James Ramsey Ullman, *Tiger of the Snows: The Autobiography of Tenzing of Everest* (New York, 1955), 206. Including the daily allowance, it was about 300 rupees a month while on the mountain.

8. *Statesman,* June 18, 1953; *Times of India,* June 19, 1953.

9. Tashi Tenzing and Judy Tenzing, *Tenzing Norgay and the Sherpas of Everest* (Camden, ME, 2001), 146–147; Ed Douglas, *Tenzing: Hero of Everest* (Washington, DC, 2003), 207.

10. Edmund Hillary, *Nothing Venture, Nothing Win* (London, 1975), 165–166.

11. *Daily Mail,* June 9, 1953; *Evening Post,* June 22, 1953; Ralph Izzard, *Innocent on Everest* (New York, 1954), 306, 310.

12. *Daily News,* June 25, 1953; *Times of India,* June 26, 1953.

13. Massimo Mila and Tensing Norkey, *Gli eroi del Chomolungma* (Turin, 1954), consisted of Mila's history of Everest and a translation of Tenzing's story as told to United Press with a postscript by his wife, Ang Lahmu. For examples, see *Times of India*, July 11–17, 1953.

14. For the joint statement, see RGS Archives, EE 90; Tenzing, *Tiger of the Snows,* 266; *Statesman, Times of India, Pioneer,* and *New York Herald Tribune,* June 22, 1953.

15. Peter H. Hansen, "The Dancing Lamas of Everest: Cinema, Orientalism, and Anglo-Tibetan Relations in the 1920s," *American Historical Review* 101 (1996): 712–747; Patrick Zander, "(Right) Wings over Everest: High Adventure, High

Technology and High Nationalism on the Roof of the World, 1932–1934," *Twentieth Century British History* 21 (2010): 300–329; Maurice Isserman and Stewart Weaver, *Fallen Giants: A History of Himalayan Mountaineering from the Age of Empire to the Age of Extremes* (New Haven, CT, 2010); Wade Davis, *Into the Silence: The Great War, Mallory and the Conquest of Everest* (New York, 2011).

16. Tenzing, *Tiger of the Snows*, 33; Jonathan Neale, *Tigers of the Snow: How One Fateful Climb Made the Sherpas Mountaineering Legends* (New York, 2002).

17. Maurice Herzog, *Annapurna, Premier 8000* (Paris, 1951); David Roberts, *True Summit: What Really Happened on the Legendary Ascent of Annapurna* (New York, 2002).

18. TNA, FO 371/92928, Kathmandu to London, November 23, 1951; FO 371/101162, minutes, January 7, 1952; *Times* (London), January 4 and 8, 1952; TNA, FO 371/92928, June 19, 1951.

19. Jane Burbank and Frederick Cooper, *Empires in World History: Power and the Politics of Difference* (Princeton, 2010); F. O. Adams and C. D. Cunningham, *The Swiss Confederation* (London, 1889), 25.

20. David Edgerton, *Warfare State: Britain 1920–1970* (Cambridge, 2006); David Egerton, *Britain's War Machine: Weapons, Resources and Experts in the Second World War* (Oxford, 2011).

21. J. R. Sutton, C. S. Houston, and G. Coates, eds., *Hypoxia and Molecular Medicine* (Burlington, 1993), 184–189; J. B. West, *High Life: A History of High-Altitude Physiology and Medicine* (New York, 1998).

22. See TNA, AVIA 54/1476, for the Ministry of Supply and oxygen equipment.

23. TNA, T 350/15, Sir Robert Knox, secretary of the Political Honours Scrutiny Committee in the Treasury.

24. *Manchester Guardian,* June 15, 1953; Hansard, *Parliamentary Debates, House of Commons,* 5th ser., vol. 516; *News Chronicle,* June 24, 1953.

25. Nehru to Azad, June 19, 1953, File No. 2 (655)/53-PMS, in *Selected Works of Jawaharlal Nehru,* 2nd ser., vol. 22 (New Delhi, 1998), 580–581. For prohibition against titles, see Indian Constitution, Article 18; cf. United States Constitution, Article 1, Section 9.

26. Hillary, *Nothing Venture,* 163–164; Hillary interview with the author, 1998.

27. *Daily Herald,* June 13, 1953.

28. *Sunday Standard,* June 21, 1953; *Life,* July 13, 1953; see also the draft of Tenzing's autobiography in James Ramsey Ullman papers, C0268, box 7, folder 1, Department of Rare Books and Special Collections, Princeton University Library. For his birthplace, Tashi Tenzing interview with the author, 1998, and later biographies of Tenzing.

29. *Bharat Jyoti,* June 21, 1953.

30. *Leader,* June 9, 1953.

31. *Times of India* and *Statesman,* June 24, 1953. Lionel Caplan, *Warrior Gentlemen: "Gurkhas" in the Western Imagination* (London, 1995); Pratyoush Onta, "Creating a Brave Nepali Nation in British India: The Rhetoric of *Jati* Improvement, Rediscovery of Bhanubhakta and the Writing of *Bir* History," *Studies in Nepali Society and History* 1 (1996): 37–76.

32. *Telegraph* (Calcutta), April 15, 2003.

33. RGS Archives, EE 89, Hunt to Kirwan, June 23, 1953; cf. TNA, FO 371/106880.

34. *Statesman,* June 24, 1953.

35. *Statesman,* June 27, 1953.

36. Nehru speeches, December 14, 1953, and January 24, 1954, in *Selected Works of Jawaharlal Nehru,* vol. 24, 66–68, 100.

37. *Times of India,* November 5, 1954.

38. Tenzing Norgay and Malcolm Barnes, *After Everest: An Autobiography* (London, 1977), 53.

39. *Statesman,* June 25 and 30, 1953; *Pioneer,* June 25 and July 3, 1953.

40. TNA, FO 371/106880; *Dr. Rajendra Prasad: Correspondence and Select Documents,* ed. Valmiki Choudhary (New Delhi, 1992), vol. 16, 422; and excerpts in *Statesman* and *Pioneer,* June 30, 1953.

41. Nehru to chief minister, July 2, 1953, File No. 25(6)/53-PMS, in *Selected Works of Jawaharlal Nehru,* vol. 23, 565–566.

42. *Selected Works of Jawaharlal Nehru,* vol. 24, 100.

43. Tenzing, *Tiger of the Snows,* 269; cf. Sherry B. Ortner, *Life and Death on Mt. Everest: Sherpas and Himalayan Mountaineering* (Princeton, 1999), 87.

44. Nehru to chief minister, July 2, 1953, File No. 25(6)/53-PMS, in *Selected Works of Jawaharlal Nehru,* vol. 23, 565–566.

45. *Statesman* and *Times of India,* between June 9 and July 2, 1953.

46. *Times of India, Statesman,* and *Times* (London), July 2, 1953; Douglas, *Tenzing,* 238.

47. *Times of India,* June 29, 1953.

48. *Pioneer,* June 26, 1953; *Times of India,* June 29, 1953; *Statesman,* July 1, 1953.

49. *Times of India,* July 2, 1953.

50. See RGS Archives, EE 89, for transcript, and BLNSA, recording T19520; *Yorkshire Post,* July 4, 1953; "Everest Heroes Home," 1953, www.britishpathe.com.

51. *Times of India,* July 5, 1953.

52. Hunt interview with the author, 1996.

53. RGS Archive, EE 89, War Office to Hunt, October 16, 1953, and Hunt to War Office, October 22, 1953.

54. TNA, CAB 124/2924, Government Hospitality Minutes, July 6, 1953; TNA, PREM 11/458 and FO 371/106880.

55. TNA, FO/371/106880, Minutes, July 15, 1953.

56. Tom Nairn, *The Enchanted Glass: Britain and Its Monarchy* (London, 1988); David Cannadine, *Ornamentalism: How the British Saw Their Empire* (Oxford, 2001).

57. RGS Archives, EE 69, Reynolds to Hunt, June 2, 1953.

58. *New Zealand Herald,* August 10, 1953. For newsreels of Hillary's return, see National Archives, Wellington, and National Film and Sound Archive, Canberra.

59. Hillary, *Nothing Venture,* 98.

60. Jock Phillips, *A Man's Country? The Image of the Pakeha Male,* rev. ed. (Auckland, 1996); Graham Langton, "A History of Mountain Climbing in New Zealand to 1953" (Ph.D. diss., University of Canterbury, Christchurch, 1996).

61. *New Zealand Herald,* August 21, 1953.

62. Mavis Davidson to W. A. Brodkin, September 11, 1953, IA 1, 152/1183, National Archives of New Zealand, Wellington.

63. *Evening Post,* September 1, 1953. See Ephemera B, Mountaineering, 1953, Alexander Turnbull Library, Wellington.

64. September 17, 1953, *New Zealand Parliamentary Debates* (Wellington, 1954), vol. 300, 1320.

65. BLNSA, recording T27351; BBC Written Archives Centre, Caversham, "Scripts, Queen's Journey," and "Relays/Christmas 1953."

66. Tom Fleming, ed., *Voices Out of the Air: The Royal Christmas Broadcasts, 1932–1981* (London, 1981), 72–74.

67. NLS, Acc. 4338, 12 (2), Graham Brown and de Beer to president of the Alpine Club, July 17, 1953.

68. Hunt, *FAMB,* v; *Times Literary Supplement,* November 29, 1957.

69. Gavin de Beer, *Science and the Humanities* (London, 1958), 18; E. J. W. Barrington, "Gavin Rylands de Beer, 1899–1972," *Biographical Memoirs of Fellows of the Royal Society* 19 (1973): 64, 80.

70. Gavin de Beer and Max H. Hey, "The First Ascent of Mont Blanc," *Notes and Records of the Royal Society of London* 11 (1955): 236–255.

71. J. G. Jones, E. M. Tansey, and D. G. Stuart, "Thomas Graham Brown (1882–1965): Behind the Scenes at the Cardiff Institute of Physiology," *Journal of the History of the Neurosciences* 20 (2011): 188–209.

72. NLS, Acc. 4338, 160 (3).

73. T. Graham Brown, *Brenva* (London, 1944); and *AJ* 71 (1966): 51–57, for the editing.

74. Graham Brown, *Brenva,* 6, 12, xiii.

75. NLS, Acc. 4338, 160 (1), themes 50–51, 59, 74, 86; Acc. 4338, 160 (15); emphasis in original.

76. NLS, Acc. 4338, 160 (12), "The Vindication of Paccard, Typed 20, 21 iii 1947."

77. *FAMB*, 6, 30, 172, 193.

78. Ibid., 151–152, 181, 186, 192.

79. Ibid., 34–36, 40.

80. Ibid., 61–62, 132–133, 138–139, 173, 208.

81. Robert K. Merton, "Priorities in Scientific Discovery: A Chapter in the Sociology of Science," *American Sociological Review* 22 (1957): 635–659.

82. George Sarton, *The Study of the History of Science* (Cambridge, 1936), 34–35, 44–45; emphasis in original.

83. François Arago, *Historical Eloge of James Watt* (London, 1839), 106; emphasis in original.

84. Thomas S. Kuhn, *The Structure of Scientific Revolutions* (Chicago, 1962), 62.

85. Ludwik Fleck, *The Genesis and Development of a Scientific Fact* (Chicago, 1979), 78; emphasis in original. Fleck, *Cognition and Fact* (Dordrecht, 1985), 79.

86. Babette Babich, "Kuhn's Paradigm as a Parable for the Cold War: Incommensurability and Its Discontents from Fuller's Tale of Harvard to Fleck's Unsung Lvov," *Social Epistemology* 17, no. 2–3 (2003): 99–109; Nicola Mößner, "Thought Styles and Paradigms—A Comparative Study of Ludwik Fleck and Thomas S. Kuhn," *Studies in History and Philosophy of Science* 42 (2011): 362–371.

87. Gavin de Beer, *Reflections of a Darwinian* (New York, 1962), 54–55.

88. Gavin de Beer, *Streams of Culture* (Philadelphia, 1969), 10, 16–17, 21; Fleck, *Genesis and Development*, 142. Cf. Thomas Robertson, *The Malthusian Moment: Global Population Growth and the Birth of American Environmentalism* (New Brunswick, 2012).

89. Graham Brown to Thorington, February 11, 1958, box 2, folder 2, J. Monroe Thorington Collection, Manuscripts Division, Department of Rare Books and Special Collections, Princeton University Library.

90. De Beer, *Streams of Culture*, 45.

91. Fleck, *Genesis and Development*, 64, to which Fleck added, "just as there is probably no limit to the development of other biological forms."

92. *Statesman*, August 9 and 10, 1953.

93. *Life*, July 13, 1953, 122; *Daily Express*, July 2, 1953.

94. Tenzing, *Tiger of the Snows*, 251; *Daily Express*, July 6, 1953.

95. Edmund Hillary, *High Adventure* (New York, 1955), 232–235; John Hunt, *The Ascent of Everest* (London, 1953), 206; Edmund Hillary, *View from the Summit* (London, 1999), 15–18; Hillary, *Nothing Venture*, 162.

96. *Age* (Melbourne), September 2, 1953, and other newspapers; *Tablet*, September 5, 1953.

97. *Catholic Herald,* September 18, 1953; *Ensign,* September 19, 1953.

98. John Hunt interview with the author, 1996; Martin Haigh, "The Crucifix on Everest," *Reader's Digest,* November 2008, United Kingdom and Asia editions.

99. RGS Archives, EE 89, Misc. Autographs file, Haigh to Hunt, July 9, 1953, and July 14, 1953.

100. BLNSA, Recording 19470, London Calling Asia, for the Far Eastern Service, July 15, 1953; cf. Hunt, *Ascent of Everest,* 7.

101. John Hunt, "Why Climb Mountains?" *Rotarian* 85 (September 1954): 28–30.

102. Shih Chan-Chun, "The Conquest of Mount Everest by the Chinese Mountaineering Team," *AJ* 66 (1961): 35; cf. Shih Chan-Chun, "We Conquered the World's Highest Peak," and Wang Fu-Chou, "On to the Summit," *China Reconstructs,* August 1960, 4–7.

103. Tenzing, *Tiger of the Snows,* 247–248, 293.

104. BLNSA, Recording 19467, Sherpa Tenzing interviewed by A. Hasan, July 14, 1953; many thanks to Anil Sethi for this translation.

10. BODIES OF ICE

1. The procès-verbal by Edmond de Catelin is quoted in Stéphen d'Arve, *Les Fastes du Mont Blanc: Ascensions célèbres et catastrophes* (Genève, 1876), 68; *Journal de Genève,* August 17 and 21, 1861; *L'Abeille de Chamonix,* June 15, 1862, and July 2, 1863; Charles Durier, *Le Mont-Blanc* (Paris, 1877), 420.

2. J. Corbel and E. Le Roy Ladurie, "Datation au C 14 d'une moraine du Mont Blanc," *Revue de Géographie Alpine* 51 (1963): 173–175; Emmanuel Le Roy Ladurie, *Times of Feast, Times of Famine: A History of Climate since the Year 1000* (New York, 1988), 167–168, 352.

3. Marc Bloch, *Apologie pour l'histoire; ou, Métier d'historien* (Paris, 1949), 35; Bloch, *The Historian's Craft* (New York, 1964), 25–26, 68; Le Roy Ladurie, *Times of Feast,* 18.

4. Le Roy Ladurie, *Times of Feast,* 4, 99.

5. Ibid., 18.

6. Paul Mougin, *Études glaciologiques en Savoie,* 6 vols. (Paris, 1909–1927); Charles Rabot, "Les débâcles glaciaires," *Bulletin de géographie historique et descriptive* 20 (1905): 413–465; Gaston Letonnelier, "Documents relatifs aux variations des glaciers dans les Alpes Françaises," *Bulletin de la Section de Géographie* 28 (1913): 288–295; Raoul Blanchard, "La crue glaciaire dans les Alpes de Savoie au XVIIe siècle," *Recueil des Travaux de L'Insitut de Géographie Alpine* 1 (1913): 443–454.

7. Le Roy Ladurie, *Times of Feast,* 17–18, 22, 119.

8. Ibid., 129–226; Jean M. Grove, "The Little Ice Age in the Massif of Mont Blanc," *Transactions of the Institute of British Geographers* 40 (1966): 129–143; see Jean M. Grove, *The Little Ice Age* (London, 1988), chaps. 4–6, for alpine glaciers.

9. Samuel U. Nussbaumer and Heinz J. Zumbühl, "The Little Ice Age History of the Glacier des Bossons (Mont Blanc Massif, France): A New High-Resolution Glacier Length Curve Based on Historical Documents," *Climatic Change* 111 (2012): 301–334; S. U. Nussbaumer, H. J. Zumbühl, and D. Steiner, "Fluctuations of the 'Mer de Glace' (Mont Blanc Area, France) AD 1500–2050: An Interdisciplinary Approach Using New Historical Data and Neural Network Simulations," *Zeitschrift für Gletscherkunde und Glazialgeologie* 40 (2005/2006).

10. *Annals of Philosophy* 9 (1817): 101; and the original in ACL, C12.

11. Mark Bowen, *Thin Ice: Unlocking the Secrets of Climate in the World's Highest Mountains* (New York, 2005), summarizes a large field.

12. Bert Bolin, *A History of the Science and Politics of Climate Change: The Role of the Intergovernmental Panel on Climate Change* (Cambridge, 2007).

13. "History without people" was a section heading for chapters on climate in Emmanuel Le Roy Ladurie, *Le territoire de l'historien* (Paris, 1973), vol. 1, 417–423; *The Territory of the Historian,* trans. B. Reynolds and S. Reynolds (New York, 1979), 285.

14. Emmanuel Le Roy Ladurie, *Histoire humaine et comparée du Climat,* 3 vols. (Paris, 2004–2009).

15. Emmanuel Le Roy Ladurie, Daniel Rousseau, and Anouchka Vasak, *Les fluctuations du climat: De l'an mil à aujourd'hui* (Paris, 2011); the parenthetical dates refer to the period of fluctuation, not the life span of its eponymous patron. On the IPCC, see Bolin, *History of the Science and Politics of Climate Change.*

16. Emmanuel Le Roy Ladurie, "Vers un désastre climatique?" *Le Monde,* December 4, 2011.

17. *Le Figaro,* August 8–10, 1986.

18. *Le Dauphiné Libéré,* August 9, 1986.

19. Ibid.; *Le Faucigny,* August 23, 1986.

20. *Le Dauphiné Libéré,* August 9, 1986; *La Stampa,* August 7 and 8, 1986.

21. *Le Figaro,* August 9–10, 1986; *Le Dauphiné Libéré,* August 10, 1986; *Le Monde,* August 8, 1986.

22. *Le Dauphiné Libéré,* August 9, 1986; *Le Figaro,* August 9–10, 1986.

23. *Journal de Genève,* June 27 and August 11, 1986; *Le Progrès,* August 11, 1986.

24. *Le Monde,* August 8, 1986; *Libération,* August 8, 1986; *L'Humanité,* August 9, 1986.

25. *Neue Zürcher Zeitung,* July 22, 1986; *Le Figaro,* August 8, 1986; Josef Auf der Maur, "Die Erstbesteigung des Mont Blanc 1786: Ein neu entdeckter Brief des Estbesteigers Dr. M. G. Paccard," *Die Alpen, Zeitschrift des SAC* 61 (1985): 28–36.

26. *Le Dauphiné,* August 9, 1986.

27. *Les Inconnus du Mont Blanc,* 1986; see the Cineteca Storica e Videoteca, Museo Nazionale della Montagna, CAI-Torino.

28. Gilbert Gardes, *Histoire monumentale des deux Savoies, Mémoire de la montagne* (Lyon, 1996), 290–291.

29. *Corriere della Sera,* August 7 and 9, 1986; *La Repubblica,* August 8, 1986. See also Biblioteca Nazionale del Club Alpino Italiano, Bust 110, Fasc. 584, Carteggio bicentenario Monte Bianco.

30. *La Stampa,* August 4 and 8, 1986.

31. *L'Osservatore Romano,* September 5, 1986, Italian daily edition.

32. Ibid., September 8–9, 1986; most were reprinted in *L'Osservatore Romano Weekly Edition in English,* September 22, 1986; I have used the Italian edition for quotations.

33. *La Stampa,* September 8 and 10, 1986.

34. *L'Osservatore Romano,* September 8–9, 1986, daily edition; cf. *La Stampa,* September 9, 1986; N. M. Ognibene and R. Poletti, eds., *Giovanni Paolo II: Papa tra i monti* (Aosta, 2004).

35. *L'Osservatore Romano Weekly Edition in English,* September 22, 1986; translation modified.

36. *L'Osservatore Romano,* September 8–9, 1986; cf. *Le Figaro,* September 8, 1986.

37. *L'Osservatore Romano,* September 8–9, 1986; *La Stampa,* September 8, 1986.

38. *La Stampa* and *La Repubblica,* July 18, 1990.

39. Cf. "Giovanni Paolo Sovrano d'Europa," *La Stampa,* July 19, 1990; "Quando il Papa va in Vacanza," *La Repubblica,* July 27, 1990.

40. *Corriere della Sera,* July 21, 1990.

41. *Fate of Mountain Glaciers in the Anthropocene: A Report by the Working Group Commissioned by the Pontifical Academy of Sciences,* May 11, 2011; J. Zalasiewicz et al., "The Anthropocene: A New Epoch of Geological Time?" *Philosophical Transactions of the Royal Society A* 369 (2011): 835; *The Stockholm Memorandum: Tipping the Scales towards Sustainability,* 3rd Nobel Laureate Symposium on Global Sustainability, Stockholm, Sweden, May 16–19, 2011.

42. Paul J. Crutzen, "Geology of Mankind," *Nature* 415 (January 3, 2002): 23; he aired similar views in a geological newsletter in 2000.

43. Jan Zalasiewicz, Mark Williams, Will Steffen, and Paul Crutzen, "The New World of the Anthropocene," *Environmental Science & Technology* 44 (2010): 2228–2231.

44. James Secord, *Controversy in Victorian Geology: The Cambrian-Silurian Dispute* (Princeton, 1986); Martin Rudwick, *The Great Devonian Controversy: The Shaping of Scientific Knowledge among Gentlemanly Specialists* (Chicago, 1985).

45. *New York Times,* February 27, 2011.

46. William E. Ruddiman, *Plows, Plagues, and Petroleum: How Humans Took Control of Climate* (Princeton, 2005).

47. Will Steffen, Jacques Grinevald, Paul Crutzen, and John McNeill, "The Anthropocene: Conceptual and Historical Perspectives," *Philosophical Transactions of the Royal Society A* 369 (2011): 842–867.

48. See Fabien Locher and Jean-Baptiste Fressoz, "Modernity's Frail Climate: A Climate History of Environmental Reflexivity," *Critical Inquiry* 38 (2012): 579–598, for discussion of theories of climate change related to deforestation and a "climatic colonialism."

49. Robert V. Davis, "Inventing the Present: Historical Roots of the Anthropocene," *Earth Sciences History* 30 (2011): 63–84, esp. 73–75.

50. Charles Lyell, *Principles of Geology* (London, 1830), vol. I, 158.

51. Samuel Haughton, *Manual of Geology* (London, 1865), 344.

52. Antonio Stoppani, *Corso di Geologia* (Milan, 1873), vol. 2, 731. Many thanks to Tina-Marie Ranalli for clarification on the translation.

53. Joseph Le Conte, *Religion and Science, a Series of Sunday Lectures* (London, 1874), 261.

54. Joseph Le Conte, "On Critical Periods in the History of the Earth and Their Relation to Evolution and on the Quaternary as Such a Period," *American Journal of Science and Arts* 14 (1877): 114.

55. For the Soviet "Anthropogenic system (period) or Anthropocene" in the 1960s, see *Great Soviet Encyclopedia* (New York, 1973), vol. 2, 139–144; Pavlov's concept has been Anglicized as both "Anthropogene" and "Anthropocene."

56. W. I. Vernadsky, "Biosphere and Noösphere," *American Scientist* 33 (January 1945): 1–12; emphasis in original.

57. Davis, "Inventing the Present: Historical Roots of the Anthropocene," 76; for Soviet schemas in the 1960s, which variously used "Recent," "post-glacial," and "Holocene," see *Great Soviet Encyclopedia,* 141–143.

58. Dipesh Chakrabarty, "The Climate of History: Four Theses," *Critical Inquiry* 35 (2009): 201.

59. A. D. Barnosky et al., "Approaching a State Shift in Earth's Biosphere," *Nature* 486 (June 7, 2012): 57

60. Steffen et al., "Anthropocene: Conceptual and Historical Perspectives," 862.

61. Tim Flannery, *The Weather Makers* (New York, 2006), 291–295; see also Mark Mazower, *Governing the World: The History of an Idea* (New York, 2012).

62. See Lauren Benton, *A Search for Sovereignty: Law and Geography in European Empires, 1400–1900* (Cambridge, 2010); Jane Burbank and Frederick Cooper, *Empires in World History: Power and the Politics of Difference* (Princeton, 2011).

63. Adrian Howkins, "Melting Empires? Climate Change and Politics in Antarctica since the International Geophysical Year," *Osiris* 26 (2011): 180–197.

64. James Rodger Fleming and Fladimir Jankovic, "Revisiting Klima," *Osiris* 26 (2011): 9–10, 14.

65. On geoengineering, see James Rodger Fleming, *Fixing the Sky: the Checkered History of Weather and Climate Control* (New York, 2010); Eli Kintisch, *Hack the Planet* (Hoboken, 2010).

66. Pontifical Academy of Sciences, *Fate of Mountain Glaciers in the Anthropocene.*

67. Chakrabarty, "Climate of History," 222.

68. Manuscript note scribbled on the title page of Marc-Théodore Bourrit, *Relation of a Journey to the Glaciers in the Dutchy* [*sic*] *of Savoy* (London, 1776), KD 24226, Houghton Library, Harvard University.

69. Sheila Jasanoff, "A New Climate for Society," *Theory, Culture and Society* 27 (2010): 233–253.

70. Julie Cruikshank, *Do Glaciers Listen? Local Knowledge, Colonial Encounters, and Social Imagination* (Vancouver, 2005); Mark Carey, *In the Shadow of Melting Glaciers: Climate Change and Andean Identity* (Oxford, 2010); for "endangered glacier narratives," see Mark Carey, "The History of Ice: How Glaciers Became an Endangered Species," *Environmental History* 12 (2007): 497–527.

71. Bowen, *Thin Ice*, 365, 332; for striking earlier examples, see Deborah R. Coen, "Imperial Climatographies from Tyrol to Turkestan," *Osiris* 26 (2011): 45–65.

72. "Allmächtiger, das ist ja ein Mensch!" *Augsburger Allgemeine,* September 13, 2011.

73. Brenda Fowler, *Iceman: Uncovering the Life and Times of a Prehistoric Man Found in an Alpine Glacier* (Chicago, 2001), on the discovery and early history; see also Angelika Fleckinger and Hubert Steiner, *Faszination Jungsteinzeit/Il fascino del Neolitico/The Fascination of the Neolithic Age* (Bolzano, 2003); and for day-by-day summaries, see Elisabeth Rastbichler Zissernig, *Der Mann im Eis: Die Fundgeschichte* (Innsbruck, 2006).

74. Konrad Spindler, *The Man in the Ice: The Discovery of a 5,000-Year-Old Body Reveals the Secrets of the Stone Age* (London, 1994).

75. P. Gostner and E. Vigl, "Insight: Report of Radiological Forensic Findings in the Iceman," *Journal of Archaeological Science* 29 (2002): 323–326; P. Pernter et al., "Radiologic Proof for the Iceman's Cause of Death," *Journal of Archaeological Science* 34 (2007): 1784–1786.

76. A. Vanzetti et al., "The Iceman as a Burial," *Antiquity* 84 (2010): 681–692, and three critical responses published in *Antiquity* 85 (2011).

77. *Focus Magazin,* November 7, 2011; *Daily Mail,* November 8, 2011.

78. *New York Times,* December 1, 1994.

79. A. Keller et al., "New Insights into the Tyrolean Iceman's Origin and Phenotype as Inferred by Whole-Genome Sequencing," *Nature Communications* 3, no. 698 (February 28, 2012): 1–9.

80. *Stern,* May 14 and December 10, 1998; *Berliner Morgenpost* and *Die Welt,* January 16, 2003.

81. *General-Anzeiger,* January 14, 2003; *Berlin Kurier,* January 15, 2003; and from Deutsche Presse-Agentur (DPA) wire services, January 16, 2003.

82. *Berliner Kurier,* January 15, 2003.

83. *Süddeutsche Zeitung,* November 4, 2003; *Nürnberg Nachrichten,* November 4 and 14, 2003; *Spiegel Online,* November 4, 2003; *Die Welt,* November 5, 2003.

84. *Independent,* October 25, 2004.

85. *Nürnberger Nachrichten* and *Le Monde,* October 20, 2004; *NRC Handelsblad,* December 4, 2004; *De Telegraaf,* December 7, 2004; and the television program *De ontdekking van Helmut Simon* (2004).

86. *Nürnberger Nachrichten,* October 25, 2004; *Observer,* April 20, 2005.

87. Guy Benhamou, *La malédiction d'Ötzi* (Paris, 2006); and innumerable newspaper stories.

88. For the quotation, see the *Observer,* October 24, 2004; for the commentary, see *La Repubblica,* October 20, 2004.

89. "Ötzi: Finderlohnstreit ist Geschichte," *Dolomiten,* August 30, 2010.

90. *Augsburger Allgemeine,* September 13, 2011.

91. Joseph Leo Koerner, *Caspar David Friedrich and the Subject of Landscape* (New Haven, 1990), 122–226.

92. Angelika Fleckinger, ed., *Ötzi 2.0: Una mummia tra scienza e mito* (Vienna, 2011); for the first model, see Fleckinger and Steiner, *Faszination Jungsteinzeit.*

93. See "Ötzi Lives!" at http://oetzi20.it/2011/02/25/14-otzi-lives/?lang=en.

94. Andrew Shryock and Daniel Lord Smail et al., *Deep History: The Architecture of Past and Present* (Berkeley, 2011), 264, 269.

Acknowledgments

It is a pleasure to thank many of the people who helped me during the writing of this book. While it is simply not possible to acknowledge everyone, I must especially thank several institutions, colleagues, and my family.

This is a Harvard book in more ways than one. At Harvard University Press, I owe special thanks to Sharmila Sen. She contacted me about a related book, but graciously accepted this one and improved it with good advice. Thanks also to Heather Hughes and many others at the press, and to Melody Negron for production editing, Fran Lyon for copyediting, Isabelle Lewis for the maps, and Jean Jesensky for the index. The extraordinary holdings of the Harvard University libraries are matched only by the generosity of its librarians, whose contributions to scholarship are vastly underestimated and, if restructuring is any indication, seriously undervalued. The dynamic international community at the Minda de Gunzberg Center for European Studies at Harvard has been a constant source of intellectual stimulation and moral support for many years. This book began to take its current form in 2005–2006, during a sabbatical in residence at the center.

Visiting fellowships at Harvard, Clare Hall, Cambridge University, and the Humanities Research Centre at the Australian National University (ANU) also provided ideal settings for research and writing. Simon Schama and Harriet Ritvo each provided crucial encouragement for this work from early stages. Thanks to Jenny Anderson, David Armitage, Chris Bayly, Gillian Beer, David Blackbourn, Arianne Chernock, Stefan Collini, Abby Collins, Mary Conley, Trisha Craig, Jim Cronin, Greg Dening, Paul Fideler, Alison Frank, Ranajit Guha, Peter Hall, Stanley Hoffmann, Laura Frader, Art Goldhammer, Patrice Higonnet, Maya Jasanoff, Fred Leventhal, Mary Lewis, David MacDougall, Charles Maier, Joyce Malcolm, Stephan Malinowski, Kris Manjapra, Iain McCalman, Leena Messina, Tom Metcalf, Simon Schaffer, Jim Secord, Sandy Seleski, Malcolm Smuts, Deborah Valenze, Chris Waters, and Peter Weiler, who were models of collegiality and intellectual generosity at Harvard, Cambridge, ANU, and the Northeast Conference on British Studies. Financial support for this research came from the National Endowment for the Humanities and Worcester Polytechnic Institute (WPI).

At WPI, I am very fortunate to teach in an interdisciplinary curriculum, department, and university. I have learned a lot from the inquisitive students who discussed earlier versions of this work in seminars, especially Felipe Polido and members of the Outing Club, who rekindled connections with current climbers. I essentially stopped climbing after becoming a parent, but pursued this research instead. In different ways, I must thank Bland Addison, Bill Baller, Kristin Boudreau, Joel Brattin, Ulrike Brisson, Margaret Brodmerkle, Steven Bullock, Fabio Carrerra, Constance Clark, Jim Cocola, Mary Cotnoir, Joseph Cullon, David Dollenmayer, Jim Doyle, Beth Eddy, Laureen Elgert, Michael Elmes, Michelle Ephraim, Lee Fontanella, Jeffrey Forgeng, Roger Gottlieb, Jim Hanlan, Karen Hassett, Scott Jiusto, Rob Krueger, Aarti Madan, JoAnn Manfra, Jennifer McWeeny, Wes Mott, Malcolm Parkinson, Creighton Peet, Tina-Marie Ranalli, David Rawson, Kent Rissmiller, Angel Rivera, Tom Robertson, Jennifer Rudolph, David Samson, John Sanbonmatsu, Lance Schachterle, Stanley Selkow, Eunmi Shim, Ingrid Shockey, Ruth Smith, Michael Sokal, David Spanagel, Gray Tuttle, John Urang, Rick Vaz, and John Zeugner. Many thanks to WPI's librarians, especially Lora Brueck, for acquiring essential materials.

I am grateful for comments on the manuscript from two anonymous readers and from Kathleen Kete, Kerwin Klein, Sherry Ortner, and Joseph Taylor. For comments on related works, thanks to Mark Curthoys, Martin Daunton, Jacques Defrance, Jaś Elsner, Olivier Hoibian, Colin Matthew, Bernhard Rieger, Joan-Pau Rubiés, Stewart Ward, and the editors of several journals. Alison Frank, Marcus Hall, Tait Keller, and Sverker Sörlin highlighted the Austrian, Italian, and environmental dimensions of this work. Mary Ashburn Miller provided valuable comments on the French Revolutionary mountain. The many participants in the interdisciplinary Making Publics project at McGill University sharpened my attention to early modern knowledge of the natural world. At the Alpine Club Library in London, thanks to Glyn Hughes for help with its archives and to Jerry Lovatt for references to Mont Blanc. Thanks also to Alessandra Ravelli and Marco Ribetti at the Museo Nazionale della Montagna in Turin, and Laurent Vittet at the Archives départementales de la Haute-Savoie, Annecy. Corinne Chorier at the Conservatoire d'art et d'histoire de la Haute-Savoie coordinated the use of images in its collection. Very belated thanks to Navid Akhtar, Mick Conefrey, and David Upshal for sharing material during the filming of documentaries on Everest and the Matterhorn. A symposium at Bolzano with David Breashears, John Cleare, Angelika Fleckinger, and Reinhold Messner convinced me that the Iceman deserved a place in this book. Thanks to Roger Teissel of the Austrian Police for permission to use their photograph, and to Matthias Fanck for material from *Der ewige Traum*. Participants at public libraries engaged with some of the ideas in the book in discussion groups sponsored by the Massachusetts Foundation for the Humanities.

My largest debt, which can scarcely be measured let alone ever repaid, is to my family. Without doubt, I never would have been interested in this topic at all if not for years traveling the country and hiking in the mountains with my parents, Hogie and Anne, and my sisters Deb and Sarah. My children, Katie and William, have grown up faster than this book. I do not regret spending more time with them than with it when they were younger, or even now. To say that my wife, Allison, has lived with this book as long as she has lived with me would be half right, but mostly give the wrong impression. For one, I have hardly worked at constant pace. Life does that. For another, any image of the stoic spouse would be the opposite of her energy, enthusiasm, and love. I owe Allison more than can be put into words.

Despite much advice and assistance, the responsibility for remaining errors or mistakes is mine. Convention dictates that I should say mine alone. In the unlikely event that these lines are reached after reading this book from beginning to end, you should already know that the solitary author is yet another of the mythologies of modern man.

Index